SIEGFRIED TREBITSCH
IN 1942

CHRONICLE OF A LIFE

by

SIEGFRIED TREBITSCH

WILLIAM HEINEMANN LTD
MELBOURNE :: LONDON :: TORONTO

Translated by
EITHNE WILKINS *and* ERNST KAISER

FIRST PUBLISHED 1953

PRINTED IN GREAT BRITAIN
AT THE WINDMILL PRESS
KINGSWOOD, SURREY

CONTENTS

ILLUSTRATIONS

I

ESCAPE INTO FREEDOM

IT is obeying the impulse, not my own heart's need, that I set about this work; for I am impelled—the kindly and at the same time serious words of friends impel me now at long last to write my reminiscences. I would gladly have complied with this request long ago, if it had not meant I was forced to speak of myself. And if I have so long hesitated to fulfil the wish of publishers and friends, it was diffidence at the thought of speaking of myself and my own life. Before I finally agreed to write a book of memoirs, as it is called, I racked my brains in the attempt to discover how it might be done without slithering straight into autobiography. I wondered if it might be possible to exclude oneself and tell the story without naming the story-teller. But then, that would mean creating the impression that the writer of the book refused to take any responsibility for the book's contents, and that would have an odious suggestion of cowardice. In short, I circled round these questions for a long time without finding any satisfactory answer. It really seems as though I would have to keep silence for ever about whatever these sixty years that I have lived with my senses alert, my judgment mature, might have of significance for myself and others, or I must march on ahead of them with a banner bearing my own poor name, a banner I do not much care to see fluttering in the breeze, if only because it has by no means always been a standard of glory or victory. Be that as it may, I mean to try honestly to say as little as possible about myself and as much as possible about my contemporaries and the conditions of my time, although I am perhaps justified only in speaking of myself, who am, I dare say, the one for whom I am most qualified to speak. So now I shall begin the venture, laying the heaviest load of responsibility for this book on the shoulders of those who so insistently urged me to bring it into being.

Then come now, ye Memories, and be gracious to me! I will descend into your deepest cellars. Open the doors for me and grant me a faint light, so that with dim eyes I once again may see what

1   A*

things have been. And impassioned truthfulness shall be like a scarlet thread guiding me through the labyrinth of my life.

It is not important, of course, on what precise day I, the octogenarian, was born in Vienna. Besides, the date is given in many a work of reference, and anyone who insists on knowing it can easily look it up. I only know that I have no particular difficulty in remembering things from my fourth year on, and my first and most intense memory is not a pleasant one. I stood at my father's death-bed—or rather, I was stood there, still so small that I could scarcely see over the edge of that bed of pain and gaze into a wan and noble face round which pallid shadows seemed to hover. Beside me my mother kneeled, no more than twenty-four years old, and sobbed, abandoned to uncontrollable grief. The man whom she had loved, the man she had stood up for with the words: "Better a few years with him than a lifetime with another!" was being torn away from her in the thirty-third year of his life. In her genuine sorrow there was doubtless also desperation at the thought that the numerous people who had time and again warned her parents and doubtless herself against a marriage with a young man suffering from grave heart-disease now, with such finality, were proved to have been right.

But here I hesitate for the first time. Is it important to learn that I had an elder brother who lived only one year and died of diphtheria, and that this grief increased the seriousness of my father's illness and brought him nearer to the final catastrophe? He must have greatly loved that child, for on the little tombstone there is a deeply moving poem of farewell written by the father to his infant son.

As a result, there was precious little sunshine or joy in my childhood and in that of a posthumously born son, whom the young father, dying so early, never knew. I did not learn to laugh in the nursery; but I saw many tears and much sorrow that was very near to despair, which left its mark of sadness and gloom on my childhood.

At the age of twenty-nine my mother contracted a second marriage. She followed her unforgettable first husband's brother to the altar —that brother who had promised the dead man on his death-bed that he would never abandon his wife and her children and would have these children brought up to their flourishing joint business and have them trained to take it over in due course.

I think he took this promise too literally, failing to form a proper estimate of the power of providence and the incalculability of destiny. In the course of the years it became apparent that in spite of his exaggeratedly great sense of duty and genuine love for the beautiful woman at his side he could neither make her happy nor find happiness himself. The only father I can say I ever really knew was this excellent man, who called me his son and whom I was taught to call 'Papa'. Years came when I entirely forgot that he was not my real father; for he did his utmost not to let us have the slightest feeling that the three sons whom my mother bore to him in the course of the years were in fact much closer to his heart than his step-children, although the latter also bore his name.

In the period from the day of my father's death to my tenth year, when it was at length time for me to leave the nursery and go to school—I had up to then been taught privately at home—scarcely anything happened that is likely to be worth recalling. I had to contend with the usual childish ailments, which left practically no traces, although among them there was an attack of scarlet fever that brought me to the very brink of death. The man who had of his own free will become my father often spent half the night sitting beside my bed, nursing the feverish child with touching devotion. I think it was then he so won my affection that, perhaps without knowing it, even when I was a youth and later as a young man I tried to fall in with his wishes, although they were far from the same as my own and set up grave psychological conflicts within me.

This fanatical devotee to his own sense of duty all too often called to mind the promise—which almost every occasion provoked him to remember—that he had given his beloved brother, who had also been his partner in business, to look after his son. He did it in his own way. He, who was the descendant of an old patrician family that had emigrated from Moravia, wanted above all to train me, the eldest, to take over the hereditary family business. What more (he thought) could he do than offer a young man such a fair future, which must inevitably bring him to a state of prosperity in which he would have no cares?

One incident I should perhaps not pass over unmentioned, because it overshadowed my whole life and always prevented me from rollicking about with jolly friends of tastes similar to my own and enjoying all the delights of young life as so many were privileged to do in those bygone days.

In my twelfth year I was fatefully stricken in body.

What happened was this. My English master, Professor Emil Seeliger, at the appointed hour in the afternoon came into my modest room, where text-books and copy-books for the lesson were, as usual, neatly laid out and I was already sitting at the table leafing through the last lesson, when suddenly I saw only half of the tall man who had just crossed the threshold. The other half was lost in darkness, through which spiral-shaped lights flashed. I must have looked horrified, for before the skilled linguist sat down beside me he asked: "What's the matter? Why are you so pale?" "I can only see half of you, Herr Professor!" I gasped.

"What does that mean?" he asked, laughing. But there was nothing to laugh at, all the less as I was now overcome by nausea, which compelled me to rush out of the room. Disconcerted and distressed, my tutor called the maid and told her to tell my mother that I was ill. My mother hurried along, saw from a glance at me that I had been vomiting, became very alarmed, asked the embarrassed man—who kept on asking: "But what's the matter with him? What's the matter with him?"—to cancel the lesson and take himself off, and then, after I had been sick once again, got me into bed. In the meantime my vision returned to normal. I gave a sigh of relief because I could see the whole of my mother's beautiful face, and I asked in profound terror: "But what's happened to me, Mamma? My head hurts like anything."

An hour later our family doctor was sitting at my bedside with her, examining me to the best of his knowledge and ability, after which he rose, greeted my father—who in the meantime had come in and been hastily informed of the situation—and said in his rather gruff but nevertheless kindly manner: "The lad has a bad migraine."

This statement actually told me nothing, for it was the first time I had heard that unfamiliar word. But meanwhile such a frightful headache had begun to throb in the left side of my head that I was no longer capable of hearing, for I abandoned myself to these new torments with all the helplessness of someone who has been ambushed. I began to weep, saying: "Mamma, I can't bear it!" But the benevolent doctor—it was the highly esteemed Professor Widerhofer, who was also physician to the Emperor, who had pronounced the grave diagnosis—was already bending over the suffering child with great sympathy, and saying: "Ah well, we've

plenty of pain-killing remedies!" at the same time putting his hand
into the case he had brought with him and in a trice preparing, in a
tumbler of water swiftly held out to him, something that was to
help me. Greedily I gulped down the remedy, which incidentally—
as I well remember—was in no hurry to begin working. All the
same, it did put me to sleep, and I only just had time to hear that
wise man saying to my father, who was on terms of close friendship
with him: "Now we must wait and see if this is going to recur
periodically, which I am slightly afraid of, or if it's only just a case
of an isolated attack, which may, after all, merely be the result of
an upset digestion."

Well, the periodic recurrence of this affliction, which began to get
a firm hold on me, was to be my lot. Now the tender little tree had
received its first shock. The attacks came and went, and only when
the years of youth were finally over and done with did they cease
to dig their claws into my body. For it did not long remain a matter
only of the one-sided agonising headache. The whole of the left
side of my body became affected by these paroxysmal attacks, and
round about my twenties the illness flourished so markedly and
took on such alarming forms that even the most cautious doctors
gave me morphia injections at the beginning of such an attack. If
I now make this obviously constitutional curse of my life a matter
of public knowledge, it is done in order that others similarly afflicted,
and likewise nurses, doctors and teachers, may learn from it and
draw their own conclusions. I should like also to mention at this
point that these attacks time and again tore to shreds the delicate
webs of my later literary work. It is they who are to blame for the
fact that I could never develop the great sweep that the large-scale
novel demands of a writer.

Professor Widerhofer, who many and many a time sat opposite
me in the first years of my illness, once said to my mother: "This
boy is a nervous cripple, though with the physical constitution of
an athlete. What syntheses there are!" This remark of his may
have had something to do with the fact that I put all I had into
holding my own with those of my own age, first of all in a physical
sense, simply paying no attention to the condition that was trying
to get the better of me. I was, furthermore, unconsciously convinced
that I could only get the upper hand over this torment by means of
great bodily strength and, so to speak, by means of gaining skill in

all my limbs, and that I must above all dominate it instead of letting it dominate me, if my constitution was not to force me into the ranks of the second-rate. I was not exactly ashamed of my unfortunate heritage, but I kept it to myself, without being able to prevent schoolfellows and friends male and female, then and much later too, from occasionally seeing and so getting to know what would come over me at lightning speed, and what it reduced me to.

It was to this chronic condition, with which I began to reckon more the older I grew, that I owed many other things, such as encounters with such great doctors as Professor Oppenheim in Berlin, Professors Wagner-Jauregg, Nothnagel, and Marburg in Vienna, and Dr. Heinrich Lahmann in Dresden. But the name of Lahmann is one I cannot simply mention in this list, for to him I owe not only a treatment that was, if not curative, at least alleviatory, but also a little human experience that should be remembered here.

Dr. Lahmann, Chief Medical Officer of the Sanatorium of the same name on the Weisse Hirsch near Dresden, was very particularly interested in my condition and was the doctor who treated me. I lodged a fair distance from his consulting-room in the villa called Elb-blick. He had, however, very earnestly impressed it upon me that I was to send for him instantly when I felt one of my attacks coming on. He seemed to expect great things from observing the course of it. The day came all too soon. I only need to shut my eyes and go back in spirit into those bygone days in order to see him again sitting at my bedside—that bearded man with the firm, grave features and the over-large black eyes that seemed to be trying to pierce through me. He had insisted that I should be in bed when he called. Outside the door an orderly waited for instructions. He had scarcely examined me and taken my pulse when he told this attendant to bring a pail of hot water, in which I had to immerse my legs up to the knees. After five minutes that unsuccessful experiment was over and I was again lying in my bed, delivered up to my pain and Dr. Lahmann. He now put a list of questions to me. My diet, which he himself had prescribed, he naturally passed as correct, and all my conscientious answers unfortunately offered him no clue. Suddenly he jumped up and walked irritably up and down the room. Then he turned to me and said: "Do you know what I feel like, my dear fellow? Like a savage who has been called into a room in order to put out a painfully glaring light and who, having no notion that there is a switch on the wall, begins to throw stones at the lamp in the ceiling. He demolishes half the room, and the light—well, of course the light goes on burning, because he doesn't know about the switch, with which it can instantly be flicked off. The day will come when one of us doctors finds the switch and with a single flick of the fingers will switch off your dreadful illness. I hope he is already born!" he said, laughing. "But I shall simply let the light of pain go on burning until it goes off of its own accord, instead of doing any further damage." He then gave me some shrewd advice about what I should do for the next few hours and days, prescribed cold compresses, pressed my hand in the most sympathetic way possible, and left me to my evil hour and the passage of time. And since then how many doctors I have seen, eager and anxious to help, sitting by sick-beds, and all they could do was throw stones; and they are still doing it to this day, because they have not found and still do not find the switch.

The hated migraine was as incalculable as a beloved woman. It almost always attacked me when I was least expecting it. It did not come, for instance, in the form of punishment for some excess, as when I had once again kicked over the traces, eaten too much or slept too little. Oh no, precisely then it spared me. But when, bearing it in mind, I had been living in a particularly careful, restrained and in every way moderate style, for example after a night when I had slept long and soundly and had wakened refreshed and full of energy to start a new day, *then* it would leap out at me, sinking its claws into my left temple as though it wanted me to understand that now I was all the better equipped to contend with it.

It is to my illness and my fight against it that I owe, above all, a certain independence of my parents. Especially my father, who would have liked to organise my education and development according to his own temperament and his own ideas, did, after all, have to consider my physical constitution and demand less of me than he would have liked to demand of me, most particularly, of course, with reference to the promise he had made to his dying, deeply beloved brother, to make a prominent industrialist of me. The paternal silk-factory was waiting for me; but I was not waiting for it.

From my fifth year onward I was expected, with my mother's enthusiastic agreement and to my later good fortune, to learn foreign languages almost as well as my native language. French and English governesses and, later, linguistically proficient tutors came and went even in the nursery. This may be connected with the fact that my mother had had a much-loved English governess whom she was always quoting, while my father had spent years of his youth with business friends in Lyons.

The German, English and French governesses to whose mercy I was more or less left as a little boy all had their various quite different attitudes to me. They left marks in me that can be traced into my early manhood. Except for two North German Protestants, they were all more or less devout Catholics and taught me to know the beauties of Vienna's churches. I often came home quite dazed from hours spent in a pew while they performed their long-drawn-out devotions. It may be said that they brought me up to, as it were, no religion, but to the beauty of the Christian—or rather, of the Catholic—form of worship.

The quarter of the town in which I was born was known in the vernacular as the Brillantengrund (Diamond Fields), because the then thriving silk industry of Austria had there had its most respected representatives and because, apparently, it was believed that this trade had made this quarter of the town rich and provided the women with the diamonds that they wore. The children of the Brillantengrund all happened to speak fairly fluent French, and my ambitious parents would not have been able to bear it if I had not kept up with them. I first beheld the darkness of the world in Number One Zieglergasse, from the windows of which one could see the old building where my ancestors had had their offices.

The Brillantengrund has had its poet too, and one who sprang from that quarter. He was the writer Emil Ertl, the son of the silk-manufacturer Ertl. His books were in the main concerned with the lives and affairs and destinies of the silk-weavers on the Schottenfeld. The most illuminating book in this respect that Emil Ertl ever wrote bears the title *Die Leute vom blauen Kuckuckshaus* (*The People of the Blue Cuckoo-House*).

It is doubtless to the physical condition already described that I also owe the fact that, although I was not bad at my lessons, I had tutors to supervise me at home, doing my exercises with me and trying to make it easier for me to contend with the school time-table. They did not exactly talk French with me; instead they took me to skittle-alleys in the suburbs where they themselves went regularly and showed me that there were people who could knock all nine of the pins flying. Some of these tutors, most of whom were Bohemians of German descent, were talented men and wrote verses, which however left no impression on my mind, perhaps because even at the age of fifteen I myself could not resist the inclination to clothe slight emotions and still slighter ideas in metre and rhyme. On this territory, therefore, in spite of their age, they had not as much of an advantage over me as they had at the skittle-alley. There is one man I must recall here, because besides myself he had also had many a famous parliamentarian and respected scientist as his pupil in the schoolroom. This was Professor Josef Nossek, who originally hailed from Leitmeritz, a genius as much gone-to-seed as unrecognised, one who—I admit—might not have got even as far as he did if he had been liberated from all the cares of which he complained and had been able to create the things that it was not granted to him to create. It is easier to live on intellectual credit than to pay in cash. At any rate, he had some imagination and a certain poetic gift.

I like to recall the dreamy evening hours when the day's tasks were done and our room, which I shared with my brother, three years my junior, filled up with darkness, which was lit only by our teacher's glowing cigar and the glimmering log in the stove, which was now going out. When he wanted to be particularly gracious to me he would lean back, drawing at his Cuban cigar, and recount very strange and exciting stories. His condition was that darkness should be gathering in the room. That stimulated him. I used to listen in breathless rapture, hailing in that queer little man the first real story-teller I had met, one whose stories made a stronger and more lasting impression on me than the little books, which I had been given as presents long before, of Nieritz and Hofmann. Who knows, perhaps it was this Josef Nossek who planted in me the seed from which later the writer developed that I pass for today.

Doubtless it is the same with human beings as it is with trees that are covered with blossoms, all of equal value, of which only a small proportion ever turns into fruit. The others, whose right to turn into fruit is, after all, no less, fall to the ground and perish, unwept, unhonoured, and unsung.

My school-leaving certificate examination I passed, not with distinction, but still very well, and now I was—free! When I left the school building in which I had, after all, spent many years without forming a single real boyhood friendship, I was overwhelmed by a severe migraine, which prevented me from taking part in the farewell party given by my schoolmates and teachers. Even at that time I was learning to spend the time of others' celebrations quietly at home by myself, which I have many and many a time in my later life done voluntarily and involuntarily.

But I should not like to create the impression that I had a joyless youth as a result of my illness. On the contrary, I especially enjoyed the splendid summer holidays, which we always spent first in the surroundings of Vienna and then in the Salzkammergut, and then for many years in Bad Ischl.

Among the thoroughly uneventful summers that were nevertheless important for the part they played in forming my character, I think I should speak of one, because it was the one when I made the first acquaintances that were to be of permanent significance.

Not far from Salzburg is a railway-station called Vöcklabruck, from which one can make a short trip by rail to the lovely shore of Attersee, on the lake of that name. There we were spending the summer holidays after a winter of hard 'swotting' under the constant threat of heavy colds.

In Attersee we met the youngest German university professor—he was then twenty-eight—Erich Schmidt, who went on the merry-go-round with us at a country fairground and took the opportunity of finding fault with our Viennese manner of speech. He could not approve of our tutor's German. Naturally we had no idea that this fiery young savant was many years later to become a luminary of the academic world, a front-rank Goethe scholar. The painter Morgan urged our mother to sit to him for her portrait, and a *diseuse*, Frau von Hustern, declaimed Mosenthal's 'Deborah' at an evening entertainment, to Professor Erich Schmidt's annoyance. Her children played with us, and much later, after many years, in Prague and Berlin I was again to be reminded of those summer holidays in Upper Austria.

It was, after all, to that beautiful woman and her good memory that I owed my first meeting with Rainer Maria Rilke, a meeting of which I shall afterwards have much more to say.

Since I, together with my brother, was almost always accompanied by either a French or an English governess, even in those times I learnt at least to speak those languages very well, although the grammar and reading lessons, which I had to have on long summer afternoons, also did much for my real knowledge of the foreign idiom, even although I did not always welcome them joyfully.

But the English that I absorbed finally and permanently, both as a language and as a mode of expression, I owe to Professor L. C. Hurt. An Englishman of very old family, who had been at home in Vienna since his twenty-first year, this tutor of ours had initiated many a distinguished pupil into the mysteries of his mother-tongue, among them ex-King Ferdinand of Bulgaria and the sons of four Egyptian rulers. His family tree went back into the fifteenth century. He was connected by marriage with the high English nobility. His great-grandmother on his mother's side was a Duchess of Rutland, and it was on her ancient family estate that Professor Hurt spent his summer holiday every year. His great-grandfather on his father's side was that celebrated Sir Richard Arkwright who invented the spinning-jenny.

Like so many of his countrymen, L. C. Hurt had been educated at Eton, preparing for the career of a 'younger son'. After extensive travels and a stay of several years in St. Petersburg, Rome, and Paris, he came to Vienna, which so much appealed to the then still youthful globe-trotter that he settled there permanently. He had no difficulty either in mixing in the Viennese society that set the tone in the 'eighties, or later when it turned out to be necessary for him to take pupils, which was made all the easier for him through his very friendly relations with Professor Palotta, the leading Viennese English scholar.

Professor Hurt above all loved passages for reading chosen from Bulwer-Lytton's *Night and Morning*, *The Lady of Lyons*, and *The Last Days of Pompeii*, as well as Byron's *Childe Harold* and *Mazeppa*. He was fond of asserting that those pupils who had learnt to read and write English from these works had been introduced to the English language and the English way of looking at things quite differently from and better than the others. This strikingly hand-some man, who looked so entirely different from what one would imagine an English gentleman to look like, was for many years extremely successful as professor of the English language at the Vienna Academy of Commerce and at the Theresianum.

Professor Hurt lived not far from the Prater meadows. He was an exceedingly keen cyclist and walker, a circumstance to which he owed an astonishing agility lasting long after his eightieth year. This unusual man still read without spectacles at the age of ninety. Even at a very great age he looked through some of my translations of the works of Bernard Shaw, for whom, admittedly, he did not care.

What is particularly worthy of mention is this venerable man's memory. He recollected all the details of his life, so rich in varied experience, back to his earliest childhood, and hence naturally had infinitely much to tell his friends and former pupils, who never ceased to visit him.

When he celebrated his ninetieth birthday this strikingly tall man was still incomparably alert in mind. On the other hand, a bad fall that he had had a few years earlier had robbed him of some of his physical agility. He died in Vienna at the great age of ninety-two.

If for no other reason than in sheer grateful memory of my step-father's endeavours to gain our love as children by marks of affection, I must not omit to mention an incident that caused me such pleasure as made my heart thump and caused me to burst out into cries of delight. It was like this.

In those hot days we went 'to the country' to Purkersdorf, a place near my native city, which enabled the hard-working head of our family to spend most evenings, but above all the week-ends, in the circle of those near and dear to him. His business made lengthy annual journeys necessary, taking him to far countries. These often came in the late summer days. Since the great express trains did not stop at the little holiday-resort on the Westbahn, but went thundering straight through, my father had to get into the train half an hour earlier, at the central station in the city. We children—I was then eleven, my brother eight—of course knew the time when the beautiful Orient Express would come roaring past the closed gates at the level-crossing, and were taken to the right place once by our mother and several times by our governess. And it was at the side of this girl, who was scarcely involved at all, that late one afternoon I experienced the joyful wonder.

Leaning forward, eagerly, tensely peering in the direction from which the steaming monster must charge down at us, impatiently tugging at my governess's stronger arm, I waited for the row of compartments in one of which I might expect my father to be sitting. I wondered whether I could get a glimpse of him as the train shot past, perhaps for one instant recognising that familiar face. . . . Then all at once a nostalgic whistling sounded, and at lightning speed a man leaned out of an open window in the train, and—oh look!—an arm stretched right out towards us, vigorously waving an enormous parcel. At first—just for a second—I was speechless. Then I uttered a scream and waved back. But the unexpected gift had already flown with a crash against the iron bars of the closed gates at the level-crossing. Our father's laughing face, which had appeared at the window from which he made the successful throw, vanished in a flash, and in its place was a fluttering handkerchief, which then in its turn disappeared as the train receded into the distance.

I was almost paralysed with joy, which was intensified to real bliss when the three of us bent over the parcel, which had burst open in one place. With every precaution we pulled this rich and precious cargo into the near-by meadow and there unpacked the glories it contained: new children's stories by Nieritz, a picture-book, a new school-satchel, a musical-box, a butterfly-net, a sailor's cap, and various other things of the kind for myself and my little brother. Each of the things had a little label attached with the name of the person for whom it was intended. Our governess also received a present, which she quickly conjured away into her pocket.

Perhaps I was able then to stammer out some words expressive of my delight; today I can find none. That was, and has remained, the greatest pleasure of my life. Quite by the way, it filled me with an entirely new childish love, surrounding my father's figure with a nimbus that transformed it for me, astonishing and delighting me. In my imaginative world a father was from this time forward one who leaned out of a nostalgically whistling express-train of the kind that makes one long for far countries, and with a beaming face threw to his children, standing waiting at the closed level-crossing gates, precious parcels containing not only practical little presents but also his whole heart. Perhaps that was why after his return he refused to have any long and detailed discussions of the incident, would not hear of gratitude, and once again displayed his accustomed grave manner.

But in that throw there clearly lay so much redemption and reconciliation that the seed of an utterly pure joy fell into the boy's receptive heart, only to blossom much later and so give that joy an indelible validity. And if today, in writing this book, I must strive to get a panorama of the great joys or at least the joyful moments of my life, I must say that I do not remember any greater cause of happiness. Neither literary awards nor fortunate accidents of any kind, nor rescues from extremity and danger, have given me that untrammelled, bright, enrapturing sense of happiness, such as did the seeming triviality I have here described.

An important event that often recurred should be quickly noted here before it is left to silence. My father always had the welfare of his workmen very much at heart, and it was doubtless in some way connected with this that in later years I many and many a time in his office met the Austrian labour-leader Dr. Victor Adler, with whom he had discussions during which he did not wish to be disturbed. I think that the result of these meetings was the 'Labour Welfare Fund' that my father founded with his own money for the working people of Mährisch-Schönberg and Wigstadtl, where our —now confiscated—factories were. He was a great philanthropist before the Lord and dried many tears for the poor, which then were shed all the more sorrowfully at his grave.

In my last years at school riding-lessons were begun. But I cannot quite manage to register the fact so simply. I must confess that the attitude of my parents—without whose agreement, indeed approval, it would of course never have occurred to me to put such a request to them—is in the highest degree incomprehensible, and that I now see the hand of providence in my being guided to take up riding as a sport. Yet my own father was the victim of this taste; it was a riding accident that my mother had to thank for the great sorrow of her youth.

My progenitor had gone on horseback to visit a spinning-mill in which his firm was interested, and from that visit he returned a gravely ill man. Before arriving at his destination he had fallen from his horse, so unluckily, as it happened, that he was flung against a tree-trunk, which he struck with his chest. The result was a cardiac lesion, and since at that time there was no possibility of undertaking a heart operation, an accident that ninety-nine times out of a hundred does no worse damage than the breaking of an arm caused him to fall ill, and after some years of the resistance put up by his youth, and by his thirst for life, he passed on.

And although this event ought, after all, to have been like a flaring danger-signal to his widow and his brother, my parents urged the youth to the riding school in order to harden him physically and in the belief that in this way his migraines would be overcome.

Naturally, in the course of the years when I was riding, I took a tumble now and then, for the most part when racing, but apart from bruises I never suffered any injury and the little accidents never had any consequence. On the other hand, this love of horses and everything to do with equestrianism did later turn out to be the misfortune of the family from which I sprang. The last head of the house, my step-brother, the son of the man whom I also always called father, had a positively pathological love of trotting-horses. For the sake of this foolish passion he neglected his duties in the business, which he had to steer through the infinitely difficult war and post-war years, and indeed neglected them so seriously that the firm was completely ruined—though admittedly with Hitler's help. It was not only because he had made horses the chief object of his attention instead of the hereditary business which had been entrusted to him, but also because his mania kept him from defending himself commercially against the new era that was about to set in, in other words, from taking proper and appropriate steps. It goes without saying that National Socialism and Bolshevism had a great deal to do with the collapse of the business. These terrible powers met with no real resistance from the frivolous heir and passionate horse-lover and had no difficulty in thrusting into the abyss what was in any case just about to fall.

To foresee all this was something that could not be expected then. No one, of course, had the faintest notion what time and the times would bring. Nor was it to be expected that my parents could have thought such a future and such an end of that great firm at all possible; but what remains eternally incomprehensible is their readiness to deliver us up to horsemanship, indeed to favour and encourage our delight in riding, when, after all, as I have described, a dear member of the family had perished of it.

Even at the early age of seventeen I was a pupil at the Spanische

Reitschule (the headquarters of *haute école*), into which an influential friend of my father's had introduced me. Riding was an exceedingly great pleasure to me and, remarkably enough, it also lent wings to my imagination. I was, as Professor Widerhofer had actually foretold, physically very deft and made more rapid progress in this no less stern school than in the intellectual field. And now that I had passed my school-leaving examination my father was hesitating whether to take me straight into the office or to leave me to do my military service while I was still pliable to demands made on me. I was now nineteen and there would have been little sense in beginning anything that I would, after all, have had to interrupt a year later under the pressure of compulsory military service. So I at once reported to the Seventh Dragoons, in order to serve my one year as a volunteer with that regiment.

In all conscientiousness I make a swift survey of the five years still to pass before this moment is reached, but apart from a long holiday journey through Sweden and Norway right to the North Cape I find nothing worth the telling. In Oslo, which at that time was still called Christiania, as a result of a train's being late I actually encountered Ibsen on the platform. He was pointed out to us by our guide. I did not know overmuch about him, but I had a lengthy conversation with him, doubtless as a consequence of the great interest that he showed in my native city of Vienna. Ibsen was at that time not yet at the height of his fame.

My constant companion, the migraine, has to be thanked for my acquaintance with a highly cultivated elderly lady, the Countess de Créange, who tried to cure me with smelling-salts, in which, oddly enough, her dear friend and helpmate, the Russian Ambassador in Norway, Krupenski by name, also believed. This was my first great journey, and it was markedly different from the little trips that had, however, taken me as far as St. Gallen. I was about sixteen years old when I first came to know Switzerland, where, being in the care of dear good relatives, I felt very much at home. On the beautiful terrace at Romanshorn I at that time met that twenty-seven-year-old favourite with the ladies, Dr. Eugen Steinach, who later became very famous and, if I am not mistaken, has an imperishable name as an early discoverer of rejuvenation hormones. But my travels to the North, on which I was allowed to set out straight after passing my examination, at that time seemed to me the peak of all attainable joys.

In the last years before my examination I had learnt not only riding but also dancing, skating and fencing, which was done in *Paukböden* (students' fencing-clubs) as well as at the fencing-school of the respected Professor Hartl. We had an aunt who, in contrast with my parents' quiet style of living, did things on a very grand scale. Then I actually came into friendly contact with the female sex for the first time.

This kind of society gave me great pleasure, and as family balls were at that time the order of the day, I entered a tremendous whirl in which especially those families were involved that had daughters to marry off. Of course I soon had all sorts of little adventures, even mild little love-affairs, which, however, passed off so harmlessly that if only for that reason they are not worth talking about. A young man's preoccupation with a young girl in those days was of quite a different character from what it is today. A young man was in fact careful not to draw too close to those more or less delicate and pretty young things in white dresses, unless he had matrimonial intentions, which he was often talked into having even if the question could not arise for years to come. Outside the house, and apart from dances given at home, there were, of course, for all that, adventures and passionate loves in plenty, which too often came to a more tragic end in those days than nowadays. Suppression of emotions was at that time actually something like an obligation, and the raw material of conflict embittered and destroyed many a budding love, while addiction to the vices was much more hypocritical and much more treacherous than in these more sincere and informal days in which we live now. There was much suffering in the 'eighties and 'nineties, because people were all too ready to fall in with ridiculous prejudices.

Quarrels, impertinences, and insults had to be settled in a 'chivalrous' way for as long as the Empire lasted and for some little while afterwards. Never since then have I heard so much talk about honour, about satisfaction, about chivalrous settlement of grave differences, as I did in my youth. Novels and plays were full of duels, and the dramas, for instance, of that great writer Arthur Schnitzler often have as their nucleus or germ the destiny-laden power of the duel. The chivalrous settlement of such an 'affair of honour', as it was called, which was often nothing but a disguised taste for brawling, or mere vengefulness, was at that time obligatory in the upper-middle and upper classes. Schnitzler's charming plays *Liebelei* (*Playing with Love* or *The Reckoning*), *Freiwild* (*Outlaws*), and *Das weite Land* (*The Far Country*) would have been impossible without this subjection to the laws of the affair of honour, which were given all too much prominence by the fact that an important writer took such a serious notice of them. The newspapers published detailed reports of duels between members of Parliament who had hurled offensive remarks at each other's heads, between officers who knew of no other way of defending their love than sword in hand, between civil servants high and low. Indeed, duelling flourished right up into the highest circles of the hierarchy of those days, and young and old, poor and rich, paid homage to a code, that is to say, to the laws that made it compulsory to settle affairs of honour according to certain definite prescriptions and along fore-ordained lines.

Even before my year of voluntary military service, which was to fling me right into the hornets' nest of these views and attitudes to life, I had to fight a duel—the weapons being swords—if I was not to lose the right, won by my passing the school-leaving examination, to service as a one-year volunteer in the army of the Emperor Franz Joseph.

In order not to let any part of the year be wasted—for so they referred to the time of reflection necessary to a young man beginning to yearn for acquaintance with his own personality—between the time of my examination and the beginning of my year of military service, I attended a course at the Vienna Commercial College. Having matriculated, one was there prepared for a career in commerce, once more thoroughly learning arithmetic, the keeping of accounts, and the names of various kinds of goods and the great commercial centres of the world. Professor Zehden, with his one arm and his pointed beard, at that time aroused a wild longing to travel in these boys so susceptible to suggestion. In his classes we were all quiet as mice. However scientific the geography was that he taught, it was linked with stories from distant latitudes which were in no way inferior in suspense and thrilling incidents to the Red Indian stories we had only laid aside such a short time ago. And this learned and at the same time so imaginative man had a way of arousing his pupils' desire to travel and discover for themselves; it was clearly his purpose to spur them on to go out into the world and seek their fortune in far countries, in those very far countries over the seas that seemed to us quite unattainable, since at that time, of course, travelling by air had not even been dreamt of.

Among Professor Zehden's pupils there were a few rough fellows, and one of them had actually done his year's military service as a volunteer and was now an officer of the reserve. He sometimes came to lectures in uniform, which was far from correct but which, nevertheless, much impressed a large number of the students. This young man had an extraordinary fund of knowledge, not in the subjects that ought to have been the purpose of his presence there, but as to the future military duties of his fellow-students. For instance, he knew for certain that I would join up in the coming autumn. He at once adopted towards me a tone that I would have expected from a sergeant-major; but the more I avoided this noisy fellow, tedious as I found him, the more violently and unpleasantly he set about me. Unasked, he informed me, and a few students sitting near me, of his political opinions, talking with especial enthusiasm about the Pan-German Deputy Schönerer, who was often enough the talk of the town and whose challenging nationalistic behaviour received comment, disapproving or approving as the case might be, in the daily newspapers.

I think there can have existed few young men as unpolitically-minded as I was. I was without the faintest interest in politics, and I have remained so to this day. I was bored with this much older fellow-student's sword-rattling harangue, and I was glad when the break that he had made use of to deliver his tirades was finally at an end. But just before the next class could begin he flung me a few sneering remarks about a young married couple, friends of mine, with whom he had seen me in the Vienna City Park the day before, though I had been unaware of it.

"You'd better not let yourself be seen about with such people if you want to be an officer," he laughed gibingly, taking up a challenging attitude in front of me. The blood rushed into my cheeks and I said—softly, because the door was just opening to admit a professor: "Mind your own business! What do you mean by talking like that anyway? It's downright impudence." "Oh, you'll see for yourself," he hissed, while my neighbour, who by that time was indeed almost a friend of mine, exclaimed in a whisper: "Be quiet now, but you must have it out with him afterwards."

I followed the lesson absent-mindedly, and what we were being told about commercial and currency law was incapable of arousing my interest. The hour that took so long to pass finally ended, and no sooner was the class alone and about to scatter that this persistent young man once more stood in front of me, drawn up to his full height, and exclaimed: "I stand by everything I said just now!" "That's because you're pushing and ill-mannered," I retorted. "Take that back!" he shouted.

"I've neither time nor inclination to do so," I answered, turning my back on him. Then fell those words, even then so thread-bare: "You shall hear from me!" I was accompanied home by two fellow-pupils who had heard it all and who said: "The whole thing's quite clear. He has provoked you, and this afternoon he'll send his seconds to you. You can rely on us. Send them straight to Doctor Palmay." This was the name of one of these two fellow-students, and one whom I liked very much. He was a lieutenant of artillery in the reserve. Many years of friendship were the result of Palmay's cool and sensible conduct of the affair.

And so it came about, in the old monotonous way, as though fore-ordained and long established as inevitable. It was evident to me—and this was confirmed by my seconds, as the two witnesses of the incident had now become—that in consideration of my approaching year as a volunteer I could not avoid a duel with the stranger, who ranked as a superior officer, if I did not want to endanger my immediate future.

The four young men agreed on a duel with swords the morning of the day after the next, and so everything was arranged for the best.

The encounter took place in a big empty classroom at the institution that I attended daily. A fairly well-known doctor had also been asked by one of my witnesses, whose cousin he was, to be present at the 'affair of honour', so that no time should be lost in getting the expected wound bandaged up. From the moment of taking off his uniform coat, in which he had appeared, my much older, taller, and stronger opponent behaved as if he were going through a not entirely unfamiliar performance, while I felt nothing but extreme cold as a result of being stripped to the waist. Then everything happened very fast. The eldest of the seconds present, my prospective friend Dr. Ludwig Palmay, who was conducting the whole affair, suddenly yelled: "Right!" and we struck out at each other. I defended myself against the wild attacker with some skill, so that his blade only gave me a not too grave wound on the forehead, while my weapon slashed him from the shoulder right down to the wrist. And the next instant a tremendous: "Stop!" was shouted by four voices, for small wounds often bleed more vigorously than big ones and it was doubtless apparent that the fight, which had hardly begun, must now come to an end.

While my opponent was dressing again with his friends' aid and was soon able to go away with his arm roughly bound up, the blood was pouring out of the small wound on my forehead and running down into my eyes, and I had to be laid flat and bandaged in expert style. Indeed, as it was what is called a 'flap-wound', the doctor even had to put in a few stitches. My opponent waited until this was done, then came up to me and held out his hand, which I slowly and somewhat disgustedly took. He quickly went away with his second while I needed longer to be taken home with my head bandaged up. While the surgeon—that is to say, my colleague's friend, who had been summoned—declared smilingly: "It's nothing to worry about, but it hurts and the bandage is a nuisance," I felt strangely sick, and I still remember how surprised I was that although I was in pain I did not get anything like an attack of migraine.

Now, as my temperature had gone up—which the doctor, however, attributed to the excitement—I was put to bed, and none of us who took part in that far from pleasing incident could have dreamt that afternoon, when I thought only of the approaching scene with my parents, that I would now be tied to my bed for weeks and be in danger of my life.

The fact is that my opponent, rushing at me with such violence and being a poor swordsman, in lashing out had trailed his sword on the dusty floor, so contaminating the blade, and with this blade he had given me the wound. The result was that about twenty hours later, when I was in the most frightful agony, what had seemed a harmless cut had turned red, in other words, it was a case of erysipelas or St. Anthony's fire, and the wound gained an importance that it had in sober truth not deserved.

Shortly before the duel I had mentioned the matter casually to my parents, and since they had evidently been half-expecting something in the nature of what was so exaggeratedly called an 'affair of honour' to take place sooner or later, they were glad that it had at least passed off as fortunately as it had. However, it was a bolt from the blue for them—and for me too—when the doctor next day informed them that I was rather gravely ill with a serious attack of erysipelas.

Now began a time of grim and dreadful suffering, which I was not able to forget for years, if for no other reason than that it at once heightened and diminished and in any case changed my nature. This illness was the cause of an early maturity that I would otherwise probably have escaped. I had opportunities to observe myself and others and the passage of time in a way that set the seeds of all sorts of things in me and also developed them too soon. For the first time I came to know solitude, for it was summer, and the others had their holidays and left town, where I remained, sunk in semiconsciousness in the quiet hum of the hot days. So long as my life was still in danger my parents of course would not leave the house, but when they knew I was no longer feverish and Professor Weinlechner, the great surgeon who was then treating me, declared me to be out of danger—when this state was at last reached—for I had lain raving in feverish delirium for many weeks, almost never quite lucid—my mother naturally had to turn her attention to her other children, remove with them to the country and have news of my steady progress sent to her by my already excessively busy father, who also had to do the work of some of his right-hand men, since many of his staff were on holiday. I spent hours, after the heat of the day had faded, leaning out of the open window, watching young and old come and go, and making up many a story in my head about the strangers I saw gliding past.

If I have lingered somewhat over this youthful experience, I think it is my duty to do so, since, after all, ten years later my first book, the novel *Genesung* (*Convalescence*), which opened the gates of intellectual freedom for me, was based on that duel and, however much I may have added out of my own imagination, or changed or improved, it would never have come into existence if this foolish episode had not, as a result of the illness that it occasioned, made me into the author of the story to which I owe the discovery of my vocation.

On the other hand I feel justified in keeping silence about the other two duels that I fought in my young days. Furthermore, I was asked more often than I liked to act as a second, and as such

I have had experiences many and various. In fact, I passed my youth in a time that was, as I have already mentioned, heavy with duelling. In Germany, France, Austria and Italy—everywhere except in England and Switzerland—the newspapers were full of accounts of duels that had taken place as a result of bitter differences of opinion, or on account of women or of insults of all sorts, including those with respect to racial differences.

It must also be said firmly that this bad custom, if it was one, did anyway prevent people from setting about each other with their fists and abusing each other in the most obscene language, such as we had our fill of in later days when nobody was under any compulsion to answer for what he said. The obligation to be represented by seconds in the case of an insult did at least train people to a mode of social behaviour. Nor must it be supposed that the *Kartellträger*, as the four seconds were called, were wild fellows, young or old, with a taste for brawling, who were out to see blood flow. On the contrary, so far as I came to know about such things, the fact was that the friends called upon in defence of one's honour—with the exception, that is, of *Couleurstudenten*, with their taste for brawling, who in any case were in less danger in their fencing-encounters—did honestly endeavour to arrive at a peaceful settlement and never tired of making attempts at reconciliation. There were at least as many statements settling an affair of honour, signed by seconds who had effected a reconciliation, as there were fights that finally had to be fought out with swords or pistols till blood was shed.

It is of course a fact that an unavoidable duel did not prove anything at all, except which of the two antagonists was the better shot or swordsman. The unfairness of destiny in this respect certainly celebrated many a triumph.

Not all duels were of as little concern to the rest of the world as my own and those of so many of those who were my friends then or later. One need only reflect that Ferdinand Lassalle, perhaps the most brilliant leader that the social-democratic movement had in those days, in the full bloom of his manhood and plans became the victim of a duel with pistols and was brought to his death by an unworthy, an utterly worthless man. In France the so tremendously popular General Boulanger was severely wounded in a prolonged contest of swordsmanship with that great orator the parliamentarian

Floquet, and was exposed to ridicule, while his opponent was able
to leave the scene of the duel without a scratch.

Many examples could be mentioned in evidence of the fact that
then one had to do as the Romans did. Especially in the literature
of that time duels were very much the order of the day. The
Parisian dramatist Henri Bernstein, for instance, had a tale to tell
in that respect. For when he was considerably over seventy he had
to cross swords with the dramatic writer Edouard Bourdet—a duel
in which Bernstein, as almost always, dealt wounds and received
none.

Little use it was indeed that at the time when the mania for
duelling was beginning to wane an edict was issued against the
practice. It was persistently ignored, and the prosecution of duellists
was something the guardians of the law set about with a twinkle
in their eye.

Ever again an incident would occur to strengthen the supporters
of duelling in their conviction that it was the only possible dignified
way of getting satisfaction for grave insults and slander of every
kind. Above all it was the large number of duelling students who
supported them vigorously. And truly, in certain cases a duel did
seem impossible to avoid; after all, the Emperor himself had
permitted his Prime Minister, Count Badeni, to fight, and on another
occasion permitted Prince Philipp of Coburg to fight a duel with
the cavalry captain, Geza Mattachich, who had run away with his
wife. The Austrian Prime Minister, Count Badeni, a Polish noble-
man of the old style, indeed had no other way out, for he was
continually being publicly insulted by the German-Nationalist
Deputy Wolf, who treated him as though he were a naughty boy.
The Badeni-Wolf duel was for weeks the talk of Vienna, and great
was the disappointment of all right-thinking people when the
newspapers announced that the Prime Minister had been shot in
the arm, while his opponent remained unscathed. From this one
can see yet again that the result of a duel is far from being a judgment
of heaven.

As for literature, duels naturally contributed a good deal to the
tension and development of the action in plays and novels. One
need only think of Maupassant's *Bel Ami*. This should be specially
emphasised by way of excuse for the Austrian writer Arthur
Schnitzler, for he is reproached with ever and again making duelling

the focus of action in his dramas; had Schnitzler used other levers
to set the action going, he would not be so much neglected on the
stage of our own era. Producers assert that the outlook of these
plays, as well as the exaggerated way in which the love-conflicts
in them are intensified to the point of catastrophe, make them
almost unintelligible to the modern generation.

And so now I wore my new uniform—red trousers, a blue coat
with yellow facings, a heavy helmet on my afflicted head—and
appeared punctually every morning, my sword girded on, in the
cavalry barracks in the Josefstadt, to go on duty. Thanks to my
long training in *haute école* I found the many hours of strenuous
riding-exercises very easy. I liked my duties, and I liked some of
my comrades too, and today I cannot remember that I had much
trouble from my migraine during my period of service. I dare say
there were severe attacks now and then, but clearly I had the good
luck that they did not afflict me at decisive moments during the
great manœuvres.

Especially during my illness with erysipelas and the long convalescence I then spent in Heligoland, where I was sent with a very
kindly tutor, I had written poems, scarcely very good ones, and
not very few in number either. They broke out of me in eruptive
fashion, and it is in vain for me to try to remember now who gave
me advice. I dare say no one did. The tutors and instructors who
came and went did not do so. I had no poetically-minded friends
at that time, or I knew nothing of those with similar aspirations,
who were in any case doubtless not to be met with among the military.
But one thing is certain: at Christmas in the year when I was doing
my military service, shortly after celebrating my twentieth birthday,
I surprised my parents with a slim volume entitled *Poems*, which
had been published by the bookseller Gerold. They were taken
aback and displayed mixed feelings.

I was not particularly proud of this little success and the modest
achievement in respect of my talent, and my parents were disturbed
at the thought that my predestined career was in danger. Oddly
enough, in my unit our commanding officer was the first to learn
of this publication. He sent for me and said something like this:
"It has been reported to me that you have published some poetry.
I am not sure that this is permissible. There is nothing to be found
about it in regimental regulations, obviously because such a thing

has never happened before. However, it only goes to show how much time we leave you young fellows for such things. An extra hour's riding-exercise and you would have been too tired to feel any inclination for scribbling poems." I clicked my heels and only replied timidly that I had not written a single poem since joining up. "Oh, I see," the captain said. "All right then, if it happened earlier on, the whole thing really has nothing to do with me." I was about to make an about-turn when he called out quickly: "Best thing is keep it dark, don't go telling the others." I had in any case precious little desire to do so, and so my final: "Very good, sir!" sounded very sincere and genuine.

I had had the feeling all the time that I had in fact done something very rash. My brother's governess, with whom I was in love and who probably liked my verses for that reason, had eagerly encouraged me to have them printed and had kept up my spirits when I hesitated.

A volume of poems was of course received quite differently by the public and the critics if one already belonged to a literary 'circle', even if this 'circle' amounted to nothing more than a large table in a café. But to dash forward, so to speak from an ambush, with printed poems was something most people were on the whole inclined to be annoyed about.

The year of voluntary service, which worked up to a climax in strenuous manœuvres, passed so quickly and was monotonous in such a healthy way, so good for me physically, that I scarcely recall any details worth recounting. Only one incident that took place at that time seems to be so characteristic of the whole nature of the Empire and the determination of its administrators to see the fundamental laws of the constitution upheld that I feel it a duty to tell the story. A quite ordinary happening resulted in a high-ranking officer's taking a memorable attitude.

Two cadets doing their one year of military service had clashed; the cause of their bitter quarrel is of no moment. Insults were uttered, which led to a challenge being issued by the young man who felt his honour impugned. This challenge was rejected, the grounds being that the challenger, being a Jew, was not entitled to demand satisfaction.

Some days passed, during which this incident was a main subject of discussion among the cadets. Then suddenly one morning a bugle-note resounded such as always heralded the appearance of a high-ranking military personage. The gate of the Josefstadt Cavalry Barracks flew wide open, and, very straight in the saddle, Feldzeugmeister Baron Gradl, Garrison Commander of Vienna, rode on to the barracks square. With a negligent touch of the bridle he pulled up his beautiful charger, which stood uneasily pawing the ground, quite near the gate, and sent for the commanding officer of the cadets' detachment, Captain von Haas, who came running up, saluted, and asked for his superior officer's instructions. These were that the whole detachment, some thirty men, was to parade in order to be addressed.

In a trice we were on parade, standing in rank and file behind our commanding officer, who had given the order.

Now von Gradl raised his tall cavalryman's figure out of the saddle and said: "I have come here today because an unpleasant incident that has taken place in your ranks has been reported to me. One of you, whose name I prefer not to mention—I dare say you all know who it is—has gravely insulted a comrade and refused to give that offended comrade honourable satisfaction, on the pretext that the challenger is of another faith and hence not entitled to demand satisfaction. To this I have the following to say:

"Anyone who has been brought up from birth to think nobly and act in a chivalrous way is entitled to demand honourable satisfaction, no matter where his cradle may have stood—even if he were a fuzzy-wuzzy!"

The General's voice was high, almost shrill, as he continued:

"This comrade of yours has taken it upon himself—in a disgraceful and dishonourable way—to refuse honourable satisfaction to a gravely offended comrade who has, like himself, the privilege of wearing the Emperor's uniform and whose previous studies have entitled him to wear on his sleeve the badge showing him to be a cadet. How miserable, how unchivalrous! As for the pretext, what infamy! Only his youth saves him from instantly having to bear the gravest consequences. My orders therefore are: Within twenty-four hours it must be reported to the corps command that the comrade-in-arms who has been insulted and has the choice of weapons has received honourable satisfaction, which he is thoroughly entitled to receive. Should this not be reported to me within the specified period, the offender who has in such a cowardly manner attempted to escape the consequences of his behaviour will not be permitted to remain in this detachment. I shall see to it that he is instantly removed."

There was a deathly hush among us. Then our commanding officer's voice rang out: "Very good, Your Excellency!" At a sign from Baron Gradl's adjutant the barracks gate flew wide open and, sitting very straight in the saddle, Vienna's brave Korpskommandant, after having saluted the detachment that was standing to attention, rode out again, his horse foaming at the mouth and nodding its head as though in approval.

Two mornings later he received the following report from our commanding officer, von Haas: "Early yesterday morning a duel was fought with swords between the two cadets X and Y. Both received somewhat severe wounds and are now in the garrison hospital."

In the course of this year I did in fact become a very respectable cavalryman. The well-known Colonel Ottokar von Pizzighelli testified as much in black and white for me. And the question was whether I imagined it or was it really a fact that my frightful migraines seemed to be favourably affected by intensive physical activity, if it did not continue into the night but was followed by a great deal of sleep.

Then, when we were granted the necessary leave for the purpose, with the help of an older artillery captain I prepared myself thoroughly for the officers' passing-out examination; and it was from him that I learned, to my high delight, that in the report on each of us that had to be sent in to regimental command I was referred to as an unusually capable horseman. I had the Imperial *haute école* training to thank for that.

I was so pleased about this that I at once began to play with the thought of doing what my comrades-in-arms, and also one younger officer, urged me to do: to stay on in the army for some months longer than my year of volunteer service and serve as a newly-fledged lieutenant. At Christmas, then, when I received my gold sword-knot and presented myself to my parents as a brand-new lieutenant—something that they did not particularly rejoice at, but nevertheless were quite pleased and glad about—I at once burst out with my wish, not, indeed, to become a professional officer but to serve a few more months now before taking up the occupation that awaited me, according to my father's decision, in his office.

The years that follow, which are those between twenty and thirty, are the darkest in my memory. I wish to be rightly understood: I do not mean to say that my memories are gloomy. Oh no, they sometimes shine in dazzling colours, positively distressing me with their blinding brightness. But over this period there lies a strange veil, which I would gladly remove, but I cannot.

At this time it had already become clear to me that anyone must fail who relied overmuch on himself and the strength of his own will. For at this period I had seen and come to recognise, almost with horror, how my father, impelled though he was by the noblest impulses, was incapable of making anyone happy or of being happy himself. He and my poor disappointed mother were soon at cross-purposes, and their marriage was held together only by their shared interest in the children.

In general the era of the 'eighties and 'nineties is regarded as 'the good old days', a sort of golden age. But if the truth be told we must admit that in those times of serene peace, free from the faintest threat of war, youth especially was a prey to terrible sufferings that penetrated into the inmost marrow of its bones. With that 'golden' age there passed away a world of prejudices that embittered our lives and which we were not strong enough to fight against. Many young men—and women too—whose friends were justified in having the fairest hopes of them sought an early death because they could not see any other way out and with their 'advanced' and yet so natural feelings ran up against a terrible wall as soon as they tried to act according to those feelings. I often wonder whether the world really had to fall in ruins before parents could be found who were ready to give their blessing to the cohabitation of young people of different sexes even though, for all sorts of reasons, marriage was impossible. What games of hide-and-seek there used to be, what a hypocritical, unhealthy denying of natural youthful instincts!

And what harsh treatment those who led sheltered lives accorded to those others whom Schnitzler called *Freiwild* (*Outlaws*, or *Fair Game*)!

Oh, that wicked belief in keeping up appearances! Whether one could do it or not, it was required of one that one should live 'in keeping with one's station in life', if one did not want to be excluded from social circles that one wished to enter for innumerable reasons to do with one's profession, connections of all kinds, chances of marriage, and so on; or one had to rely on one's own resources and build up a life of one's own, which of course only some rare spirits succeeded in doing. The rest led a miserable existence, their emotions stunted, making others unhappy, unhappy themselves, as a punishment for following the fine examples shown them on all rungs of the social ladder.

So far as myself and my family are concerned, I suppose one reason why we were all not social climbers was that the older generation had already carved out their place in the world and the younger of us had been born with a silver spoon in our mouths. In addition there was the fact that we had very strong instincts of independence and our father, at any rate, had set an example of how to go one's way regardless of the chatter and the incomprehension of the world in matters of emotion, giving an account of oneself only to oneself.

I was a strange product, concocted of many years of changing methods of education under my various native and foreign governesses, some of whom had made quite a deep impression on me and caused quite a stir in my adolescent heart, and under the tutors who had followed in their brisk footsteps. The tutors had steered me in a quite different direction and made me forget the earlier upheavals occasioned by the governesses, most of whom had been very pretty and cultivated persons. But there was one feeling that was aroused in me by both the female and the male supervisors of my younger years, and that was pity. This feeling was the strongest one I had. It was especially the men, of whom the younger ones did not know what to do with themselves and the elder were embittered, who even during lessons in some peculiar way became objects of study for me; and if I worked hard at my lessons, it was partly in order to help my teachers to be successful. That has always been the scarlet thread running through my life: anyone for whom I was sorry, or who managed to make me sorry for him, always won hands down and could get me over to his side.

I was different from others of my age during my army period too, in that materially and physically I was still almost quite uncorrupted —and yet at the same time much more corrupted than others, with all their boasting,because my imagination had early gone roaming far afield. I was more than feverish in my longing for all the

unknown potential pleasures. I knew—and I took the fact seriously
—that I was about to enter on a career for which I did not feel
myself in the slightest way suited, one for which I had neither love
nor longing; but I relied on my luck to put me in my right place
sooner or later and lead me the right way.

From round about my seventeenth year onward I was a great
reader. Every free hour I had I spent with the books that came
flooding in from all sides for me. Dumas' *Three Musketeers*, which
I devoured, I owed to a French governess, Bulwer-Lytton's *Last
Days of Pompeii* and *Night and Morning* to a very conscientious
English governess who, precisely like Professor Hurt later on,
attached the highest possible importance to my acquaintance with
these books and very gravely and strictly insisted on my reading
them, which I in any case found infinitely enjoyable. I read and read,
often indiscriminately and at random, until the classics caused such
a stir in my emotions that for years I was unable to tear myself
away from them.

Even during the three months of military service that I did after
my year as a volunteer, when I was training my captain's horses
for the officers' race (I then weighed 110 pounds) and giving fencing
instruction to the volunteers of the year after mine, I had translated
into German verse an Indian verse-drama that the great Sanskrit
scholar, Angelo de Gubernatis, had translated from the original
Indian language into Italian. My father had agreed to my doing
these three months' extra service on the condition that I should
now seriously set about learning Italian, because as soon as I was
completely at his disposal he intended sending me to a silk-spinnery
in Italy. My Italian master, the Triestino Leon Senigaglia, brought
me this work, which he regarded as an especially fine example of
Italian rhythm and the peculiar melody of the Italian language.
This Indian fairy-tale, which was called *Savitri*, greatly took my
fancy, and so there came about, first as an exercise, but then quite
freely adapted in German verse, a work that obliged me to get into
touch with Angelo de Gubernatis, first of all by letter. He was a
person who on closer acquaintance turned out to be one of the most
appealing personalities I came to know in my youth. This *Savitri*
very nearly made me into a Burgtheater author even before I had
begun my career, for Baron Alfred Berger, who was at that time
the secretary of the theatre, liked it so much that he recommended

it to the production committee then in temporary control. But it did not meet with sufficient approval. Today, alas, I no longer have a copy of this work, which was published by Gerold.

Perhaps because my master was a particularly good teacher, I learned Italian much faster and more pleasantly than any other language. My father shrewdly turned this to account by sending me to a silk mill near Bergamo, the owner of which was an extremely close personal and business friend of his. There I was to set about learning my future job. And so this brought me to the country of my heart's desire—to Italy.

This is perhaps the place to speak of the persistence with which the directors of great firms, the heads—often as proud as they were modest—of respected businesses known beyond the frontiers of their own country, as soon as they had sons of their own could think only of one thing: keeping up those businesses, inherited in earlier times but vastly enlarged in the reign of the Emperor Franz Joseph, and knowing that they would be carried on in future by men bearing their own name. And on top of that there was the consideration, in this case, that my step-father had promised his dying brother to give his son a proper start in life, which meant material security. However patiently this man may have agreed to constant postponements right down to my thirtieth year, which brought the decision, acknowledged by him too to be the right one, he nevertheless had no other thought than some day to see me at his side at the head of this beloved business, which he had endowed with a reputation and commercial importance extending far beyond the frontiers of our native country.

I dreaded the thought of it. Among all the feelings I had, none was so strong as the conviction that I should never be able to fulfil that wish, even if I were to do everything in my power to extinguish my own personality. But I was equally aware of my powerlessness and was sensible enough not to make too great a parade of that conviction. And I have time and again discovered that my father was far from being an exception. The other heads of firms, large and small, at least in those days thought exactly as he did. Let me here give an example that I think deserves to be recorded.

Many years later, while on my way to Karlsbad, I once happened to be having tea in Prague at the house of the parents of my friend Franz Werfel. He himself, unfortunately, was away, conducting important negotiations with his publisher in Germany, while I had to give a lecture in the German students' assembly hall. I believed and indeed hoped that the old man would turn out to be the proudest and happiest of his famous son's admirers. It must be borne in mind that at that time Franz Werfel had already written, among other great works, *Die Geschwister von Neapel* (*The Pascarella Family*) and that immortal work *Musa Dagh* (*The Forty Days of Musa Dagh*). He was already one of the few writers using the German language who had gained a world-wide reputation. It was only natural that, if only for the sake of honouring old Werfel, I should speak of his son and his son's writings with great enthusiasm. To my astonishment—and I was so astonished that I was speechless for the rest of my visit—the elder Werfel exclaimed: "Ah yes, that's just my bad luck! There's the reason why my glove-factory's going to wrack and ruin. I had intended Franz to go into the business. If he prefers travelling round the world and writing, instead of working in my business and enlarging what I've built up, I must write my life off as a failure. You must excuse me for not being able to share your ecstasy. I have been disappointed by my only son."

Only about twenty-five years have passed since I had that memorable conversation. Now, it seems to me that everyone who has created anything is so penetrated with the sense of his achievement that if he is not an artist and has no imagination he remains far too wrapped up in his own life and his own work to be capable of recognising differences in value and of understanding that the most eminent achievements in the realm of commerce can, after all, never compare with deeds and doers who are able to bestow some precious happiness on the whole world by means of their works. It should be said, to soften the impression given by this remarkably gruff attitude on the part of an otherwise model father, that old Frau Werfel all the time sat there smiling and exchanging glances with me that relieved me of the necessity of speaking up for her son.

The six months I spent in Upper Italy were very welcome, although they did for the first time take me away from my riding, which had become something I could hardly get on without at all. It had been really delightful, after all, and a sort of liberation, to go cantering through the Prater meadows on beautiful horses, exactly as I liked and whenever and for as long as I liked, whereas up to then I had been in the saddle almost always only as a pupil of the Spanische Reitschule or when on duty. This was also the only activity during which I ceased to have forebodings of my difficult situation and the approaching struggles, reflecting on them all too optimistically or pessimistically; and this release from my own ego was something I had not experienced so delightfully and liberatingly in any other occupation as I did on the back of spirited, sometimes even slightly unmanageable, horses, with which I quickly got on excellent terms. This was now for a while to be a thing of the past. I was to enter strange surroundings, in a strange country.

Not on my own account, of course, but as my father's son, I was very kindly and expectantly received into the patrician family-circle of these silk-spinners. I did what was expected of me, and not only at work but after work attached myself to the extremely pleasant sons of the house that had so hospitably opened its doors to me. From this there grew up a lifelong friendship that we toasted in Milan only a year ago, remembering our youth. Naturally I made use of every free day to get to know the glorious country in the North of which I was working, at Alzano Maggiore near Bergamo.

A further reason for my readiness to fall in with my father's wish and go abroad for the first time, although my attitude was connected with the future he intended for me, was the prospect of making the personal acquaintance of the man, so many years my senior, who through his letters had become my friend—Angelo de Gubernatis, the author of *Savitri*. The meeting took place in Florence, for the first time bringing me together with one who was internationally celebrated as a scholar. I was received with downright enthusiasm by him and his little family, which consisted of mother and daughter. He could not sufficiently praise the work I had devoted to his creation—work that he had already, I dare say to some extent from vanity, sent to his patroness, the Marchesa di Villamarina, lady-in-waiting to the Queen. And I did in fact receive from this benevolent lady a charming letter in which there was no lack of the over-enthusiastic phrases typical of the great kindliness of the Italians.

I confessed to the scholar who was by many decades my elder that I wanted to dedicate my life to poetry—or, to put it more precisely, to writing—and told him how great the obstacles were that I would have to overcome, for the career my father had planned for me was meant to lead me into quite other, fundamentally different, paths very little appealing to my temperament. Angelo de Gubernatis listened with thoughtful gaze, looking into the far distance, but with genuine sympathy; and he advised me to leave the decision of this vital question to fate with a good heart, since fate managed to lead on to the right road precisely him whom a lack of self-confidence or a lack of energy prevented from obstinately fighting for aims that did, after all, lie in darkness. I did not leave this man without having to promise to come often and often again and to remain in contact with him. This promise I did indeed keep in so far as was feasible; I visited him again some years later, for the last time, in Rome, where he was teaching Sanskrit at the university. But it was not long before I received news of his death, which had been preceded by that of his wife. I never heard from his daughter again.

In memory of him and not only in order to re-discover works of my own, I do not cease to hope that the little volume with the title *Savitri* will turn up again some time in a second-hand bookshop or out-of-the-way library.

My stay in Upper Italy had been intended by my father to last about a year, but an incident with which neither he nor, remarkably enough, I myself had reckoned put an end to my visit before that time was over. I was called up for my first period of military training, and because of my outstanding abilities as a horseman I was made adjutant. It was in this capacity that I was to do my first period of active service in the Austrian Army, which would last twenty-eight days. I did not like having to part so suddenly from my new friends, but orders were orders.

It was the first time that I had to join my regiment as an officer, and there could of course be no delay. Even my parents, who very much regretted this interruption—particularly my father, who mistakenly believed I had perhaps been won over to my new career after all—merely took it as a matter of course that they were now seeing me again for this reason. Like myself, they knew that afterwards I could not very well go back and continue various little jobs I had begun there. Nor did I come home entirely without some knowledge of silk-weaving matters; even my weekly correspondence with my father's firm had shown that I had made progress and acquired knowledge that would be of use to an industrialist later.

My orders were to report in Prague; but from there I was

transferred to the Imperial manœuvres at Pilsen. This period of training, which would have been quite uninteresting if I had been on ordinary service with the regiment—so my former comrades-in-arms, who had also been called up, told me—in my case was as stimulating as it was exhausting, for I had been attached to a general as his adjutant. Suddenly, immediately after I had reported for duty, I found myself involved in a technical hitch. The cavalry regiment under the command of my general for the duration of the manœuvres had to supply me with a horse, but refused to do this because an epidemic had broken out among its horses and it naturally needed the few sound horses for itself and the manœuvres now beginning. My general sent for me and said: "It is your duty to ride beside me at seven o'clock every morning, carrying out my orders, but as the result of the incident with which you are acquainted there is no horse that can be placed at your disposal by us. Hence, against my will and your own—at least I assume so, Lieutenant!—you are off duty, unless you are successful in getting hold of a horse, on your own account, that would be suitable for the duties you have to perform. I give you two days. Then we must move to Pilsen. If I find you at my side at seven o'clock on the morning of the day after tomorrow, I shall reckon the achievement highly to your credit and remember it. If I do not see you then, I shall simply have to manage without an adjutant or only with one lent me from time to time, and shall know that your bad luck has made you unsuccessful in your attempt to remain at my disposal." With these words he dismissed me and galloped away.

In so doing this strange but very likeable general, who was distinguished from his brothers-in-arms in that he spoke with a North German accent, which was, incidentally, very much in keeping with his name, Fleck von Falkhausen, aroused in me an ambition hitherto unknown to me. At that moment there was nothing I longed for so much as a rideable horse, and I set out in search of one. I went to all the taverns in the outlying districts, asking for the hire of a riding horse, a request that generally met with the greatest of amazement and shaking of heads. A waiter called out to me irritably: "If you want a horse, you'd better go to the circus!"

This piece of repartee gave me the right idea. I did in fact go to the circus, the presence of which had already been made known to me by placards, and asked to see the manager. I explained my bad luck to him and also described my disappointed ambition. The man, who had been a soldier himself, laughed amiably and said: "Well, Lieutenant, I can think of a way of helping you, but it isn't much good suggesting it. I have here a riding horse that really isn't fit for riding any more, because a fairly lengthy period of service with an undertaker has spoilt him for his original function. If you like to try your luck with him, especially if you like to break him in by riding round my ring before you take him out into the open, I'll gladly put both at your disposal."

I literally heaved a sigh of relief and exclaimed: "Bring me the horse!"

In the course of the next quarter of an hour he was brought to me, at the bidding of the sympathetic manager, but with thoroughly shabby head-harness. Without waiting for the explanations that were now showered upon me, I swung into the saddle. Now a thorough-going struggle began between the very handsome animal and myself. It was a long time before he remembered having carried a rider, and he caused me a great deal of trouble in my attempts to get him going in the paces known as walking, trotting, and galloping. I soon left the ring and spent hours, without even a thought of eating, racing about in the open, in the fields and meadows around Prague, with this animal. In the end, too, I had my reward, for the astonished horse soon began to make progress. In any case, if only in order to show my good intentions, after spending another day from dawn to dusk practising my arts on the bewildered animal, I meant to try to appear at the place I knew of at my general's side the following morning.

It all went really quite tolerably, and as I had also provided myself with a rather better saddle and bridle, which the batman allotted me obtained with great skill and adjusted to the animal, now at the appointed hour I rode gaily out to the place of assembly. But there something unexpected happened. A funeral came past, and suddenly the horse began to behave in the way one would expect of an animal that had been all too long used in funeral processions. He pranced along with me in time with the dead-march in such a way as to make my hopes that I had won him over to his new function sink again. There was still something of a prance in his paces when to my general's great astonishment I suddenly appeared at his side. He laughed full-throatedly, held out his hand to me, and said:

"Splendid, splendid—how did you manage it? I congratulate you. You can be proud of this. You're a real cavalryman."

However delighted I was to hear this praise from so high a superior officer, I nevertheless continued to tremble inwardly at the thought of what might happen if the animal remembered its past. Not for nothing had I feared that moment. The same funeral procession that I had already met came past our brigade half an hour later, after we had set out, and to the high delight of my chief and all the officers riding and marching around him the funeral horse that I had with such trouble and persistence restored to being a riding horse once more began its solemn pacing. I would not give in, and my general was kind enough not to leave me in the lurch and send me straight home again. And indeed it did become possible to make the horse behave sensibly, especially when galloping. But one can as little be galloping all the time as one can be always declaiming. I soon discovered this. Luckily for me less than a week passed before the regiment provided me with a proper mount, which had apparently more or less got over the infection that had been going around among the regiment's horses. To this little episode I owed the very good report I got from my general, to whose entire satisfaction, of course, I performed my duties in the second half of the manœuvres. However, I was also helped by a strange coincidence that is so characteristic of the game of playing at soldiers popular among the youth of that time that I cannot pass over it without mention.

I had a great and respectful liking for the old Emperor who had suffered so much and endured such terrible blows of fate, which he had done with an exemplary bearing that it was almost beyond mortal power to understand. It had always been my childish wish to get into his presence somehow. This wish impelled me to ride in the Emperor's suite—as, being a cavalry officer in the reserve, I was entitled to—at the annual Imperial parade in the spring, which was held on the Schmelz, a heath in the suburbs of Vienna. I was always waiting for some chance to bring me close to him, but this never happened, until the aforementioned manœuvres did at last bring me into his presence in the course of duty. He actually addressed two words to me, and perhaps the story of this very short speech is interesting enough to be told here.

As I have already said, I did my part in the Imperial manœuvres in Bohemia at the side of that distinguished General, Fleck von Falkhausen, and as a sign of his great satisfaction with several successfully accomplished long-distance rides he relinquished me, on one of the hottest days of the manœuvres, to Colonel von R., who was in charge of the attacking party of a brigade and enjoyed the privilege of being attached to the Emperor Franz Joseph for his personal guidance in the sector.

On the decisive day the Emperor sent for the divisional commandant, and I galloped along to the point of assembly behind my superior officer. After reporting and receiving an order my brigade-commander beckoned me over to him, and when I pulled my horse up before him and saluted, I found myself at the same time confronting the splendid horsemanly figure of the Emperor. A long-dreamed-of desire was fulfilled. In the presence of the Supreme Commander of the Armed Forces the colonel now turned to me and said: "Lieutenant, you are to convey the two following orders. The artillery regiment under the command of Colonel von Koller is to march without delay up the Tafelberg and there unlimber ordnance. Then ride to General von Sloninka's Brigade and inform the General that after carrying out a successful outflanking manœuvre he is to occupy the Fichtelberg, with both his regiments."

I had listened tensely, breathlessly, and was concentrating on the order I had received when the colonel added: "Lieutenant, repeat the message." That was his duty; it was a military regulation. I had just opened my mouth, when the Emperor, who had been patting the beautiful neck of the thoroughbred on which he was mounted, struck his shining right boot with his thin yellow riding-crop, flashed a glance at me out of his large kindly blue eyes and, turning to us both, exclaimed impatiently: "*Wird's, wird's!*" ("Get going, get going!") The colonel made a sign to me that I understood. Tightening the reins, I saluted and dashed away, giving my horse the spurs, in order to carry the instructions I had received to the place for which they were intended without a moment's delay. I had almost reached the artillery commander's position when an icy feeling of horror overcame me, nearly wrenching me out of the saddle. Which unit was to occupy the Tafelberg and which the Fichtelberg? Fear of confusing the two hills almost robbed me of my senses. But I had no time for reflection; I plucked up my courage and delivered the important messages at random. It struck me especially that General von Sloninka received the order with a nod of agreement and instantly began to pass it on. But I was soon back at my commanding officer's side. Armed with a large pair of binoculars, he was watching the movement for which he had given orders. I pressed the bridle tight between the palms of my hands and sent up silent prayers that all might be well.

All at once the colonel turned his tall figure towards me and held out his hand. Disconcerted and delighted, I took it, completely put at ease by the smile on his furrowed face. And then, believe it or not, he said to me: "I congratulate you, Lieutenant, on your precocious generalship. You instantly recognised that under the stress of His Imperial Majesty's impatience I uttered the names in the wrong order, confusing the Tafelberg with the Fichtelberg, which I would of course have noticed if you had been permitted to repeat the order. You corrected the error on your own responsibility, as a result of which victory will go to the troops I command. Thank you. I should be glad to have such an adjutant in the event of real fighting, face to face with the enemy." Overjoyed, unable to believe my ears, I saluted.

By that evening in the mess the story had already gone round and I was cheered, almost fêted, by my younger brothers-in-arms. In my own mind I knew, of course, how disgracefully I had confused the two orders and that it must have been a wise man who had introduced into the army the regulation that all important orders must be repeated.

Rainy days, working up to cloud-bursts, put an end to these first manœuvres of mine and obediently I returned to my parents' house. Now the time had come to fulfil the wishes that were not my own, or at least to try honestly to do so, and out of gratitude, if for no other reason, to enter upon the preparations for my future career, for which I felt myself utterly unsuited.

I still remember the first morning when I entered my father's office in the Schottenfeldgasse punctually at eight o'clock and sat down at the place that had been made vacant for me. Here I was now to make entries day after day, adding and subtracting, even, indeed, multiplying—in other words, practising the three forms of arithmetic in which I was tolerably skilled. I wondered whether I should also be expected to do division, which was difficult. I can still see my father's beaming gaze as he welcomed me that morning.

In front of me and next to me, not particularly far away, sat clerks, and each of them had his little sphere of activity in which he was at home, while I went to an incredible amount of trouble to develop some taste for the life that I had now begun.

After some weeks of fumbling my day passed more or less as follows. First thing in the morning I went to the Spanische Reitschule in order to get some physical exercise and go to work all the stronger for it. On the noble white Lipizzaner's broad back I learned cheerfully to shake off the greyness of everyday things and master the emotional conflict that might otherwise have been a heavy burden to me psychologically. Then till noon, under the observation not only of my father, who would come up to me every now and then, but also of so many other people, strangers to me, I would sit at my desk, which was big enough and covered with enough blotting-paper for me to write, underneath it, things that meant more to me than the dry work allotted to me, which utterly failed to appeal to me. About one o'clock the office was closed and we went down to the first floor to lunch with my mother. My brother and my step-brothers, who had come in from school, would already be there to share the meal with us. After lunching we would chat while our parents lay down and rested for an hour or so. Then I went up to the office again and mechanically carried out whatever was demanded of me. Shortly before six, or thereabouts, I was free.

So that was to be my youth and my life. I would never have dared to say so in so many words, but I felt as if I were in a state of very mild captivity with no threats to make it unbearable.

However, I do not feel justified in describing the monotony of the days that gradually mounted up into years, with all the little incidents that occurred in the way of business. They are as unimportant as the man who describes this epoch of his life. What does seem important to me is all the things that happened outside the limits of life in my father's firm. To my way of thinking my own life began only when I had left the office to which I was condemned.

However full of variety life in my native city might be for a young man, with however many adventures beckoning one from every nook and cranny, I was on the look-out for a chance to travel in order to escape from the ordinariness of my existence; and there were chances enough, particularly when I began to cheat and associated them with the needs of the business, which I really had not at heart at all. My father, who had himself always had a great liking for travel but who never got any farther than France, took the remarkably unselfish point of view that his sons should have and do what had not been granted to him.

In the office I secretly had under all the piles of blotting-paper a little literary workshop—loose sheets on which I not only scribbled poems but also produced a fairly long narrative, entitled 'The Smile that was Sold', which, with two other stories, 'The Cot' and 'The Buried Doll' appeared in the Wiener Verlag as the ninth volume of the Library of Modern German Authors, though admittedly that was much later, not till the year 1905. I have always called these signs of my underground industry my 'ledger'. When I went to my room after these stolen hours I always felt pretty tired, but I do not recollect that I was ever punished by a vengeful migraine for the offence I had committed against the obligations that I had, after all, accepted, and also against my own health.

Shortly after I had completed the stories I have just mentioned I went on a holiday, which took me to Constantinople and Greece. The visit to the Acropolis, Olympia and Salamis filled me with such a great sense of sublime happiness that today I still look back gratefully to those places that have long ago been so effectively and significantly described by others.

I managed to get permission for this journey because my father wanted to form connections in Brussa and Smyrna, and chose me to open negotiations. In this I was helped, oddly enough, by an English family I got to know in the Anatolian hotel at Brussa—the naval captain Gambier and his lovely companions, a very cultivated English lady with a quite delightful daughter. This hotel acquaintance developed into a friendship that I was able to keep up on my first visits to England many years later.

At that time I came to know old Turkey under the rule of the Sultan Abdul Hamid, and on the day I left there began one of those terrible massacres of the Armenians that Franz Werfel portrayed unforgettably in his novel *Musa Dagh*. At that time there were still swarms of dogs in the streets of Constantinople, and right to the door of the Pera Palace Hotel, where most so-called 'distinguished foreigners' stayed, came that dreadful howling, which resounded in the sultry nights, at once ominous and heartbreaking and really like a cry for help. The women were still heavily veiled, and the well-known Freshwater Corso, with the gaily decorated *kaiks*, looked like a cavalcade of people from a masked ball. But the high-spot of my Turkish memories is an expedition I made to the island of Prinkipio, whose fairy-tale groves were of such a sort as to give one a glimpse of the wonders of the Orient. Yet the memory that still takes precedence over much more important and even more beautiful and more magnificent impressions is that of sailing into the Bosphorus. This harbour was at that time, I am sure, the most beautiful in the world, and even the joy of seeing Naples suddenly looming up out of the sea when one comes from, say, Brindisi, cannot be compared with that splendour.

When I came home from that expedition, which had actually only taken some weeks, I remained for a long time in my native city, which was as rich in mysteries as a city can be, and which I was only now, when I had acquired some feeling for comparative values, to begin to appreciate properly. I was a Viennese and I seldom stood before locked doors when I wanted to see something of what they concealed and to explore it.

Vienna was even then the city of dancers and fiddlers, as Anton Wildgans some decades later said all the people of Austria were. Almost everyone whether rich or poor had a vision of the future that was carefree compared with the picture of what is to come that modern men and women carry about with them, and which is built up out of dreadful experiences. Naturally there was no lack of sorrow and anxiety. And out of it arose many an experience that today would only arouse a smile. But it was truly a city of dancing merriment and joyful song, and there can scarcely have been so many people of talent—and even more than one genius—anywhere else as there were in Vienna.

There was much hospitality. Private balls competed with public dances and with the great festival balls that at the same time had a certain official function. I remember weeks when I had to get into evening dress every evening, I had so many invitations and was so glad to answer the calls of hostesses, whether the balls they were giving were in private houses or in the beautiful Sophiensäle, where most public balls were given.

I was unspeakably eager to know people and have experiences, even if they were too small to have any claim to be noticed in a book of reminiscences. Affairs of the heart, amorous adventures, exist in order to be passed over in silence! As a result of my affliction and the warning I had been given against alcohol and nicotine I became a teetotaller and non-smoker once and for all, and have remained so to this day. Hence my entire interest was concentrated on the female sex, against which I had not been warned, if for no other reason perhaps than that, young as I was, I would be bound to burst out of such a tight circle of prohibitions in some direction or other. But this is not intended to be an introduction to love-stories, which, heaven knows, I do not wish to recount. I cannot mention the girls and women who meant nothing to me, and those who played a fateful rôle in my life, for weal or woe, I consider it my duty to leave in an obscurity lightened only by grateful memories. Everyone may have the right to expose his own secrets to view, but not, after all, those of his trustful female partners, who can never lose their claim to his silence.

About that time there was in Vienna a world-famous pianist, a virtuoso who was also a very much sought-after internationally known teacher. This was Professor Leschetitzky, who had a great attraction especially for American music-students of both sexes. In the autumn they came from great distances to take lessons from the great master and enjoy the Viennese carnival, the Viennese theatres, the Viennese spring with the revels in the Prater and at Schönbrunn, and also went a great deal to social gatherings at private houses, where they were easily introduced and liked to go. In their circle it was Emily Hutchinson and Jenny Baker who were accounted the most good-looking feminine representatives of their country beyond the seas, and oddly enough they were also Leschetitzky's best pupils. Twice both of them had gone home in the summer and returned punctually in the autumn—so great was their yearning for Vienna, for their Viennese friends male and female, but also for their memorable lessons with Maestro Leschetitzky. They were also stars of the glittering private balls given by great industrialists and banking magnates. The famous music-master could hardly ever be persuaded to accompany one of his favourite girl-pupils to such entertainments, but there was *one* challenge that he did accept.

It came to his ears that these same two girls obstinately refused to go to the piano that was to be found almost everywhere and give a small circle of friends a display of the skill they had acquired in Vienna. One of them, Emily Hutchinson, of whom Professor Leschetitzky was particularly fond, complained to him about being asked so often and he asked hastily: "Would you play if I were to come along and be one of your audience?" She instantly agreed, and so it came about that at least one of the young ladies sat down at the piano in the house of a family with whom she was on terms of friendship; it was a small event but eagerly looked forward to by the numerous acquaintances who were present. The applause that broke out was, however—to her astonishment, though not at all to her distress—meant for Maestro Leschetitzky, who had sat down in a row of chairs at the back, just opposite her. The affair developed into a thorough-going little concert, which produced enthusiastic applause and approval, in which the music-master, who had been a delighted listener, heartily joined. From this evening on it was no longer doubted that the American girls who came to Vienna every year for the sake of music and a music-master were able not only to flirt, as it was hinted of them, but also to become first-class musicians.

This circle, of which I gradually grew tired, was one I very soon left in order to find more serious attachments and more satisfying ways of spending my evenings.

The great lure was that of the Viennese theatres, particularly the splendid Burgtheater. To be produced at the Burgtheater some day was every young writer's dream. But so much has been written about this theatre in admirable essays, even in whole volumes, that I can scarcely bring myself, in the framework of these reminiscences, to utter a reminder of the sensational experiences we owed to the artists Sonnenthal, Gabillon, Baumeister, Robert, Hartmann, Mitterwurzer, and the ladies Charlotte Wolter, Stella von Hohenfels, and others whose names can never be forgotten and are ever on the lips of all Viennese.

But when things began to be difficult in my private life, when I was overwhelmed by love-affairs and the coming and going of violent passions, sometimes so much so that it took my breath away and I could not get relief even on horseback, then it was a dreamt-of journey that saved me from many a danger and from myself. This longing was at that time even stronger than any other, and it burst asunder the chains that I all too quickly and all too gladly wore when they were forged for me by seductive Viennese maidens.

My father had a representative in America, and as he did not know him personally he was completely dependent on correspondence with him and his partners. He had sometimes said in passing that he would like me to visit this man some time and discuss with him some plans for extending the business. At a time when business was flourishing to an extent that reinforced this wish of my father's, I was asked to give my opinion on these questions, and I joyfully agreed, but asked for permission not only to visit New York, where we had our branch, but to travel across the United States from North to South and from East to West.

So August approached in the year 1893. According to the ideas of that time I was really still too young, at the age of scarcely twenty-four, for such a long journey, which meant going such a great distance from my parents and the protection of my native city. To cross the seas was then still considered a very serious matter. Even when the undertaking had been resolved on, my parents seem to have had qualms about it, and it must doubtless be ascribed to this fact that my father applied to the well-known Stangen travel-bureau, which was then collecting travellers and material for a round-trip through the United States. The worthy Stangen, with whom I soon came into contact, won my liking at once, and I fell in with the wish that had brought me to him and entered my name on the list of pilgrims, who, however, would be conducted through the States by Stangen only from New York onwards.

My father surprised me with a berth in a first-class cabin in the then largest German steamer, the *Fürst Bismarck*, which I boarded in Hamburg, in order to travel to the New World armed with letters of recommendation.

But what instantly set me free from any paralysing homesickness on board the ship was the sudden encounter on deck with Jenny Baker, Leschetitzky's pupil, whom I already greatly admired. During the whole time she was in the centre of the flirtation-movement that was well able to compete with the very stormy movement of the ship itself. I at any rate attached myself to this lovely girl's heels and was her always welcome escort on moonlight strolls round the deck. It was of course easy for this young lady, some years older than myself, to keep my excitability, whose cause she herself was, within bounds. Nevertheless, she very cordially, and as though it were a matter of course, invited me in the name of her parents to call at her hotel in New York and also to visit her temporary home in Chicago. On board this ship there were also Herr and Frau Goldschmidt with their children. He had been the American Consul-General in Vienna and was now on his way to Milwaukee, where he also invited me in the friendliest way possible. In the course of my journey I was to have the opportunity of making use of this invitation, which I had accepted.

At that time the journey from Hamburg to New York still took ten days, and even that I suppose only if one was lucky enough to travel in a steamer of the size and power of the *Fürst Bismarck*, which of course was not in the least comparable to modern luxury steamers in all matters of comfort and splendour.

In New York the first thing was to settle my business. I was hailed in the most spectacular way by my father's business-friend Mr. Hoeninghaus, and his colleagues Ehrbacher and Klaus, but there was genuine kindliness and helpfulness concealed under the frequent shouting and exclaiming of 'My dear boy!' These three men, immigrants from the Rhineland, took it in turns to show me round New York and almost never left me alone. Their taste was not always mine; I found it especially difficult to get any pleasure out of the down-town variety-halls and negro drinking-places which they thought I would particularly enjoy. On the other hand, I found the theatres to which I was taken very interesting.

In the hotel where my friend Jenny Baker was staying I also met the second pianist to whom I had paid homage in Vienna, namely Emily Hutchinson, and now I was given invitations right and left by these two young ladies and dragged about now to this and now to that 'sight'.

The impression that New York made on me was of course overwhelming, although the reader must not think of the modern city of that name—a fact that I myself had the opportunity of noting when I went to America again decades later. However, it was then possible to make the round of all the sights that I was allowed to enjoy under the guidance of my three mentors.

During none of my stay in New York did I have the feeling of travelling for pleasure, for by the elaborate questionnaire he had given me my father had seen to it that my daily correspondence with his firm in Vienna was by no means easy. I had to spend hours with Mr. Hoeninghaus, the former silk specialist from Krefeld, discussing questions that really scarcely interested me at all and making notes in order to be able, when I was back in my room at the hotel, to write the letters that were expected of me.

Now the time was approaching for me to join Stangen's travel-party on the journey through the United States. In this party I made the acquaintance of young contemporaries and also of much older travellers who were able to arouse my interest. People from all parts of Germany had placed themselves in Stangen's charge in order to get to know 'the States' in so far as that was possible on a three-months' trip.

We did not always remain slavishly together; since it was impossible to fulfil everyone's wishes and carry out all ideas for diverging from the programme, our guide sometimes gave us several days 'off', on the condition that we reassembled at a certain place on a certain day in order to resume our tour along its predestined lines. In this way I turned aside in order to see the watering-places of Saratoga Springs and Newport, where I was astonished by luxury generally undreamt-of in those days and by the standards then prevailing; I also dashed off to visit the interesting town of Buffalo and the Niagara Falls. The latter to this day remain, I suppose, the most overwhelming and magnificent natural spectacle it has been my privilege to behold. Pale in comparison are the strange Mormon town, Salt Lake City, and even Denver, with the Garden of the Gods, a natural park formed of red sandstone blocks, which only lingers in my memory because it was from there that the funicular railway—at that time doubtless the highest in the world—led up to the summit of Pike's Peak.

When I had reached this peak, after far too speedy a journey, and stepped out into the open at a height of 4,000 metres, as a result of the abrupt change of air I became unconscious for the first time, and so far as I can remember also for the last time, in my life. I soon regained consciousness, recalled to life by countless bottles of smelling-salts brought to bear upon me by my feminine fellow-travellers, but recalled also to a frightful migraine, which prevented me from enjoying the wonderful view. I had to go down to the valley again immediately and be put to bed.

I did better on an expedition into the rocky region of the Grand Canyon, whither Stangen directed a regular caravan of vehicles containing his guests, while I had the good fortune to get a horse and ride to the meeting-place in the company of a cow-man—or I suppose I should call him a 'cow-boy'. My delight in the familiar exercise caused my companion to utter the suspicion that I must be a colleague of his in disguise, or at least once have been one.

Under Stangen's guidance we got to know Yellowstone Park and its wonders, and in the further course of our journey towards the West drove, in open carriages hired as occasion arose, through the archways cut in the gigantic trees in the Yosemite Valley. It was to California that I owed the most heart-stirring and rapturous impressions, as a result of the combination of the beauties of land and sea, and in my memory San Francisco remains the most beautiful city in the world; especially the arrival from Oakland through the Golden Gate has remained unforgettable in my mind to this day.

I spent two days recuperating in a place called Monterey, on the coast, which to my amazement is little mentioned nowadays. At that time I was lodged in the delightful Cliff House Hotel. I had a room looking out on to the sparkling, gold-tipped sea and was simply overwhelmed by a sunset that I admired while leaning out of my window. Opposite me, almost near enough to touch, were rocks towering up out of the sea, and here sea-lions sported about in the evening light. It seemed to me they were performing a ballet, so gaily and swiftly did they dance, ever again plunging into the water and ever again storming up the little mountains on which they sunned themselves.

At the open window of the Cliff House Hotel I wrote home in high spirits, wanderlust such as I had never known before impelling me to ask for permission to make my way home not with Stangen and his party but via Japan, which amounted to making a journey right round the world. I asked for a reply by telegram, which reached me while I was still in San Francisco. It was somewhat curt in tone, asking whether I really thought that time and money existed only for me to waste. I was to return home instantly by the shortest and quickest route, via New York, where Mr. Hoeninghaus was already waiting for me with very important new plans, which I was to bring with me.

On the return journey we visited the World Fair at Chicago. This was to be the culminating point of our trip. An international exhibition in America was of course the goal of innumerable people from all parts of the earth,and I was particularly proud to see that in the very heart of the exhibition there was an 'Old Vienna', where the charms of my native city were displayed to foreigners, admittedly in a language that they would not have been able to understand even if they had ever learned German.

In Chicago my two friends Emily Hutchinson and Jenny Baker were at home, or rather, not at home, for it was actually Pasadena in California whence Jenny Baker had set forth in order to become Leschetitzky's pupil. Now she was staying at the Lexington Hotel with her parents, only in order to be able to spread over several weeks the strenuous business of visiting the colossal exhibition. I was often her guest, and she always put a rose in my button-hole— a rose, however, that was always taken away from me, though not without being replaced by another of a different colour, in the course of the evening meal to which I was fairly regularly invited by Emily Hutchinson and her circle. I always went out adorned by the one and took care not to betray the fact that the other would not hear of my wearing this button-hole and replaced it by a more permanent one. In a confession that I made—but only to one of them—on the day before my departure I called this 'the War of the Roses', freely adapted from the English history to which I had devoted my last studies before leaving my native city.

Since the Stangen party let us have only one little week for Chicago, we were on our feet from morn till night and were glad to rest when it was time for us to get into the Pullman car and begin our return journey to New York.

The leave-taking from my two young lady friends had been very hard. Of course we promised each other to write often until there should be a reunion somewhere in Europe, presumably in Vienna. But I recall only one single letter, which was written by me and remained unanswered.

I never again saw that strange bewitching being, Jenny Baker, who was surrounded by such an aura of passions, of unfulfilled dreams and desires. But many years later I happened to read among the 'incidental news' in a foreign newspaper, and that only by accident, that a very smart American woman had one evening left her hotel in Geneva in the company of a young Portuguese, with whom she had got into a rowing-boat and rowed out on to the lake. The empty boat had been washed up on the shore the next morning; the bodies of the two unfortunates had not been recovered until much later. What a romance! What tragedies of the heart had there been laid to rest at last? So Leschetitzky's mysterious pupil, who by her *bravura* as a pianist had filled two continents with his fame, ended in mystery.

In New York the serious side of life caught up with me again in the three figures of Hoeninghaus, Ehrbacher and Klaus, and I had to spend many hours in this trinity's office, where everything had been arranged for me to pack at the bottom of my trunk and take back home to my father.

On arrival in New York I separated from the leader of the Stangen party, and likewise from my travelling-companions, not a single one of whom had become a friend. The thoughtful representatives of my father's firm had already long ago booked me a cabin on the *Fürst Bismarck* for my return journey.

Here I should like to be allowed to recall a travelling-acquaintance I made by chance, for it lives on in my memory more vividly than any of the random company that Stangen had brought along. I met him in the dining-car of the Pullman train going from Chicago to New York. He was sitting opposite me, and we were just embarking on a commonplace conversation about the weather and the speed at which we were travelling, when he suddenly said to me: "You are still so young—how is it you speak our language so well and how is it that you take such a great interest in America, which you know better than most Americans do?" I was giving some embarrassed answers when he said, without transition: "I should like you to take home with you a lasting souvenir of your wonderful journey, and so you shall be one of the first to hear the news that I am now starting on a journey to England in order to sell my silver-mine to a great bank, for the doctor has ordered me to give up my strenuous activities. I want to place two hundred shares at your disposal at the price of a pound each, a price intended only for foundation shareholders. So far as one can be humanly sure, you will make a great deal of money and remember me and America for the rest of your life."

Somewhat surprised and taken aback, I asked for the address in Europe of the stranger who so generously wanted to silver-plate my path through life. I merely told him that I had not got two hundred pounds at my disposal, but would tell my father all this and did not doubt that I would then get the money to buy the shares. My travelling-companion was agreeable to this, and I kept my word. It consisted of a letter of refusal, for when I told my father of this remarkable adventure he said, laughing: "There you are, you see, if I weren't here and you had the means, you'd be the victim of every rascal. Write and say I have no confidence in such business deals and won't give you the money."

From this little episode I very quickly proceeded to the order of the day and was quite ready to have the lie given to my good impression of the man, but when some twenty years later I learnt by chance that the shares offered me at a pound each were now quoted at a hundred pounds, I suddenly realised that with my father's help I had turned down the only opportunity in my life of becoming a millionaire.

And so now I was at home again. It is hard at this date to describe how queerly strange I felt, and as though I did not 'belong', in the first weeks at home, and even after that. It was then that I realised for the first time that there is something special about travelling and that other home that we call 'abroad'. Is it the fault of a young man's freedom when he is away from home? Is it the fault of the pleasant, oppressive, and delightful impressions one has received? Or of the adventures sought for and unsought for, some of which may be quite painful? It seems to me that an inexplicable state of, as it were, floating follows every long absence from home, which has not held one fast but let one go at one's desire.

The homesickness of which there is so much talk fades when one is away, giving place to other feelings, and anyone who returns home after a lengthy absence suddenly no longer knows where 'abroad' is, where it begins and where it ends, and how it comes that the great blissful joy of being once more in the place from where he started out somehow does not gush up in his heart as it should.

Until that fateful year 1938 I never again felt as much of a stranger in Vienna as at that time, perhaps because I never again went so far and for so long. But today it seems to me that the cosmopolitan, the man who is at home everywhere, who can even feel at home everywhere, is actually not so anywhere. People, even when they were old acquaintances, seemed estranged and as though at a remove. How often it happened to me to hear sentences beginning with the words: 'Oh yes, and have you heard——?' and then I was told something that ought to have interested me and actually no longer concerned me.

Then, when all the moods and impressions that had flooded in upon me were assimilated, I nevertheless felt—however long the strange state had lasted—that this was where I belonged and it was from here that I must make my way, which would inevitably always bring me back from the farthest distances to this point of origin, and that this point of origin, which would never fail me, would be the support that would prevent me from stumbling into the void in my thoughts and feelings and actions as well. Passing acquaintances, particularly those from the regiments in which I had served, had naturally forgotten me, but they heard about me and did then quickly find their way back to me, in so far as they had ever been close to me at all.

And now the ordinary everyday monotony of my life was resumed. I had to spend weeks with my father going over the results of my journey, which I dare say had not been very fruitful in a commercial respect. When, during my father's explanations, I all at once and against my own will began listening to my own thoughts and became absent-minded, he would sometimes ask me impatiently: "Well, what are you thinking about?" Ah, if I had only known! I had an obscure longing for myself, a longing to recognise those notions and wishes that so suddenly fled from me again. On my travels I had written down new verses of my own composition and also recorded material for stories that sometimes pressed me hard. But I now adapted myself to the rhythm of things much more energetically than before, was scrupulous about keeping office-hours, and looked forward to beginning the day at the Spanische Reitschule and to the evenings when my time was my own.

Perhaps before I go any further I should speak of a morbid mood that began to gain a hold on me and never left me or let me go for the whole of the rest of my life, not even today. The thing was that I found Sundays unendurable; they made me miserable. From my early waking to my late falling asleep Sunday was an enemy that paralysed me, reducing me to physical and spiritual misery. It is no use demanding any explanation of me; I could never find one.

The sudden paralysis of everydayness, the new colour that the hours took on, now so different from those of our week-days, bore the blame for my feeling the sensation of having been torn out of my environment and thrust into a dungeon out of which it was useless to attempt to escape. Round about noon I felt myself suddenly up against an imaginary fence. Beyond it lay all the other possibilities from which I was cut off, everything else that one might still have become and which one is allowed to taste when everyday routine sets one free. Hence the Sunday sportsmen, the Sunday horsemen, the Sunday writers.

In order to liberate myself I wrote the story 'The End of the World,' the hero of which suffered from my own affliction, which drove him to his death. When it appeared, much later, in a volume of stories, it was Rainer Maria Rilke who drew attention to it, praised it to the skies and, understanding it as fully as he did, accorded it the highest rank.

It was about this time that my father founded the Vienna Chess Club, whose president he became and remained to the end of his life. He introduced me to this scene of his own recreation, which gave him a great deal of pleasure, and I was amazed at the number of people that very soon came flocking to join this new kind of undertaking. However much I try to get to the bottom of it, with the best will in the world I cannot say when and through whom I learnt to play chess. Suddenly I had grasped the elements of the game and acquired a feeling for it. I think I must have got my slight knowledge of it through often watching others play.

When I began to become absorbed in this unique game I could not have dreamt that some years later I would be utterly in the grip of chess. It displaced pretty well everything that had previously begun to stir me, and there was a time when I wondered whether I should not dedicate my whole life exclusively to chess—this my father would have been more likely to understand than anything else—in order to become a champion like one of those who had world-famous names and whom my father did everything in his power to support, financing their journeys to tournaments and even at his own expense arranging a world-championship tournament in Vienna. This taste, which my father smiled upon, he did however, as I have said already, understand a good deal better than that other taste that had so early driven me into the arms of literature.

He did not suspect that I had written the story, 'The Smile that was Sold', in the office in spite of scrupulously carrying out my duties there.

The following years passed monotonously enough, brightened only by various little adventures. All at once, with the suddenness of an illumination, I felt the impossibility of any longer sharing my room with anyone, even with my own brother. When I came home from the office I felt a need amounting to anguish to be alone, but above all to have a chance of setting about 'my' work without being disturbed. I complained to my father about this and was greatly pleased to hear him first mention the idea of bachelor lodgings, which was my secret wish. It was also he who generously helped me towards a new home. Evidently remembering a similar state of affairs in his own youth, although perhaps in another town, he found it amusing to assist me in my search for a flat, and when this was by chance found in the centre of the city, in the Nibelungengasse, I had to thank him for setting me up very comfortably and pleasantly. It was a day of great rejoicing when I was suddenly able to move in and spend the first night under my own roof. When I woke in the morning I was for a long time overcome by rapture and rejoiced to myself about my liberty and my untrammelled disposal over many an hour.

I had three very pretty rooms, and a former factotum from my father's business became my first servant, keeping the apartment tidy, getting me my breakfast, looking after my clothes and to the best of his ability trying to make up for what I had lost in leaving my parents' house.

I was twenty-six years old when this event took place and I moved from my room in the Schottenfeldgasse into a rather smart bachelor apartment in the First District; and in those rooms, where I was to experience so much, I stayed up to my marriage, that is to say, for twelve long years. It is remarkable that I had no sooner settled down there than I had no other thought than to begin my work, which was not that imposed on me and expected of me. Only now did I really begin to write regularly. But since I came home from the office feeling rather worn out, it quickly tired me, and my all too faithful migraine attacked me often enough, evidently in order to make me realise that one cannot serve two masters with impunity. In my apartment I got the first morphia injections from our very cautious family doctor. The pain was at that period sometimes terrible and simply had to be stopped; after the painless semitrance of the morphia I felt much better, somehow stronger and with blunted feelings. I had no tendency to become an addict and I have never in all my life given myself an injection.

I was, however, now torn away from many doubts and scruples, and also from tender ties that were threatening to become too permanent, by being called up for my second period of military training.

This time too I was ordered to report to Prague, where I was again an adjutant, this time attached to a Feldzeugmeister by the name of Probst von Ostorff, a high-ranking Austrian Government official on horseback. This time everything went off quite smoothly. I only had to go from my hotel, zum Blauen Stern, in Prague, to a certain place in the Karolinenthal, where my horse was waiting for me and where I would receive instructions as to where I should report to my chief. The first week of manœuvres passed off without a hitch, but even if I have forgotten the details of it, there is one positively fateful experience that imprinted itself on my heart and brain for ever, and nothing could ever happen to make me forget it. A pale, forlorn yearning sometimes makes me long for it even now.

I came home from a day's duty and found a letter from a Frau von Oesteren, who wrote that she remembered me from bygone summer days that we had both spent by the Attersee and that she expected the same of me, perhaps even more so. She invited me to an evening party at Schloss Veleslavin, a castle about an hour's journey from Prague, where she lived with her three children; it was going to be a great event, so she wrote, and would celebrate a number of occasions in her honour. And then came the startling conclusion:

'There will be few young men of your own age present. But so that you shall not feel lonely I have asked the young Prague poet René Rilke, whose parents are friends of mine, to come too, and have seen to it that he is informed of your visit. At my request he will call for you at your hotel, the Blaue Stern, at seven o'clock in the evening, in a carriage. You must of course introduce yourself to this somewhat shy young man, and the longish carriage journey will certainly do its part in making you both better acquainted and in giving you a chance of exchanging views. So I shall expect you both and am already greatly looking forward to seeing you again. You must tell me about Vienna, your dear sweet mother and the circle in which I first met you. I am also looking forward to seeing the impassioned little swimmer of those days (I was a keen swimmer and have remained so) as a young officer of dragoons. Then followed her almost indecipherable signature.

In those days the name Rilke could not, of course, mean anything to me. I had never heard it before and was merely glad that I would not have to make the long carriage trip alone and looked forward to perhaps getting to know a like-minded young man. I of course at once remembered the writer of the letter and was uncommonly pleased at the prospect of again meeting the great lady who had then recited Mosenthal's 'Deborah' to Professor Erich Schmidt's disapproval and now, as the writing-paper showed, inhabited a castle. Down to this day, however, it is a mystery to me how and through whom she can have discovered that I was in Prague and was identical with the little boy she had got to know so long before.

The carriage arrived with the greatest of punctuality at the door of the hotel and the pale, slender René Rilke got out. I went towards him in my dress uniform, such as was regulation attire for such occasions, and, smiling, he stretched both hands out towards me. I took his hands and told him my name, which he already knew, having a little white card with him on which it was written down. Some minutes later we were sitting in the carriage, and set off at a rapid trot for Veleslavin, a village some distance from Prague. Rilke told me very many delightful things about the castle, which belonged to a Prince Palffy, and about Frau von Oesteren, who was a friend of his mother's. He also lost no time in preparing me for the beauty of our hostess' two daughters; and looking back at it all today it seems to me in keeping with Rilke's destiny that from the time of his very first poetic stammerings he received invitations from great ladies to their castles.

Our first conversation was a timid groping and feeling of our way. I learned that Rilke was still a student and about six years younger than myself, although in spite of his youth and frail appearance he showed by his manner of speaking that he had plenty of confidence and resolution. I find it quite difficult, because

c

it is so obvious, to say now that I liked this young man particularly because of his quiet firmness and the smile that hardly ever ceased to play about his mouth; I liked him particularly because everything about him was so utterly unlike the young men with whom I was together on duty all day. On the journey, which took somewhat over an hour, I at once confided in him far more than in many a young man of my own age whom I had known for years.

But now we were hurrying up the steps of the wonderfully illuminated house, and Rilke, who even then was quite familiar with the usages of the great world, introduced me to our hostess, elegant in her gala dress. I instantly recognised her and found it extremely difficult to put a damper on my high delight when, as I was kissing her hand, she drew me closer to her, smiling, and said: "It is easy to recognise you again, although you are completely changed. Your beautiful uniform takes care of that, if nothing else does!" She went on laughing, and then introduced me to her daughters, who had just approached, after which she herself turned away to chat for a few minutes with Rilke, whom she knew well, but who kept on glancing over at me as though he had taken on some sort of responsibility for me.

That evening Frau von Oesteren shone in the glory of her personality, to which I am sure she was mainly indebted for the homage she was receiving. The rooms quickly filled with people, many of whom wore uniform, as I did, many of them with decorations and orders of all kinds, but all of them in ceremonial dress, as were also the ladies they had brought with them.

Rilke and I made for each other, and soon we were both together observing the ever denser throngs of guests. Suddenly everyone streamed into one room, in which our hostess's beautiful and intellectual elder daughter, whose name was Laska, did some incredibly successful imitations of the greatest living actresses, Eleonora Duse and Sarah Bernhardt. She was enthusiastically applauded, and I remembered the Attersee, where her mother had attempted something similar with less success, and guessed how the lovely girl came to have her talent.

The younger sister—I think her name was Stella—was a great deal prettier even than Laska, doubtless what one could call a thorough-going beauty, and she was much courted by a cavalry captain of the name of Löffler, the classical type of the handsome

man, who came of an old military family and knew how to gain the
affections of this much admired and charming girl, whom he some
years later led home as his bride. This couple, whose marriage was
very happy, nevertheless left the world long before the highly
cultivated and elegant sister Laska, who lived to a moderately great
age at the side of her husband, von Hönl, an under-secretary in one
of the ministries, whom I met at the house of friends once again
before the great catastrophe broke over the whole earth. The word
'Veleslavín' flashed up between us, but it soon sank to the ground
with weary wings, in almost unrecognisable greyness.

It was quite a while before all the guests had found their places
at the wonderfully decorated horseshoe-shaped table and sat down.
The far-seeing lady of the house had saved both herself and us
trouble by putting Rilke on one side of me as my 'lady'. On the
other side was an elderly lady who from the moment of sitting down
was in such intense conversation with her neighbour, who to judge
by his appearance must have been an eminent lawyer, that I scarcely
felt much obligation to startle her out of her perhaps important
discussion with any commonplace supper-table chatter.

During the first courses, which were served by numerous footmen,
Rilke and I were both not very talkative. During the rather long-
drawn-out meal we suddenly saw through the high windows of the
great room how the Chinese lanterns were casting their glimmering
light in the garden outside. Towards the end of the meal, during
which a few speeches were thrown off at a long distance away from
us, near our hostess, we did at last become somewhat more talkative,
and young Rilke pointed to the gaily lighted park-like garden outside
and said: "As soon as this is over, let's go outside. There we can
have a talk without being disturbed or overheard." I eagerly
agreed.

At that moment soft music began to play, and at a tolerably
great distance, at the other end of the long room, we saw Laska,
our hostess' slender daughter, opening the dance. That was doubtless the sign for everyone to rise from the table. We saw too that
other couples were following the example of our hostess' daughter,
and now our moment had come. We hurried into the garden, where
we began to stroll around, chatting, in the pleasantly faint light
from the Chinese lanterns.

Nobody bothered about us; we were certainly the youngest in

this gathering and could not have been of interest to anyone. As we strolled along the carefully tended gravel paths of the princely castle where we were guests Rilke suddenly confessed to me, with utter candour and frankness, that he was a poet. I can still see his smile and hear the strangely energetic tone in which he said: "My father, and now my mother too—they are set on bringing me up to be a government official. But nothing can come of that. I don't dream of it. Mother knows that by now, and perhaps she is telling her husband how it is at this very moment while I am confiding in you this secret that is important only for myself. I shall either become a poet that people will listen to, or leave this earth, disappearing into the darkness."

Such foreboding words loosened my tongue. Here was a fellow-sufferer, so much younger than myself, who had summoned up the courage to declare his unconditional faith in himself and leave his parents in not the slightest doubt as to his destiny, whether they wanted to admit it or not. And I—in what struggles of excuses, procrastinations, and futile beatings around the bush I was exhausting my poor powers! For precisely this was my own case too, and it had nothing to do with the degree of our talent. Or *had* it? I now poured out the suffering of my whole youth to my newly won friend, telling him of my parents' house, my migraine, my father's occupation and his inexorable decision to yoke me into his own activities for the sake of a vow he had once taken and to make me into his own image, something for which I was no use and of which there could be no question. Rilke listened gravely, almost breathlessly. Growing pale, he said: "You must make a clean sweep when these manœuvres are over. We have a right to our own life. 'Become what you are' is God's eleventh commandment. It is *His* Will we must fulfil and no other. We must develop whatever has been implanted in us by higher powers. That is our sacred duty, believe me!"

I pricked up my ears at these words. Swinging round, I looked at the pale young man, so much my junior, who could so effortlessly give utterance to all that I had often and often felt, hesitantly and doubtingly and in bewilderment. Over our heads a glittering sky of stars spread out its blessing over our groping youth.

I felt a hitherto unknown courage pulse through me, and in the gleam from the faintly flickering Chinese lanterns I clearly saw my

path marked out before me. In an upsurge of joy over the decision
that had so unexpectedly come upon me, I put my arm through that
of my companion, who had now so suddenly become my friend,
and we began to talk eagerly. I learned that Rilke was working not
only at poems but also at a drama, *Das tägliche Brot* (*Our Daily
Bread*), and that he had a great yearning to go far, far away and
was very envious of me for the travels I had undertaken, of which
I now told him.

We would doubtless have gone on gossiping together all night,
if the great lady to whom we owed this highly fortunate turn of
events, which was an illumination to my whole youth, had not come
up to us, evidently in search of her protégés, and said, smiling:
"Well, you two *do* seem to have a lot to tell each other! It's just as
I thought. What a pity my son Werner isn't here. Like René, he
wants to be a writer. Do you know," she said, turning to me,
"some of my guests have gone by now, and some are getting ready
to leave? The driver of your carriage is becoming impatient, too,
and gladly as I would still keep you both, I must remind you to be
starting back homeward. René, you're tired," she said laughingly
to Rilke. "I can see that. And you," she said, turning to me again
"must be in the saddle again at seven o'clock in the morning. So
hurry along, you two."

Obediently, we followed this lady, so concerned for our welfare,
into the vestibule and quickly got ready for the return journey.
The carriage that had brought us drove up to the door, we kissed
our hostess' hand, showered her with expressions of thanks for the
unforgettable evening, and got in. The impatient coachman drove
us away at a quick trot, while we gazed longingly back at the castle
that soon disappeared in the darkness of the night into which we
were being borne in a state of grace.

Rilke had aroused my loquacity, and when he had finished
reciting a few of his own verses and leaned back, smilingly
acknowledging my enthusiastic applause, something gushed up in
me, and to Rilke's great amazement I now unleashed a whole pack
of my poems at him. With bowed head, he listened, and when at
last, drawing a deep breath, I fell silent, he exclaimed: "My dear
fellow, but you are already what you want to become! And now
promise me one thing more—that you will not only be a brave
cavalry officer, but also a brave man in the battle of life that awaits

you. You must liberate yourself, and since you have already written stories, too, you are under an obligation to sweep aside every distraction and dedicate yourself with all your powers to the work that destiny sets you. We have no choice—men like you and me. Or else some day we shall go into gardens, worn out and broken in mind, to bewail our lot."

I was astonished and held out my hand to him. There was something like the swearing of an oath in my promising to do and carry through what he—and in my heart of hearts I myself—considered my duty.

On that unforgettable evening I twice had to fight down a very violent desire. I wanted to show young René Rilke my liking and my confidence by suggesting that we should use the intimate 'thou' in addressing each other: the first time was when we were strolling in the twinkling, lamp-lit garden, and the next when we said good-bye outside my hotel in Prague. But both times I was stopped by the peculiar feeling that by so doing I would in some way reduce the young hero of a unique encounter to the level of my brothers-in-arms, with whom I was on terms of 'thou and thou'—which, for all the liking I had for some of them, it seemed to me simply impossible to do. These were different worlds, in which forms of speech must also be different.

And so then, in spite of a friendship lasting decades, with the river of youth rippling away below, we remained on terms of the formal 'you'.

During my stay in Prague we met several times again, in a café, and worked out plans for the future. My period of military training was over in a few weeks. The second half called me away to Budweis, without there being any episodes that would deserve particular mention here or even need to be described at all. On the last day of manœuvres I had my first migraine on horseback. By the exertion of will-power beyond the limits of my strength, I finished the day in an upright position, and when I made my final report to my commanding officer he held out his hand to me and said: "You are terribly pale. I think you ought to have a few days in bed."

I cannot remember whether I paid a farewell call on Frau von Oesteren or merely wrote her a letter of thanks. Her son a few years later became quite a well-known writer, under the name of Werner von Oesteren, with a book entitled *Christ, not Jesus*. I met him too, if I am not mistaken, in Prague or Vienna; then he suddenly disappeared not only from my gaze but, after an unsuccessful attempt at suicide, also out of the ranks of those whose endeavours were similar to his. In those bygone days he was also among those who knew and honoured Rilke, whom he had of course learned to admire in his mother's house.

Rilke wrote to me once again at that period and informed me that he had given his first, very successful recitation performance one evening at Veleslavin. The following spring I received an unforgettable and imperishable sign of life from my dear carriage-companion. He sent me a copy of his little book *Larenopfer*, which had just been published—and what did I find, still signed 'René Rilke', written in his own handwriting on the first page? This poem!

On the rough cobbles rattled loud and hard
the rapid carriage rolling through the silence of the night.
'Twas there I heard you speak those quiet verses
in which a poet's soul lay bright, entire.

And I no longer heard the quick beat of the wheels,
for with a voice loud as the spheres themselves he spake;
and more than in the gleam of footlights ever
his words' true ring there moved my heart.

It seemed to me the blue night chimed,
through which the stars like pious pilgrims moved,
and my own dreams unfolded wide their wings. . . .
Take for that blessed hour these thanks that yearn to bless!

In the margin was the dedication: 'To the writer Siegfried Trebitsch, that hidden, sensitive poet, in remembrance of driving home from Veleslavin.'

Deeply moved, I read these lines again and again, feeling as though knighted by René Rilke's delicate hand and made a member of his order. Once again he had clearly shown me my path, and I owed it to my newly won friend now to take this path and not to disappoint my young mentor by my work, if my gifts were adequate.

I remained in touch with Rainer Maria Rilke by means of an

intensive correspondence that was, however, sometimes interrupted for years, and this until his all too early end. He will appear often again in this account of my life.

Before I went to see my parents, I remained in my own apartment for two days, physically and spiritually quite exhausted; my presence there was not betrayed to anyone. When I had more or less recuperated, I could scarcely wait to confront my father and keep the promise I had made to Rilke.

When he appeared, only just returned from his summer vacation, we greeted each other with extreme cordiality. He enquired in great detail as to how I was, but I recognised that this moment was really not the right one to take him away from his business and involve him in a serious discussion. He would probably have listened to me with only half an ear. Later, then, I asked him for an interview the next afternoon, and insisted that it should take place in his private office, where we would be safe from interruption and no one would overhear us. My father gazed at me sharply for a moment before he agreed. I then withdrew somewhat hastily and went down to the first floor to greet my mother, who was by this time somewhat worried, and remained with her for quite a time, not without giving her a detailed account of Frau von Oesteren's hospitality and her wonderful castle.

The next day I lunched with my parents and was glad to see my brother and step-brothers again. When the very gay, stimulating meal had come to an end and my parents had withdrawn for their siesta, I went up to my place on the second floor and awaited what was to come, thinking out everything I intended to say and vowing to myself that I would settle things with my father and not disappoint my distant friend, to whom I must of course report as soon as the die had been cast.

"Well, what can I do for you, Lieutenant?" were the words with which my father, who had sat down opposite me, began our conversation. It would be foolish to try to reproduce word for word, at this date, a talk that took place so many decades ago. It seems to me, however, important to mention that a little work of mine, an article that had appeared in the *Neue Freie Presse*, had made some impression on my father; for up to then, if I am not mistaken, only poems had appeared from time to time in the *Blaue Donau* and *Jugend*, papers that he scarcely ever saw. And so he began, not unamiably, by referring to this, as though he wanted to give me to understand that he had already guessed the drift of the interview for which I had asked. In this way he made my task somewhat easier, for of course I knew that the *Neue Freie Presse* enjoyed the very high esteem of the Viennese bourgeoisie and that anyone who could get himself published there would be noticed and not merely smiled upon by them.

Anyway, I now burst out with my attempt to make it perfectly clear to my father that life in his office was becoming ever more and more unendurable to me and that I had in fact no other destiny in this world than to be a writer, and this even if I should fail and become a complete wreck for sheer lack of ability. While I held forth about this I naturally thought of the shining conversations I had had with René Rilke and the verses he had dedicated to me, which inspired me and made me talk with more confidence than I would have been able to summon up without that memory— dispirited and full of self-doubts as I was. My father listened to me without interrupting, and then said something I had not expected: "Now I am myself afraid you are going to be lost to our firm, and if I had not given your father such a solemn promise to get you to the top in our line of business, I would let you go your own way now, with a light heart, for nobody can do anything in any sphere without taking a pride in his work. Work done against one's will means bad work. But as this case lies, I must after all see to it, in so far as it is humanly possible, that you do not fall a prey to your own fancies and become a mere dilettante. Therefore I should like to suggest to you that you should continue your work in our firm, for the most part abroad, until some unquestionable success proves to you, to me, and to the rest of the world that the new road you want to take really is the right road for you. After all, so many young men of your age write. Your own father, for that matter, used to produce poems, especially when he was in love. Neverthe- less he realised he could not become a writer, because he was, after all, an industrialist. I shall not be over-hasty in holding out a hand to help you to end in disappointment, for once you have left here you can scarcely come back again. It would be far too humiliating for you, after all, and I don't think you want the firm to keep a back door open for you—no, you want to slam the door once and for all. So take my advice, work as well as you can in your free time, and

c*

if in those circumstances you achieve a real success, I shall be the first to set you free and give you my good wishes for a career in which you will already be able to point to an achievement."

He rose, while I was still considering this proposal in some dismay and trying to take it in. Then he held out his hand to me. "I mean it for your own good. Is it a deal?"

Even for anyone else confronted with this man it would not have been easy to turn down a suggestion so full of wisdom and kindliness. Besides, the way I had always pictured things was, after all, that even after leaving the firm my ancestors had founded I would remain on the best of terms with my parents. Furthermore, I had to think of my mother, whose delicate health meant that I must not cause her any great stress of mind. So I shook hands with this superior man and declared my agreement and readiness to submit to his condition.

I then hurried home, where I once again in my own mind went over the discussion and its outcome very carefully, reflecting on the whole thing. It seemed as though a fundamental change had now taken place in my life. I suddenly had a new aim before my eyes, one that I must work towards with all my power. I also had plans for literary work, and there were notes for the novel *Convalescence*, which was to become my first novel and in fact was to open the gates of freedom for me. Now I began to long for a thorough talk with like-minded people, even though I could have no illusion that I would encounter another René Rilke.

May I at this point stress the fact that we unfortunately learn to value the decisive encounters in our life much too late? Today I know that I ought to have followed Rilke—ever and again appearing, wherever he might go, ever and again disappearing, but nevertheless always in his vicinity, ever and again returning to him. As soon as one is in the public eye, encounters follow each other posthaste, and in my life there have certainly been some that can rightly be ranked as the equals of that with Rainer Maria Rilke. But one's first great meeting, like one's last great love, remains decisive.

Since the *Neue Freie Presse* had made the above-recorded discussion easier for me, I naturally wanted to go on working for it from time to time. With this end in view I went to see the feuilleton editor, Theodor Herzl, whom I had already met socially and come to know slightly. He received me in a very friendly

manner and discussed with me, in a complimentary way, the essay
I had written on Georges Rhodenbach, whose novel *Bruges la morte*
had made such a deep impression on me that I had been impelled
to take up my pen. At that time I could not know that many years
later I would become acquainted with his widow and be entrusted
with the German adaptation of his play, *Le mirage*, based on that
same novel. Even less did I suspect that I would then not only see
my version performed in the Lessing-Theater in Berlin, under Otto
Brahm, but also place it at the disposal of the young Erich Korngold
for the opera, *Die tote Stadt*, that he was then to write.

Theodor Herzl was charming in a kindly, somewhat condescend-
ing way, and his lordly airs were far from being forbidding, but
only made his human sympathy seem all the stronger and more
encouraging. He sent me away with the assurance that he would
promptly read everything I sent in and whenever possible publish it.

In the following summer at Ischl, at a tea-party, I made the
acquaintance of that handsome man of the world Arthur Schnitzler,
whom I congratulated on his moving story 'Sterben' ('Dying'),
which had just been published. He gazed at me in a way that made
it clear how pleased he was with my veneration. At that time the
seven-years-older doctor had not yet devoted himself exclusively
to his literary work, but was still working at the clinic of his great
father, the famous laryngologist.

In order to pay me some trifling compliment in return, Schnitzler
mentioned that he had read my essay on Rhodenbach's masterpiece
in the *Neue Freie Presse*. I was uncommonly pleased, and I at once
confessed to him that I also had greater and longer works in my
desk.

The next winter I went to Egypt to recover from an obstinate
catarrh. There I absorbed the tremendous impressions that Cairo
inevitably made and recuperated particularly well on the Nile trip
that took me via Luxor to Assuan.

Returning home in better health, I plunged into the joys of spring,
and even more doggedly into my work. This work was for the most
part that on my novel, *Convalescence*, which had already been
begun.

At that time cycling was becoming something of an epidemic in
Vienna. There was scarcely any young person who did not possess
a Cleveland bicycle. Anyone who, like myself, loved the Burgtheater

like a woman, bought it from the brother of Arnold Korff, the great actor. On a fine May morning it was delightful to exchange the usual Lipizzaner for a bicycle and ride to have breakfast in the Prater. From my apartment the lovely Krieau could easily be reached in under an hour, and it was truly delicious and refreshing to drink one's coffee under the trees in the Prater and eat the glorious freshly-baked milk-bread that went with it, not to speak of the little rolls called *Kaisersemmeln* that looked so alluring on the rustically decked tables.

On one of these expeditions I had some minor trouble with my bicycle and stopped outside the café garden, trying to put it right. A good-looking young man, who had just leaned his own bicycle against the wall, came up to me and asked: "What has gone wrong?" While he was bending over my machine, he told me his name: Felix Salten. With his aid everything was soon all right again, and now we sat at a table together, chatting and eating, while the spring wove its veil over us.

At that moment Theodor Herzl came past, responded smilingly to our eager greetings, and sat down at the same table as a young man who was striking on account of his large head and who, like Herzl, wore a flowing beard, even though his was less well-groomed. Felix Salten, who had been exchanging greetings with people on all sides and knew many more literary people than I did, said to me: "Look, that's Hermann Bahr, of whom I am sure you have heard and read a great deal."

After that I used to meet Felix Salten regularly in the Krieau, where he also introduced me to the elegant Fräulein Metzl, from the Burgtheater, who was later to become his wife. I kept in touch with both of them, of course with long interruptions, caused by my own and Salten's extensive travels if by nothing else, all through my life, until they both closed their eyes for ever in Zurich, where I am now writing these pages.

Salten was actually the first to say—as he did quite unexpectedly, as we were cycling side by side from the Krieau back into town: "I should like to get to know something more of your writings. And I like having young poets read aloud to me. I am very fond of doing so myself."

In those days there was also a writer living in Vienna whom one is bound to call a German, because his books were written in

German, although by name and descent he was an Englishman. This was Houston Stewart Chamberlain, the author of the much-read *Foundations of the 19th Century*. During his short stay in Vienna, which nevertheless lasted some months, he held himself painstakingly aloof from Viennese literature and its representatives.

I had made his acquaintance in the house of that highly cultivated and outstanding actress, Lili Petri, and since she was, as Chamberlain once confessed to me, the woman whom he had most loved, I suppose it was to this friendship that I owed his liking for me. He had moved into a modest apartment in the Gumpendorferstrasse with his somewhat older wife, but spent many hours a day working at his 'Goethe' in the home of the actress I have just mentioned, even when she was out at rehearsals.

As a result of my travels I then lost sight of him, after hearing that he had tried to get a divorce from his wife and that she had died during the divorce proceedings. But to my astonishment Houston Stewart Chamberlain after a year and a day had passed did not marry Lili Petri at all, but a daughter of Frau Cosima Wagner, and from that time on spent his life in Bayreuth, where he died.

At that time I had not only literary interests. At least four times a week I went to Professor Hartl's fencing classes, where I got to know the eighteen-year-old Loris, otherwise Hugo von Hofmannsthal. He was toughening himself up for his year as a cadet. There I learnt—and as it happened from the best amateur swordsman in Vienna, the locomotive-manufacturer Max Friedmann—that this frail young lad with the glowing eyes had written a small work with the title 'Gestern' ('Yesterday'), which was arousing general interest. By the next day I had read it myself.

My fencing-master, who was delighted with my progress, then made me enter the international fencing tournament that was being held in Vienna, and I did in fact fight in it, winning a splendid certificate for, I think, about fourth place. I cannot help feeling that I collected all these physical successes, which I extorted from myself, only, as it were, in order to show my migraine that it would never be allowed to reign sovereign over my physical life.

Fencing at that time not only gave me a great deal of pleasure, but the word went round that I wielded a useful blade, and it is perhaps to be ascribed to this circumstance that I was not exposed to challenges and bloody affairs of honour as in my early days.

But I was all the more in demand as a second to others when they had affairs on their hands, and I succeeded in settling many a quarrel by means of written statements of reconciliation.

Human beings would perhaps not be capable of living and going on their way, doing what they have to do, regardless of all that is seemingly unendurable, if they could never shake off the memory of illnesses, and above all of pain they have borne. But it so happens that Nature has seen to it that there is nothing one is so sure of forgetting as physical agonies one has suffered. It is not given to us to measure our pains, to compare them, to establish on what day they were less, once they are over and done with. The causes of our pains shape us, leaving their traces behind. We remember how the catastrophes that have befallen our bodies came about, but the pain itself is forgotten in a way that no other powerful sensation is.

In Sicily, while I was travelling through Southern Italy, I fell a prey to a grave attack of malaria, which at first transformed me into a hopeless wreck. I contracted this appalling illness in the stone-quarries of Syracuse, where I experienced the torments of a thirst such as I had never known before. I must then, forgetting all precautions, have gulped down a glass of fresh water, as though I had not been in a fever-area but in the mountains of my native country. On the journey back, in Milan, where I wished to visit the friends of my youth, the storm in my infected blood broke loose. My migraine, ever ready to attack me, positively shrank before this much more powerful and autocratic sister, which crushed all resistance. I hurried home, and combating this terrible affliction, in addition to everything else, tried the elasticity of my youth to the highest degree.

Now once again it was the great doctors who decided the course of my life and to whom my father deferred. I was sent to the Engadine, and from there to Ostende; and when the attacks of fever were only somewhat alleviated wherever I went, but nowhere really successfully disposed of, I was summoned back home. It was in Ischl, within call and sight of my parents, that the final liberation came to me. Malaria enlarges the spleen, and high fever weakens the soundest heart. If one wanted to strike at the heart of the disease, at that time at least one had no better weapon than quinine.

Similarly as I have described it in the case of Dr. Lahmann, it was the well-known consultant Professor Oser who sat by my bedside during an attack of malaria. He made careful observations, and after many vain attempts he succeeded in giving me such strong doses of quinine at the right moment that the evil toxins were defeated by the anti-toxin.

Then again there was a winter when after finishing my work I was able to spend the evening skating at ice-rinks. And once again a summer came that permitted me to swim in the waters of our glorious lakes. Apart from the noble equestrian art, I never loved any sport so much or found any so refreshing as swimming.

Wherever I went—I mean of course in the summer—my first question was where to find a swimming-pool, as anyone else's question would have been where was the best restaurant or café.

My malaria had cost me much of my strength and also much time, and when at last I was liberated from it, I felt slightly older and mature enough, now at last, to go the way that Rilke had pointed out to me. And so, regardless of how weary I was by evening, I plunged into my work and got well ahead with my novel, not without time and again laying it aside in order to write little stories, which would thrust themselves on me, and poems, which often flooded into my mind immediately on waking.

At that period Vienna shone in its most enchanting colours, and its magical surroundings lured me into the open more than I liked, all the more since I had discovered in myself an inclination to follow the call of life much more obediently and resolutely than the call of my awakening, slowly growing art. People, even if they were dear to me, found it difficult to distract me; but it was all the easier for things, moods and small events that occurred in my life, to do so.

But the hour had not yet come when I could utter the great words: "The vow of Veleslavin is fulfilled. I am no longer a restless waverer between two occupations, of which the one is for me as unrealisable as it is unendurable. Now I can come to terms with myself and follow God's eleventh commandment, 'Become what you are', which you, René Rilke, taught me."

To my great delight my father's firm was coquetting with the idea of more extensive commercial relations in Paris. As always, when it was a matter of plans abroad, I was sent there, which, as

always, meant much greater freedom than the daily routine that
was imposed on me in Vienna. Like almost all young people, I
loved Paris and felt thoroughly happy in that city. As often as
I could I got myself sent there, although at that time Rilke was not
yet there; in the later course of my life I was to meet him in Paris
time and again.

Now, however, a very eventful summer was approaching. I was
on very close terms of friendship with a great actress who shared
my passion for France, as a result of which we decided to spend
the holidays in the Pyrenees. I had spent the most beautiful part
of the early summer doing business in Paris, where we met in order
to travel together to the mountain resort of Cauteret in the
Pyrenees. We were so charmed with this district that we decided
to take the waters in Bagnière de Luchon.

It was in Luchon that I had a great literary adventure. In our hotel
—I think it was the Scaron—there were large posters announcing
the performance of a play at the summer theatre: this play was
entitled *Boubouroche* and the author's name was Georges Courteline.
This was the Parisian poet of Montmartre. He was also going to
play a leading rôle in his play. The strange title caused us to decide
to see the performance of this comedy.

We had expected a frivolous, unimportant, cabaret-like entertainment. But after the very first scene, the setting of which was a Paris
café, it was clear to us that we were present at the performance of
a little masterpiece. When the curtain fell, I made use of the long
interval, in which numerous refreshments were handed round, to
air my enthusiasm. My fair companion was completely of the
same opinion as myself and supported me in my ecstatic wish to
get to know the author of the play, who had not yet come on the
stage, and to congratulate him on his work, of which we had as yet
seen only half.

It was not so easy to get hold of Georges Courteline. All those
taking part in the little comedy seemed to have made up their minds
to frustrate the attempt; but, alarmed by the sound of many raised
voices, he suddenly came down the three steps that separated me
from the holy of holies, and I instantly hurried up to him, introduced
myself and expressed my admiration of what I had seen up to now.
Courteline laughed and said: "But that's nothing, you know. The
second act, which is coming now, is the real play. Besides, I'm

playing the main part in this act, and so I must leave you at once."
I dare say he had hardly caught my name, which he might have
heard. I just had time to call out: "Where can I see you after the
play?" He hastily named a restaurant in which he would be having
supper with his wife, who was playing the leading female rôle,
shortly after the end of the performance. "Come along too," he
called out to me, in a way that reinforced my feeling that I had not
made a bad impression on him. I went back quickly to my
companion and told her what had happened. "Good," she said,
"let's go there afterwards, if the second act doesn't disappoint
us."

This second act, which has since become immortal and which is
perhaps the most outstanding comedy of cuckoldry that has ever
been written in France, caused gales of applause, in which we joined
with all our strength. We also cheered the actor who had been
unsurpassable in the now celebrated rôle of the man in the cupboard.
However undeniably superb his performance was, I could not help
having the feeling that it was as if he were only at a dress rehearsal
showing his leading actor how he wished the part to be played,
but perhaps this criticism only flashed through my mind because I
knew that Courteline was the author and actor in one person. His
opposite number, Adèle, the heroine of the little masterpiece, seemed
to us to be inimitable in the way she brought out the wit. In any
case, nothing was lost that would have been important to the writer
of the play. His leading actress managed to achieve the wonderful
collaboration that is necessary to lift a work written for the stage
to the heights of an unusual success.

Boubouroche had caught my fancy, although I had of course
seen many a brilliant play in Paris. At that time Maurice Donnay,
Henri Bataille, Alfred Capus, and others whose names are almost
forgotten today dominated the French theatre. But here was something quite different. This, as I believed, still unknown Courteline
was a successor to Molière, and he was not concerned, like his
colleagues, with arousing sensuality and touching all the chords
of the griefs and joys of love and playing variations on them. Here
a delineator of human beings was at work, one who was beyond
the sufferings to which French youth, if one was to believe their
poets, was a prey and of which it sometimes even perished.

When after countless curtain-calls the curtain fell for the last

time, we went to the restaurant that Courteline had named, took a
fairly large table in a corner and waited for what was to come. It
did not take them long to remove their make-up and change, for
soon Courteline and his leading actress came through the glass door
on which our gaze had been fixed. We rose, but he was already
standing before us, holding out his hand to me with a smile and
introducing me to his fair companion, whereupon I did the same,
and some minutes later, after the waiter had taken our order, we
sat opposite each other sunk in conversation.

We were soon so absorbed in our stimulating conversation that
we scarcely noticed that the two ladies were doing the same and,
although they had only just become acquainted, seemed to have a
great deal to tell each other. Afterwards it did strike me, of course,
and when my friend and I were going home, I had it explained to
me how much two actresses have to tell each other even if they come
from different countries.

It was not altogether possible to be particularly reserved with
young Courteline, and without reflecting on the consequences I
immediately made the suggestion to him that I should translate
the comedy, *Boubouroche*, which had so delighted me, into German.
Courteline laughed, and his companion was positively enthusiastic.
She kept on asking, however, whether the Germans would be able
to understand such a comedy. I said, laughing in my turn, that I
could not answer for the Germans, but I was prepared to bet that
my countrymen, the Viennese, would probably receive the play, if
well performed, particularly if my own companion were to play
Adèle, no less enthusiastically than the summer visitors at Luchon
had just done.

Courteline was very enthusiastic about my suggestion, or at least
very much flattered; with a Parisian author it is difficult to
distinguish. But suddenly he said: "*Vous me proposez une affaire.
Venez me voir à Paris*," at the same time writing his address in
Paris on the menu and handing it to me across the table. I promised
to come and carry out all the formalities that must precede an
authorised translation. This was, I suppose, the first time that I
recognised how artistic enthusiasm and approval must finally be
reduced to a business agreement.

At that period I could not dream that this enthusiasm—the
transports of which were put to a stop to by the lateness of the hour,

however stimulating the time was that we spent together—was to be the beginning of a friendship that ended only with Georges Courteline's death.

On the way home Courteline asked me what my occupation was a question that caused me some embarrassment. I was not given to boasting and did not dare to utter the premature assertion that I was a writer. I answered evasively that I had not yet quite finished my studies but that I had already occasionally done some journalism and even finished several little stories. This confession did not seem to discourage Courteline at all; and when we separated from him and his companion outside the little villa where they were staying, he vigorously repeated his invitation to me to visit him in his apartment in Paris, the address of which he had written down for me, in about ten days' time.

In Paris I went along at the agreed time to see the actor-writer in the Rue Lepic in Montmartre. He received me with lively outbursts of the Latin temperament and pressed me into the chair reserved for visitors beside his desk. He began by making it clear to me that except 'on tour' he was not an actor and had no intention of ever appearing on the stage in Paris. He used a phrase that made me prick up my ears and laugh. What he said was: "What I do is a kind of military exercise in order not to lose the living contact with the theatre. It is singularly helpful to me in the writing of my little plays, into which I have to cram as much as my colleagues do into the longest of comedies with many acts." His actual words were: "*Je fais mes vingt-huit jours!*"

I left my new friend—for so he had called me over and over again and had even embraced me on my departure—with a contract signed by both of us, the first one that I had made with a foreign writer. Secretly I rejoiced that this work would not take up much of my time and so would not cause any diversion from my own literary activity, for which I as yet had but little time to spare.

Once I had returned home I wanted to strike while the iron was hot, and so I immediately set about putting the two acts into my mother-tongue. Only then did I discover the difficulties of my undertaking, for it turned out—something that I had of course already felt vividly in Luchon—that the dialogue and the rhythmic quality of the language in this work were so fundamentally French, so very Gallic in tone, that the exuberance and the bitter irony that flashed out of all the conversations were something that could scarcely be reproduced.

But this discovery did not dishearten me, for the little masterpiece in two acts cried out to be performed on the stage, a fact that would certainly be apparent to every man of the theatre who set eyes on it. And I had the pleasure of interesting the then director of the Raimundtheater in the play, which was difficult to produce mainly for the reason that, being only two acts long, it would have to be supplemented by other plays on the same evening. Soon after this I was to see the première and the great success of *Boubouroche* in a production that was made especially charming by the performance of the first German 'Adèle'. Critics of the rank of Hermann Bahr naturally recognised at once how important the author was and what rank he must be accorded. Now my parents and relatives also learned that this little deviation from the aims I was supposed to be making for had once again taken me a little further off the road that they wanted to see me follow. But a successful joke causes even those to laugh who are otherwise not very pleased by it.

The fame of the German actress, which was by no means second to that of the French actress whom we had seen together in Luchon, if only because she was much better-looking, grew quite considerably and connected her name with that of Georges Courteline, who was now much talked of in literary circles.

I now wrote Courteline detailed letters about this Viennese success, which caused him the utmost delight, the epistolary expression of which I at first took merely for politeness, whereas it turned out that this strange, highly original writer had always wished to have his work performed on a German stage. And indeed shortly afterwards I succeeded in bringing this about at the Residenztheater in Berlin, which was then under the direction of the well-known Lautenburg; but apart from Alfred Kerr and Julius Elias only a few of the Berlin critics could make anything of what one of them called 'the jargon of this French comedy'.

Much later it was Courteline's pleasant lot to know that *Boubouroche* was being given an exemplary production, surpassing any French production, at the Burgtheater in Vienna, with Rosa Retty and Otto Tressler in the principal rôles.

But soon after the first modest success on German-speaking territory Courteline did in fact display enthusiastic friendship for me in my youthful audacity; this made me very happy and I responded warmly. In these memoirs there will often be mention of the man, the only one among his professional contemporaries whose little plays are still acted from time to time, while his books, especially *Le train de 8 h. 47* and *Les gaîtés de l'escadron* have never ceased to delight French readers and are time and again reprinted in all sorts of editions.

Perhaps this is now the place where I should make a confession that I have never before had an opportunity to make in public. I was evidently born with an unusual delight in discovering men of genius. In the moment of making such a discovery I have never thought of the consequences, which, because one thing leads to another, are inevitably bound up with translations when the people concerned are foreigners. No sooner had I succeeded in paving the way to my own career than I created new difficulties for myself by the discoveries, or, as it might be, translations, that I myself put between myself and my work.

It is a fortunate chance that Georges Courteline gave me relatively little work. To make up for that, in the most important years of my own creative work, fascinated by the art of Bernard Shaw, which had not even been performed in his native country, I hid my own light under a bushel for years, without letting it occur to me even in my dreams that in this way I would in the eyes of the world, in the crude general judgment of those taking a merely superficial interest in me, suddenly and quietly be ejected from the ranks of the creative and be classified among the translators.

Here I wish swiftly to record an experience that occurred at that time, but which actually became an experience in the full sense of the word only later, as a result of the strange circumstances that were associated with it.

It was on a journey home from Switzerland, where I had been spending pleasant but short holidays, and I had made sure of my seat in Buchs and, getting into the train again after going through the Customs, found my place occupied by a stranger. Being in those days much more vehement in my insistence on small rights than I am today, I indicated my claim, which had been made quite clear by the presence on the seat of a straw hat that had now been unjustifiably removed. The exchange of words that now arose was on the point of becoming violent and unpleasant when a slim, clean-shaven young man of great elegance, to all appearances an English-man, of his own accord intervened as an eye-witness, vigorously and energetically took my part and, pointing to the hat now hanging in the luggage-net, insisted that I should have restored to me the seat of which this inconsiderate person had tried to deprive me. Impatiently and somewhat shamefacedly the wrong-doer left the compartment in which the quarrel had taken place. I thanked my travelling-companion for his kind assistance and introduced myself. With a vivid smile he introduced himself as follows: "My name is Dr. Hau of New York. Anyone who can suppress his sense of justice in trifling matters is too easy-going and will fail when faced with greater tasks." So he pronounced didactically. "I am an American," he added with quiet pride.

We soon got into conversation, and half an hour later we were no longer sitting opposite each other but beside each other, exchanging stories, views, experiences, and plans for the future. I soon found myself admiring the great knowledge, the considerable skill as a linguist, and the genuine culture of a man who not only seemed to have enjoyed a careful upbringing, but also to have his head full of magnificent plans, which he began to expound, not in the manner of a self-important travelling-acquaintance, but in a hesitant, thoughtful way, as though talking to himself. He had just come from Paris and was on his way to Constantinople, if I remember rightly, entrusted with some mission or other to the Turkish court. He promised to visit me in Vienna on his return journey and show me the high Ottoman decoration, a star, which he was expecting to be given.

I was struck by the fact that he seemed to know the family of the Russian Ambassador in Washington, Count Kapnist, very well and spoke in a tone of special admiration of the ambassador's daughter, with whom, so he said, he had opened a ball there.

Some weeks later Dr. Karl Hau, whom I had not forgotten and to whose visit I was in fact looking forward, was my guest in Vienna. Dressed in an exquisite summer suit, he knocked at my door one morning, the picture of gay and carefree youth, and in such high spirits, in such a mood of joviality as can only be caused by success and easy triumph.

Hau stayed in Vienna for two days, and I still remember that I fulfilled his wish to get to know the Prater, showing him the glories of those wonderful meadows and walks, in the midst of that very gay society, now vanished, that was so utterly different from that of today and which greatly charmed my guest, whose standards were very high. In the beautiful Krieau, which I have already mentioned and which was the afternoon rendezvous of the leisured, smart Vienna of bygone days, I took tea with Karl Hau.

Afterwards he accompanied me back to my apartment, unable to say enough in his grateful enthusiasm for everything he had seen, smoked a cigarette with me, then suddenly looked at the clock, became restless, and declared that his time was up and that he must now go at once, so that we parted sooner than I had intended. I just had time to wish him a good journey and quite casually to suggest that we might meet again 'in Paris or London', being a little taken aback by his abrupt departure.

He did not keep his unasked-for promise to write to me and I never saw him again; but I was aghast to read horrible things about him approximately a year later. All the newspapers in the world were full of the mysterious murder of a certain Frau Molitor in Baden-Baden, whose daughter was to marry the young lawyer Dr. Hau. The description tallied so completely with the strange visitor I had had in Vienna that it was impossible to doubt. The Dr. Karl Hau who was charged with murder was the same man as had taken my side in the train and then visited me in Vienna. Perhaps he had even then conceived his dreadful plan. And perhaps everything that he had told me had been mere invention; perhaps his journey to Turkey had merely been an attempt at providing himself with an alibi. That very talkative man was very silent during the trial, which was very fully reported in all newspapers; but he never ceased to declare that he was innocent. He was then sentenced to lifelong imprisonment on circumstantial evidence, but a few years later died in jail of tuberculosis.

Jakob Wassermann made him the hero of his popular novel *Der Fall Mauritius* (*The Mauritius Case*). Nobody ever found out for certain, or will now, of course, ever be able to find out, whether he really fired the fatal shots at his future mother-in-law in a quiet avenue in Baden-Baden, or not. Frau Molitor is said to have been as rich as she was avaricious, and Hau's accusers asserted that he had been after the inheritance.

At that time, of course, I knew nothing of all this. I was now once more living the everyday life of my native city with its duties and joys and was also beginning to take a certain pleasure in the café-life that was such a feature of Vienna. My favourite cafés were those where I knew Schnitzler, Hermann Bahr, and Salten went.

Round about this time, too, I got to know Peter Altenberg, who was much older and who interested me mainly on account of his benevolent father, of whom he was a pale copy. This father—I think his name was Moritz—I had got to know in the office, for he had business relations with my step-father. There I had many and many a time hastened to meet him when he came in, his gaze at once seeking me out, and then he would always forget the main purpose of his business visit and would tell me a great many remarkable things. He was almost always in the highest of spirits. But once he said to me, not without making a deep impression on me: "My son Peter goes and prints all the things I have been saying all these years. All over the place I keep reading my own sayings, by Peter Altenberg. If I had dreamt that the things I say and write to my friends would ever be worth so much, I would have published them under my own name. It's all very well for a son—for plagiarism of one's own father doesn't really count as plagiarism. The son is only making his father's arm longer when he touches upon the same things."

In the top right-hand corner of old Herr Moritz Engländer's letter-paper was a saying by Victor Hugo, whose works he knew through and through. He had a hundred sheets of this paper printed, and on each was a different quotation from the work of his French idol. He was an eccentric old man, who gazed upon the world out of very large blue eyes and who—I may as well confess that this is my opinion—was by no means inferior to his son in the originality of his expressions and the unique quality of his views and outlook.

'Fame attaches itself to the latest name'—so, if I am not mistaken, Jakob Wassermann once said, and it happened that Peter Altenberg was this latest name, behind which the talent of the old business man, Moritz Engländer, lay hidden.

These facts were not known to Egon Friedell, Peter Altenberg's much younger friend, who, although he himself was much more important, condescended to be Altenberg's Eckermann; and he remained speechless for several minutes when on one occasion I enlightened him as to these remarkable circumstances.

I had at that time already met young Friedell, who was my junior. Even before I was captivated by his original mind, he interested me if for no other reason than that he was, after Emil Ertl, *the* writer whose father was also a silk-manufacturer, in other words, a colleague of my father. For him there had not been much in the way of struggles; he took everything much more lightly, and from his earliest youth onwards, with extraordinary assurance, he laughingly carried out whatever he thought right, without racking his brains about the feelings of the people around him. So it was that he once said to me:

"It was of course obvious to my parents at once, when they became acquainted with me, that I could not continue what they had begun. Even as a baby I wouldn't stand any nonsense in such matters. Nor did I, like you, put up with the name with which they burdened me. Your name is not a very fortunate one for success or, if it comes to that, great fame. You ought to have handed it back to them and chosen one for yourself. 'Friedmann,' I said to myself. 'But that's what my brother is called—the animal.' (For that was what he called him). 'To hell with it, I'm not called Friedmann. There are far too many of them.' And in a wink I'd changed my name into Friedell, because I didn't know anyone with that name, and that's the way it'll stay, too, as I have no intention of bringing another Friedell into the world. It's only me. And that's the end of it. Egon—well, I could put up with that all right. E.F. are quite tolerable initials. I did it at once, as soon as I'd left school. Once a name has got firmly attached to you, you can't do anything but bear it, groaning and moaning."

Egon Friedell was, I suppose, the most unprejudiced man in our circle at that time. Hermann Bahr very quickly took a fancy to him and pulled strings for him wherever he could. Today, of course, we know that this laughing philosopher possessed vast knowledge and that his *History of Civilisation* constitutes an imperishable enrichment of the human mind, even though, if regarded from the point of view of profound scholarship and historical research, the work may seem superficial.

Now came a summer that was very decisive for me. I wanted to settle down somewhere at last and make a first draft, from beginning to end, of my novel, *Convalescence*, of which I had now and then written a fragment. This I did in Madonna di Campiglio, that incomparably beautiful mountain-resort in Southern Tyrol. I had four weeks of August at my disposal. I made use of them and there wrote down that first work, which I had approached so very timidly, from the first to the last line, working about eight hours a day.

In Vienna I had told few people of my intention and the purpose of my summer holiday. One of the few was Felix Salten, because he showed the most lively interest in my work. I remember to this day the pleasure I felt when on the day of beginning my work I received a telegram from him, the wording of which I have never forgotten: 'The Madonna di Campiglio give you strength and make your work successful.'

When I returned home from those mountains I had my manuscript with me and could now begin with the work of polishing. The material and contents were now laid and could not be wrested from me any more. The most urgent need I felt was to be read by those who had doubts of me, and here again I was helped by the *Neue Freie Presse*.

I published a long essay, 'Summer's End'. Some weeks later there appeared in the same paper a little story, 'The Buried Doll', which received a good deal of notice and must have indicated to my father that my change of occupation might perhaps soon become a real issue.

Perhaps it was connected with his fear of that moment and his wish at least to postpone it for as long as possible that he summoned me and put it to me that I should go to London for him and his firm. He had already started small business relations there, but what he planned was a large branch, a sister firm to that in Vienna.

Since he was evidently not entirely displeased with the small commercial successes that I had already had abroad, he suggested that I should for once do something that would be remembered in the annals of his firm. I was to found this undertaking, was to stay on the banks of the Thames for many months and, of course under his guidance and instruction, seek and find employment and commissions for his factories, which were constantly increasing in size.

I did not object, if for no other reason than that I would at any rate not be under observation in London and would not be tied to office-hours, which were always subject to being checked. And then, I had for a long time had the conviction that the hour would soon strike for my change of occupation, not only because I felt myself bound by the promise I had given to Rilke, but also because my sense of self-preservation apparently forced me to believe in the success of the book that was now perhaps to be published.

Before I went to London for a stay lasting some time, I therefore wanted to try to arrange for the publication of this book. I did of course say to myself, full of gloomy forebodings, that there would be as many rejections as publishers and that my prospect of reaching my immediate aim in life with this little novel was fairly slight. Now I considered very carefully what I should do. I very quickly said to myself that a rejection from a large publishing-firm would perhaps be less painful than the same thing from one or more small publishers; and so I resolved to choose for my purpose the firm of S. Fischer in Berlin, already famous and at that time the most respected of all, and for the present to let my fate be decided by his acceptance or rejection. From conversation I knew that Arthur Schnitzler and Hermann Bahr published with Fischer and were on excellent personal terms with him. Very timidly, and apologising all the time, I asked them both for a few lines of recommendation, which I wanted to enclose with the manuscript I intended to send to the publisher. To my great surprise the almost wordless but very vigorous nods of agreement with which both reacted were no mere formality, for only the morning after the next I received the very kindly couched letters of recommendation to the man on whose decision so infinitely much would depend for me. My constantly repolished manuscript had in the meantime been beautifully typed out, with two carbon copies, and I carried my hope, neatly packed up with my accompanying letter and the two letters of recommendation, to the post office myself. And so now my first book had gone off to Berlin, to S. Fischer.

Then I once again said farewell to Vienna and to much that had become dear to me in my native city, and travelled to London.

Now came very sober, and to some extent tormenting, weeks for me in this huge city, in which I did not even know a single interesting person. I was for the first time really in a strange country. The office of my father's representative was in the City, and every morning I had to make a very long journey by bus in order to get there from my hotel in Blackfriars.

I remember that I tried to brighten my days somewhat; and since in Vienna I had, after all, been a dyed-in-the-wool theatre-goer, here too in a foreign city I wanted to have brighter, more comforting evenings to follow the more sombre days. For this reason, in defiance of my physical fatigue, which was chiefly caused by the entirely unaccustomed climate, I went to the London theatres fairly often.

When I had said good-bye to Hermann Bahr and Felix Salten, it had struck me that, oddly enough, both had shaken hands with the same parting words: "Do send accounts of the English theatre, of which people here know practically nothing." So I could in any case turn to two Viennese newspapers, the *Wiener Allgemeine Zeitung* and the *Neue Wiener Tagblatt*, on which the two above-mentioned critics held important positions. The editors of both papers had not made any promises, but had nodded amiably with the remark: "If you send in anything interesting, we might publish something on and off."

Now in my spare time, which was paralysingly dreary, especially on Sundays, I began to write home to Vienna about the cheerless evenings that I was spending at the theatre in London. This distraction refreshed me, and now, when my critical feuilletons were actually published from time to time, I went on with this side-line fairly frequently.

If I am not mistaken, I crossed the Channel for the first time in October, and round about Christmas I had got under way, not entirely without a lucky hand, what had been demanded of me, reinforced almost daily by letters full of instructions. I was glad to return home, at long last again to enjoy evenings at the theatre and not to be bored by melodramas that all resembled each other as one egg does another and by musical comedies that could not be surpassed for sheer lack of wit. But it was worst of all when an author tried to write in style and subject-matter like the famous French boulevard-playwrights. It was here that the reign of an incomprehensible prudery really became apparent.

From a human and artistic point of view London was at first a great disappointment to me, and in contrast with my perpetual longing for Paris I felt horror at the thought of a return to London, which was inevitable sooner or later.

I had not yet quite settled down again in my old familiar surroundings and had as yet had little opportunity to have talks with like-
minded people, when, unexpectedly fast, a letter came from
S. Fischer in Berlin, accepting my *Convalescence* in principle, a
communication that made me completely speechless. I could never
have dreamt of such a detailed analysis, such understanding, of
another person's work. This letter, which positively churned up
my feelings, was signed by Moritz Heimann, the firm's 'reader', who
urgently suggested several small changes to me. I could not help
reading this memorable letter over and over again, for I felt I had
been recognised and seen in my true colours in such a way that I
felt as if the clothes had been stripped from my body. Here was
a stranger who knew almost more of me and my struggles than I
did myself and unconcernedly uttered words that for me were
veritably like a healing medicine.

In spite of his affirmative attitude, the writer's objections were at
least as numerous as his words of approval, and the outpouring
ended with more or less these words: 'We want to publish this
magnificent first novel because it is our kind of thing and we believe
we may expect many and various things from its author.' Added
to this was the suggestion, likewise in S. Fischer's name, that
I should as soon as possible go to Berlin for a personal talk.

I had a long struggle with myself as to whether I should not rush
straight off to my father with this letter; but then I should have
robbed myself of the effect for which I had, after all, always been
preparing myself in my own mind, the effect that it would inevitably
make when I laid the printed book on the table before my father.
I therefore took refuge in a little stratagem, telling that conscientious
man I had learned in London that our representative in Berlin would
be able to give useful information on various questions that I could
not settle properly from London. My father naturally had no
objection to my going to Berlin first of all in order to clear up these
problems, which to him seemed so important.

When the holidays and New Year were past, I at once began to
talk of my journey to Germany, and the time was very quickly
fixed. In Vienna I informed Schnitzler, Bahr, and, I think, Felix
Salten too, of my success, so arousing in these writers a fairly lively
curiosity about my book.

Admittedly, I had wavered as to whether I should not wait until publication and then go to Berlin already an independent writer. On the other hand, Heimann's letter left me no peace, and I did of course want to have a discussion with him by word of mouth and then make the alterations he desired directly before the book went to the printer. I was also very curious to meet the remarkable writer of the letter.

I was immediately utterly charmed with Berlin, and I also liked the people I met. But I was afraid of becoming enthusiastic. I said to myself: Your time here will come when you are really free, when only you yourself have to decide the length of your stay.

My first visit to the great, flourishing, turbulent German capital was therefore of very short duration. I was very kindly received by the great publisher S. Fischer, in whom I at once believed I recognised a quite unusual man. He eagerly asked me about Hermann Bahr, Schnitzler, and Altenberg. He was particularly charmed with Schnitzler, who was just his type. "He's a writer after my own heart," he said. Then he called Moritz Heimann, whom I was already burning to set eyes on, into his office and introduced us. Before Heimann could get down to the main purpose of my visit, the discussion about the book, Fischer said to me, in his presence: "We like your *Convalescence* in many ways. Heimann will talk to you about the few places we should like changed. I shall send the contract to your hotel today." This was more or less how this first memorable interview passed, which marked the beginning of decades of collaboration and a friendship of which I often received touching tokens that made me deeply devoted to that wonderful man, Samuel Fischer.

Now I sat opposite Moritz Heimann, who was already a respected essayist and critic, and although, intellectually speaking, he was fairly hard on me in that first conversation and was not sparing with adverse criticism, I immediately felt myself captivated by his grave benevolence, and I felt quite at ease. But he had aroused the spirit of contradiction in me, and now I defended my standpoint as well as I could, and indeed not quite without success; for it did not always agree with his æsthetic views.

He was, however, anything but obstinate or set upon dictating, and I remember that our talk ended with his saying: "All right, in these three cases you may be right, and I will gladly give way on these points if, to make up for that, you will make fairly radical

changes in the other passages," and he pointed them out to me in
the manuscript lying open before him. I at once made notes of
what I had agreed to change, and Heimann rapidly passed on to
other matters, wanting to know more about my development than
I could tell him in one somewhat harassing hour in an office, and
then said good-bye to me cordially, remarking in more or less the
following words: "Once your book has appeared I hope to see you
here on a longer stay and to help you to become not only a poet
but what you are already well on the way to becoming—a writer!"

On one occasion much later, when we were already firm friends,
Heimann said something that deserves to be recorded, something
that hardly anyone was as much entitled to say as he was, for he
had pruned many a tender literary tree, and taken care that it
should grow straight, and spared it many a blow. He was a teacher;
and no less a man than Jakob Wassermann, not to speak of others,
had been through his school. The prospect of being allowed to do
the same delighted me, and I have never forgotten his words:
"Nobody is surprised if a singer takes singing-lessons or a musician
music-lessons, but most people think everyone can become a writer
the moment he wants to and sits down at a table determined to do
some writing. That is a great mistake. In our profession there is
much to learn, and one is still not very far advanced when one has
learnt that. But if one can't do that, however great one's gifts may
be, one is likely to come to a bad end."

Now I hastened back to Vienna full of intellectual impressions
received from two utterly different men, a publisher and his 'reader',
in order to work at finishing my book, making the alterations and
corrections. The alterations were mainly in connection with the
way that feelings were represented, a way of which Heimann did
not quite approve. The teacher in him wanted to see the young
adept more disciplined, more matter-of-fact, more economical, but
also more profound, in the use of words. He pruned back the superabundance of emotion. "If you want to move the reader, you must
not let it be seen how moved you are yourself," he impressed upon
me. And I think the changes he had got me to make did satisfy
him, for my corrections first went through his hands, and to my
delight I read on many a margin the words: 'That's right!'

And now the great day came when the first copies of my novel
reached me.

It was actually the first book that came through the post to me as 'printed matter', whereas the other ten copies followed by book-post. I put it down in front of me, firmly resolved that the next day I would pay my father a visit that would in some sense be a farewell visit.

I must give his due to the man who managed to keep me on a short rein so long, like a young horse, and say that he had an unusual knowledge of human nature and could anticipate many a word that another found it difficult to utter. When I entered his office with the evidence of my crime in my hand, in the quiet third hour of the afternoon, he rose from behind his desk and came towards me with the words: "You want something from me. I can tell by looking at you. Well, come on, out with it!"

Thereupon he went ahead of me into his private office. I now went up to him and not without a certain agonised embarrassment I held out my book to him and said: "Well, here you have the first success that you made the condition for my leaving our firm."

Extremely interested, he took the book, sat down, invited me to do so too, leafed through it, smiling, and said: "And so you have succeeded after all? Well, well!"

I now quickly explained to him that the success on which he had insisted was to be seen in the fact that the most respected German publishing-house had published my first book. Favourable reviews were only a matter of time, and of very little time, at that. They would confirm the success for him.

At this he laughed and said: "I don't need to wait for them, I can read for myself." Then he looked at me enquiringly. I did not quite know what to say. The main thing was not to say anything exaggerated, high-falutin', anything like: "Now you shall never see me here again!" Oh, no; everything that lay before me seemed too difficult and vague for that.

He made the transition easier for me by asking: "Well, what do you mean to do now?" Thereupon I said quite simply: "I want to ask you to let me go. One really can't serve two masters, as you have so often said, and it is my duty to dedicate myself exclusively to the vocation to which I was born, and to become, to the highest degree that is granted me, what I have, after all, always been."

At this my father nodded and said: "Evidently one can't play providence, after all. Anyway, so far as you are concerned, I have lost. It isn't quite unexpected. I have had my own thoughts about it for some time and made some provisions for the event of the striking of the hour that has now struck."

"I should just like to hand over my desk to you, and all the notes I brought back from London," I said. At this he nodded and followed me to my desk, where I cleared everything out of the drawers and laid it before him, feeling exceedingly relieved and also sparing him a dialogue that might have gone on indefinitely.

"I assume," he now said, smiling, "that you will now want to go home in order to recover from the blow, which will, however, not be a blow at all, if I have my way. You will now have to live much more modestly than I had intended you should and have hitherto made it possible for you to do. You proved yourself in London in such a manner that you would have been sure of a partnership soon, which you will from now on of course have to do without. Have you any plans for travel?" he asked me suddenly.

At this I said: "Yes, I want to go to Berlin again to see my publisher and there wait a while to see the effect my book has, but I shall certainly be back here again in a fortnight."

My father became very grave and said: "One thing I cannot save you from, which you would have been saved from if you had turned out to be a less good business man that you have been. You must go to London again and get your successor started in the job. We shall have a talk about this later, if you will put yourself at my disposal for this brief relapse into your former occupation." Then this superior man came up to me, embraced me and said: "Yes, today I myself believe you would be wasted if you went the way your forefathers went. You have fought honestly for your own road. Well, good luck to you now! Now devote yourself with all your strength and all your talent to your dreamt-of profession and do us all as much honour as ever you can. In this way you will also place the readiness with which I now let you go in the right light, and in spite of my failure, which is your success, I shall then come out of the whole thing better."

But now I could not bear any more. I tore myself free, and I could not help noticing that this man, who was fighting down a certain amount of emotion, accompanied me to the outer door, and as it closed behind me, the sound waked me as though from sleep. "Good-bye!" I called back over my shoulder, though there was no longer anyone to hear, and then I ran down the stairs, towards my new life.

When I was between my own four walls, joy and grief overwhelmed me. "I am free!" I am free!" I exclaimed aloud in the twilight that filled my study, and collapsed in mingled ecstasy and exhaustion.

II

FRIENDSHIPS

NOW I was thirty years of age, had an apartment of my own and a career I had chosen for myself.

Naturally I did not rush straight to the railway-station to travel to Berlin, but first of all settled all sorts of things at home that seemed to me important. First of all, for instance, I finished the story 'The End of the World', which was to give the title to a volume of stories later on, but at the same time, in a heightened mood of creativeness that did not, perhaps, always produce creative power, I wrote my first drama, *A Last Will*. Much earlier on I had already been guilty of a play with the title *Lou*, which I had, with the aged Frau Maria Ebner von Eschenbach's permission, based on her thrilling story 'Das Schädliche' ('What Does the Damage'), though scarcely thinking or believing that a performance would come about.

To my delight my journey to Berlin was already accompanied by very kind reviews of my *Convalescence*. For the newcomer Berlin was an experience. It was not only the reception that Fischer accorded the young writer, inviting me to his hospitable house, but also the great, even eager interest taken in me by Moritz Heimann, who some days later took me from the office to his home and introduced me to his wife, a sister-in-law of Gerhart Hauptmann, that stimulated my wavering emotions and increased my self-confidence, which was always ready to collapse into an impotence, even despair, with which I was familiar.

Heimann quite unconsciously encouraged my confidence in future works, about which he questioned me impatiently and searchingly. He also showed me many a kind review of *Genesung* that had already appeared in newspapers inside Germany. There were hours spent sitting at his desk in conversation that illumined me and aroused in me a strong desire to work.

At the house of Fischer, who saw me, from the publisher's point of view, as a coming man, I had met Julius Elias, the art critic and translator of Ibsen's works, and his wonderful wife, Julie, both of whom at once invited me to visit them. Julius Elias had almost the

greatest thirst for information of any man I ever met. But I had no
intention of surrendering to him, as to Moritz Heimann, all that
he would have liked to know and pass judgment on. When I talked
to Julius Elias enthusiastically about the Viennese theatres, above
all about the Burgtheater, at the same time stressing my disappointment with the London theatres, he hesitated for a moment and
then said to me: "If you go to London again, you must go and see
my friend William Archer, who is Ibsen's English translator. He
often writes to me in utter despair about the English theatre, and
I think a discussion with him ought to give you a good idea of the
lie of the land."

I accepted this suggestion very gratefully, for I had not forgotten
that I would have to go to London again and that I was not to escape
this last journey. In fact, I had the intention of getting it over as
soon as possible, and so I very cordially thanked the man who was
very soon to be one of my intimate friends in Berlin, looking forward
to at last meeting a man of intellect in the foggy city on the Thames.

But this was not merely a dinner-table conversation. When I
returned to my hotel that evening I already found, together with
Julius Elias' card, the letter of introduction to William Archer that
was to play such a great part in my life.

In the same year Thomas Mann and Hermann Hesse, to mention
only those who attained to world fame, also received their literary
baptism in the S. Fischer Verlag. Gerhart Hauptmann had already
some years earlier aroused great interest with his story 'Bahnwärter
Thiel' ('Signalman Thiel') and his first drama *Vor Sonnenaufgang*
(*Before Sunrise*).

Returning to Vienna, I felt an increased desire to consort with
Viennese writers, but I simply had no time to pay regular visits
to the cafés they frequented. I felt myself most drawn towards
Arthur Schnitzler, seven years my senior, whom I also met most
often and with whom I was soon on terms of friendship. He read
each new work of mine with great interest, after he had discussed
Genesung with me in detail. He explained his qualms, like his
approval, in a way that was as matter-of-fact as it was witty, and
from this I learned to understand the differences between his
creative power and my own as yet not fully developed poetic
eloquence.

I sometimes visited Hermann Bahr on the Semmering, where he

spent many a week-end recuperating. This witty, high-spirited, and good-tempered great European loosened my tongue on our strolls together and liked to have me tell him of the subject-matter that I meant to use in stories or dramas. It happened a few times that he stopped and said to me: "I say, I like that! Make me a present of it!" so making me very proud and receiving the material for his own use. That writer who was so over-brimming with ideas could well afford, precisely because he did not need to do so, to treat himself to such a little plant from my modest garden of ideas.

Round about the same time Hermann Bahr had in his stormy, even turbulently challenging way taken up the cudgels for Hugo von Hofmannsthal, with whom he kept in very close touch. Hermann Bahr had been the editor of the weekly paper, *Die Zeit*, before he went to the *Wiener Tagblatt*, and even then, in that paper, he had greatly boosted his favourite, whom he constantly and without mincing any words about it called a genius, a term that the young, modestly proud poet was well pleased to accept, without particularly taking his herald to his heart.

Hermann Bahr's incorruptibility can be seen in a *bon mot* that he made in my presence, when some of us—I think Schnitzler and Salten were among the company—made it quite clear to him that the young poet from the Salesianergasse whom he so much admired showed no trace of gratitude for the way in which he was furthering his cause—encouragement that the young poet nevertheless was direly in need of, if one considered the scepticism with which the public regarded his first beginnings. Hermann Bahr nodded and said: "Unlike you, I don't ask a tenor for gratitude and family feeling, but for a high C. So long as he can sing that, I'll stand up for him."

It was about the same time, too, that Hermann Bahr did as much for a woman, whom he did not shrink from calling 'more than earthly'. This was an Italian actress by the name of Eleonor Duse. The Carltheater in Vienna became the cradle of her world-wide fame. After her first appearance in Sardou's pot-boiler *Fedora* Hermann Bahr, that critic with the infallible eye for new talent, hailed this noble actress as a wonder. His essays—columns of description of her art—were no longer criticism but bugle-calls, stirring calls summoning the public not to miss a single performance given by this divinely inspired Italian woman with the indescribably beautiful eyes and hands.

And Hermann Bahr succeeded in driving people to the theatre to see this foreign actress, so turning what had been an empty house into a theatre where there was not a ticket to be had. Other countries also pricked up their ears and sent invitations to this inimitable actress. But she always gratefully returned to Vienna, where her star had first risen.

Meanwhile I was still being nagged by the thought of the promise I had given my father to settle everything for him in London and hand the job over to my successor. Until I had done that I was not really free. There was still something left over, which tugged at me, and so one day I specially announced that I was coming to dinner with my parents, in whose house I in any case regularly appeared at lunch-time. And now I explained to the man who looked at me questioningly, betraying some slight impatience, that I was now at his disposal for my last journey to London in the service of his firm.

He smiled. 'I didn't want to raise the matter myself, but I was become rather curious to know how long it would take you to think of fulfilling your last duty, which you do, after all, somewhat owe it to me to fulfil. I am glad that you have now spoken of it yourself. Well, it's not too late yet. Everything goes so slowly over there. But it is high time. We will discuss details later.' And he made an appointment for me to see him in his office the next day.

And so there again I sat facing this man, in the same place as so often before, but with quite different feelings. Now I was not a prisoner of his will, but as it were a guest who had come freely and open-handedly, eager to make some return for many wishes gladly fulfilled and kindnesses received. My father had already prepared everything, and our session did not last long. Three days later I set off on my journey, with my last instructions from a world that had very quickly become alien to me.

This time, at the beginning of spring, I liked London much better than before, and it no longer wore all the signs of my dependence. It was with quite different feelings that I went to the office there, where, as the departing envoy of a great firm, I received a much more friendly reception than ever before. All the arrangements for my last visit had already been made from Vienna, and so the work was got through much faster than I had supposed it would be. In several days I had performed my tasks and conscientiously carried out my mission to the best of my ability. I wanted to stay a short while longer and be within reach in the event of anything important having been overlooked and needing to be gone over again. But secretly I wanted this time in order to pay the to me so valuable call on William Archer. I wrote to him, asking for an appointment with him, a wish I justified by enclosing the letter from his German colleague, Julius Elias.

I had not to wait long for an answer. It reached me the very next morning. The great critic asked me to tea at the National Liberal Club, where he also used to work.

The day following, about five o'clock, the club page took my card to William Archer, who was already waiting for me. He was very different from the Englishmen I had met hitherto; what struck me as so different was the briskness with which he rose, holding a newspaper in his left hand and stretching out his right hand to me. He invited me to sit down. Tea was brought, and no sooner had the waiter gone away than Archer said to me without more ado: "I have read almost everything you have published in Viennese newspapers about the English theatre, and I am grateful to my friend Elias for sending you to me, for it has struck me how similar our judgments are, although, after all, we arrive at our opinions of dramatic works from such different worlds."

And now he hardly let me get a word in edgewise, so much did he tell me about the plays that drove him to despair and about the authors, Grundy, Jones, and Pinero, who unjustly dominated the London stage. In the course of our conversation he suddenly and unexpectedly said: "Your mistake and your misrepresentations lie in the fact that in your articles on the English theatre you always only mentioned the plays that are being performed. But there are unperformed plays that are outstanding dramatic works, which hardly anyone knows at present. The most important writer among them, one with whom I am on terms of close friendship, is a dramatist to his finger-tips, but a West End theatre would never put on a play of his. He has to make do with experimental theatres. In your country people go to the theatre before dinner, here they go after dinner. That makes a tremendous difference. Your public is receptive and combative. The English theatre-goer is tired and battle-weary and wants to have only light fare set before him and to be amused."

I interrupted Archer with the assurance that I would now write no more about the English theatre, and therefore would never again be able to commit the error for which he had reproached me. Then, however, since my curiosity had been aroused, I asked him: "Who *is* this unrecognised genius?" Then for the first time I heard the name of Bernard Shaw.

I asked Archer to write it down for me, because I wanted to try —if only in order to show him what a high value I attached to his judgment—to get the dramatic works of this unknown writer in a bookshop. At this Archer exclaimed: "Wait, I'll also write down the name of a bookshop for you where you can probably get the three volumes he has published so far. He is not in demand with the public, and you will seek his works in vain in the windows of our bookshops." And in the same moment he tore a sheet off a note-pad and wrote down for me the name of the author and the titles of the three volumes.

My visit had already lasted overlong, and I rose, after I had put the slip of paper in my pocket, thanking this original man for his kind reception and his instructive conversation and promising, as he asked me, that after I had read these works, if they should convert me to his opinion, I would not fail to meet him again.

Two days later I began my journey home with the three volumes, *Plays Unpleasant, Plays Pleasant,* and *Plays for Puritans.* In the train I leafed through the books and, attracted by the title, read *Candida.* Never before had the long journey seemed so short. I enjoyed the strange fairy-tale of this poetic work as one of the most exquisite gifts of a new and individual dramatic poetry. And afterwards, in the tranquillity of my study, my enthusiasm grew and did not let me rest until I had read all the ten plays.

I had to let off steam in some way, for although I recognised that an unexpected stroke of luck had led me to a veritable treasure-trove, I was by no means intent on guarding this revelation like a secret. On the contrary, I proclaimed my admiration from the house-tops, and my first thought was to campaign—at least in Germany and Austria—for this man, in whom I saw an epoch-making personality and the future conqueror of the stage throughout the world, and to do it in a way that would with one stroke put him in the right light. I thought I owed this to William Archer too.

At that time it did not yet occur to me to become the interpreter of Shaw's works, for I was much too involved in my own writings, in my *own* dreams. My head was full of plans and I was by no means willing to put that all aside in order to yoke myself into anyone else's team, even if he was a genius. It was only the resistance that I encountered eveiywhere, the cool rejection of my enthusiasm, and the resentment that rose up in me as a consequence, that made me into Bernard Shaw's translator.

Admittedly, with this intention I had already intervened in a foreign sphere and acted contrary to all current usage. How did a foreign play find its way on to the German stage in those days, and for that matter probably down to the present day? It went like this. A bustling theatrical agent saw, perhaps in Paris, a new play whose reputation had lured him into going and seeing it, and decided it would be a great success in German too. He now approached the society of authors, bought the piece for cash, took it home, and looked through his list of professional translators to see which of them would be the most suitable man for this play. He then summoned this translator and commissioned him to translate the newly acquired foreign work. The specialist went to work, and the usual fee, which he received on delivery of the German translation, was at that time generally about five hundred gold marks.

Exactly the same thing happened when the theatrical agent went to London because of a great theatrical success, saw it, judged it, and bought the rights for the German stage. This was the normal business procedure, which of course could not be applied to Shaw's plays, for no resounding success called any agent to London to see them. And the very fact that I was poaching on the preserves of those very honourable business men, who generally had a great deal of good taste and almost always had a flair for new work, made my task much more difficult. I was not a professional translator, only a cobbler who would not stick to his last.

To give only one example of the irritated indifference and lack of understanding with which I had to contend, I should like to recall here a remark made by the proprietor of the Entsch theatrical publishing firm in Berlin, to whose attention I had time and again recommended Bernard Shaw's plays.

Entsch, to whom I had at that time given my drama, *A Last Will*, asked me to come and see him when I was staying in Berlin and showed me three telegrams accepting my drama: one from the Deutsche Volkstheater in my native city, one from the Stadttheater in Leipzig, and one from the Stadttheater in Hanover.

"I should like you to regard this as evidence," he said, "that I take an interest in you and have a high opinion of you. But I refuse to have anything to do with this crazy Irishman whose plays you are always trying to foist on me. It simply won't do. I can't waste my time on such a lost cause. But I should like to beg you to listen to me and stop being so obstinate. Heaven knows you have enough to do with your own work, which you are only likely to endanger by escapades of this kind. Take the advice of an experienced man of the theatre and keep your hands off foreign plays that have not the slightest chance of success now or at any other time."

Naturally I never again offered Entsch a new play by Shaw, something for which he was to bear me a severe grudge in a future as yet distant.

The refusals from theatrical agents and publishers, whom I tried more or less at random, were so radical for yet another reason. To the question put to me by sober men of business—and that, after all, is what theatrical publishers always are at the decisive moment, even when they take an interest in art—namely the question: "Well, how do people in England like these plays you praise so highly?" I could only answer: "So far they have not been produced in any proper theatre at all. Only the Stage Society, under the direction of J. T. Grein, has felt an obligation to perform plays by Bernard Shaw."

By uttering this statement of the truth, which I had also learned from Archer, I myself condemned to failure my attempts to find a German agent for this unrecognised writer; for in London, as also among the initiated in Germany, the Stage Society was regarded as an experimental theatre for unactable dramas, although it alone really deserved well of the then modern English theatre.

What people said was: "You know that even English comedies that have a great success in their own country often don't succeed in Continental theatres. How should it be possible to gain an international public for plays that can't even get produced in their country of origin?" And I realised that if I wanted to get a great writer already in the prime of his life the hearing he had long deserved, I must go into the breach myself and toil and labour for him as his herald in my native city and in Germany.

But for the present I had to content myself with a long letter to William Archer, in which I spared him the little disappointments described above, speaking only of my unqualified enthusiasm and expressing the hope that I would be able to call on him again in the autumn. My volume of stories, *The End of the World*, now only had to be put together. The individual parts, eight short stories and the story that gave the title, were finished, and Fischer had already informed me that he would like to follow up my first work, *Convalescence*, with a collection of stories. The manuscript was soon arranged and sent off.

In the meantime, however, my military service and the experiences I had had in the provinces as a young officer had provided me with some curious subject-matter, which so urgently demanded to be dealt with that I had to set about work on it. So there came into existence the novel *Das Haus am Abhang* (*The House on the Hillside*), which was later also published by S. Fischer.

Now my life in Vienna was gradually beginning to become the life of a writer. Greater and lesser poets had always thronged around Arthur Schnitzler and his table, and one afternoon a very smart, *soigné*, raven-haired young man wearing a monocle on a broad ribbon sat beside him. This young man he introduced to me as Dr. Richard Beer-Hofmann. What struck me at this first meeting, apart from his exceedingly carefully chosen clothes and his red cheeks, was his loquacity. Not only on that afternoon, but as often as I met him in the same place, he was in rollicking good spirits and very vigorously criticised everything he happened to see, although he himself had as yet scarcely published anything but his first work, the story 'Das Kind' ('The Child'). He was older than I and had a self-assurance of manner that amazed me, all the more since it had not yet been earned by great achievements. Apart from his acquaintance with Arthur Schnitzler, he was even at that time very close friends with the young poet Loris, that is to say, with Hugo von Hofmannsthal, and was so to speak the mentor of that prince from the land of genius.

If today I cast a retrospective gaze back at that circle, some members of which attained to world fame, Beer-Hofmann seems to me to have been the most fortunate of us all. He was not only the most healthy, vigorous and energetic, but also by far the richest and most independent of all Viennese writers, and I think destiny did not make things as easy for anyone as for him. Battles such as we all had to fight, such as Arthur Schnitzler resumed with almost every new work of his, such as Hugo von Hofmannsthal had to go through until his delicate physique was exhausted, were something that the robust, laughter-loving Beer-Hofmann, with his belief in himself firm as a rock and his apparent indifference to successes, was spared. His small productivity may have had something to do with this. The fewer works one puts out, the less antagonism they can arouse and the less they can be attacked. Beer-Hofmann also had uncanny skill in getting to know the right people and attaching himself particularly to those whose liking he was able to gain by his personality and his convincing attitude.

Only a few years after the meeting I have just described he became almost world-famous through a poem entitled 'Miriams Schlaflied' ('Miriam's Lullaby'). Admittedly, the poem is of extraordinary beauty, but so are other poems that were not, like this one, instantly lifted into the limelight of fame. Those who praise it even manage to overlook the fact that its author made the impossible rhyme of *rollt's* with *Stolz*.

Beer-Hofmann, who made a love-match with a very beautiful Viennese girl, was a born patriarch. His paternal character was in his blood, as was also his despotic love of his children, which, however, in the case of his son Gabriel oddly enough met with no response.

He had an unusual gift for the living theatre and was, when it was demanded of him, an outstanding and sensitive producer. It was Max Reinhardt who first made him so, and later he had the honour of being allowed to arrange Goethe's *Faust*, Parts I and II, for a one-evening performance at the Burgtheater.

Beer-Hofmann's great material independence was perhaps not so very fortunate for his creativeness. He built himself a princely house, which he filled with antiques and in which he received distinguished guests. But in so doing he imposed on himself so many little worries and things to keep him busy that it was only seldom he had time for any creative work. What surprised me in connection with his wealth, which came to him from two fathers, one real and one by adoption, was the strange fact of his very under-developed sense of charity. I do not know of his ever having lightened the weary way of people engaged in a hard fight and almost defeated.

His first play, *Der Graf von Charolais*, first performed at the Deutsche Theater in Berlin, brought Beer-Hofmann an unexpectedly great success. A little episode of which I was a witness is charac-teristic of his belief in himself. On the occasion of the première, Fischer gave a wonderful evening party at his house in the Grünewald in honour of Beer-Hofmann. Gerhart Hauptmann, who was among those present, engaged Beer-Hofmann in a lengthy conversation. When a fairly large company of us set out on the homeward journey at a late hour of the night, a lady asked the author of *Charolais* what the famous Gerhart Hauptmann, the creator of *Florian Geyer*, *The Weavers*, and *Hannele*, had talked to him about. Beer-Hofmann turned swiftly to this lady and answered somewhat irritably: "I really can't remember. But perhaps you'll ask him what *I* talked about!" This overweening remark suddenly made Gerhart Hauptmann seem very great.

Characteristic of Beer-Hofmann's gift for repartee is the remark he made to an admirer who somewhat naïvely asked him his opinion of the *Graf von Charolais*. Beer-Hofmann gazed at him meditatively for a moment and then said: "I consider the play excellent. If I am mistaken, God grant that I may never discover the fact!"

Beer-Hofmann was an oddity, and indeed really eccentric. It cannot otherwise be explained that a man of his education should not know a word of French or English. And yet I recall having heard from Schnitzler that Beer-Hofmann was most enthusiastic about Flaubert and Maupassant. These two French novelists, together with Prosper Mérimée and Stendhal, he ranked among the greatest writers that France had given the world, but he could not read them in their original language.

While I was now in my native city, living through days full of material and emotional stress, I by no means neglected my corres-pondence with my friends René Rilke and Georges Courteline. The latter impatiently summoned me to Paris; but since summer was approaching, we had to put it off till the end of September, because he himself was again on the point of starting one of his 'periods of military training' in the French provinces, in one of his little plays, and then was going to Hendaye to recuperate. For this resort on the Basque coast was the place that most inspired the poet in him, where work for him went even faster than at the marble-topped tables of the cafés in Montmartre.

But what I had in mind was the Austrian mountains, where I hoped to push on with writings I had begun and also recuperate in such a way as to ward off the affliction I had had from my youth. I chose the Ampezzo valley, and after having roamed through those glorious spots, Toblach and Landro, on excursions, I settled down for a stay of several weeks on Lake Misurina. Never could I have dreamt of the memorable encounter I was to have on the shores of this beautiful but little-known lake in the Tyrol. Nor would I have thought it possible that a French family could stray there for a summer holiday.

The respected Protestant family of Puaux, from Paris, had chosen this glorious place for the holidays of their children, who were, however, no longer small. One son was over twenty, and the other was only a few years younger. To my surprise these two young Frenchmen spoke a fairly fluent, though of course Gallic-tinged, German, but they were nevertheless glad to be able to converse with me in their native language. It soon turned out that René Puaux, the elder brother, had already won his spurs as a writer and, strangely enough, had begun to work on a book about Finland. Naturally I had brought a few copies of *Convalescence* with me in my bag, and I gave René Puaux this story to read. Some days later he rushed up to me, congratulating me in the most exaggerated terms on my first work, and without more ado asked for my permission to translate the book and publish it in Paris. My joy was great. If I *was* translated, I enjoyed it all the more to translate myself, and I now told Puaux that I had done for Georges Courteline precisely what he wanted to do for me, and that I was a very close friend of that wonderful French boulevard writer. Puaux now revealed himself to be a great admirer of his not yet generally recognised countryman, whose works he knew very well.

We drew up a proper written agreement, and René Puaux instantly fixed a meeting with me in Paris in the event of my carrying out my intention and going there for some time in the autumn, which I, having long made up my mind to that visit, solemnly promised.

And so that summer had given me not only physical refreshment but a translator, who, after the publication of *Convalescence* by that respected publishing-house, 'La Plume', also became one of my life-long foreign friends. Decades later René Puaux became the editor of *Le Temps*, while his brother was the French Ambassador in Vienna. And many years later still, his hair now grey and suffering from serious heart-disease, René Puaux wrote a biographical introduction to my novel *Heimkehr zum Ich* (*Return Home to Myself*), which the occasional authoress, Hélène Chaudoir, had translated.

I naturally told my Viennese friends and colleagues that I was to have the good fortune to have my first book translated into French. Hermann Bahr seemed to be particularly pleased about it, and this time talked a great deal to me about Georges Courteline, of whose work he had in the meantime, after *Boubouroche*, read a few delightful one-act plays, among them *Schwebebahn* (*Funicular*) and *Ein Stammgast* (*Un client sérieux*). Hermann Bahr was very sparing with expressions like 'genius' and 'unique', but hardly any word seemed to him too great for Courteline. He himself had lived in France for a year and had also visited Morocco and Tangier. He now told me a number of things about that period, to which he owed the novel *Die gute Schule* (*The Good School*).

Hermann Bahr, who had, after all, been born in Linz, that is to say, in provincial Austria, was perhaps not the most important of the writers of those days. But assuredly he was the greatest European, the one with the broadest horizon, the most receptive and also the most eager for experiences, of all our circle. That is also the reason why he could present Maurice Barrès, who was scarcely known among us, so superbly that an interest in that French man of intellect arose that did not fade for many a day. It was also from Hermann Bahr that I first heard the name of Catulle Mendès, who was not only among Courteline's most intimate friends, but the master to whom he all through his life looked up with as much love as admiration.

On my return Paris was aglow with all the colours of autumn. Shortly after my arrival twilight fell over the city. A moment later a thousand lights glittered forth, promising the stranger thousands of delights and like glow-worms lighting up his every step. The people streamed in throngs along the boulevards, and the cafés were filling up.

Things were particularly lively in the Café Napolitain, where I went to meet Courteline. The finest flower of Montmartre was gathered here, people who years ago had sat in the Chat Noir high up on the hill and at that time had tended to avoid the Café Napolitain as a place of extreme luxury. There, all jostling together, were known and unknown quantities of the day— painters, musicians, and poets who were not yet what they set out to be, some who achieved their purpose, and others who never did.

I sat down beside Courteline, who was just breaking a lance for Dreyfus, while Lajeunesse, sitting opposite him, continued to put the case for the other side, in the shrillest tones his high voice could produce. He was supported by a plump officer, who looked less like a warrior than like the prototype of Boubouroche. The grave vaudevillist Grenet-Dancour, whose *Fils surnaturel* had set all Paris rocking with laughter, listened quietly, with a detached air; then he glanced at the clock, rose, and went. Boutet, Alfred Capus, Francis de Croisset, and other figures of the day belonging to the theatre and to literature, including some actors who were among Courteline's daily companions, sat at neighbouring tables and talked to him across the intervening space. The theatrical producer Antoine, who was the first to bring Georges Courteline's little works to the footlights, also frequently appeared in this circle, although his theatre left him little time for visiting cafés.

As most of his friends gradually rose and strolled out into the warm, whispering evening, Courteline also glanced at the clock, but he remained seated, saying he must wait for 'Catulle', who was sure to come soon. I already knew that this was none other than the celebrated poet, critic and *conférencier*, Catulle Mendès. While I was trying to picture the man whose photograph I had often seen, he suddenly came up to our table and greeted his friend, and like-wise the others who were still present, with urbane cordiality. That evening we made each other's acquaintance, and I immediately noticed the unusual, universal knowledge this man possessed, his questions and comments revealing an exact knowledge of all literatures and their aims.

At that time I had the pleasure of being present at the première of the little play, *Un client sérieux*, which, together with *Le commissaire est bon enfant* and *Le gendarme est sans pitié*, filled an evening and turned out to be the raging success that Courteline was sure of having in that milieu.

I have already mentioned the peculiar quality that made it impossible for Georges Courteline to write a comedy that would fill an evening, although the contents of many of his one-act plays would really have been sufficient to make a play several acts long. Hence his achievement remained slighter in quantity than that of most other writers; yet with regard to quality of work scarcely anyone could touch him. His plays are full of that truly Gallic humour that so many of his French colleagues have wrongly been praised for. The spirit of Molière undeniably hovered over his work. Courteline's manner has not the slightest trace of anything cosmopolitan; he is French through and through. And as a man, too, he was the typical Frenchman, as the foreigner and the tourist in Paris does not picture him to be: simple, constant, honest, thrifty, helpful, roguish and kindly, naïve, and out to turn things to his own advantage.

His name 'Courteline' may serve as evidence of one of the qualities just mentioned, as a sign that he, like almost every artist striving to get on in the world, was determined to owe everything to his own resources. Few people know that 'Courteline' is a pseudonym for Moinaux. This name was made generally known, indeed famous, by his father, Jules Moinaux, when he was a contributor to the *Tribunaux Comiques*. The son did not want any unfair advantage; he did not want to be merely his father's son.

Georges Courteline was born in Tours. His father took him to school in Meaux at the time of the Commune. He has described his life there in a way that could probably be applied to many such institutions: "A school is usually a large building, dismal as autumn and dirty as a comb. The small shopkeepers of the town are, as a rule, proud of it, and usually without the slightest cause. The school building is spring-cleaned once a year, during the summer holidays, which is why when the boys return everything smells of fresh distemper and glue, an odour mingled also with a stale smell of larders and greasy soup that rises irresistibly from the kitchen, filling the corridors and staircases."

Even in his early youth Courteline refused to follow the career for which his father had destined him at the Collège Rollin in Paris. He failed to matriculate. He was attracted by the common people, towards Montmartre and Montparnasse. Left to his own resources, for a short time he worked in the well-known Duval restaurants. Then his sturdy fitness compelled him to do his military service. To his observations and experiences of this period the French owe the superb sketches of barracks life entitled *Les gaîetés de l'escadron* and *Lidoire*. This too was the period when he wrote the book that was to establish his fame: *Le train de 8 h. 47*. After this period Courteline underwent new hardships, to which he put an end by entering the Ministry of Education as a government official. This occupation, however, did not satisfy him; it even seemed like slavery to him.

Courteline found a way out. He offered half his salary to a colleague, who was to do his work for him. The arrangement worked all right, but one day the colleague wanted to go on vacation and asked Courteline to do his work himself for just one month. Courteline had to agree, but found the burden so immense that he preferred to resign. He then discovered in his chief a man who took such an interest in the writer Courteline that he asked the official Courteline to stay on and do whatever he liked. And Courteline stayed.

Courteline's European reputation seems, like that of so many of his colleagues from Montmartre and the Chat Noir, to be linked with the name of Antoine. That shrewd discoverer of talent did all honour to Courteline's little plays, although he knew that their author did not possess the staying-power necessary to write a drama of several acts. In 1893 Antoine produced Courteline's *Boubouroche*, which was one of the most rewarding things he ever did.

Then followed the well-known one-act plays that were also repeatedly performed in Vienna. Courteline was not only a master of modern French prose, but also a highly skilful versifier. For instance, continuing Molière's *Misanthrope*, he wrote 'La conversion d' Alceste' in the metre Molière had used.

Like all French writers, Courteline was a great believer in craftsmanship in art. In order to learn and practise his métier, he for many years himself acted the principal rôles in his plays in the provinces. As already mentioned, he always called this his 'military training', the 'dramatist's military training'.

I told Courteline about my experience in the summer and my acquaintance with René Puaux, of whom he did not yet know. The delight he expressed at this happy turn of events, to which I was to owe my book's appearance in French, showed me his heart-felt interest in all that concerned me. I had naturally already called on René Puaux and had from him received the joyful news that the publishing-house of 'La Plume' would very soon be beginning with the publication of *Guérison*, which put me in the best of good spirits.

The beginning of this most bloodstained of centuries was unimaginably beautiful. One must have lived through it in order to know what has vanished for ever. Those were the great days of sublime friendships, of trifling affairs of the heart and great loves in all their harmless and dangerous variations. One had leisure enough, and the inclination too, to abandon oneself to one's emotions and somewhat exaggeratedly to call their myriad reflections 'life'.

Above all, the poets of that vanished epoch greedily relished their observations, tormenting themselves by heightening pain and pleasure, and did not keep their experiences to themselves, but passed them on, in a didactic spirit, to smaller or larger circles of the elect, those who were considered worthy to be initiated into the secrets of the human soul.

Courteline was above all others one of the most remarkable lovers, indeed worshippers, of his time, and he liked to tell his friends instructive stories of his experiences. His interest in the fair sex burnt brightest, and his emotions struck root most deeply, where a woman's attractions were combined with unique originality of mind and feeling in such a way as to be fruitful not only to his heart but also to his work. So it came that this great successor of Molière's had stranger amorous adventures than others, who were seduced by simpler and more natural charms. But the cause of this perversity, which was really not perversity at all, was connected with his métier as a writer of comedies. He wanted to paint life straight from nature, and if he had to suffer, he wanted at least to be able to celebrate his sufferings afterwards, turning them to account and extracting from them those delightful characters that were so true to life. If a mistress could fulfil that mission, she was not only immortalised but took her well-earned place in his memories for ever.

On one occasion an enchanting Parisienne put Courteline's

kindness of heart, which seemed boundless when he was in love, to a particularly hard test. One day when he entered her apartment he found her bathed in tears, and for a long time his sympathetic questions as to what her trouble was were answered only by renewed outbursts of sobbing. At last a dreadful confession broke from her trembling lips. Gaston had left her. He had refused once and for all to go on believing that Courteline took a merely paternal interest in her, and cast the celebrated name of his rival at her lovely head with the accusation that it *was* the name of his rival. All was now over. "He does not love me any more! He does not love me any more!" she kept on wailing. Speechless, the deceived lover in this way discovered that he had not been the only one. But how did he react to this? What did he do? Moved by her despair, he overcame his own disappointment and exclaimed almost tenderly: "If you will instantly cease to weep so heart-breakingly, miserable woman, I shall bring your Gaston back myself and restore him to you. Then he will have no choice but to believe that he cannot have any grounds for jealousy!"

Startled and stricken by such undeserved generosity, the woman whose treachery had been unmasked embraced the sage, and at the same instant her tears ceased to flow.

"You would—you could do that?" she stammered and flew to cast her arms round his neck. It must have been overwhelming.

"I hasten away this moment, my poor darling!" the poet sighed and set out on his way to his fellow-sufferer. His persuasive power soon achieved a well-deserved triumph. The hypocritical beauty did not suspect, of course, that by taking this sacrifice upon himself her friend had not only regained his own freedom but had also, to say the least of it, seen to it that his lucky rival was now the biter bit. He had brought peace to a poor erring heart, for Gaston willingly accompanied him and believed in the lie with which he was so drastically confronted. However, Courteline stayed to witness the grotesque reconciliation scene that now followed. He shared the wicked woman's enjoyment of her victory, feeling as if they were acting a play, all three of them—one of his own little pieces for the stage. Cheerfully the disillusioned lover, who in losing a mistress had won a partner, hastened towards the approaching hour of separation, which had now become inevitable.

But another and even more remarkable amorous adventure had

a much graver effect on the master, who might have suffered unendurable consequences if it had gone on as it had been going.

He had given his heart to an enchanting blonde whose wit and grace, combined with truly French femininity, in spite of her own unpardonable vice succeeded in holding her famous fellow-country-men captive for a long time. She was possessed with a mania for all the desirable trinkets that Paris surpassed all other cities in the world in dangling before women's gaze.

The smart shops had a tremendous power of attraction for the little Parisienne, and since her lover was very free with his money she could indulge in many a luxury and many a trifle as charming as it was superfluous, trifles without which she could neither be happy nor give happiness. Disastrously both for herself and her friend, she did not always buy everything she took a fancy to— there was probably not money enough for that—but she nevertheless acquired it, by conjuring away, with uncanny skill, whatever there was on the loaded counters that irresistibly attracted her. Veils, ribbons, frills, laces, kerchiefs, shawls—all these gossamer things, which a harassed shop-assistant had difficulty in keeping check on in the whirl of displaying wares, would slide into her capacious shopping-bag together with goods that she had acquired honestly.

Since Yvonne practised her wicked arts without any trace of embarrassment or fear of being caught, and was also untroubled by her conscience, she would unpack all her treasures at home before the looking-glass, preferably in the presence of her friend, and deck herself out with all these things in the most charming manner, with the sweetest of expressions on her face.

"But where on earth did you get all these things?" her friend exclaimed time and again, suspecting the worst. "You can't be spending so much money. At any rate you didn't get it from me!" "One doesn't always have to pay for everything!" came the defiant answer. "Oh, so you're running up debts!" "Yes, I could do that!" the stubborn woman laughed. "I would only have to give your name and hint at our relations and I would have credit—but I don't like that. Anyone who suffers from kleptomania doesn't get into debt!" "So you steal what you can't afford to pay for!" the horrified poet exclaimed, clearly recognising what the situation was. "Fie, aren't you ashamed to speak in that horrid way to a woman you love? You only have to give me more money, that's the best treatment for my illness."

Yvonne was really ill. The shop detectives in the shops she visited daily had long ago come to this conclusion, and the bills for the things she stole were mounting up. It was well known that Madame suffered from severe kleptomania. *Volomanie* her horrified lover called it. It was a nice mess.

"Please control your disease better in future, it's becoming more than I can afford!"

"So you mean to deny me the only cure there is!" Yvonne exclaimed irritably, losing her temper.

Now the poet spoke to her seriously: "I've told you a hundred times, if you like a thing so much that you think you must have it, come and tell me. And if I can afford it, you shall have it. But don't go and steal. And above all, don't give *my* address when you're caught red-handed, the way you did recently." "And supposing you can't afford it?" Yvonne exclaimed, as if she had not heard all the rest. "Then you will simply have to do without it, like millions of other people. No woman can have everything she wants to have." "It's all very well for you to talk!" the desirable little person sighed. "But for your sake I'll try my best."

Yvonne's affliction became ever graver, and the charm of luxuries exercised an ever greater spell on her. One day her affliction made her brazen and careless in 'Printemps'—it was spring outside too, tempting her to squander. She was under observation, because she was known, and suddenly a police-sergeant stood beside her just as she was slipping a sparkling crystal bowl into her bag, without having asked to see it or enquired what the price was. This was really going too far. This time the thing was taken seriously and she was arrested just as if she had not been suffering from kleptomania. When the myrmidon of the law was about to lead her away, Yvonne resisted, calling out: "Don't you dare touch me! I'm engaged to Georges Courteline!"

This claim did in fact have its effect. This was quite something! The shop-assistant and the policeman exchanged glances. The light-fingered lady was taken into the manager's private room, whence the poet was informed of the annoying incident and asked to come in order to confirm the guilty woman's statement, to bail her out or give her the lie and leave her to the fate she deserved.

Scandal was looming on the horizon and had to be avoided. Full of bitter feelings, the man so compromised hurried to the shop and liberated his loved one, by confirming her statement of their relationship and, moreover, by immediately making good the damage.

At his side the incorrigible woman, now with grave warnings ringing in her ears, left the shop she had so often robbed. Beaming for happiness, she tripped along beside her rescuer as though in triumph, not yet suspecting that now, however, she had overstepped the limits of what his love would bear. Not even his love could stand up to this test.

Once back in their apartment they had a furious argument, leading up to a last, a positively final scene—to a complete break. This man who understood women so well knew that even if he was a thousand times right, she would never admit it. Now he had to listen to the bitterest of reproaches, flung at him amidst floods of tears. Whether patient or impatient, his attempts to make her see reason were all in vain. He and he alone was to blame for everything, because he had never provided her with money enough to enable her to satisfy her modest wishes. She was the pitiable victim of his meanness. He made no further answer, but once more gazed for a long time at the beautiful woman before leaving her for ever. Once again he had learnt what he already knew and now expressed as follows to his friend:

"*Une femme ne sait jamais ce qu'on a fait pour elle, mais elle sait toujours ce qu'on aurait pu faire encore.*"

Among other things, Courteline had confessed to me how greatly he venerated his friend Catulle Mendès, who was like a father to him. *Jean d'Habit* and *La femme du Tabarin* were much-performed plays. *Zohar*, *La première maîtresse*, to name only two of a long series, were novels that had made Mendès one of the most read Parisian writers. Apart from this, Catulle Mendès had covered himself with glory as one who had early taken up the cudgels for Richard Wagner, and he had been the first to recognise Courteline's genius and had once clearly stated what was so important for the author of what seemed to be everyday comedies—that this portrayer of Montmartre was among those to whom it was granted to write the best French prose of their time.

Courteline's veneration for this aristocrat of the mind was great, and he had shown his liking for me by introducing me to him. The questions and answers that I had exchanged with Catulle Mendès on that first evening, which had been interrupted all too quickly, had aroused the wish for a more thorough discussion. I was therefore very pleased to accept Mendès' invitation to breakfast with him, together with Courteline, on one of the following days. Courteline drew my attention to the fact that Mendès' second wife—his first marriage had been to a daughter of Théophile Gautier—was accounted one of the most celebrated beauties of Paris, but that she was unfortunately in the habit of covering the great charms of her noble countenance with cosmetics. "I tell you this so that you may not be startled."

Close to the quiet splendour of the Champs Elysées, somewhat tucked away in the little Rue Bocador, and several storeys up, was the writer's light and airy apartment.

The master of this delightful abode, now opening up before me, gave the kindest of receptions to his 'little German colleague'. I was reminded of the studies of our savants at home by the busts of Nietzsche and Wagner, as by the works of our classics, which formed part of his immense library.

The urbane luxury, the love of splendour, that I saw in Mendès' dwelling did not strike me particularly, in spite of the comparisons I was quietly making, because they could be explained by the nature and temperament of this man, from whom they were indeed to be expected. In every artist there is, after all, something of a pasha. Dreams of purple and ermine and precious jewels frequently fill the souls of creative men. Grey life, with its cares and griefs, only blurs those visions and sets more sombre pictures in their place. Catulle's life lay for the most part in radiant sunshine. This had advanced his artistic and physical development. For in his case it is not unfitting to speak of that too. Anyone who once saw Mendès would not easily forget his proudly lifted Olympian head, his abundant fair mane, and the eyes that seemed to pierce deeply into people and things.

Before long we sat down to breakfast. The master of the house went on, in a lively manner, with our conversation, in which his really bewitchingly beautiful wife and his charming little boy also joined. But it was only after the meal, when we were alone, that we began to speak of all those problems that we both had at heart.

For me it was of particular interest to hear Catulles' judgments on his contemporaries, and even though I took care not to ask the analogous banal questions: "Which is greater, Schiller or Goethe, Heine or Lenau?" I was nevertheless grateful to learn what Mendès thought of the great dead of his own nation and the often petty immortals among his contemporaries.

I was struck by his high regard for Paul Hervieu as a dramatist. Since the performance of this promising young artist's drama, *La course des flambeaux*, he ranked him equal with Edmond Rostand, whom he referred to as the only one qualified to take the place left empty by Victor Hugo. This flattering judgment also covered all the limitations: even a distinguished heir must be an epigone—an opinion that I found all the more startling since so many critics hailed Rostand as an innovator.

For Georges Courteline, who—apart from formally very polished novelettes—had written nothing but one-act plays—for which reason he must be denied the sweep necessary for the writing of a drama that could fill a whole evening—Mendès had had quite specially high praise. He ranked him among the classics of modern prose; he admired his chiselled ten-line periods, such as were also characteristic of the great writers of the eighteenth century. He particularly mentioned Courteline's habit of telling his stories over and over again to a small circle of friends before beginning to write them down, and gave it as his opinion that this method was of inestimable value in achieving formal precision.

After speaking of the great successes that Mirbeau's *Les affaires sont les affaires* and Lavedan's *Marquis de Priola* were having at that time, Mendès bemoaned the recent growth of the deplorable star-system. He saw this as a very serious danger not only to the art of acting, but—what was far worse—to the development of those authors who were poets and had not yet learnt to make concessions to the theatres and those in power there—the concessions that were the sole means by which one could get a chance and arrive at great success. He bemoaned the fact that any actor who had become known at all began to refer to his 'individuality' and tried to make all the rôles he had to fill conform with it. This, he said, was the reason why more and more rôles and fewer and fewer plays were being written. The public was encouraging this deplorable state of affairs ever more eagerly. A play that did not have quite definite parts for quite definite actors could hardly be produced in Paris any longer, he said. I sighed, thinking of the only too similar conditions in the German theatre of the time.

Mendès complained that abroad, especially in German-speaking territory, the most peculiar views were held about many French writers of the nineteenth century. For many of those who were already forgotten in France the dawn of fame was only just beginning there. A great revision of literary values was urgently needed, he said. Many a stylist whom we counted among the greatest had already been outmoded by Anatole France's masterly modern prose. Modestly, Catulle passed over his own deserving part in the development of modern French prose. After much pleading, he treated us to an example of his brilliant art of declamation, reading us an act of his celebrated drama, *Les mères ennemies*.

Afterwards he spoke at length about Wagner and Nietzsche, Schiller and Goethe, and about the impossibility of really translating a poet who had sprung not from literature but out of the heart of a nation; and he concluded with wise words about the far-reaching differences between German and French verse and about our great lyric poets, above all Heine, who in his opinion had drenched German poetry with an element quite foreign to it, namely irony. And everything he said was far from being chauvinistic or put from the point of view of the French intelligentsia. On the contrary, Mendès made a point of showing that he was well able to slip into any mentality and also that he was capable of recognising a talent's point of origin and the seeds of a creative urge.

Before we left this man who knew so much and was so kind Courteline especially recommended me to him, quickly telling about me, exaggerating my talent and my still rather poor achievements. But the few hastily uttered words were quite enough, for Mendès held out both hands to me as we took our leave, and said: "My house is open to you at any time. In the evening I am at the Café Américain, and wherever you visit me I shall be greatly pleased. If you want any literary information, I am naturally at your disposal, and similarly, if at any time you want to see one of the premières that are due any time now, my box is at your disposal."

I felt truly enriched and elevated when, with Courteline, I left Catulle Mendès' hospitable house, and the first thing I did was to buy his most important books in order to devour them as soon as possible.

Perhaps the spiritualists are right and everything we experience is really fore-ordained and every accident that startles is something meant for us and no one else. So it was evidently pre-destined that Courteline should find in his so highly venerated and boundlessly esteemed friend the hero of his immortal comedy of cuckoldry, *Boubouroche*.

Courteline, whose second wife, Marie-Jeanne, was a highly gifted, charming and kindly woman, at that time enjoyed the comforts of a well-ordered household. His friends were no longer forced to seek him out in the brasseries where he had formerly done his work. Into his life there had now come that much despised virtue, regularity, and it was pleasant to chat in his cosy home. Of course, now he could no longer hide his address from his friends with the ease with which he had done so in earlier days, when a remarkable adventure provided him with the material for *Boubouroche*. At that time he used to meet Catulle Mendès regularly, and as often as they separated and Mendès asked him: "Where do you live?" Courteline would answer: "I won't tell you." This recurrent refusal to say where he lived puzzled Mendès, but he soon accepted the whim, thinking his friend was a little odd and would have reasons of his own, which must be respected.

Among men in France love-affairs are usually no secret. Courteline knew too that Mendès, who had in the meantime had a divorce, had a sweetheart over whom he kept a jealous watch. His affair with this girl lasted for years and might, as such things go, have lasted a whole lifetime or have come to an end overnight. One evening Courteline's friend came to his table, somewhat agitated, and told him that he had broken with his *amie*. Courteline could scarcely believe his ears. "But that's impossible!" he exclaimed. "After so long? All at once? Quite suddenly?"

"Yes," said Mendès. "I have always had a dark suspicion that she was deceiving me, and today I know it."

Courteline wanted to be sure. "Tomorrow you will have forgotten all about it."

"There is no 'tomorrow'. It is finished for ever. Finished, I tell you. I shall never see her again."

"Are you quite sure?"

"Here is my hand on it!"

Courteline was still not satisfied. "Is it settled? Irrevocably? You will never see her again?" he pressed.

"Never, never, never!" his friend exclaimed.

Now Courteline hitched his chair up closer and said: "Very well then! Then I will fulfil a wish of yours."

"That might be some consolation. Go on."

"You always wanted to know my address, didn't you?" And calmly Courteline now announced the name of the street, the number of the house, and the floor on which he lodged there.

His friend struck the table. "What? So you live in the same house as she does?"

Courteline nodded. "Yes. I was her neighbour through all the years of your love."

His friend leaped up. "That's a bit steep! And you tell me this today? There's something behind this!"

"My poor friend," Courteline replied. "For years I was involuntarily and against my will a witness of the shameful way that girl deceived you. I was silent because you loved her."

"So she was your mistress, was she?"

Courteline shook his head. "What do you take me for? How can you think such a thing?"

His friend pressed his hand soothingly and stammered an apology. "Yes, but how then do you know——?"

"Oh, the walls in these houses of ours are mere cardboard. I know your step, and I got used to hearing that of someone else, who was always there when you came and always went away after you had gone."

Bitterly triumphant, his friend exclaimed: "I knew it, I always knew she was deceiving me all the time! But now the scales have fallen from my eyes. That's why I saw no one coming and no one going!"

"Yes, indeed," Courteline answered. "She discovered that the best way of erasing all traces of a man is to keep him in the place, shut up in a closet, a wardrobe, a cupboard or heaven knows where, when the 'rightful lover' comes."

Deeply moved, Mendès pressed this sensitive poet's hand and exclaimed: "Thank you, thank you! Now for the first time I am really free of her, and for ever!"

Then they sat together in silence, their spirits lulled by the

monotonous clatter of the dominoes from neighbouring tables and
the unremitting din, coming from outside, of Paris rushing to work
and love. Smilingly the two friends parted that day. But before
Courteline's eyes there rose up the plan for his famous comedy of
cuckoldry.

Of course he did his very best and exerted himself to the utmost
in order to alter the prototype of *Boubouroche*, who, alas, had been
his dearest friend, until the figure was unrecognisable. It was quite
deliberately that the deceived lover was transformed from a witty
writer into a stolid respectable bourgeois.

"Est-ce qu'on sait?" said Georges Courteline, who sometimes
wrote what he experienced in real life and at other times experienced
in real life what he himself had written. At the time when the
following incident took place he was living in the Avenue de Saint-
Mandé, the street that bears the name of the place that had become
his real home. In Saint-Mandé stood the house through the garden
gate of which the faithful son every evening hurried to his aged but
still very spry mother. Now it stands empty.

A few months before the old lady's death this little house was
the scene of an episode that might have happened specially for the
great humorist's sake. Till Eulenspiegel himself, if he had been
there, would have lowered his rascally eyes in homage before the
invisible producer of the house-breaking episode in Saint-Mandé,
the story of which here follows.

Georges Courteline, who lived in a little hotel not far from his
mother's house, was one night—and in the darkest hour, at the very
dead of night—wakened by loud and violent knocking at his door.
He leapt up, opened the door, and recognised the faithful genie
from his mother's little villa, now standing before him, stammering
and shaking in her shoes. The poet, who was always prepared for
the very worst, instantly exclaimed in great agitation: "My mother
has been murdered!" The old woman stammered: "No, no Madame
Courteline is fast asleep, safe and sound. But there has been a
tremendous burglary! A tramp has stolen all the silver. We saw
him escaping. He knew he had been discovered, for he turned
threateningly, waving a large revolver at us. Jean and I would both
be corpses by now if we had caught him red-handed!"

During her telling of this story Courteline had quickly slipped
on some clothes, and now followed the maid, who had hurried on

ahead. He had only one thought—at any cost to keep the whole incident from his mother, for he knew that her tranquillity and sleep in all nights to come depended on this. So the first thing he did was to give instructions that the old lady should be allowed to go on quietly sleeping, and, when she woke, she was not to be told a word of what had happened. Meanwhile he meant to regain possession of the things that had been stolen, before she could notice that they were missing: that is to say, before luncheon. The tramp, after whom the hunt was already up, could scarcely as yet have got his booty to a place of safety. Courteline went to see the commissaire of Saint-Mandé, who was very well acquainted with him personally and who also knew the aspect that public functionaries took on in the poet's mind. It was with the most marked amiability that the guardian of the law received the agitated humorist. Without letting him finish what he wanted to say, he shook hands with him as if he were an old friend, and said:

"Don't worry, the burglar is under arrest and your property is safe. Will you examine it and make sure that nothing is missing?"

Beaming with joy, Courteline agreed. Here for once the arm of the law had stretched out at the right instant. Overcome with happiness, Courteline soon identified the lost valuables, and not even a salt-cellar was missing. Arranged in neat rows, there the things stood before his happy eyes. He only had to reach out and return everything to its proper place, and it would be as if nothing had happened.

However, the commissaire stopped the hands that were reaching out for their property, shook his head, and said:

"Gently, gently! Not so fast! The thief is in a cell next door. Let us see what he has to say and how he will behave when confronted with you. For it depends solely on him whether I can fulfil your wish and hand the things over to you."

The poet stared at the guardian of the law, horror in his amazed little eyes. It seemed to him he was hearing something that only himself could have invented.

"What? You admit you have arrested the burglar and you refuse to restore to me what he stole and what belongs to me?" he exclaimed.

"Calm yourself. There is nothing I have more at heart than to fall in with your wishes," the commissaire said soothingly.

Then he went into the next room, and a short while later, escorted by a gendarme, there followed the ruffian who had carried out the bold robbery. Nobody would have credited him with the feline dexterity necessary in order to fix a rope-ladder in position and swing himself into a house through an open kitchen-window. Pointing at the criminal, the commissaire went on to say that they were dealing with a fellow who was capable of anything, for two loaded revolvers had been found on his person. So the maid was right in saying she was lucky not to have caught him by the sleeve or to have crossed his path while he was escaping. The prisoner was led up to the table, which looked like a silversmith's shop-window, laden with old Madame Courteline's property.

The commissaire then began to harangue the prisoner in vigorous terms, pointing now to him, now to the objects that had been taken from him. The fellow seemed to see this movement as a demand that he should make a confession, but since he did not understand a word of French, simply for the sake of peace and quiet he stammered something in a gibberish that the commissaire declared was Russian, and nodded. The commissaire turned to Courteline with the words:

"He confesses to the theft."

Courteline felt as if he were hearing heavenly music, and once again he stretched out his hands in yearning.

"Stop!" the commissaire exclaimed. "After all, I'm not going to believe a fellow of this kind!"

"That's enough of this nonsense!" Courteline shouted, now beside himself. "Give me what belongs to me and make an end of this grotesque scene, or I shall immortalise you."

The commissaire shook his head, saying: "Gently! Do you really expect me to steal from this man because he has stolen from your mother? To rob him because he robbed you? He has not been *convicted* of theft. He has not yet been condemned."

"But he has confessed!" Courteline insisted.

"His confession doesn't empower me to do anything," the police officer retorted. "All the less since he cannot make it in any language we understand, and we can't, after all, rely on his gestures."

Courteline clutched his head and cast imploring glances at the beloved objects that must be back in their usual places within two hours if his mother was to be spared the knowledge of the burglary, which was the only thing that mattered to her son. What was to be done? The citizen and the functionary stared at each other in helpless bewilderment. Then an idea flashed across the commissaire's brain, and he exclaimed in relief:

"If the man gives me written permission to hand the silver over to you, I shall be covered and can do it!"

He obligingly hurried to his desk and handed the burglar a form, indicating to him, while he thrust a pen into the astonished man's hand, that he was to sign it. Apparently the man did not understand either the demand that was being made or the meaning of all that was going on in the scene he was witnessing. His eyes showing more terror even than when he had been arrested, he stared now at Courteline, now at the commissaire, both of whom displayed such a wealth of virtuosity in pantomime that the prisoner, if for no other reason than to put an end to this frightening scene, set pen to paper and—after a brief pause for reflection—made a few scrawls that could doubtless be regarded as his signature. He was then taken away. The commissaire now handed the delighted Courteline his property, and the men parted with the most exquisite assurances of mutual admiration, overwhelming each other with politeness. The stolen goods were back in their proper places half an hour later. So it was granted to Courteline to spare his aged mother a dreadful shock, and she closed her eyes for ever without having learnt what unusual events she had slept through one night.

I have always accounted it a high merit of Courteline's that he took such a noble stand by the unhappy Captain Dreyfus, regardless of the views of contemporaries whom he himself valued. He was an ardent supporter of that brave and powerful writer, Emile Zola, and passionately approved of his pamphlet, 'J'accuse!', which he called a great document. He served in the ranks, which had wonderful consequences for French literature, in that, besides the works already mentioned, *Le train de 8 h. 47*, *Lidoire*, and *Les gaietés de l'escadron*, he wrote other masterpieces too, which are untranslatable. Both in plays and in the book *Les messieurs du rond-de-cuir* he drew a bead on French officialdom and made the most of all his own little sufferings during his time as an official.

Much later I collected my friend's most important plays, *Boubouroche* chief among them, in one volume, which I called *Everyday Comedies* and which was published by Georg Müller in Munich in 1912. Although Courteline did not know a word of

German, he never stopped telling me how delighted he was about this and always kept the German book among his favourite works.

With this I had fulfilled what I felt was my literary obligation to Georges Courteline. If for no other reason than that his plays were one-act pieces, they could never be expected to be more than stop-gaps on the German stage. Indeed they were scarcely more than that even in France, but paradoxically enough they attained an immortality that was not granted to the full-length dramas of Courteline's contemporaries. Donay, Portoriche, Capus, Bataille, and Bruyère, to mention only a handful at random, are today forgotten, and the name of Catulle Mendès must unfortunately be added to the list; they are all names that have such a strange, remote sound for the French youth of today that there is no point in naming their works. They all did their part in honestly fulfilling the needs of their own time, and now sleep peacefully, awaiting an awakening that is always still possible—some of them, like Anatole France, in the Panthèon.

Meanwhile, however, October was drawing to an end. I had just seen the galley-proofs of *Guérison*, thanks to René Puaux's fiery zeal, when an impatient letter came from William Archer, reminding me in fairly urgent terms of my promise to appear in London, an appearance that he considered now long overdue.

This urgent reminder lent wings to my heels and I set out across the Channel. I remember to this day that it was the most terrible crossing I have ever experienced. I have always been a good sailor, but in those hours one migraine after the other befell me, and when at last, late in the evening, I lay in my room at my hotel in London, there was no end to the nervous paroxysms from which I suffered —and how far I was from any helping hand that would give me a morphia injection!

Only complete rest could bring relief. And so the next day I pulled myself together only in order to write a letter to William Archer, briefly informing him that I had arrived and was holding myself at his disposal. Then I stayed in the darkened room for many hours, eating almost nothing, and towards evening was more or less recovered.

That lonely evening was brightened by an express letter from William Archer, asking me to come and see him the next day at the National Liberal Club, with which I was already familiar.

E

Even more lively than the first time, and more cordial too, was the reception given me by Ibsen's successful interpreter, whose literary essays had caused a sensation among the few English people qualified to judge. "What do you think of my Shaw?" he exclaimed. "Out with it, now!"

I displayed plenty of enthusiasm and went far beyond anything that Archer could have expected from me. His delight was, however, not as great as it ought to have been.

"No, no," he said, "you're exaggerating. All that you say is true only in comparison with the plays that drive us to desperation here evening after evening. But you will soon see for yourself: this obstinate fellow Shaw will not achieve anything more than fleeting success even in Germany, supposing, that is, that you ever succeed in gaining a following for him there and finding theatres that will perform his work."

I eagerly contradicted him and tried to defend my own point of view and give reasons for my confidence. Archer smiled, pleased that he had achieved what he wanted. Before my own eyes he wrote me a warm letter of introduction to Bernard Shaw. Even though unknown and a controversial figure as a creative artist, his friend was at that time a prominent and highly regarded music-critic, in which capacity he had plenty to do, writing under the pseudonym 'Corno di Bassetto'.

It was with rather a heavy heart that I set out on my pilgrimage to the man whose personal acquaintance I was now positively burning to make. Because of the great distances to be covered in London, one often has time to become hesitant and turn back before reaching one's goal. Shaw was at that time living in Adelphi Terrace, in the heart of that city of many millions, and I was standing outside his door before my qualms had become clear to me or been settled. When, as I went up the steps, I thought of my own poor plans, for an instant I started back. . . . An inner voice was still holding me back as I stretched out my hand to the knocker. Then I recalled an infinitely beautiful poetic passage from *Candida* that I had already translated, by way of experiment, into German. This rapidly silenced all my doubts. I felt that a decisive hour had struck in my life, and I knocked at the door. The maid who opened the door took Archer's letter and ran upstairs with it.

First of all I was received by Mrs. Shaw, a lady who made an uncommonly likeable impression at the very first glance and whose understanding gaze revealed the intense vigour of her mind. Asking me to sit down, she told me that her husband would appear in a moment, and chatted with me about matters of no importance. I realised that this conversation was a pretext in order to be able to observe the visitor without his being aware of it and to form a proper picture of him: either to get rid of him again as quickly as possible or to introduce him to her husband. We had just got slightly warmed up when George Bernard Shaw, who had meanwhile read Archer's note, made an impatient appearance in the doorway and held out his hand to me. His wife now vanished as soundlessly as she had appeared.

And so now I beheld the man whose work had set me afire. Physically, too, he was of unusual stature, and bright, merry eyes gazed at me out of a face that was framed in a reddish beard trimmed to a point—features that showed how the dreamer had given up the unequal struggle with the thinker. He looked somewhat awkward as he stood there, an amiably mirthful giant. It suddenly flashed upon me then and there, as I gazed upon him, with his high, sculptured forehead, that this man's work was his over-lifesize toy.

After I had held forth for quite a while about his plays and had then somewhat shyly begun to work up to the real subject of my visit, he interrupted me with the words: "Upon my word, you have made a pretty thorough study of my works! And what is it you are really after? What do you mean to do with me?"

At this I said roundly and boldly that I was determined to translate his plays into German and had set myself the aim of conquering the German stage for him.

Shaw jumped up and ran upstairs in a flash. I heard him call out: "Charlotte, here's a young lunatic Archer's sent me whom I won't be able to make see reason! You come and try to calm him down. Perhaps you'll manage it."

Once again Mrs. Shaw came in, and now, in some embarrassment, I expounded my intentions to her. She nodded in smiling agreement, apologised for her impatient husband, and spoke words of encouragement to me. But to him, upstairs, she called out: "The young man seems uncommonly sensible. Come down and listen to what he has to say." Hesitantly, the man so summoned now returned and sat down beside us, his penetrating gaze fixed on me.

"He is quite right," Mrs. Shaw said, taking my part. "Why should the German theatre, which has made Shakespeare into a German poet, not also give you the satisfaction that is still denied you in your own country?" Shaw smiled incredulously, and exclaimed: "So you want to be my Schlegel and Tieck, do you? Well now, but then we ought first of all to go into a whole lot of purely business questions, above all the extremely important matter of copyright. After all, I can't entrust to you my whole life's work up to now, just like that, and then wait to see what comes of it. Besides, and above all: what have you done of your own?" Archer had prepared me for the fact that Shaw did not understand a word of German, and so I shyly produced the galley-proofs of the French translation of my first novel, *Convalescence*, out of my bag, together with the short list of my books that were about to appear in German, and handed it all to him.

"So you want to do for me what someone has already done for you, in spite of your youth? You want to make my work accessible to your countrymen?" Shaw asked and again began talking about copyright, a matter of which I knew nothing. He was very surprised that I seemed to see no difficulties in a matter that was—as he put it—so difficult.

Our long business-like discussion was interrupted by the announcement of a meal, to which he hospitably invited me. Shaw, who at that time had just become a vegetarian, urged me to follow his example. "Become a vegetarian, like me. That's the only way you'll be able to get a lot of work done. Above all, give up those poisons, black coffee and wine."

After the meal Mrs. Shaw withdrew, and we remained alone. I now once more expounded to Shaw, in a more business-like and matter-of-fact manner, the reason why I had come to see him, naturally concealing from him the failures there had been hitherto in the search for agents and translators. He now instantly and very amiably accepted my proposals, though of course with the faint mistrust that a lonely man feels for the approval and admiration that he prefers to consider a misunderstanding until he knows the source from which they come. But after the very first brief verbal skirmishes we understood each other very well, and by this time Shaw listened to my resolution, which I kept on emphasising, with a smile and without repeating the many objections and qualms that he at first produced. Nevertheless, the friendlier our conversation became, the more anxiously he returned to the matter of copyright and the legal problems that might be connected with it.

And as, in this first conversation, the thin crust of embitterment that covered the real character of this under-estimated writer, who though in the prime of life was not yet recognised, began to crumble, I recognised that this was a kindly man, a tower of strength for all who trusted him and would entrust themselves to him.

Finally I put a proposition to him. "Give me a year," I said. "In that time I will translate three of your plays and try my luck with them. If at the end of that period I have not found either a publisher or a stage for your works, I shall hand back the rights to you." He agreed and asked with interest which three plays I wanted to begin with. I asked for time to think it over. Swiftly now I rose to my feet, as though there were no time to be lost and I must get to work immediately. Shaw exclaimed: "*Auf Wiedersehen!*" and I laughed: "Good-bye, I shall soon have to come back again!"

Filled with the great impression that Bernard Shaw had made on me, I started out on my way back to Vienna and went to work.

It was no small shock to me when, at home, I for the first time realised fully what difficulties I had to face. It is singularly difficult to reproduce Shaw perfectly without sharing his amazing knowledge in all spheres, without being, as he was, profoundly versed in politics, history, religion, music, painting, socialism and all the intellectual and technical achievements of the age.

I now never wearied of urgently drawing the attention of everyone with literary interests to Bernard Shaw. I had remarkably little luck in this. Only a few listened to me, some smiled, and others said I ought to get on with my own work. One of my friends expressed his doubts in the following words: "If an alien mind kindles such enthusiasm in you and alien writings get into your system like this, there is a greater danger that you will not remain an original writer." And this was, as a matter of fact, the only qualm that might have made me abandon my resolve. Even my day had only twelve hours, and if I devoted many of them to somebody else—how few would be left over for me! If I was to bring another man's work to life in my language—how tired I would be afterwards when I wanted to go to my own work! Gazing upwards, I saw the summit of the mountain. But I did not yet know that it was a mountain-range of which I could see only a few crags and one peak: *Candida*.

In order to feel my way and prepare the ground a little, before setting about my actual task I published an article on Shaw in the *Neue Freie Presse*, an article that the *feuilleton* editor, Theodor Herzl, accepted with the words: "Look here, my dear fellow, you can tell me quite frankly—this man with the pious name is a mystification, isn't he?—some hoax or other of yours—we'll get to the bottom of it sooner or later. I'll put your article in, because it's interesting. But our readers won't believe in this devil of a chap of yours any more than I do or you yourself." Quite taken aback and disconcerted, I assured Herzl that he would soon have the opportunity of getting to know in German the works the authenticity of which he now doubted.

'This devil of a chap' was what Herzl had called the author of the comedy, *The Devil's Disciple*, which was the first work I now began to translate. The hero really did seem to me to be akin to the author in the innermost core of his being, and so I began—partly too for superstitious reasons—by calling the play *Ein Teufelskerl* (*The Devil of a Chap*). When this first work was finished, I put it aside for a while and set about translating *Candida*, the play I was so much in love with. I worked feverishly, usually the whole day, often half the night as well, for, after all, I had a time-limit. And what is a year when what has to be done is to find a publisher, a theatrical agent, and a theatre that would open its doors to this new man? In order to show Shaw's genius sparkling in all its aspects, I chose *Arms and the Man* for the third play, giving it the popular-sounding, theatrical title, *Helden* (*Heroes*). A literal translation would doubtless have been unthinkable. Shaw had used for his title the first words of the English translation of Virgil's *Æneid*. The corresponding German words would have had to be '*Waffentaten besingt mein Gesang und den Mann*'—which was impossible.

I kept these three plays ceaselessly circulating among publishers, theatrical people, producers, and so on, and at last I managed to talk Director Gettke of the Raimundtheater in Vienna into accepting *The Devil's Disciple*. It goes without saying that I turned the approaching production of the play to account in order to find a publisher for Shaw, and again offered the 'Three Plays" to Cotta, after that great publishing-house had already once refused them. Once again I pressed these masterpieces on Cotta's directors, and here too I enjoyed success. Cotta declared themselves prepared to publish the plays under the title *Drei Dramen von Bernard Shaw*. At that time I did not approach S. Fischer, because I wanted to keep my production and Shaw's quite separate.

About nine months had passed since my agreement had been made with Shaw when the Raimundtheater announced the première of the *Teufelskerl*, as I had first called the play. But things had not reached this point without great difficulty and all kinds of trouble. The title-rôle called for a youthful actor, but Director Gettke had not got one in his company, and he regarded it as too expensive by far to bring one from Germany specially to act in this production, apart from the consideration that it would have been rash in the case of a play that was such an unknown quantity. I had the feeling that he was very glad of this excuse, which was not really an excuse at all; for at that time there was nothing he wanted more than a chance to get rid of the play again.

After we had discussed the rest of the casting, which made it seem that the production was quite possible, I was somewhat desperate. But I did not lose heart. I was determined to provide the hero myself, and I asked Gettke for two weeks' grace. The fact was that since my frequent visits to the Weisse Hirsch in Dresden I had been well acquainted with the actor Karl Wiené, of the Court Theatre, and I knew too that Gettke was negotiating with him about coming to Vienna. Although Wiené was an ageing actor shortly before his retirement, he was keen—perhaps for that very reason —to act youthful parts and so to belie the view taken by those on whom his position at the Court Theatre depended.

When I mentioned his name to Gettke, the latter shook his head and said: "Wiené will never do it. He's not going to expose himself to reproaches for going on acting youthful parts." "Let me look after that!" I exclaimed. "I shall start out for Dresden this evening and I hope to bring you Wiené's acceptance in a few days." "If you can manage that," Gettke said, "we can go into rehearsal a week after your return. Then at least it'll be the first play in which Wiené acts in Vienna."

It was in high spirits that I stepped out of the train in Dresden the next morning. A short time later I was with Wiené, for whom

I had brought a copy of the play. I immediately recognised, of course, that it would not be a very convincing choice for the title-rôle, but I only told him of the advantages and the great theatrical possibilities of the part. We then made another appointment for that evening. By that time Wiené, who was eager to act in Vienna and who had not been very pleased with the parts Gettke had offered him so far—with the exception of *Der Andere* by Paul Lindau—would have read the play.

To my delight he came towards me full of enthusiasm, and the evening brought more than the morning had promised, for Wiené was all on fire to play the part and exclaimed over and over again that it was as though it had been written for him—which was a sheer delusion, but one that I naturally confirmed with lively expressions of agreement.

I could very well take this responsibility on myself, for Wiené was a very good, experienced actor, extremely lively and supple. And he would doubtless be able to convince an audience that was seeing *The Devil's Disciple* for the first time of all that the action and words of the text demanded of him.

I should like at this point to mention that no less an actor than Albert Bassermann was the last *Devil's Disciple*, in a masterly production given in Berlin many decades later under Director Robert. In this rôle, too, Bassermann had his usual triumph, and as he too could then no longer be described as a youthful hero, that seemed to me a belated absolution for my having chosen the elderly Karl Wiené, instead of a youthful hero, for the première of this box-office success among Shaw's plays.

I returned to Vienna, in my pocket a letter from Wiené in which he implored Gettke to let him act the title-rôle in the *Teufelskerl*. And after Gettke had read these outpourings, he greeted me with the words: "You're really the devil of a chap yourself! What a pity *you* can't act the part!"

Then everything went singularly fast. Wiené followed a few days later, and the rehearsals began.

The first night itself was one of the most remarkable I have ever experienced. One could feel a breath of something alien in the air; one could feel the impact of a new atmosphere; and so far as the spokesmen of criticism were concerned, Shaw had got a foothold on German-speaking territory even then, on that memorable evening. The audience was not grudging with its applause, above all for Wiené, and truly I had no cause to regret my choice. For me, however, the evening was given its imperishable splendour by Willy Thaller's performance as General Bourgoyne.

The second play in the volume—the above-mentioned *Helden* (*Arms and the Man*)—some years later had a quite different and less difficult fate. When it was performed for the first time in Vienna and Berlin, this carefree comedy, which in its high spirits did not shrink even from some national allusions that might have given one pause, did its part in making Shaw's name widely known.

The first performance was given at the Berliner Theater, which at that time was under the direction of no less a figure than the famous writer and successful dramatist Paul Lindau; the cast was a very brilliant one, and it deserves special mention that the idol of the gallery and the hero of the Berlin State Theater, Sommerstorf, played the part of the Bulgarian major, Sergius Saranoff.

Before he acquired the play, Paul Lindau wrote me a very remarkable letter that pleased and surprised me because at that time I would never have expected a man who had passed his seventieth year to show so much understanding of an ultra-modern new playwright. Paul Lindau recognised Bernard Shaw from the moment he read his *Three Plays* in the volume published by Cotta.

Strangely enough *Arms and the Man* seemed to have to wait for a performance in Vienna until Josef Jarno, the director of the Theater in der Josefstadt, who had with positively furious, raging insistence taken up the cudgels for August Strindberg, who at that time was also little known and often rejected, one day decided that he simply must produce this play. What attracted him to it was not only the satisfaction it gave to his own delight in making discoveries but also the rewarding main part of the Swiss captain, Bluntschli. The success it had was great, but the theatre in which it was produced was not influential enough for the effect to be far-reaching.

The first production of my favourite, *Candida*, took place in Dresden only later. I shall give an account of this in the proper place.

My joy at the speed with which I had succeeded was dimmed only by the awareness that, having translated the three plays under the pressure of the short period of grace granted me, I had had to

E*

be more superficial than I wanted to be and ought to have been. Even then I resolved that at some later, calmer period, when Shaw's influence and reputation would justify my doing so, I would issue a thoroughly revised new edition. Years later it was my privilege to fulfil this duty to Shaw and myself.

Meanwhile, however, I felt an inner voice, which had really always shown me my road, reminding me to think of myself once more and to submerge myself in my own world, so infinitely different from Shaw's. For I had thrust aside a play I had begun, *Ein Muttersohn* (*Mother's Boy*), in order to bring about the above-described success of a far-off genius. So now, all through several weeks I merely dealt as quickly as I could with all the everyday matters that thrust themselves upon me, and completed my play, *Ein Muttersohn*. I had learnt something from Shaw's patience and knew that between the finishing of a play and its performance many months, if not years, might pass.

It made a very great impression on Shaw that I had kept my word and accomplished what I set out to do. He overwhelmed me with tokens of his confidence in me, and yet it was not easy for me to get on with him. We both had the same goal: building up his reputation. But he was tempestuous, and I was steadfast. He wanted to demand, and I wanted to convince.

Year by year Shaw's plays now appeared on the German stage, with various degrees of success. The strangest fate was that of *Mrs. Warren's Profession*, at that time perhaps the most successful of all his works. At the time when there was already a demand for Shaw's plays, it was rejected by all the theatres. Only the Raimund-theater, in remembrance of its part in the discovery of this writer, accepted the play, complaining again and again that it was a gravely over-hasty decision. As late as at the dress-rehearsal Director Gettke said to me: "If they let us get to the end at all, we won't have more than three performances. Stop being so obstinate and give up the whole production!"

My answer to him was: "If I were condemned to death and were to die on Saturday, I would still refuse to hang myself on the previous Friday. Let us meet the catastrophe without anticipating it."

The play was the greatest success of the season. It caused uproarious tumult—one more piece of evidence that nobody, least of all anyone concerned, can foresee what will come of a first night.

The title-rôle was at that time taken by the very gifted Alice Hetsey, the wife of the talented writer Rudolf Holzer, who later followed in the footsteps of Hermann Bahr, who had discovered him, and became a respected literary figure. As a leading critic in Vienna, he still does Bahr credit. The part of Vivie Warren was taken by Fräulein Wertheim, later the wife of Leo Slezak.

The part of Mrs. Warren proved to have immense attractions for the leading actresses of the day. In Berlin it was acted by that respected actress Rosa Bertens, after her by Rosa Valetti, and finally, quite recently, by that outstanding actress Maria Fein in Zurich. What greatly helped me in my task of campaigning for Shaw, from the days of those first productions onwards, was the recognition that here was a writer for the theatre who was—perhaps without intending it—at the same time a pre-eminent writer of great rôles.

Since I had by now actually done more than I had promised in London, and was also receiving quite enraptured letters from Shaw, whom I naturally did not trouble with the details of my struggles, and since the ever-present copyright danger had been exorcised by the legal steps I had undertaken with regard to my hastily accomplished translations, I supposed I had the right to think again of myself and look around me in my *own* life.

Meanwhile changes had taken place in the Burgtheater. That fiery spirit, Max Burckhard, recognised Arthur Schnitzler's stature before others did. Under his direction this dramatist, who was making slow headway, achieved great things with his *Liebelei*, his success drawing all eyes to him and opening up the way for him as a writer. Christine, the principal rôle in this play, which could only have originated in the Viennese milieu, soon became a favourite part for the greatest German actresses. In Vienna it was Lotte Medelsky who in this part made such a great leap ahead in her career; in Berlin the celebrated Agnes Sorma, perhaps the greatest actress Germany has ever had, helped the Viennese writer to a great triumph and then, touring in many German cities, carried this moving work to fame and glory. Max Burckhard's successor was the North German critic Paul Schlenther.

In the years that now followed success came to yet other Viennese writers in whom high hopes had been set: there was Hermann Bahr with his *Star*, Hugo von Hoffmansthal with *Der Tor und der Tod*

(*Death and the Fool*) and *Der Abenteurer und die Sängerin* (*The Adventurer and the Singer*), and, above all, that tempestuous and incredibly energetic figure from the Tyrol, Karl Schönherr, whose *Sonnwendtag* (*Solstice*) quickly relieved him of all material cares and made it possible for him to give up his dentist's surgery in a Viennese suburb.

So two great Austrian dramatists, Arthur Schnitzler and Karl Schönherr, had originally belonged to the medical profession. For the fact was that in those distant times the audience and the public took an excessively great interest in where a writer 'came from'— which is why I mention it here. If one was not the son of a government official or at least what was called '*bodenständig*' ('Austrian born and bred'), people were inclined to think the worse of a writer for giving up his original occupation for that of his own choice. But it was useless to protest. Apart from Hermann Bahr, who was the son of a notary in Linz, which to some extent satisfied the demands of his critics, Hofmannsthal was the son of a banker, Felix Salten and Peter Altenberg were the sons of business men, Beer-Hofmann, Stefan Zweig, Rudolf Kassner, Egon Friedell, and my insignificant self the sons of industrialists. Franz Werfel, the great poet and seer in the old Empire, came, of course, from Prague and was, as I have already mentioned, the son of a glove-manu-facturer.

It can truly be said that as a critic Hermann Bahr did not lack observant and eager conscientiousness. There was scarcely any talent that he overlooked, and he himself scored a triumph at the Deutsche Volkstheater with his play *Der Star* (*The Star*), which was a resoundingly great success. The title-rôle was taken by Helene Odilon, at that time the most popular actress in Vienna.

Hermann Bahr was a born fighter, and his fighting-spirit was very often greater than his creative urge. It could not be suppressed either by his will-power, which was, moreover, very strong, or by the violent opposition he met with whenever he took up the cause of a man or an idea, ever and again determined to establish some-thing that provoked the crowd to reject it. Hermann Bahr fought for Klimt, trumpeted abroad the genius of the boy Hofmannsthal, and was impassioned in his campaigning for Richard Strauss, Gustav Mahler, Hugo Wolf, and Bruckner when these pioneer artists had scarcely done more than show the first signs of their great ability.

But, in contrast with other spokesmen and standard-bearers of culture, Hermann Bahr fought for his ideals not only with his pen, but, doubtless thanks to the possession of a fortunate physical constitution, if need be also with his entire person.

As an old *Couleurstudent* and a former soldier in the Emperor Franz Joseph's army, Hermann Bahr was well acquainted with and practised in the use of arms. In his days as a student in Upper Austria he had belonged to a fencing fraternity, a fact revealed to the initiate by the scar on his bearded face. And so it came about that this great writer, instead of concentrating all his energies on his work, in the overflowing high spirits that he owed to his iron constitution was always ready to take up the sword in defence of his opinion or of some expression, used in a verbal skirmish, that his opponent had found insulting.

During my time in the army I was present at many a duel in the capacity of a second, but never before had I seen a duellist approach the matter in such a gay mood, with such detachment, treating it condescendingly, as if it were a mere trifle; for this reason alone Hermann Bahr was superior to most of his opponents. In his own mind he treated this deeply rooted, bad old custom as a joke, but he had to—and he wanted to –do as the Romans did, if for no other reason than to test his own reliability, his confidence in himself and his belief in his vocation. It was doubtless for this reason that he was so successful with the two dramas that he wrote against duelling, *Der Meister* (*The Master*) and *Der Athlet* (*The Athlete*), both first acted by Brahm in Berlin.

After Ludwig Speidel's death Hermann Bahr was for a time the leading dramatic critic in Vienna, having the privilege of fulfilling this function, which he took far from lightly, on a respected Viennese daily newspaper. Here too he often revelled in the joys of discovery, and many an actor, many an actress, and not a few authors had to thank him for their ascent and reputation. Naturally whenever Hermann Bahr rejected anything, he was just as intense and vehement as when he gave signs of his approval. This was the reverse side of the medal; neither could exist without the other. Hence he had not only enthusiastic, grateful friends and admirers, but also embittered antagonists, even enemies—Karl Kraus was among them—and it may be said without exaggeration that Hermann Bahr was at that time the most loved and most hated man in artistic circles.

I still well remember two episodes from those far-off, long-lost days.

A very pretty young actress was making her début 'on trial' at the Deutsche Volkstheater. It was clear, not only to Hermann Bahr, that she was not yet well out of the school of dramatic art. Unfortunately for her she had a little speech-defect, which, particularly in moments when she was trying to rise to the heights of tragedy, was noticeable in a not altogether agreeable way, producing, in those who were struck by it, a hilarity that was truly not in keeping with the occasion. After a detailed appreciation of the play, Hermann Bahr wrote more or less the following about this young lady making her début:

'Fräulein J. makes it difficult for one to arrive at a proper opinion of her talent, always supposing she has any. She lisps, and this regrettable speech-defect in itself makes it impossible for her to achieve many an effect that her acting might have achieved in combination with her pleasing appearance.' Hermann Bahr, of course, was far from thinking of making the young actress' career difficult or, indeed, impossible. Since, however, although he was not the only one who had noticed this speech-defect, he was certainly the only one to mention it, the young woman may have supposed hat Hermann Bahr's review was to blame for the subsequent communication she received from the producer, saying that he regretted he was unable to offer her a permanent engagement.

Two days after this incident, which Bahr, who was exceedingly busy, had probably forgotten already, he received a letter from the young lady's brother, a professional army officer serving in Pressburg. The letter rebuked the reviewer, in extremely sharp terms, which could not fail to be understood, for his attitude to the writer's sister. This malicious criticism, the letter-writer said, had ruined her stage-career, although it was, to crown everything, a mere invention to say that she had any speech-defect. It was only at moments of great emotion that the occasional weakness of her tongue became apparent, which was a thing that happened to many people. The letter concluded with the statement that the writer would not leave the matter at that, but demanded satisfaction from Hermann Bahr for the insulting way in which he had made the writer's sister ridiculous.

In discussing this letter with two friends, Bahr said, in a first moment of justifiable bitterness: "After all, I'm not under any obligation to give personal satisfaction for words used in the carrying out of my professional work, as this man apparently insists that I should." His advisers eagerly supported him in this opinion. But at once Bahr's sense of humour and his dare-devil recklessness got the upper hand, and he said: "No, no, I can't disappoint the young man who wants to come from Pressburg to Vienna for the special purpose of fighting for his sister's honour. I can't deny him satisfaction by the cheap device of taking refuge in professional privilege. He seems to be a nice chap. I must accept his proposal." And so Bahr's two friends, shaking their heads over the affair, became his seconds. One of them wrote to the lieutenant in Pressburg, saying that their principal was prepared to give the desired satisfaction and suggesting that swords should be the weapons.

The answer came quickly. It came by telegram. The lieutenant asked that the weapons might be pistols, since he had dislocated his right arm on manœuvres. Hermann Bahr somewhat impatiently told his seconds to answer that he had no objection. It was not so easy to find a suitable place for the duel, since the whole affair had to be settled within twenty-four hours: finally a building-site was chosen which was fairly well screened by a fence. "Brother and sister are evidently not in a very good state physically," Hermann Bahr said. "The young warrior is quite right to prefer a quick shot to more protracted sword-play. Well, I mustn't disappoint him there either."

It was only on the scene itself, where Bahr arrived in the highest of good spirits, although he knew very well that in any such enterprise some diabolic turn of fate might bring about one's downfall, that he first met his opponent, who was much his junior. The usual formalities were quickly disposed of, since the lieutenant's two friends seemed to be in an uncommonly great hurry.

When the cry of "Fire!" went up, the two duellists fired at almost the same instant and both missed each other. On both sides the wooden fence was splintered, and a small piece of wood struck Hermann Bahr on the right arm, leaving him with a bruise that he laughingly displayed to his friends a few days afterwards.

The duellists then parted, their reconciliation sealed by a rapid handshake. Chivalrous as ever, Hermann Bahr assured the young defender of his country that there had not really been any insult. "Oh yes, yes, there was," the courageous brother stammered, his words accompanied by vigorous nodding on the part of his seconds. Then all three saluted smartly and took swift leave of the astonished civilians, who quite correctly concluded that the gentlemen had to catch a certain train in order to return punctually—now that everything had passed off quite smoothly—to resume their military duties.

Four days later, after Hermann Bahr had succeeded, not without some trouble, in preventing the whole affair from being made public, he received a letter addressed to him at his newspaper office. The contents were more or less as follows:

'Sir, I know all. First you attempted to make my stage-career impossible, by publicising a speech-defect that I do not have and which nobody except you has noticed. But this did not satisfy you. Shortly afterwards you tried to murder my brother. These two grave episodes, one following so swiftly upon the other, have made me resolve to renounce a career that would evidently be a fateful one for my family. Thus you have achieved your purpose. I am returning home to my parents' roof, where everyone always was opposed to my going on the stage, anyway. But who could have foreseen such consequences! I owe this resolution also to my poor chivalrous brother, who so self-sacrificingly took my part. Thus you have achieved your wicked purpose, and I wish you all the luck that you so highly deserve. Yours in disgust, M. J.'

Hermann Bahr showed this letter to a colleague who could be trusted to keep the matter a secret, and said, not without some emotion even as he smiled: "So I've learnt something once again!"

If I now recount another story of a duel in which Bahr was concerned, it is partly because this affair was much more serious and had a much more complicated background, affording deeper insight into that period when Austria was a prey to nationalist struggles. In the duel of which I am about to give an account Hermann Bahr was not a principal, but, with myself, one of the seconds to his chief, the editor of *Die Zeit*, a Viennese newspaper of that time. This paper was the successor to the weekly of the same name which Hermann Bahr had founded in collaboration with Professor Singer and the economist Heinrich Kanner. These three then some years later transformed the weekly, which had a very high reputation, particularly from the literary point of view, into a daily newspaper.

Professor Singer, who taught that dry subject, statistics, at the university, believed he had discovered himself to be a politician, which his co-editor, Dr. Kanner, perhaps really was. In any case, at that time, when the great statesman Count Aehrenthal was trying to guide the destinies of the Austrian Empire, not without success, he was writing quite readable leading-articles, to which much attention was paid.

Like almost all the Austrian writers of his generation, Hermann Bahr had little feeling for politics, all the less since at that time he had his work cut out campaigning for struggling writers, painters and musicians. Nevertheless, being one who was always putting his oar into other people's subjects, he had at that time written an answer to a highly controversial pamphlet, *Die Aussichtslosigkeit des Sozialismus* (*The Hopelessness of Socialism*), whose author was a certain Herr von Schäffle, his retort bearing the title *Die Einsichtslosigkeit des Herrn von Schäffle* (*The Senselessness of Herr von Schäffle*). Professor Singer, however, believed it was his duty to use the newspaper, which he was, after all, financing, mainly in order to combat corruption of every sort in Austria. And after some years of the varying fortunes of this war, in which this over-zealous man often overstepped the mark, his ambition led to the duel that I am about to describe.

The bellicose professor had made an unusually sharp attack on the Kanzleidirektor (secretary) of the House of Deputies, who was a Pole by descent, and since this man at first met all his accusations by maintaining a dogged silence, the professor, increasingly enraged and evidently confirmed in his opinion by the fact that his victim did not reply, began to make ever fiercer onslaughts on the alleged offender.

All at once Director H.'s patience evidently came to an end. He had suddenly had enough of being the target for scorn and mockery and having aspersions cast on his honour, doubtless also because he was being wronged and slandered, something that it is of course very difficult to make sure of today. On being urged to do so by supporters, colleagues, and friends, he one day furiously demanded that the newspaper-editor should afford him satisfaction. According to the prevailing code of honour, it was not possible to refuse to give satisfaction to a man whom one had for months been insulting in a hitherto almost unheard-of manner, if he finally took a stand in the fashion that was then customary. A settlement in court would, furthermore, have caused a scandal, which all the parties involved wished to avoid. Today it is doubtless irrelevant, and in any case my memory of the affair is not clear enough to say, whether the editor of *Die Zeit* had wronged his opponent all along the line or not. From the formal point of view, he had certainly done so.

I still clearly remember the day when Professor Singer asked Hermann Bahr and myself, as a young officer in the reserve, to act as his seconds in this distressing affair of honour and approach the seconds of the gravely offended Kanzleidirektor. We instantly got in touch with the two men, one of whom was a well-known dentist equally well known as a shot, the other, on the other hand, a cousin of the offended official, who, like myself, had just been made an officer.

When the four of us were sitting together, discussing this extremely regrettable affair, the excellent Medizinalrat, Dr. Thomas, took the management of the whole thing into his own hands, which, as we were later to realise, turned out to be a very fortunate circumstance for all concerned.

Since neither of the antagonists had ever learned to handle a sabre or a rapier, pistols were naturally very soon agreed upon. The duel was to take place two days later, before seven o'clock in the morning, in a somewhat remote meadow in the Prater.

Because of my humble military rank I was asked to take charge of the sealed pistol-case and keep it in my apartment until the grave drive to the Prater. The above-mentioned Dr. Thomas had already, at our first meeting, been appointed referee. After our meeting Hermann Bahr and I went to call on our principal, to whom we reported and who then suddenly became very solemn, which was anything but in keeping with our own mood of confidence. I recall how Professor Singer asked us to come with him to his safe, from which, with slightly trembling hands, he took a document, which he laid before himself, Pointing to it, he said: "This is my last will, which I shall now make known to you." Hermann Bahr now lost patience and, turning to me, he exclaimed: "This is very instructive. Do you see what comes of reading the bad novels that your relative" (for such he was) "spends every evening reading? Well, my dear professor—nothing doing. Pack the document up again nicely and put it back where you took it from. It's quite enough that your seconds now know where it can be found in the event of fate having the grotesque notion of putting an undeservedly happy end to your life. Please don't forget that it's a duel and not an execution you're going to tomorrow morning. I see a much greater danger in the slipperiness of the ground now that it's begun to freeze. Take care! Breaking your leg before the duel would look rather too much like trying to get out of it!"

The man who had become so grave could not bear the irresistible Bahr any ill-will and accordingly locked his will up again in the safe from which he had taken it. Soon afterwards we took leave of him, since he needed rest, and asked him to meet us outside the front door of his house at six o'clock the next morning. I was taken aback by the sigh with which he released my hand, for nobody could have more wilfully brought about a situation faced with which he now showed feelings and sentiments that proved the professor of statistics to be no match for it.

It was a beautiful spring morning on which we called for our principal. The soberness of the very early hour seemed solely to blame for the gravity with which we got into our carriage. We were the first to arrive at the rendezvous, apart from one person, actually the most important, who had reached it before us. The celebrated anatomist, Hofrat Dr. Emil Zuckerkandl, who had agreed to be present in the capacity of physician, out of friendship for Dr. Thomas, was already impatiently walking up and down with his black bag, which contained all sorts of disinfectants and bandages. We had scarcely exchanged greetings when the Kanzleidirektor came driving up, with his friends.

Dr. Thomas came up to me, took the pistol-case from me and opened it on a long wooden table that he had evidently brought to the place the day before. Professor Zuckerkandl's confidence-inspiring bag was already lying on it. The antagonists, who from hostility or absent-mindedness or most probably from embarrassment had scarcely greeted each other, were now led to their positions by their seconds. Some metres behind the place where they stood there was a ditch, which Bahr discovered and into which he immediately took Professor Zuckerkandl. Looking at the two opponents, he said, laughing: "You know, Professor, if anyone's in danger here, it's the seconds and the doctor." Some minutes later I was to learn that Hermann Bahr had not been so wrong with this exuberant joke.

When I noticed that the Kanzleidirektor's cousin was handing his relative one of the pistols that had been brought along, I thought it my duty to do as much for Professor Singer. I handed out to the man the weapon for which he was stretching out his hand and I was about to withdraw to join the others, when I was struck by the intense pallor of the man who had been challenged. And as Dr. Thomas was just talking to the Kanzleidirektor, I hastened up to Professor Singer and, startled by his appearance, whispered to him: "Do pull yourself together! You must keep up appearances now. After all, it'll be over in a moment, and, you know, you mustn't let him have the satisfaction of . . ."

I got no further, for a shot rang out and a bullet whizzed past between me and my principal, striking a tree, from which some splinters hit my leg like little harmless darts. The Kanzleidirektor, who was unused to fire-arms, had evidently pulled the trigger by accident. As I quickly jumped back, Bahr exclaimed: "What did I tell you? People who can't shoot are a menace to everyone. Now keep down here with us." Not without anxious glances at the professor, pale but now somewhat more composed, I obeyed this sensible injunction. Meanwhile Dr. Thomas, showing signs of marked annoyance, was occupied with the over-hasty Kanzleidirektor, to whom he was obviously giving a piece of his mind. The incident was however very quickly brought to an end. Jumping up on the table, the Medizinalrat spread out his arms to right and to left and, when the Kanzleidirektor had also withdrawn, he addressed both the duellists in a loud voice:

"Now, gentlemen, be careful. Pay attention only to me. I shall count slowly up to three. That is all the time you will have to busy yourself with your weapons. Then I shall call out 'Fire!', whereupon you are to shoot immediately."

The eyes of both the unaccustomed shots were fixed on the speaker, both of them naturally resolved to obey him scrupulously. And now we heard: 'One! Two! Three!' And then something remarkable happened. At the same instant as the word 'Fire!' resounded, the Medizinalrat's broad-rimmed black trilby hat flew into the air. To our boundless amazement, it seemed to draw the barrels of both pistols upward with it. The shots rang out, and, penetrated by two bullets, the hat fell on to the green grass.

Medizinalrat Thomas jumped down from the table, laughing, as though he had succeeded in a prank, and disarmed his principal. I quickly did as much with the somewhat puzzled newspaper-man, who did not quite understand the situation but was relieved, as I could see with pleasure from the blood returning to his pale cheeks and colourless lips. Now Hermann Bahr and Professor Zuckerkandl also came up, and once again it was Medizinalrat Thomas who brought about a reconciliation between the Kanzleidirektor and Professor Singer. At the same time he informed us all that he had booked a table in the Krieau for all of us to have breakfast together and that we were all to be his guests. Who could have brought himself to refuse?

And so a little Round Table in the as yet empty, neat room united two great enemies, whose reconciliation could hardly be very serious, but who, bearing themselves rather better than a short time earlier, put the best possible face on it. Now that splendid fellow, Dr. Thomas, the morning's real victor, opened up and began to talk. Hermann Bahr, who had just suppressed his own inclination to make a speech, joined us all in listening when Thomas, in the gayest of moods, explained that many a huntsman was familiar with the trick he had just played in order to play providence and with which he had indeed been successful. Experience teaches that if one is directing men who are about to fire, or if one is the man in charge, as the referee of a duel is, of course, and one throws an object into the air when calling out 'Fire!', ninety-nine times out of a hundred they will aim and shoot at this object, even if their intention has been to shoot in quite a different direction. At first, naturally, we were taken aback and also pleased to be given this glimpse into the world of a sport in which Thomas was so much at home, but almost at the same time we all burst out into hearty laughter; and in some way or other each of us thanked this bravest of all dentists for his direction of the irresponsible bullets that were sent forth on their flight by irresponsible hands.

Decades have now passed over this episode in which Hermann Bahr was involved, but it deserves to be recorded perhaps not only for his sake but also for the sake of a splendid, true Austrian who knew the prejudices of his time only too well and suffered under them, and who, knowing as he did the foolishness of the whole undertaking to which he nevertheless had to lend his aid, in the goodness of his heart prevented a possible calamity.

When Hermann Bahr took an interest in someone, his unfailing acuity always discovered the gaps in the knowledge, in the intellectual equipment, in the philosophic views, of his protégé—for that was what one always was in such a case. So he detected that my musical interests were nil. He often castigated this deficiency and tried to make me enthusiastic about Anton Bruckner, Hugo Wolf and, above all, Gustav Mahler; but he also went back much further and declared it was inexcusable that I should go on being a stranger to the mighty works of Richard Wagner.

He resorted to a drastic remedy and, with his rough-and-ready manner of sweeping aside any objection in advance, he insisted that I should accompany him to the Bayreuth Festival, acting as esquire to the knight of the pen that he was, his essays on Bayreuth at that time being eagerly read by all and sundry.

Our journey took us through Salzburg and Munich, that is to say, first through a part of Austria to which Bahr was very attached and which he had known well since his childhood, and then into Bavaria, where he felt so much more at home than in North Germany. In Munich I came to know young Franz Blei, Max Halbe and Wedekind. However, Bahr had little time to linger there, although Blei, especially, was someone whom he particularly valued and for whom he had done a great deal.

In Bayreuth we stayed in a private house. Seats had been booked for us for three performances, which were, I think, *Valkyrie*, *Siegfried* and *Tristan*. Truly, on those afternoons the great and strange world of Richard Wagner's work was revealed to me.

About this time Bahr had separated from his first wife, who was one of the most beautiful girls in Vienna. His life's star, only newly risen, was Anna von Mildenburg, who was singing the rôles of Kundry and Isolde in Bayreuth. His marriage to this great artist lasted until the end of his life. It was in her arms that he closed his eyes for ever in Munich, at the age of seventy.

Now I could return once more to my ordinary everyday existence, which was not so very ordinary, and I can reveal that meanwhile my volume of stories *Weltuntergang* and, shortly afterwards, the novel *Das Haus am Abhang* had been published by S. Fischer. Both books had not inconsiderable consequences, which I cannot pass over in silence. I had read various things by and heard various things of Rainer Maria Rilke (he had now changed his name from René to Rainer), although there had been rather a lull in our private correspondence. But now something happened that swept me back again, with all the delight and the intensity of that time, to the memory of our first meeting; for this great man, my friend, who had never lost sight of me, had this time sent me a token of quite a special kind.

That wonderful publisher, S. Fischer, whose eye nothing escaped, surprised me by sending me a review of my book *Weltuntergang* (*The End of the World*), which was only some months old. The review was penned by Rilke and went as follows:

'This book contains nine stories, but actually only one of them stands out, the first, which gives the book its title. One does wisely if one calls it, without reservation, a masterpiece, it is so simple, so genuine, so out-and-out good. It ought to be read in schools. *The End of the World* is the story of a man who is destroyed by his Sundays—nothing more. This is one of those subjects that hundreds pass by. Seekers do not find such subjects; it is those who are born lucky who pick them up. This story is wonderfully told, calmly, justly, without a redundant word. Does one feel how here profundity is drawn from a destiny, and greatness and great gravity? Once again: we shall only do this story justice if we place it beside the best of what we possess.'

Fischer at that time complimented me in writing, and in the nicest way, on this success, adding that the gentle poet Rainer Maria Rilke as a critic wielded a very sharp blade and that even books that had appeared under the imprint of S. Fischer did not fare lightly with the poet of the *Neue Gedichte*, which had just appeared.

When I had read all of this and had written to Rilke about it my qualms as to whether I should succeed in going on my road were put at rest for the first time.

But there are two sides to everything, and as a result of this over-enthusiastic review my publisher's expectations, like those of my few adherents, were pitched very high and they were all looking forward expectantly to the appearance of my first more lengthy novel. It followed the volume of stories about two years later. Its title was *Das Haus am Abhang* (*The House on the Hillside*), and now once again fate willed it that an important and successful young poet was to pass judgment on it.

There was at that time a very much respected literary periodical that appeared in Munich, with the name *Der März* (*March*). I think its editor's name was Kurt Aram. No lesser man than Hermann Hesse, whom I had already met casually at Fischer's office, had written in this periodical a lengthy review of *The House on the Hillside*. It was not couched in such high terms of praise as Rilke's review of *The End of the World*, but it contained some prophetic advice, which I did in fact try to follow until Bernard Shaw's great successes made it impossible for me to continue alone the road on which I had set out. For in this review Hermann Hesse had urged me to write plays. He said he had sensed the dramatist in the author of *The House on the Hillside*.

This candour on the part of so experienced a critic caused me, before I did anything else, to finish the play I had begun, *Ein Muttersohn* (*Mother's Boy*). In the course of my life I have naturally found myself confronted with innumerable reviews, some appreciative and some with reservations, and most of them are forgotten, never having made any deep impression on me. Only these two, that of Rainer Maria Rilke and that of Hermann Hesse, I have never forgotten down to this day, because, after all, they did somehow point out to me the way I had to go.

At that time there was a very well-known restaurant on the Kurfürstendamm in Berlin. A group gradually formed to meet in a private room there; one of the members was Moritz Heimann, who used to appear regularly for dinner, and there were many very interesting rising artists among those who came. Heimann often took me along to these gatherings, where I came to know Martin Buber, Felix Holländer, Manfred Hausmann, and the painters Ernst Weiss, Emil Orlik, Walser and Lesser-Ury, to name only those whom I remember most clearly. Before I was robbed of all I possessed by the Nazis, my study in Vienna was adorned with very beautiful flower-pieces by Ernst Weiss and Lesser-Ury's celebrated painting, 'Das Café des Westens'. It was Moritz Heimann who chose these pictures, as he also gave me Buber's writings, into the study of which, at his earnest request, I entered with as much interest as joy.

It was a matter of course that even then I told Moritz Heimann, as well as Fischer, about Bernard Shaw. Fischer of course knew that three plays by this dramatist, so little performed in his own country, had been published by Cotta, and he asked me from now on to show him everything that I was going to translate. "Perhaps I can take Shaw over," he suggested. "After all, it would be much simpler for you to know everything was in the same hands, instead of having to correspond with various different publishers." "Yes," I said, "I have thought of that. But I would rather keep my works separate from those of a foreigner whom so many people regard as dubious and have them published by different firms."

Fischer entirely understood this point of view, but it was not long before—if only for reasons of friendship and because Moritz Heimann wanted me to—I regularly sent him all the works of the Irishman, whom he soon came to admire, together with my own.

My—as I assume—quite original play, *Ein letzter Wille* (*A Last Will*) had attained quite a pleasant success at the Deutsche Volkstheater in my native city, but it was much too gloomy to harvest more than literary recognition. I naturally went also to the performances in Leipzig and Hanover, and there I had more or less the same experiences. That great critic, at that time the director of the Deutsche Theater in Berlin, Otto Brahm, who well understood how to make an event of each one of Gerhart Hauptmann's new plays, had advised me not to try to have a production in Berlin itself, for he expected little pleasure for himself or me from such an enterprise; and I agreed with him.

I now went back to my work on behalf of Bernard Shaw with renewed zeal. Above all I wanted to see a production of my beloved mystery, *Candida*, after the success *The Devil's Disciple* and *Mrs. Warren's Profession* had had at the Raimundtheater.

About this time a little company, the Berliner Sezessionsbühne, under the direction of the young actor Max Reinhardt, was performing at the Theater in der Josefstadt in Vienna. This company went in especially for plays by Ibsen, producing them in a way that was hitherto unheard of. Reinhardt had working with him those highly gifted actors Emanuel Reicher, Fritz Kayssler, Winterstein, and Wassmann, and the lovely young actress Else Heims. He very soon had an extraordinary success, for which no one did more to pave the way than Hermann Bahr and Felix Salten.

At a cosy supper after one of the performances I met Max Reinhardt and his company, and told him about my discovery, Bernard Shaw, the fellow-countryman of Oscar Wilde, whose *Salome* Reinhardt knew and was determined to produce. I talked to him enthusiastically about *Candida*, and I remember that I succeeded in interesting him to such a degree that he made me tell him the most important points about that wonderful play, which interested him especially because of the great parts it contained, above all that of Candida and that of the young poet Eugene Marchbanks. He at once began to talk of the possibility of casting and producing it.

I was very well satisfied with the success this supper had turned out to be for my purposes, all the more since Reinhardt asked me to read *Cæsar and Cleopatra* aloud to him, Felix Holländer and Arthur Kahane, his dramatists, in my apartment. However, I knew how much could come between the proposal and its realisation as soon as this young actor, at this time tied to Otto Brahm for some months more, was back in Berlin. My impatience on Shaw's behalf was at that time—and I believe it was so over and over again—much greater than for myself; and so it came about that I took the manuscript of *Candida* along with me to the Weisse Hirsch in Dresden, whither I once again betook myself with my old affliction. There I gave the manuscript to Paul Wiecke, the leading actor at the Dresden Hoftheater, for him to read. That great young actor, with his enormous capacity for enthusiasm, passed the manuscript on to his chief, Count Seebach, asking him to read it at once, since it contained a terrific part for himself, that of a young poet, while the title-rôle cried out for the most popular of Dresden actresses, Klara Salbach.

Count Seebach, who was one of those who were always on the look-out for new work, at once read the play and asked me to come and see him. He wanted to be the first to produce it in Germany. When I told him that the work was half promised to the young director of the Berlin Sezessionsbühne, he laughed: "But I want to see it entirely promised to our Hoftheater!"

However, a theatrical season passes quickly, whereas it takes some time to complete a production. Max Reinhardt had meanwhile realised a youthful dream by becoming director of the Deutsche Theater (where he had, incidentally, decided to produce *Candida*), in the place of Otto Brahm, who had taken over the Lessingtheater. However, to my delight he agreed to my suggestion to let the première production take place in Dresden and to maintain an attitude of benevolent reserve, awaiting further developments; he was glad to agree to this, since he did not want to have the title-rôle acted by anyone but Agnes Sorma, whom he could not engage at that time, since she still had previously-made engagements to fulfil.

So it came about that this great literary event, the first production of one of the most interesting, remarkable and significant plays of that time, and perhaps of the present time as well, took place at the Court Theatre in Dresden, with Klara Salbach in the title-rôle.

The production turned out to be a sensation, if for no other reason than that the leading Berlin critics, as well as other writers who had gathered around Max Reinhardt—among them Christian Morgenstern—hurried off to Dresden with me in order to be present at the first night. There were present, besides, my dear friend Moritz Heimann, who on this occasion suggested that we should now use the intimate 'thou' as a token of our friendship, and Alfred Kerr, who was one of the earliest to recognise Shaw.

Count Seebach, who had attended all rehearsals from the first to the last and had quite fallen in love with the play, like so many people of that time, old and young, was enraptured to see that by this choice of a play he had forced the most distinguished literary figures in Germany to visit his theatre. The first night itself, carried by Paul Wiecke and Klara Salbach, was no disappointment; it turned out to be a great and far-reaching success, which not only received enthusiastic reviews in the Dresden newspapers, but also— a thing that had hardly ever happened before—made a great stir in the leading Berlin newspapers, which was due to the presence of the celebrated representatives of those newspapers.

Christian Morgenstern said to me after the first performance: "Now I know who the poet is whom I've been waiting for all this time. I don't mean your Bernard Shaw, but that wonderful figure of his, Eugene Marchbanks."

When I returned home, it was of course an easy matter for me to get *Candida* accepted at the Deutsche Volkstheater. The Burgtheater had at that time, oddly enough (it was then still under the direction of Schlenther), chosen the comedy *You Never Can Tell*, which I had meanwhile submitted. It was performed even before

Candida, with young Arnold Korff, Hugo Thimig, Hedwig Bleibtreu and Lotte Witt in the principal rôles.

In relation to Shaw's work as a whole, and for Shaw himself, *Candida* is a harmless and amusing, though of course very original, play; and as such it was treated, with a certain sense of relief at the fact that the by now much discussed man in England should be able to write for a wider public too.

Hermann Bahr had of course reviewed *Candida* after reading it, even before its production in Vienna. He called it a counterpart to Ibsen's *Nora*, over which it had, however, as he said, the advantage of spiritual cheerfulness and the superiority of a truly human heart. It was Hermann Bahr, again, who produced *Candida* at the Deutsche Volkstheater. He was a brilliant producer, staging his own plays so well (above all in Berlin) that Max Reinhardt engaged him in that capacity. Together with the poet Robert Michel and the actor Max Devrient he also for a short time managed the Burgtheater, where he produced Anton Wildgans' new play *Dies Iræ*.

Among the great figures of my youth Theodor Herzl occupies an important place. His name shines from the fields of my past with particular radiance, down to the present day, for he was among the first who helped me to get on in the world—and who that knows what gratitude is could ever forget that? He was the almighty feuilleton editor of the most powerful newspaper in my native country which covered such vast territories, and the road of a young writer who wanted to reach the public naturally led into the office where Herzl, with his exquisite taste, dominated the æsthetic affairs of the *Neue Freie Presse*.

The first decisive steps leave traces that one comes upon ever and again whenever faithful memory turns back into the twilit distances; and so, whenever I recall my bitter-sweet youth, I swiftly and easily recall that extremely handsome bearded man whose eyes were full of wrathful kindliness, eyes that sought to penetrate one in a flash, impatiently summing up whoever was demanding admittance. It was not so easy to face up to those Jupiter-like eyes. One had to have a clear conscience and feel one's pilgrimage was justified and legitimised by utterly honest determination and a matter-of-fact humility before the unconquerable powers of Success and Ability, the doors of which this just man gracefully and sublimely opened in order that fame might pass through.

Theodor Herzl possessed the divine gift of being able to distinguish the false from the true, and the fine ear of one whose fate was early marked out made it easy for him to discriminate and sift, to approve and to mistrust. So for us beginners his judgment was something beyond which there was no appeal, which was the reason too for the excitement with which each of us sat opposite him.

For me he made things easy. He published my first essays and my first stories and encouraged my work without flattering words; on the contrary, he was more like a teacher, endeavouring to moderate my joy at being accepted by uttering well-founded qualms and warnings.

Even at that time I naturally knew what it was that filled his mind and aroused him to feverish enthusiasm in a way that his art could not—those incomparable poetic emanations that he modestly called feuilletons, laying them on the altar of his newspaper. This was the object of his old faith and his new confidence, Zionism, as the uncrowned king of which he closed his sunlit eyes. This was a holy of holies of his being into which he did not admit me, feeling as he did how much a stranger I was to that movement, which was not yet rightly understood. He did not let anyone touch upon those things with ignorant words or, worse still, with inquisitive questions, and it was only to initiates, to those who were profoundly convinced of the same beliefs as he held himself, that he granted the privilege of a real discussion on the subject of his life's dream.

So the bond linking me with this unique man was not of the strongest kind. I, who was filled only with poetic plans, could not come quite close to him. He took to his heart only those who had both dreams—the artist's and, beside it or above it, the dream of the revival of Judaism.

The idea of the Jewish National Home was first produced by him. What it meant to him can be seen from a discussion he only had with his chief, Moritz Benedikt, the editor of the *Neue Freie Presse*. This autocratic, hot-tempered man, who did, after all, put all his energies into taking his part in the conduct of political affairs in Austria, on this memorable occasion angrily shouted at Theodor Herzl: "You must choose! Either the *Neue Freie Presse* or Zionism!" whereupon Herzl instantly answered: "I have chosen!" rose and left the room, never to enter it again.

His job was taken over by Hugo Wittmann. Long before this scene occurred, Herzl had brought a cousin of his, Raoul Auernheimer, to the *Neue Freie Presse*, with his first graceful writings, and as a result of his resignation, Auernheimer's road, which would in any case have led him into the editorial offices of the paper Theodor Herzl had helped to make great, seemed almost predestined.

In the company of Herzl and his wife I once attended the first night of a play by this relative of his, in the Theater in der Josefstadt. This wistful comedy bore the title *Talent*, a quality that could certainly not be denied the author, Raoul Auernheimer, after this first night, which was one of the last theatrical performances Theodor Herzl attended. After this Herzl all too swiftly fell a victim to the grave disease that the greatest doctors of those days had diagnosed, which now dominated his life and of which he was to die all too soon.

It was known in the circle of Theodor Herzl's friends and admirers that this healthy-looking, strikingly handsome man was suffering from heart-disease. But almost everybody whose soul soared all too high was stigmatised by some physical suffering or other, and when the first rumours of the evil that had befallen Herzl went round, scarcely anyone among his acquaintances dreamt of taking it particularly seriously.

A few years later, however, almost all those who were in contact with him could feel that he was doomed, and what even today seems to me the worst of it, the greatest tragedy of his dying, was that he himself knew better than anyone else what his condition was. And the way he bore this knowledge, the way he came to terms with his destiny, and settled his affairs, the way he limited his mission, his high-soaring dreams for the future, and his poetic creativeness, setting his aims not further than the day of his approaching end— all these amazing proofs of his greatness as a man made of him for ever the heroic figure, the example that lives on in, and is an inspiration to, those who had the good fortune to come into his orbit and receive encouragement from him.

In the last weeks of his life, when he was still in what should have been his prime, he increasingly cut down the great number of the visitors who thronged to see him, and only a small circle, selected by himself, was allowed to approach his sick-bed. He found me worthy to be among these, and few experiences of my youth have remained as vividly in my mind as my last visit to that dying apostle.

It had surprised me and stirred me deeply when one morning I was informed by Professor Joseph Redlich that Theodor Herzl was expecting me to visit him in Edlach, where he was slowly and quietly dying. We agreed to make a pilgrimage together on the following Sunday to his bed of pain in the Sanatorium near Reichenau, some hours from Vienna, a place that he was very fond of, as his unforgettable feuilletons bear witness. He saw me alone, after his consultation with Professor Redlich, who was one of his intimates and who had priority, was over.

The evening radiance that lay on the sufferer's pale countenance, the wide stare of the wonderful eyes, which seemed to penetrate the visitor with almost physical anguish, moved me so much that for a long time I fought to find words. With a tired smile, Theodor Herzl made the transition to a conversation easier for me, and as though to anticipate the banal question as to how he was, which was naturally in my eyes and on my lips, he said with an indescribably ironical smile: "Yes, yes, my dear fellow, I'm going downhill. The old clock inside won't go on ticking much longer. But I still have some time left." I gave a sigh of relief. Then, raising his beautiful white hand, he added: "But not very long." Then he turned the conversation into easier channels, enquired after various books and a few new plays that he had not seen, and asked me about my work and plans. I had the pleasure of hearing from his own lips that *Candida* had converted him to Shaw, whose *Devil's Disciple* he had not liked.

Meanwhile dusk had fallen. The beautiful autumn day was fading, and it seemed to me that the sick man shivered faintly. I rose, and seeing that he was trying to do the same, I helped him out of his deck-chair. With short but firm steps he walked towards the house in which he had his rooms on the ground floor. His youthful appearance and undiminished charm filled me with deceptive hopes. I accompanied him to his doorstep. There he turned, surprisingly, and stood facing me, drawn up to his full height.

With a positively regal gesture he pointed to the evening sky, glimmering in weary colours, and said: "*Le soir.*" Then his keen eyes followed a passing cloud. I held my breath. Starting out of his reverie, he suddenly added: "*Mon soir,*" while a smile of indescribable melancholy flickered round the pale curve of his mouth. At the same time he held out his hand, which I hastily took, and for a few seconds we stood wordlessly facing each other, he in thought miles away from me, I immeasurably shaken and incapable of uttering any word of farewell.

"Adieu, my dear fellow," he said suddenly, quite a different, sober tone now in his melodious voice, suggestive of the matter-of-fact wish to be left alone. At the same time his left hand was already reaching out for the knob of the door to his room. I now took my leave of him with many words, pouring out floods of wishes for his recovery, and the last of these many words of mine were, I am sure, the banal: "*Auf Wiedersehen.*" He nodded to me with infinite friendliness and vanished so quickly that, suddenly and painfully feeling myself alone, it seemed to me almost as though I had been turned away from his door.

After a few weeks, during which I heard only that Herzl's condition was unchanged, the news of his death reached me on a journey in the Carpathians. It was a hard and terrible blow, however much I had been prepared for his end.

I had an appointment with Hermann Bahr to meet him at Theodor Herzl's funeral. It was the greatest and most moving funeral at which I have ever been present. The overpowering impression literally made us speechless. We sat side by side in silence, Hermann Bahr strikingly pale and reflective.

Then we went together to Arthur Schnitzler's house, where we were invited to a meal after the obsequies on this memorable day. Only after the meal, when the magic of that writer's unforgettable home began to work its spell on us, did the stormy waves of our grief slowly begin to ebb. The image of the man who had gone from us, his mission on earth and his early death—all this was deeply alive in our minds, and only the awareness that we could never again lose our knowledge of him who had passed away stilled the agitation that we could not and did not want to control.

Arthur Schnitzler agreed with us that it had been a great experience to know Theodor Herzl. He too had been affected, and doubtless that was the reason why he was even more melancholy than usual. Then Bahr suddenly began to do something he seldom did, namely to speak of himself. He complained of cardiac symptoms of which he had never told us before, and I think I still recall his words: "I am suffering from the same disease that brought Herzl to his grave so early. My heart is in a very bad state, and who knows how soon I shall have to follow him!"

We looked at each other. We had never before heard the carefree
Hermann Bahr talk so gloomily, with such resignation and such
helpless sincerity. Arthur Schnitzler, the doctor, instantly took up
this confession, saying: "You must go and consult a heart specialist,
without fail." Hermann Bahr looked up, half surprised, half
irritated. And I added: "You must give us your word of honour
that you won't lose any time but will go to the best Viennese
specialist tomorrow." Like so many people, Bahr did not believe in
doctors so long as he did not believe he was ill. Now that his own
condition taught him to think differently, he began to waver. Urged,
even implored, by us, and doubtless also still under the influence of
the sombre morning we had spent, he solemnly promised to find out
for certain what his condition was, and to do so immediately. His
face relaxed and he smiled, letting us feel how glad he was now at
long last to have to think of himself.

The next day Bahr went to a famous specialist, who came from the
same part of the country as he did himself and in whom for that
reason he doubtless had more confidence than in any other celebrated
heart specialist.

We had agreed to meet after the decisive consultation, and I still
remember the impatience with which we waited for Bahr, who
seemed to us to be far too long with the doctor of his choice. At last
he came, pale and agitated, and sat down hastily at our table. "I am
done for!" he stammered. "My feeling did not deceive me! Professor
Ortner said to me in so many words: 'You have come to me after the
eleventh hour.' "

Arthur Schnitzler smiled sceptically and replied: "Patients have a
way of retaliating for such a diagnosis by outliving their doctor."

This remark had a miraculous effect on Bahr. He suddenly, as
though relieved, seemed almost restored to his old mischievousness.
I asked what the doctor's orders were with regard to his way of
living. Thereupon he crumpled up and explained: "I can only be
saved if I completely give up my way of life in Vienna, stop working
at night, go right out of journalism, and henceforth live only for my
health. Then, he says, I might be able to think of getting back to my
work some time later—if I'm lucky. The first thing is to have a
change of scene, a rest-cure on Lake Constance."

"A decision hard to face," I said thoughtfully.

"Very easy to face," Arthur Schnitzler contradicted me, "if it's a

F

matter of life and death. An overworked, nervous smoker's heart has a chance of recovery, but of course you have no choice. Do it, however hard it is." Hermann Bahr nodded in agreement and sank into deep brooding, in which we did not dare to disturb him. When we parted, we knew that the beautiful days of frequent association with him were gone for ever.

The next day he packed up and left Vienna for good. What came now was the time-consuming rest-cure on Lake Constance that transformed him into an apparently healthy man; and then followed years of solitude, after he had abandoned journalism, in which he had been so prominent and had everywhere encouraged the younger generation. For Hermann Bahr these years became an epoch of poetic creativeness rich in blessing. To them we owe his finest and most mature works.

A man of his temperament, to whom writing was so effortless, whenever he was called upon to do so could with the greatest of ease deliver impressive speeches, which bore witness to his amazing knowledge, on the most difficult of problems. Afterwards he was capable of spending a night over the profound writings of the philosopher Mach or sitting at a friend's table talking and laughing, his mood increasingly gay under the influence of wine, to go off then, apparently not in the least the worse for wear, and cycle to the Prater meadows for breakfast. When such energy is harboured in a body bristling with inexhaustible youthfulness, so that there seems to be no such thing as over-exertion for it, the doors are obviously wide open to the evil demons of disease.

If in addition to all the rich gifts that fate had positively showered upon him Hermann Bahr had also received the gift of moderation and had been able to recognise under what conditions he should live, he would still have made the impression of being very well preserved at the time of his death, which came all too early for us. The thirty years that he wrested from destiny after his great collapse are exemplary and must be accounted highly to his credit—as highly as any mighty work of his youth, when he had mown all obstacles down before him. Doomed, by his own fault, to an early death, with admirable elasticity, forethought, and right conduct of his emotions he nevertheless redeemed his life. He was capable of pulling up short the chariot of his life, which had set so much dust whirling, in the very last moment when it was racing headlong toward the invisible precipice. That too must be accounted a work of art, a piece of virtuosity, which scarcely any other contemporary would have succeeded in achieving.

Anyone who had the rare privilege of seeing and speaking to Hermann Bahr in those times of transition, when he lived in retirement, almost quite cut off from society, learned to understand what is meant by the process that begins with a conversation and ends with a transformation. When something so difficult, indeed almost impossible, has to be performed, one cannot draw all the strength one needs in the struggle out of one's own life. To the man engaged in that struggle there must come an angel who will bless him in the end. And this redeeming, salvation-bearing Ariel, who had always sung in Hermann Bahr's blood, was faith.

In the hour of his greatest need, when he still wanted to embrace life with all the fibres of his being and yet already stood before the gates of death, Hermann Bahr found his way back to the prayers of his childhood. The gravity of his illness led him back to the tranquil radiance of his parental home, making the enlightened man devout again. Much has been said and written, and far too little has been understood, about this transformation that took place in a free-thinker, a man who had fallen victim to the natural sciences, as Hermann Bahr had in his vigorous youth. Many an unsympathetic, indeed many a scornful, word has been spoken on this subject by those who knew nothing of the inner procesess I have just described. No such word could hurt him, could even touch him. For those who understand it is precisely on account of this nostalgic return to his home in God that Hermann Bahr stands for ever in his unchangeable loyalty to himself, which is nothing but loyalty to the vows of his beginnings and to his own destiny, to which every man is bound from the cradle to the grave.

After the cruel pronouncement made by his fellow-countryman from Upper Austria, Professor Ortner, who did, however, perhaps save Hermann Bahr's life, this man with the exemplary will-power unflinchingly carried through what he had taken on himself to do, for he felt that his life and his most highly creative period still lay ahead of him and he must not be allowed to break off such because of the inadequacy of a muscle. He immediately resigned from his newspaper, laying down his office as the first critic and feuilleton editor of the *Neue Wiener Tagblatt*, left his beautiful villa in Ober-

Sankt-Veit, which his friend Olbrich had built and decorated according to his own exact designs and wishes, and moved to Salzburg. Now he was, for the first time, out of the way, and could no longer be overrun by colleagues, admirers, and people who wanted to get on in the world. Now at last he belonged only to himself and could give all his attention to the battle against his illness, a battle that he waged with amazing patience and resolution until his recovery.

Now the time had come to test and prove what he had said more than once: "I don't need all these stimulants, like alcohol and nicotine—I have the intoxication of sheer ability in my brain!" It was to this intoxication that Hermann Bahr now gave himself up for years, until he later moved again to Munich. A very spacious apartment in Schloss Arenberg, where he had a large study with a gigantic writing-desk and a colossal number of books, became the sphere of his activity. It was from here that he sent the comedy *Das Konzert* (*The Concert*) out into the world, to become his greatest and most far-reaching success, one, indeed, that was almost unparalleled in its day, and one that made him financially entirely independent.

Hermann Bahr showed us, his time, and his doctors that a human heart that would gladly cease to beat at the age of forty can be persuaded to serve a creative will for another thirty years after that, continuing to beat until the task that has been begun is at last accomplished.

In Vienna everything now went on its course without Hermann Bahr, and once again we saw the melancholy truth of the saying that no one is indispensable. The theatres flourished. The 'folk-play', ennobled by the great Anzengruber, and before him by Raimund and Nestroy, was then much in demand and much produced, being resurrected time and time again. Another friend of Hermann Bahr's, J. Karlweis, whose career had not been begun in literature, became a particularly popular author with his comedies *Ein kleiner Mann* (*A Little Man*) and *Das liebe Ich* (*Self Comes First*), while Gans von Ludassy, a newspaper editor by occupation, tried to compete with him, which he could not manage to do in spite of the success of his comedies, such as *Der letzte Knopf* (*The Last Button*), in which Girardi had his triumphs.

One who was to gain a much firmer foothold and have a much more tremendous rise in the world was the novelist Jakob Wassermann, who had come to Vienna from Germany and began to attach

himself enthusiastically to Schnitzler and Hofmannsthal. Wassermann was undoubtedly an outstanding literary phenomenon, even
for those who could not wholly sympathise with his works. He had
something of the tremendous narrative force of Balzac, without
possessing his richness of colour, his grace, his wideness of horizon
or his art of fathoming all human passions. Jakob Wassermann,
too, soon had his house in Döbling and from that time on was
counted among Austria's writers. This was just the same time as
Arthur Schnitzler left his modest dwelling in the Spöttelgasse and
moved into a beautiful house in the 'Cottage', which, as he always
said, he only did in order 'to have enough room at last' and not, for
instance, to follow the example of Bahr, Beer-Hofmann and Hofmannsthal, the last of whom had long ago set up house in Rodaun
near Vienna. It was about this time that Schnitzler embarked on
matrimony, and the issue with which his union was blessed, Heinrich
and Lily, grew up in his beautiful literary home, until much later a
great misfortune—the cause of it a carelessly handled revolver—was
to deprive this most sensitive of all writers of his newly married
daughter.

Another man who joined this circle at that time and who also
came from a long way off was Richard Specht, who had, however,
come to literature from music and later returned to music again. We
have to thank him for important works on Johannes Brahms and
Richard Strauss. Specht was a particularly close friend of Felix
Salten.

Apart from Arthur Schnitzler, the Viennese writers, even those
who did not have to do so professionally like Auernheimer, Sil-Vara
and the above-mentioned Richard Specht, enjoyed writing criticism.
For the most part they did so at length, using the essay, a form to
which Hugo von Hofmannsthal and, ever again, Rainer Maria Rilke,
felt themselves strongly attracted.

A writer of genius, though not equally welcome to all, but certainly
one who towered over most, was the satirist Karl Kraus, whose work
is only now being properly appreciated for the first time. Even in his
own lifetime scarcely anyone had as great an influence on the younger
generation as he did, less as a great poet than as the judge and
interpreter of his age. He cannot be denied a certain prophetic gift,
and this brought him a following, at first in private and then in
increasingly large circles, which became increasingly vocal.

Egon Friedell was among the first to become a follower of his, careless of approval or contradiction, just as he was also one of the first admirers of Georges Courteline and Bernard Shaw. *Die Fackel* (*The Torch*) was a widely-read paper, and the only thing for which its variegated and aggressive contents could be criticised was perhaps that Karl Kraus took unnoticed persons far too seriously, persons who, remaining almost unknown, had scarcely any real influence on the public or on a readership of any size. It happened more than once that people asked me: "Who is So-and-so, about whom there is a long article in today's *Fackel*?"

Karl Kraus wrote exemplary German prose, which was not at all deserved by many whom he chastised with it. It would often have been worthy of loftier objects and more dangerous enemies of the people than some few journalists, male and female, who kept Vienna amused without having any dubious influence.

About the same time a young writer for the theatre attracted some notice, even more as a result of his youth, which was bent on embracing success, than for his work itself. This was Hans Müller, who conquered the Burgtheater at an unusually early age, with an effective play. I must take this opportunity of saying that both in Austria and in Germany there were some dramatists who were not only under-valued but also too badly treated by the leading critics of the day. The Austrian was Hans Müller, the German Ludwig Fulda; Hermann Sudermann also shared their fate. They had great theatrical successes, apparent for all to see, but the poet's laurels were obstinately refused them. The competence and effectiveness of their plays had to be some compensation to them for much heart-ache. They had been born with the infallible sense of the theatre that can create the great scene—something that they would not miss at any price—and this was the very thing that seemed to annoy their antagonists. They constantly met with hostility and as constantly had their successes. They were doubtless compensated by the public's applause and the material rewards that the theatre can provide, but they remained embittered.

Ludwig Fulda translated Rostand's *Cyrano de Bergerac* into really superb verse, and his versions of Molière's plays have also for the most part remained extremely actable and are entirely successful. Fulda's own plays, which a critic as severe as Otto Brahm was always determined to produce at his Deutsche Theater—whence there was a

Fulda first night once every year—never suffered a defeat. Success never abandoned them; but their author was discontented, going through life feeling injured and dissatisfied, and indeed later, in his disappointment and being threatened and persecuted by Hitler's minions, took his own life.

I myself had meanwhile been in Paris again with my friends and had carried out a mission to Catulle Mendès which Bahr had urged upon me. In one of Mendès' novels, *La première maîtresse*, there was a scene between an ageing woman and her fifteen-years-younger lover, which contained a secret that was enough to arouse anyone's curiosity. I had got Bahr to read this book, and he now shared my curiosity; so now on his behalf I could ask the French writer a question that I would doubtless have suppressed if I had been left to myself. The passage that we wanted to have cleared up went more or less as follows: 'When he was on the point of saying farewell to her for ever, she bent to his ear once again and whispered to him those infamous words that made him shudder to the very bone and linked him to the woman whom he did not want to go on loving any longer so firmly that he was incapable of leaving her'. What could the poison be that this experienced woman had trickled into the ear of the man fettered by his senses?

Hermann Bahr, who had read the book with great interest, said to me, laughing: "Do me the favour of asking that old juggler what the wretched woman whispered to her lover. I should really like to know!" This mission from a writer whom Catulle Mendès knew and respected was one that I lost no time in carrying out. But what answer did the master give me, not without irritated embarrassment? "What? You expect me to tell you that today? Isn't it enough that I wrote it and that it fulfils its function so well? Now you people go to the lengths of expecting me to know—and word for word, into the bargain—what a woman said in her impassioned determination to keep the man who was trying to slip away from her! No, no, my dear fellow, tell Bahr—and note the fact for your own benefit too— it is the reader's business to know that, or to guess it, and I have nothing against everyone's having his own notions about it and even imagining that he's the only person who knows what I meant."

I wrote to Bahr telling him this. The letter I received from him then was full of whimsical approval and appreciation. Nor was the word 'swindle' absent, I believe.

When I told Courteline of this little incident, he was delighted at his friend's answer and said that Alphonse Daudet had made use of similar tricks in his very moving love story, *Sappho*, in order to show how his hero was held in fatal bondage.

The aim of my visit to Paris was in the main connected with the appearance of the French translation of my book *Convalescence*. It gave me a child-like pleasure to see everything that had already been left so far behind me, but which had preoccupied me so deeply, once again coming to life in the French language, under the title *Guérison*. I felt as if I were being handed an exquisite dish on a strange plate, for me to consider it and decide now whether it had remained my favourite food.

Then, however, I hastened home, disturbed by news of my father's serious illness. I plunged into my work, in order to distract my mind from various depressing matters, and for the last time went through my new volume of stories, which was to be published by S. Fischer within a month, making corrections. The title was *Tagwandler* (*Day-Dream-Walker*), and the nine stories it contained for years served me very well when I gave public readings. Over and over again, right down to the present day, I have gone back to individual passages.

This is perhaps now the place to expend a few words on the matter of my material situation at that time. I was always regarded as the son of a very rich man and a great industrialist, which I never was. Even though I read the word 'step-son' for the first time in my step-father's will, I did always know that I could never count among his heirs and that all he had carefully and conscientiously held in trust for me was the modest property that I had inherited from my real father. On the other hand, his elder brother, who was fourteen years older than he, had died childless years before, leaving a respectable fortune, which was divided among seven heirs, of which I was one. This inheritance meant that I was materially very comfortably situated in life.

Meanwhile one of my step-brothers, my father's presumed successor, who was to direct the concern that had now become so large, had married and moreover had done so into an environment that did not have a beneficial influence on him. I cannot shake off the conviction that this marriage sowed the seeds of the later ruin, hastened on by Hitler and the popular democracies. In this circle he became acquainted with views and attitudes that drew the twenty-year-old into a direction from which for him, so weak and uncontrolled, there was no turning back. His father had indeed seen this and spoken of it, but he could not and would not take serious steps to intervene lest he should entirely lose his son, who had become so involved in another way of life.

The fateful horse, which in such a remarkable way turned up over and over again in our family, was now actually conducting the affairs of our firm. It multiplied in an alarming way, becoming an expensive stud and a racing stable, taking complete control of this wealthy heir's time and money and slowly leading him towards ruin.

When at that time I returned from Paris the only thing the doctors were sure of was the gravity of our father's illness. They did not agree in their diagnosis; but that lasted only a few months. The heart-disease that suddenly came into the foreground was recognisable and evident to all, and it did indeed become the cause of his death at the age of only sixty-four. Our mother survived her deeply mourned husband by some ten years.

Now that supporting wall had fallen against which we human beings, without knowing it, lean because it gives us a sense of security and protection so long as it stands. Only the collapse of our parental home makes us recognise and feel that we stand helplessly outside doors closed for ever, the wind howling and the storm raging around us, solitary and left entirely to our own devices, menaced by hostile powers. The image of a father accompanies us through life for a long while—and where is the son who, standing at his mother's grave, would not make up for whatever he has done, even though he never knowingly did anything to shorten the life of the human being who brought him into the world?

My step-father died in December 1906, that is to say, eight years before the beginning of the First World War, an evil time that my mother lived to experience, trembling for her sons. He died after a life that had at least outwardly been a happy one. His motto was: 'You reap as you have sown'. And whenever he was asked how things were going with him, he would always answer, pedantically enough: "In health and in business I reap as I sow."

For at that time people had a sense of security. One may think whatever one will of Emperor Franz Joseph of Austro-Hungary,

F*

holding him responsible for the collapse of his Empire or acquitting him of all guilt—the fact remains, nevertheless, that under him Vienna and Austria prospered, the inhabitants of his realms— realms so painstakingly glued together and always striving to break apart—were not unhappy, and those generations that lived during his reign and were dependent on his government were granted a long era of peace.

That age of peace seemed to us all to be so solidly established that we simply could not imagine a war. Precisely because the youth of Austro-Hungary had to do a period of compulsory military service, our fathers especially seemed convinced that the peace would last for ever. The same conviction was apparent in the speeches of parliamentarians and members of the government. They all thought anything was possible; only a war seemed to them unthinkable.

We who saw a world collapse in ruins, to such an extent that we scarcely dare to bemoan our own, often so bitter, fate, because it can never compare with the yet worse fate of others, look back not without a certain envy at our forefathers, who in their worst nightmares could not have imagined a fraction of what we all then had to go through in our lives.

In later years, when ties of close friendship bound me to Stefan Zweig, I often talked with him about this outlook on the part of our elders. He considered their lack of imagination partly responsible for the catastrophe in store for us, their sons.

About a year after my father's death, I at the age of thirty-eight did after all decide to marry too. A brother and a step-brother had already set me this example, neither good nor bad in itself. I myself was for a long time surprised at this step of mine, because I had actually been resolved to remain a bachelor. The fact that I suddenly changed my mind must have been somehow connected with the spiritual and human qualities of the beautiful woman whom I chose.

Now the moment had come to set up a home of my own. The fortune I had inherited from my uncle, which had been well invested, and which I would not at any price have put into my step-brother's firm, now so quite differently managed, was at my disposal, and so, on the site that my wife had selected, opposite the Schönbrunn Park in Hietzing, the spacious house was built at 20 Maxingstrasse where I lived and suffered, enjoyed pleasures and, above all, worked more than ever before, all through thirty years.

Moritz Heimann said: "Now the nomadic snail has its house." That exceedingly witty and amusing man, Egon Friedell, was, I believe, the originator of the expression 'owner of a literary workshop' (*Schriftstellereibesitzer*). Since, shortly after we had moved into our house, I had acquired a secretary, being so overwhelmed with my very various literary activities, in comparison with my former method of work I did seem to myself something like the owner of a 'literary workshop'. But the fact was really that during my long honeymoon, the time during which the house was having the finishing touches put to it under the direction of the architect Ernst von Gotthilf, I had lost a great deal of time, and had also not yet translated plays of Bernard Shaw's that had come into existence meanwhile.

Even before this there was a very pleasant success at the newly-founded theatre, the Wiener Volksbühne, which was managed by the writers Stefan Grossmann and Arthur Rundt. There we had the German première of Bernard Shaw's very first play, *Widowers' Houses*, which he had written in collaboration with William Archer. Archer later gave a very amusing account of how impossible Bernard Shaw had been as a collaborator. Archer had brought him the material, which was to be used for a three-act play, but after some weeks Shaw came to Archer, saying: "I have used up all your material on the first act. What now?"

Horrified, Archer withdrew from the collaboration, leaving the continuation and completion of the play to his self-willed friend. Shaw dedicated this play to that section of the population in which he took such a lively interest—the working-class, with its joys and sorrows. At that time, after all, he was already the leader of the Fabian Society, from which the present-day Labour Party originated, with its spokesmen one and all disciples of Bernard Shaw.

The success of this bitter comedy was so great that it was repeated in the following theatrical season in Berlin. I had of course already long ago translated the ten plays in the much-talked of first three volumes. That delightful comedy *Der Liebhaber* (*The Philanderer*) was beginning to interest theatrical people, and so did that sparkling comedy, *Arms and the Man*, which I had little trouble in bringing on to the stage. However, eight years had now passed, during which *Captain Brassbound's Conversion* and likewise that masterpiece *Cæsar and Cleopatra* had aroused the interest of German producers.

It was uncommonly difficult, and sometimes rather dangerous to one's psychological balance, to make a proper plan of work for a writer who always had one foot in another writer's territory and did not want to withdraw the other from his own original ground. In all this, of course, where I myself and my own work were concerned I had the feeling of being perfectly free, because after all I had not to give an account of myself to anyone but myself; but on the other hand, where Shaw, who had now begun to believe in me and count on me, was concerned I had a great feeling of responsibility. As a rule the issue was decided by the urgency with which work clamoured to be dealt with. I then had the feeling that I must fulfil my duty to myself as quickly as possible, in order then to return with complete devotion to the duty I had assumed.

Before me now lay the task giving Shaw's *Man and Superman* the proper form for the German stage, which was all the more difficult since this work involved not only a play but also an important open letter to Arthur Walkley, at that time, with William Archer, the leading critic, and also the appendix, entitled 'The Revolutionist's Handbook', as well as the extremely witty 'Maxims for Revolutionists'. This meant sacrificing time—time, time, which is what creative people receive an allocation of from destiny and of which they always have too little.

I was at that time fascinated by a subject that I had linked with one of my favourite heroes of antiquity, the general, Epaminondas. I now made it my main task to complete this work, and the industry with which I applied myself to it was anything but strenuous. The story—its title was *The General's First Dream*—was easy to write, and when it was finished I went to Berlin to offer it, as I did every new work of mine, to my friends Fischer and Heimann.

Also staying in the same hotel was Hugo von Hofmannsthal, who had come to Berlin to see the rehearsals of Max Reinhardt's production of his *Elektra*. After a swift exchange of greetings, he hurried away to the Deutsche Theater. I too went out shortly after my arrival, on my familiar way to Fischer, and soon my little work lay on my publisher's desk.

Some days later, in expectant mood, I took the same walk to the Bülowstrasse in order to hear Fischer's verdict. He came up to me in as friendly a manner as ever and at once began to speak eagerly about my opus. "You have," he said, "made a note at the head of your manuscript, saying 'thick paper, antique-style type', which is quite right but at the same time indicates the reasons compelling me to turn down this highly original piece of work. It simply doesn't go with my list. This little work, which I myself, personally and humanly speaking, found very moving, is not on a sufficiently large scale to be published as a single story, and on the other hand is on too large a scale and too individual to be put into a future volume of stories, all the more since the subject-matter, which is utterly different from the general run of your stories, would make it impossible to put it into such a volume."

I was considerably taken aback, although I ought to have been prepared for such a turn of events. As though to cheer me up and show me that he was expecting something from me, he said more or less the following words: "I hope you are working on a novel that will be more in my line and will give us both much pleasure." These were promises for the future. But the present hour had brought me disappointment.

When I walked through the lounge of my hotel, the rejected manuscript under my arm, I must have looked rather mournful, and without looking up I walked past someone who called me by my name. It was Hofmannsthal. When I went up to him, he said: "Why so disheartened? Did our friend Fischer reject the manuscript that you're so noticeably carrying, like an open wound?" Now we both laughed, and I bemoaned my fate to him, telling him the reason for our publisher's refusal to publish my story.

Hofmannsthal listened as only he could listen, his gaze lowered. Then he looked up and said: "Let me have the manuscript for a few days. Perhaps I can offer some consolation. After all, we're both staying under the same roof and can easily get in touch with each other." Unable to guess what he might have in mind, I handed him the blue copy-book, remarking, with a grieved smile: "There's no hurry about it." When something like a week had passed without Hofmannsthal's having given me any sign, I rang him up, and heard that he had returned home the previous day. Somewhat ill-humoured, I followed his example.

But the very morning after my arrival I received a memorable and lengthy letter from Rodaun, written in the poet's own handwriting. He thoroughly analysed my work, which he fathomed to the depths, and I still recall the passage in which he wrote: 'Like my own *Elektra*, your *Epaminondas* is a great experiment. It seems to me so important that I have sent your manuscript to Anton Kippenberg, the director of the Insel Verlag, urging him to publish your little book. Perhaps we shall have better luck in that quarter than you had with Fischer.'

Made very happy by this unforgettable letter, I sent it, with a letter mentioning Hofmannsthal's name, to Professor Anton Kippenberg, who was as yet unknown to me; this was after I had sent off my outpourings of gratitude to Hofmannsthal. And never did I receive that precious document back again, although I asked for its return again and again and ever more urgently. To this very day I have never got over it.

The answer from the Insel Verlag was not long in coming. With a reference to Hofmannsthal, it contained words of approval, as well as a contract assuring me of an early date of publication and that the book would be produced in the style that I felt to be so important. It appeared punctually in October 1910. Hofmannsthal's literary mission in my life was not yet quite accomplished. I feel there is something else I have to thank him for: and this is the Bauernfeld Prize, which was awarded to the book *Des Feldherrn erster Traum* (*The General's First Dream*) shortly after its publication, and the detailed appreciation of this little work that the eminent and celebrated Danish literary historian, Georg Brandes, published in a very prominent place. Here were three beautiful milestones on my winding road, which I owed to the sympathetic kindness and encouragement of that great poet, Hugo von Hofmannsthal.

It was the leading Viennese Germanic scholar, Professor Jakob Minor, who, as I later heard, had proposed my little work for this award at a meeting of the Bauernfeld Prize committee. The first congratulations that I received on this honour, which had been reported in the Viennese newspapers, came from Berlin, from S. Fischer, who was sincerely pleased and put round the books of mine that he had already published slips announcing this little event, which deserves to be called very unselfish of him, seeing that the book had not been published by his firm. Heimann wrote to me: 'You see what good can come from a rejection. First of all, if it hadn't been for that, Hofmannsthal would never have been able to do anything for you. What it really comes to is what your friend Shaw says: you never can tell.'

And when a short time later I read a detailed appreciation of this story in the *Neue Freie Presse*, written by no less a man, again, than Georg Brandes, it seemed to me as though I could still feel Hofmannsthal's hand hovering over my work.

Herewith I pay the great debt of gratitude that I would have settled long ago if it had not truly been far too difficult for me to talk about myself in so doing, thrusting myself into the foreground, which is, after all, unavoidable if I am at long last to confess that Hugo von Hofmannsthal, the great German poet of my native city, Vienna, furthered my artistic career at an important moment, and not, as he might have done, with one of his negligently weary gestures, but by exerting the full force of his already very influential personality.

Meanwhile Bernard Shaw had invited me to come to London to be with him at the rehearsals of his new Don Juan comedy, *Man and Superman*, which already existed in German by that time. Naturally I was not going to miss this. It was, indeed, most interesting to watch the writer carefully conducting rehearsals of this remarkable comedy, supported by his then favourite actor, the gifted Granville Barker, who was also not unimportant as a dramatist. Granville Barker had already acted the part of Eugene Marchbanks in *Candida* to perfection, just as he always gave a masterly rendering of almost every one of the main parts written by the master whom he at that time so much revered.

Man and Superman in the German translation never entirely got a foothold, although the play has naturally been produced many times, both with and without the interlude in Hell. There is no fathoming what is to blame for the cool reception given to this sparkingly witty work. The cause has probably always been the same: the public was not yet ready for this completely new kind of Don Juan, who had so completely broken with tradition. Only now has *Mensch und Uebermensch* had the great success it deserves, in a wonderful production in Zurich.

My play *Ein Muttersohn* (*Mother's Boy*) had been accepted by Baron Alfred Berger, that perpetual applicant for the lofty position of direction of the Burgtheater, in Hamburg, where he had for years been admirably directing the Deutsche Schauspielhaus. This man was one of Austria's tragic figures, such as many others there have been. Destiny did not grant it to him to reach his life's goal and fulfil the mission that he believed in with every fibre of his being.

Baron Berger was a writer of importance, and his Greek tragedy, *Oenone*, was performed at the Burgtheater. Through his marriage to the celebrated Burgtheater actress, Stella von Hohenfels, he became even more closely attached to this theatre, which was truly a temple to him, and he suffered all the more deeply under the fate that compelled him to show abroad what he could have done at home and wanted to do with all his strength. Then, much too late, worn out by long waiting and, alas, also gravely ill, he was summoned to take over the direction of the Burgtheater, which was likewise failing in strength; but when he moved into his house in Hietzing he knew—and his closest friends also knew—that the days of his life were numbered. He had no chance now to show what he was capable of achieving—either as a producer nor as a discoverer of talent, either in authors or in actors. His high-soaring plans had to remain plans, and he had to take the dark road to which his sick body had doomed him.

My *Mother's Boy* was later produced at the Burgtheater too, under the direction of Hugo Thimig, and this great actor and man of the theatre must doubtless have expected a success, for he cast two actresses for the leading female part. It success, however, was fairly modest. It was only much later, after the First World War, that I had the privilege of enjoying a real success at the Burgtheater, with the drama *Frau Gitta's Sühne* (*Jitta's Atonement*).

This questionable play, *Ein Muttersohn*, met with a mixed reception. All that I can now remember clearly is a remark made by Richard Dehmel, who was then among Fischer's most favoured authors and received all that firm's new publications. He, the severely critical, cool, mistrustful judge of his contemporaries, concluded his memorable letter to me with the words: 'I did not know that you had got so far.'

Up to this moment I had gone through life carefree and, so far as I knew, untroubled, surrounded by people who meant well by me. But now I had enemies. One acquires enemies suddenly, overnight, just as one gets measles. One doesn't do anything to deserve them and one cannot do anything to get rid of them, scarcely even to appease them; and all reflection and brooding on the causes of an enmity lead nowhere in the case of someone who is not compelled by his profession to cross people's path, causing them grief or joy, wounding them or comforting them. All this, however, was not the case with

me, for I had almost never done any public criticism, and when I did
so it was, after all, in a positive way, because I was enthusiastic about
a work.

Baron Berger had acquired the rights of Shaw's historical comedy
Cæsar and Cleopatra for the Burgtheater, even living to see the first
night' which caused him great pleasure for two reasons. One was
that he had brought one of the most important works of the by this
time admittedly established literary figure, Bernard Shaw, into the
brightest limelight, and the other was that he had discovered a young
actress who was probably the best Cleopatra the German stage has
seen down to the present day. This was the sixteen-year-old
Iphigenie Buchmann. She was the sensation of the evening, in a play
that was a sensation in any case, in a wonderful production by Albert
Heine, the young beginner's teacher. Heine himself took the part of
Cæsar, and there was no moment when he was not much more
worried about the fate of Cleopatra than about his own, which got
him into a peculiar conflict with his rôle, one that was only overcome
by his great artistry.

It cannot even be said that Iphigenie Buchmann acted herself into
the front rank on that memorable evening, since that would, after all,
pre-suppose that she had been in any rank at all, even the last, and
had been noticed there. She had fallen as though from the clouds on
to the boards of the Burgtheater, which she left at the end of that
evening a recognised and applauded actress.

I, however, hastened to Berlin, where Max Reinhardt had begun
rehearsing *Candida*, a few days after he had succeeded, at long last, in
engaging that great actress Agnes Sorma for the title-rôle, at his
Deutsche Theater.

Agnes Sorma's Candida was perhaps the most perfect study of this
part that has ever been seen on any stage. Never was there a more
convincing picture of high-minded femininity intimately bound up
with seductive charm, and of devotion and grace bound up with the
most dangerous promises of a great knowledge of the danger that
could doubtless be lulled but yet remains ever ready to spring up at
the right summons. Agnes Sorma needed only to plumb the depths
of her own nature in order to lay bare the final mysteries that Shaw
put into his *Candida*.

This was the first of the many memorable Shaw premières for
which I must always feel indebted to Max Reinhardt. Sitting in a

row at the back during rehearsals, brooding, his eyes flashing in the darkness of the auditorium, was the young actor Alexander Moissi, while up on the stage, for which this Germanico-Italian so impatiently yearned, Max Eisfeld was dealing as best he could with the part of the young writer in love.

From the time of this brilliant first production onwards I enjoyed Agnes Sorma's friendship for many years. But when after the first rehearsals I tried to speak of Reinhardt's pupil, Alexander Moissi, she waved the subject away rather impatiently, so that I never dared to confide in her my inmost conviction that this unremarkable-looking young actor was probably born, as it were, for the part of Eugene Marchbanks. This was also Max Reinhardt's opinion. It took him several years to give Moissi the scope that his tremendous gifts demanded.

It would be idle here to give a detailed description of the sun-like ascent that Alexander Moissi's career became. After the early death of Joseph Kainz, after that radiant figure's light had been extinguished—for ever mourned by those who had the privilege of seeing and admiring him in his most brilliant rôles—Alexander Moissi must be considered the most important 'male lead' actor of the great days of the German theatre. This acknowledgment of Moissi's position was confirmed much later when his colleague, that very different kind of actor, the tremendous Albert Bassermann, handed him the Iffland Ring.

This time I remained in Berlin longer than usual, in order to attend the first night of *Cæsar and Cleopatra*, which took place at the Neue Theater (rented for this purpose) in a production by Max Reinhardt. It was a great success, as was admitted, either enthusiastically or patronisingly, by all concerned, as is usually the way with the first production of a new play. The worst of it was that the box-office results did not correspond to the admiration this work met with from those best qualified to judge. It then, I am sorry to say, disappeared from the stage fairly quickly, like most of Shaw's plays in the first eight years; they were almost always a success at the first night and in the reviews they received, but were dropped by the public much faster than was understandable.

If today I ask myself how it could be that that splendid comedy, *The Doctor's Dilemma*, with young Wegener, young Durieux, young Moissi, and the rest of that remarkable cast, could disappear from

the Deutsche Theater's repertory programme after a few performances and then, three years later, play to full houses for a
hundred nights, I simply cannot find any sensible answer. It was only
after a good ten years that the stormy demand arose for the Irish
master's new plays, which were then all without exception great
box-office successes.

What was particularly queer was the fate of this comedy, *The
Doctor's Dilemma*. The first German performance was at the
Deutsche Theater in Berlin, in a production by Max Reinhardt,
which was indeed one of the most wonderful productions I can
remember. And in spite of this it was an out-and-out failure, which
was most strikingly summed up by Paul Goldmann, the *Neue Freie
Presse* correspondent, in the words he uttered as he rushed past my
wife after the first night: "Your husband really might have spared us
this disgusting stuff!"

The consequence of this was that my very sensitive and rather
easily offended wife said to me on our way home: "*Do* drop this
Irish friend of yours now! People simply don't want him, and you
can't force them to share your taste."

But three years later, at the same place and with the same cast,
The Doctor's Dilemma was such an uproarious success that it had
to be given a hundred-and-seventy-five times and also held an
important place in the programmes of the other great German
theatres for weeks. This is an example of the incalculable way things
go in the theatre, especially when a theatre is in its evolutionary
stages, which was then the case with the Deutsche Theater under
Reinhardt.

The Doctor's Dilemma did not cause such surprise at the Burgtheater, the most conservative German stage. It was there too that
Major Barbara, which I also translated about this time, made its
first appearance. The leading male part, that of the armaments
magnate, was taken by Albert Heine, who also produced the play.
Later in Berlin Eugen Klöpfer and Käthe Dorsch were a great and
well-deserved success, without, however, being able to keep the play
going for any length of time. Its day had not yet come.

At that time I could still take refuge from such semi-disappoint-
ments and semi-fulfilments in my own work and there try to find
consolation for not yet being able to give the great man, whom I had,
after all, become fond of in the course of this first decade of our

collaboration, the pleasure that I had imagined for him and which his unusual dramatic achievements did indeed deserve.

Burying myself in my own writing, therefore, I completed a volume of stories that had been begun much earlier and had ever and again been pushed aside by more urgent day-to-day work. It was entitled *Der Tod und die Liebe* (*Death and Love*) and was destined to be another splendid literary success for the S. Fischer Verlag. *Genesung* (*Convalescence*) had in the meantime been included in Fischer's 'Novel Library', where it went through many editions.

Suddenly I once again felt a strong urge to travel abroad. This time I went to Spain, where in Madrid I met Emil Broutà, the correspondent of the *Vossische Zeitung*, to which I had meanwhile become a contributor. Under the well-informed guidance of this witty and charming man I wandered through Madrid and learnt to know the unforgettable Prado Museum, which left me with an inextinguishable love for the paintings of Greco and Goya. In Seville then I saw a bull-fight for the first time in my life, and to the present day it has remained incomprehensible to me how cultivated men and women can enjoy this horrible perversion, and that even in our present age. It was a long time before I could get over the horrible pictures of the horses with their bodies torn open and the bleeding steers, wounded to the death, finally receiving the *coup de grâce*, by which the matadors achieved indescribable triumphs.

In my memory the strange beauties of Granada, Cordova, Toledo and, above all, the glorious marble Escurial surpass the greatest imperishable impressions I have of the artistic treasures of Italy. It seemed to me that there is no way leading from the great painters to the heroes of the bull-fights, who are, nevertheless, more loudly and triumphantly hailed than those artists whose works, on the other hand, not being merely transient, bear witness for them to all ages, while the names of those skilled bull-fighters hardly live for more than some years.

On my way home I visited Lisbon and Paris, where I did not find all my friends in the same state as I had left them. The dearest of them, Georges Courteline, had suddenly become very ill with diabetes, and the treatment of his illness was a cause of great anxiety to his friends, but above all to his wife, Marie-Jeanne. When I told him that the best of his little masterpieces, including, of course,

Boubouroche, would very soon be appearing in book form, in my translation, published by that respected German publisher, Georg Müller, in Munich and that it had turned out to be a fairly considerable volume, he rejoiced about it more than the occasion deserved.

A letter from Bernard Shaw unexpectedly summoned me to London.

He surprised me with two plays that were fundamentally different from each other, proving to me once again how great was the scope of his talent, which made it possible for him to treat the most different and antagonistic themes in quick succession and both in a masterly way.

The one comedy was entitled *Androcles and the Lion*; the other was called *Pygmalion*. Being particularly attracted by the title, I read the latter first, the very next evening, and it did not really need my own by now quite experienced faculty of judgment to recognise that the work I had in my hand was one of which the dramatic effect might well be far-reaching. When later, at table, I held forth to Shaw and his wife in almost garrulous detail about the possibilities of this play, so quite delighting Mrs. Shaw, who had become somewhat impatient, Shaw himself, not in the least surprised, said: "Yes, yes, that was just what I was after. One has to write a box-office success now and then."

And then he told me of the decision he had taken, which excited and also moved me very deeply. He had resolved, as a token of his gratitude for the poor services I had rendered him, to leave me the privilege of the world première of the comedy, *Pygmalion,* which meant that I was to have the right of bringing this highly promising play to the footlights for the first time in the German language and in whatever theatre I chose, while the English production, both in Great Britain and in America, was to take place only after the German.

My responsibility was great this time, much greater than ever before, for this play really did not need any help from me in order to establish itself. Was there anywhere a producer who would not have recognised this instantly? I was under the obligation to set about the work without delay and carefully and calmly to produce a version that would in every way justify Shaw's confidence in me. I knew only too well that, pressed for time as I had been, I had not translated his first plays as irreproachably as they would have deserved. This was naturally discovered, too, by professional philologists, who chalked it up against me accordingly. I could not explain to these Beckmessers, after all, that I was utterly sure of some day publishing a collected edition which would once and for all make good all the mistakes and superficialities.

It was at that time mainly the stylistic achievement with which I was concerned. The text was to be such that the translation would not be noticeable. That was more important to me than philological exactitude. At that time I did not have the time always to explore the dictionary thoroughly whenever I was not certain of having chosen the correct German expression. I freely confessed all this to Shaw more than once; but it was nothing new to him. He knew about it from innumerable anonymous and signed letters, to which he gave his answer in his foreword to the German collected edition, in the essay 'What I owe to German Culture'.

I hurried back to Vienna as fast as I could and set about this work so laden with responsibility.

I had quietly come to the conclusion that this world première must without fail take place in my native city, and of course at the Burgtheater. At that time Hugo Thimig was the director of this leading German theatre, and when I had finished my work I first showed it to him, for he was an extraordinary actor and man of the theatre. He was all on fire with enthusiasm for the Burgtheater to pay and receive this honour.

And so there came about the brilliant and thrilling première in October 1910, a first night that had been looked forward to, at home and abroad, with the grestest of interest. Once again the success of the production did not disappoint the highest expectations. The performance, with young Lili Marberg as Eliza and young Max Paulsen as Professor Higgins, was, I am sure, one of the best that has ever been given of this play, which has been performed so many times since then.

Strange was the fate that *Pygmalion* then had in Berlin, in that Max Reinhardt, for whom it had naturally been intended, generously waived his claim because he had already acquired the rights of *Androcles and the Lion* (which had been written, and also translated by me, almost at the same time) and could not produce another play by the same author either immediately before or immediately after it. So Viktor Barnowsky of the Lessingtheater, to his delight and much to the improvement of his none-too-secure financial position, obtained the chance he had so much wished for—to produce this great box-office success.

Barnowsky had to wait impatiently until the Burgtheater première had taken place before he could produce the play himself, which he did as fast as circumstances and the necessary rehearsals permitted. The reception the play received in Berlin was no less enthusiastic than in Vienna, and initiated, financially interested circles suddenly discovered that this English dramatist whom they had once avoided so nervously could write sensationally successful plays as well as anyone.

After the phenomenal triumph that *Pygmalion* had in German I was at last out of the wood, and Bernard Shaw, the hero of so many wanderings, had reached firm ground.

In coming into harbour thus we had, however, had the help of a pilot who stilled the stormy waves for us by means of his work. This was the young German literary historian, Julius Bab, a critic who had come from the circle around Siegfried Jakobsohn, the editor of the *Schaubühne* in Berlin. Julius Bab had written a very readable and illuminating biography of Bernard Shaw, and this fact alone, of course, aroused a certain stir. Today this book, the completion of which was published in 1926, is obsolete, for the sole reason that, as goes without saying, it could not deal with those works of Shaw's that only came into existence later. In any case, Julius Bab was among the first to recognise the great Irish master.

I myself soon reaped a modest success, not to be compared with Shaw's triumphal progress, with my play *Gefährliche Jahre* (*Dangerous Years*), which was first performed at the Deutsche Volkstheater, Vienna and also met with a very good reception later on in Munich and Hamburg where it was produced by Hermann Röbbeling, later the director of the Vienna Burgtheater, with the Viennese actress Lina Woiwode in the leading rôle.

By way of exception, because this play did, after all, grow out of the moods and outlook of that period, I shall here give a short account of its theme.

There was a family, and it was not the only one, in which the sons and daughters, who had had a sheltered upbringing, all threw away their lives in one way or another while still in their adolescence. One daughter was unhappily in love with her piano-teacher and sought liberation from the anguish of her heart by flinging herself out of the window of her room, high above the ground. The sons actually perished on adventures undertaken because they were unhappily in love, plunging their parents into mortal sorrow.

And now, for the subject of my drama, I chose the last son of such a family, hard tried by fate, a son whom the parents wanted at any price to protect from these disappointments. They are resolved to make any sacrifice in order not to lose their last child, in order not to experience again in his case what had already made them so unhappy in earlier years. Therefore the father has his son, a philosophy student, kept under continuous observation, and to his horror he soon learns that the young man is spending every free hour in paying court to a young girl whose occupation ties her to the place where she works. He knows the exact time when she leaves this place and now waits for the chosen girl at the corner of the street. At first she does not notice him; then she pretends she does not notice him; and finally, when he speaks to her, she discourages him, but not in over-harsh terms. She pays no attention to his protestations of love.

When the youth's parents discover this state of affairs, they resolve to do something to save their last son from being driven down the path that has already led his brothers and sisters into the abyss.

After a discussion with his wife, which opens the play, the father sends for the young lady, asking her to come to his office for a business interview. When finally she sits opposite him in all the freshness of her youth, pretty, intelligent, practical, and not without education, he brings himself to the point of making her a strange suggestion. She is to be in league with him, to respond to his son and make him happy, behaving to him in such a way that he shall believe he is loved—but all the time she is to be the father's ally and in continuous touch with him, keeping a watch over his son.

Highly astonished, the young lady, whose life is far from easy and who feels this suggestion portends a great chance for her, smilingly accepts and makes her new employer certain of success by confessing to him that she has only one wish, namely to give up her job and go on the stage. "There you are!" the anxious father thereupon exclaims. "Then it was a stroke of luck that brought you to me! If you are successful in carrying out the task I set you, then you will incidentally have proved your talent. It will mean that you are even now an actress who must make her way, which I will of course make easier for you by every means in my power."

It is, above all, this prospect that causes the young lady, now very thoughtful, to agree and enter into the strange agreement, which is that she must keep the father of the young man, who must now be the central figure in her life, constantly informed and confer with him to decide when the time has come to set the young man, now so much in love, free again—free as one who has gained his object and been made happy, as one who is now on the side of life, the life to which his passion would in any case lead him back sooner or later.

In the acts that follow this first one what actually appears is the impossibility of playing such a game with destiny. The young man's happiness is only of short duration, because, although he is being loved and spoilt seemingly for his own sake, he nevertheless always feels that there is something wrong in their relationship. The play ends with the young man's discovery of the plan that had originated in his father's pathetic anxiety about him and he goes over, as it were, to his father's side, mainly because he has for a long time had only one desire—to free himself again from that 'great love' in order to abandon himself to a new dream.

It will be seen that this play had its origins in a world now long forgotten and today almost incomprehensible. Both father and son would today have quite different things to worry about. It was only in order to make this distinction quite clear that I let myself be tempted into making this excursion. I now return to the fate of Shaw's last plays.

Max Reinhardt, who, because of the circumstances already described, had with such a heavy heart renounced *Pygmalion*, made use of its great success in order to produce *Androcles and the Lion* as quickly as possible. This play, which was first staged by the Deutsche Theater, naturally did not achieve the same financial success as *Pygmalion*, but it aroused great and fascinated interest, not the least contribution to which was the fact that the Viennese, Egon Friedell, acted the important part of the Roman Emperor. This was a decisive event for this unusual writer, who one day discovered that he was an actor and quickly convinced those whose word counted that in fact he was one. His performance also confirmed the belief that he was one of those who knew and understood Shaw's work best; and it cannot be sufficiently emphasised that he made this claim for himself at once smilingly and with the greatest of conviction.

This rôle, which Friedell acted with a passionate enthusiasm he brought to none before or afterwards, kept him for a long time in Berlin. He looked rather ill during this period, a fact that was noticed by many of his friends and acquaintances. When one of them asked him: "What's the matter with you, Egon? You really look frightful. Don't you get enough to eat, acting for Reinhardt?" Friedell answered with a sigh: "Oh, what ideas you have! I get plenty to eat, but I don't get enough sleep! That's why I'm so thin."

The Berlin newspapers were even more enthusiastic about *Androcles and the Lion* than about *Pygmalion,* according a very high rank to this charming comedy that now moves one to tears, now arouses merry laughter.

Perhaps at this point I may disregard chronology in order to record the fact that Max Reinhardt also once, as an actor, contributed to the success of a Shaw play. This was in *The Man of Destiny,* the play about Napoleon, in which no less an actress than Agnes Sorma played the part of the 'strange lady'. Max Reinhardt had always hesitated to take the part of Napoleon himself, although he had no one for the part who could have done it nearly as well. He had these scruples because he had very often jokingly, and also maliciously, been compared to Napoleon in his capacity as the conqueror of the German stage.

It was a rare pleasure to see that great actor—for such Max Reinhardt never ceased to be—achieving the greatest effects in those tempestuously brilliant dialogues with Agnes Sorma. They positively excelled each other, and shared a roaring success.

Bernard Shaw, however, had the good fortune of a third triumph with a brilliant piece of acting by Agnes Sorma, after those she had already achieved as Candida and the 'strange lady'. It was on the evening when this so gifted and enchanting actress played the part of Lady Cicely in the comedy *Captain Brassbound's Conversion.*

She was really too young for the part at that time, but she possessed noble womanliness and the power of influencing people to a very high degree. Bernard Shaw, as it happened, had, quite contrary to his usual custom, written this part for a particular actress; this was Ellen Terry, whom he wanted to show that she was wrong to complain so bitterly that, having just become a grandmother, she was now too old ever again to act the part of a woman capable of making anyone fall in love with her. This Lady Cicely, a part written for Ellen Terry, proved Bernard Shaw right, as he had intended it should, when the actress who had begun to doubt her own powers came to perform it on the stage.

When Agnes Sorma, who was married to a Count Minotto, followed her husband overseas as he was taking up a diplomatic post, she not only had to leave this rôle behind in Berlin, but had to take leave of the theatre, even though she did not say good-bye to it for ever. However, the effect of the comedy in which she had created the main part was so great that after her departure, even though it was then some years later, Helene Fehdmer was able to act Lady Cicely with considerable success. Her husband, Fritz Kayssler, who was one of the pillars of the Deutsche Theater and one of its best actors, also gave the most convincing performance as Captain Brassbound.

But now may I be permitted to look around me once again in my own life in the Vienna of those days and give a retrospective account of what I did and left undone?

My wife had in her first marriage gained the experience of how to run a large house, and since the number of rooms in our villa justified its being so described, it came about quite automatically that, possessing an extensive circle of acquaintances and friends, as we did, we were able to entertain many people, most of them quite inestimable. Among Viennese writers it was Arthur Schnitzler with whom my wife very quickly found a way of establishing agreeable relations, having known and loved his works before she had known and loved me; and it always remained one of her great delights to have long and intimate discussions with him. Arthur Schnitzler often visited us and was particularly fond of our very old garden. We also kept up a lively exchange of visits with Felix Salten and his wife, and we knew their children from the time of their first babblings, remaining to this very day in friendly contact with those of them who are still alive.

This beautiful, spacious house, the library of which had been equipped for me by that bookseller of genius, Hugo Heller—who naturally bore in mind the writers I myself was particularly fond of —very quickly made me forget my youthful passion for horsemanship, to which I had been devoted for so long.

It was at Hugo Heller's that the most interesting literary readings of those days used to take place. He himself and his ever-tactful wife knew how to attract the writers of Austria and of Germany into their spacious bookshop, which was as though made for intimate readings, and I remember that my very first successful reading, which was later followed by so many others, indeed by tours devoted to public readings, took place in Hugo Heller's bookshop.

It is permissible, and no exaggeration, to say that all the considerable writers of my country, which was very large at that time, were discovered, or proved their worth, at Hugo Heller's. One of them, whose 'evening' developed into a sensation, was Franz Werfel from Prague, who there at Heller's read aloud in a trembling voice from his books *Wir Sind* (*We Are*) and *Der Weltfreund* (*The Friend of all the World*), leaving behind him the impression that here a great actor had united with a great poet to achieve triumphs in a poetic revelation never heard before.

At this reading there were a great many girls and women; but Alma Mahler, who was later to become Werfel's wife, was not among those present. This young lady, so richly endowed with graces of body and mind, was at that time already the wife of Gustav Mahler, whom she had followed to America at the height of his triumphs and whom she then brought back to Vienna a dying man. As the daughter of the celebrated Viennese painter, Schindler, she was as though intended by destiny to lighten the burden of life for great artists with her profound understanding. In the days when a new literary generation was given a hearing for the first time at Heller's, from Rainer Maria Rilke to Felix Braun and Werfel's friend from Prague, Max Brod, young Frau Mahler was at her husband's side, fighting the battle for the rejuvenation of that venerable ancient institution, the Hofoper (the Imperial Court Opera), and for the birth of modern music and a new kind of composition.

After the great success of Shaw's *Pygmalion* at the Vienna Burgtheater, quiet but remarkable changes took place both in my life and in my now alarmingly increasing obligations to my English friend. Up to this time there had actually been no agency for his works in Germany that had extended its activities to Austria, that is to say, since Entsch had rashly turned them down, for which reason he was now tearing his grey hair. Now, however, all the large theatrical publishers in Germany suddenly wanted to be our representatives and to tie me down permanently for the future.

What had led up to this state of affairs was something that did

considerable credit to S. Fischer's great powers of judgment. It had
in fact become almost impossible to work with two publishers if I
wanted to maintain my own work by the side of Shaw's. In order
to simplify my plan of work I had to unite the two of us in one
concern, and I feel myself under a great debt of gratitude to the
Cotta Verlag because they saw this point when I put it to them. Cotta
even agreed to my having the rights of the first three plays, which he
had published, for a later collected edition to be published by S.
Fischer, under whose imprint all the plays of this author—who was
now, as it were, in the centre of literary-theatrical interest—had for
some time been appearing.

Now, however, my shrewd friend S. Fischer approached me with
another request. Trusting in the attraction of Shaw's future works,
in which he firmly believed since the great success of *Pygmalion* and
the popular revival of *The Doctor's Dilemma*, he was thinking of
starting a special publishing company for plays. His old-established
authors, above all Gerhart Hauptmann, who was nearest and dearest
to Fischer, and also Henrik Ibsen, whose work he was now about to
publish in a complete German edition, were still tied, for another ten
years, to the largest German agency, Felix Bloch's successors.
Hauptmann could not get away from there, although, of course,
being the most important living German dramatist, he would have
been even more welcome to Fischer in this enterprise than Shaw. I
remember the memorable discussion that Fischer concluded with the
words: "If you cannot let me have Shaw's works for this agency or if,
for reasons that I can perfectly appreciate, you hesitate to let me have
them, I will drop the entire plan and stick to my last, which is
publishing books."

However, I knew in what excellent hands the theatrical rights
would be with such a scrupulously conscientious man as Fischer was,
and gladly agreed, though not without first of all informing Shaw,
who in this matter naturally had no opinion. Right down to the
much too early death of that wonderful publisher and far-sighted
friend I never had cause to regret it.

Fischer was soon at the head of all the agencies dealing with
theatrical work, having such distinguished authors as Shaw,
Schnitzler, Hofmannsthal and many others who had hopefully and
confidently associated themselves with this new enterprise and were
only too glad to know it was their publisher who was also dealing

with the performing rights of their works. If I am not mistaken, the first person to whom Fischer entrusted the management of his new undertaking was my friend, the Austrian Leo Greiner, who had written an outstanding biography of Lenau. He did the job extraordinarily well, considering what an eccentric he was and what an unworldly poet. He was later followed by Dr. Konrad Maril, a very experienced man who knew the theatre inside out. Fischer always had a remarkable dislike of the obvious man for the job. "People who come fresh to the work," he used to say, "have many more ideas and get on with things in a much more untrammelled way."

I think Fischer had a great deal of pleasure and satisfaction from this enterprise, but not much in the way of material reward. He was modest in what he asked by way of commission, for the most part, too, printed acting-copies at his own expense, and, finally, took on a number of employees when the demand for the works he handled increased.

Incidentally, this undertaking of Fischer's was preceded by another which was much more important. What he had done, though naturally not at a moment's notice, but after many discussions and calculations and much pondering of the matter, was to found the *Neue Rundschau* in 1889. This was a great monthly paper, which was intended to be for the new literary generation what Julius Rodenberg's *Deutsche Rundschau* had been to the old. We called this latter review *The Almshouse*, for it was there that one found the works of Paul Heyse, Adolf Wilbrandt, Julius Wolf, Baumbach, Ebert, Felix Dahn and all those who were doubtless very famous but could no longer mean much to the German youth of those days. Fischer gathered around him and in his periodical Gerhart Hauptmann, Thomas Mann, Hermann Hesse, Emil Strauss, Jakob Wassermann, Moritz Heimann, Peter Nansen, and Gustaf Gejerstam; and, of the Viennese, Hugo von Hofmannsthal, Hermann Bahr, and Arthur Schnitzler, to mention only the most important and striking names of that younger generation. Extracts from the new works of these writers appeared fairly regularly in the *Neue Rundschau*, which, to put it quite simply, became the mirror of the new age. At their head stood Fischer himself, supported by the musicologist Oskar Bie, Moritz Heimann, Professor Saenger, Alfred Doeblin and, later on, Rudolf Kayser. Those who wrote regularly on economics and sociology were Werner Sombart and Georg Simmel; but Fischer's paper on principle opened its columns to all who had something new to say and could say it in an impeccable style.

With the founding of the agency that Fischer had started in order to handle theatrical rights, I had, it seemed to me, been relieved of a great responsibility, which was now in other, equally reliable hands. It goes without saying that Fischer had also taken over the rights of my own plays; but the dramatic activity that Hermann Hesse had once urged me to take up now very soon came to an inglorious end. The story is as follows.

I naturally sent my plays in, like every author, to theatre directors I knew, quite independently of Bernard Shaw's work, and now, still in connection with the great success of *Pygmalion*, I found myself in a situation that soon became intolerable. The very same theatrical directors who in my youth had shown great interest in my own plays, and had irritably refused even to read one by Shaw, now approached me with what I then felt to be strange and indeed almost outrageous suggestions. One, for instance—and he was not the last—said to me: "Your play is very interesting, and I would produce it if you would promise me that I shall get the rights for the première of Bernard Shaw's next play."

I was almost stunned. What was expected of me was that I should do something that was practically blackmail! With annoyance I asked: "If you are offered a play by Max Dreyer, do you also make Shaw's next play a condition for accepting it?" At this the man of the theatre laughed awkwardly and stammered: "Well, of course he hasn't got a Shaw! But you don't seem to be separable from your Irish wizard of the stage any more."

Thereupon I went home, completed my new play, which was at that time entitled *Der Geliebte* (*The Man She Loved*), and wrestled with the resolution never again to write a play of my own, or at least to submit it under a pseudonym. When in the course of the following years such improper suggestions mounted up, I did in fact make a clean sweep and stopped writing plays myself, after the last— it was called *Das Land der Treue* (*The Land of Constancy*)—had been acquired by Max Reinhardt.

However, destiny did grant me one great theatrical success before that. I mention it in this connection although some fifteen years lay between the two productions. The fact was that in 1922, that is to say, soon after the First World War, the Burgtheater produced my drama *Frau Gitta's Sühne* (*Jitta's Atonement*), which had a greater success than any other of my dramas. Bernard Shaw, who had in any case always sought an opportunity to compensate me for many a trouble of my youth, adapted this play, which made a strong impression on him when he was told the plot of it and which somehow fascinated him, for the English stage and brought about a great success for it both in his own country and also in America.

At this point I cannot resist recounting a rather amusing episode. When he had begun the work of translation, Shaw suddenly wrote me a despairing letter in which he exclaimed: 'None of the words you choose seem to be in any dictionary! I have to guess most of it, and the secretaries who claim to know German and whom I have set to work are practically incapable of being any use to me. So you must rely completely on my intuition.'

I naturally answered by return: 'Do you think that the words of which your plays consist are to be found in the dictionary?'

He thought that very funny, and answered: 'Yes, that's the way it is, we have to invent our own language. One can't write new plays with what there is at one's disposal.'

I then also wrote a historical drama in verse, which was entitled *Emperor Diocletian* and which has remained unperformed down to this day. It did however have a remarkably great interim success, for on my sixtieth birthday it was given a matinée reading in the Theater in der Josefstadt by that eminent actor and interpreter of poetry, Wilhelm Klitsch. Its success was extraordinarily great, and the Intendant of the Burgtheater, Schneiderhan, who was present, came round to me in the interval and exclaimed: "Things of this kind exist, and the Burgtheater doesn't do anything about it!" I laughed and said: "I shall be the last to insist on preventing it!"

But now, however, the sacrifice had been made: I would not express myself in drama any more. It would have been bound to lead to the most unpleasant feelings and incidents and would in the end also have imperilled my friendship with Bernard Shaw, if I had gone on submitting plays by both of us. Since, furthermore, my inner world was so entirely different from his, there could be no thought of, as it were, bridging the gap in such a way as to make my plays admittedly somehow dependent on his. I was, after all, anything but an imitator of his, and it was precisely the fact that he was so utterly different from me and all the German dramatists of my time that had led me to him in the first place.

But at that time there were unusual intellectual pleasures awaiting me in Paris. Not only were my old friends assembled as they had always been, not only were Courteline, René Puaux and Mendès here, not to speak of all of other, more recent friendships, but the dear friend of my youth and my discoverer, Rainer Maria Rilke, had now become the secretary to that great, indeed tremendous sculptor Auguste Rodin—and whom had Rodin just begun to do a bust of, as I had already heard from two quarters as well as from himself? The English writer Bernard Shaw!

But this period in Paris, to which I was looking forward so very much, was something that I wanted to earn first by finishing a piece of work, the story *Die Frau ohne Dienstag* (*The Woman who had no Tuesday*). It was so far advanced that I was able to get it finished in two weeks by working many hours every day.

What had led up to this story was a remarkable little adventure, which had for some years prevented me from making the closer acquaintance of a very great man and his epoch-making work. Ever and again tormented to the last degree by my neuralgic migraines, I had also sought help from that great doctor Professor Siegmund Freud, in the hope that it might be his destiny to find the 'switch' of which Lahmann had spoken and to bring my torments to an end.

Scarcely however had I begun to describe my sufferings when my kind listener asked me, without any real transition, how I got on with my parents and whether my father made it very difficult for me to be with my mother. This question left me quite speechless. "By no means," I stammered. But the great savant went on: "I mean, do you particularly dislike your father? Does he stand in your way? And do you expect all the help, all the liberation, of your youth to come from your mother?" I felt myself turning pale, but I shook my head and said: "Herr Professor, you don't know my parents. My father has always only been pleased when, instead of always going out, I have for once stayed at home with my mother. He only encouraged me in this wish, which I must say I have had very rarely, and he himself is such a nice person that it would be impossible for me to hate him. Nor have I any reason to do so, although he has in fact not made my vocation easy for me, trying—but this sounds exaggerated—to keep me from my mission."

G

Professor Freud smiled. "Yes, I know you're a poet, and of course in the eyes of the old generation that is always something forbidden." With these words he seemed to suggest a bridge of understanding between us; but he rose, spoke in passing of my migraines, which would soon pass off if I lived in a sensible way, held out his hand to me and sent me away with the usual encouraging words.

I still remember how I went down the stairs feeling discomfort and regret at having made this visit. This experience prevented me for many years to come from giving my attention to the work of that great psychologist, as I ought to have done. For then the *Frau ohne Dienstag* might have come into being under his influence, whereas, as things were, it arose quite spontaneously, side by side with his work, and everything there is in it of insight into the psyche and knowledge of the human heart I owe only to myself. No other work of mine was as easy to write as this was. It was not only the thought of Paris that lent me wings, but also the feeling that I would complete this work either in the first storm of creative activity or not at all.

When I had finished it I showed it first to a friend of whom I have not yet spoken here. This was the then editor-in-chief of the *Berliner Tageblatt*, Theodor Wolff, with whom I had also spent many pleasant hours in Paris and with whom I used to exchange impressions and experiences, which brought to light a remarkable likeness of outlook and a great similarity in our opinions. In our Paris days Theodor Wolff was the correspondent of the *Berliner Tageblatt*, the proprietor of which, Rudolf Mosse, was keeping him in France until he could summon him to the responsible position that he later held in Berlin. Wolff was a nephew of the great newspaper proprietor, but this relationship would have been more of a hindrance to him in trying to reach his high position if it had not been that every line he wrote proved to his uncle that no one else could carry the heavy burden of editing his newspaper as easily and with such noble strength as Theodor Wolff.

It was my good fortune that my friend, who had now moved to Berlin, liked *Die Frau ohne Dienstag* extremely and pressed it upon his feuilleton editor. So it was that this story soon appeared in the *Berliner Tageblatt*, where the numerous letters that both the editor and I received showed that it had caused some stir. Later on it was published as a slim volume by S. Fischer. Shortly after its appearance the rights were bought by a new film company, called Larus

Film A.G., and only a year later I enjoyed the minor sensation of being present at the showing of an unfortunately rather bad film version of my work at the Berliner Marmor-Lichtspiele. The film, furthermore, was less successful than the book.

In Paris I was impatiently awaited by Bernard Shaw, Rainer Maria Rilke and Georges Courteline. Secretly I was looking forward most to seeing Rilke, whom I had after all not seen for such a long time and whose letters could never be a real substitute for meeting him, so far as I was concerned. So I did not keep strictly to my appointment to meet Shaw in Meudon, but arrived much earlier and had in fact the pleasure of finding Rilke not yet so much taken up by his Master, Rodin. We were joyfully stirred at seeing each other again and brimmed over with the most important events of our recent years, often both talking at the same time. I was, however, taken aback by Rilke's appearance. I should scarcely have recognised him, and I am sure I should have walked past him in the street. He wore a long fair beard, which was very fluffy, for the draught from the open window of the room in which we met was enough to keep it fluttering about. This made Rilke look much more French than he had done with his narrow, noble, clean-shaven face, as I had last seen him and remembered him. He spoke in terms of boundless enthusiasm of Rodin and the genius of that wonderfully kind and yet so tremendous man.

Rilke knew, of course, that I had come partly to see Shaw and because of Shaw, and spoke of this model of Rodin's—and, what was more, without using those threadbare expressions 'mocker, talker, preacher, juggler with words'. On the contrary, he had fully recognised Bernard Shaw's immense seriousness and told me how instructive these sittings always were, especially for him; how that great writer looked up to the sculptor with all the modesty of one who felt he was himself a learner; and how honoured, indeed almost flattered, Shaw felt at being immortalised by Rodin's chisel, much more certainly than he would be through his own work. Later he was to say, with a smile: "Some day my name will be in the encyclopædias followed by the phrase: sat for the celebrated sculptor Auguste Rodin."

I thought it more appropriate to call on Shaw and his wife for the first time in their hotel on the Quai d'Orsay and let him take me along with him to a sitting, instead of suddenly popping up in Rodin's studio at Rilke's side. This first meeting in Paris was extremely stimulating. Shaw was never tired of talking about Rodin and his sittings and invited me to come to one of them the next day, saying he and my friend Rilke had already prepared the Master for this visit.

Mrs. Shaw, who was generally not very talkative, was also in the best of spirits. It was she who had insisted on having Rodin do a bust of her husband, but now that she had attained her object she was turning again to other plans, the central point of which was, of course, as ever, her husband's new work, which this time was *Back to Methuselah*.

I well remember that silent sitting, with three people present who hardly dared to breathe, while the fourth, the artist at work, filled the studio with his raging activity, his gigantic movements and exclamations, which were not always quite intelligible and doubtless were meant only for himself. What delighted me as much as it astonished me was the great understanding Bernard Shaw showed for Rainer Maria Rilke, whom he called the *prima materia* of a poet who in innocence and goodness excelled even myself.

Mrs. Shaw some days later invited us to a delightful dinner at the Grand Hotel on the Quai d'Orsay, where they were staying while Shaw sat to Rodin. Long indeed did we sit together, Shaw, Rilke, and I, absorbed in profound talk about God and the universe, and it was not least due to the outstanding personality of Charlotte Shaw that this evening never ceased to live in our memories.

Things were not easy for the wife of so eminent and brilliant a writer, even if she always kept in the background with positively insistent modesty, which went so far that in spite of all urging she would never let herself be photographed. If it had not been for some undaunted persons who slyly took snapshots of her, few people today would know what she looked like. Yet she was among those who knew and understood French literature best, apart from her own. She was particularly interested in Eugène Brieux, with his daring revolutionary dramas, of which she thought so highly that she translated three of the most important of them into English, and did so excellently; with her husband's help she also brought about successful performances of these works in London.

Her lofty mind and her sound taste in artistic matters enabled her to enter into her husband's works with quite special sureness of judgment. She knew there was scarcely any dramatist of those days who found the invention of an exciting plot as easy as Shaw did. That, truly, was something he had proved up to the hilt with his early plays. If he later tried to do without the crude medium of action, making up for it with unsurpassable dialogue, penetrating into the furthest depths of human understanding, this was doubtless because he wanted, as it were, to challenge himself to keep his audience as spellbound by the presentation and illumination of important problems of the age as they could ever be, in their hours of leisure, by detective stories. In this, naturally, he did not always succeed, and he would then always quickly prove once again that he was capable of making up for it with plays containing plenty of action.

Charlotte Shaw knew that this much-discussed man was, in any case, the most serious man likely to be met with far and wide. I myself have never met anyone more pedantically serious. He took everything seriously, trying to think everything out to the final conclusions, and never leaving to anyone else what he could do himself. Indeed, the future of mankind was something he cared about to an extent that was almost beyond the limits of the permissible. In his rejection of everyday happiness for himself and in his violent acceptance of all the annoyances of life for himself there lies, perhaps, the proof of his heroic individuality and eccentricity.

Mrs. Shaw gave evidence of her great independence of mind in many a debate at the Fabian Society. And this too was the place where her future husband learnt to admire her, while she in her very reserved way made the acquaintance of the man at whose side she was then to spend many happy and extraordinarily stimulating decades.

I have mentioned the orgies of modesty that Shaw went through in placing himself so infinitely far below Rodin as an artist. His admiration for a master in a very different territory was somehow touching and disproved the accusations that were often enough made against him, namely that he was the noisy herald of his own fame. Shaw had commissioned a second bronze cast from the bust that Rodin had made; this was intended for me, as a new and permanent token of friendship, and it reached me in Vienna in June 1914, immediately before the outbreak of the First World War.

Now the bust of Shaw was finished, and there were no more evenings to be spent together at the theatre or in conversation. Among other things, I had gone with Shaw to the Grand Guignol, that theatre of dread and horror. The plays, most of them by de Lorde, interested Shaw very much, but the more blood-curdling and frightful they became, the more of an effort he had to make not to burst out laughing. Nothing could frighten him; he was not frightened even when, coming out of the theatre one evening, we suddenly met with formations of police and small units of armed cavalry outside the Madeleine, because, as sensation-hungry evening newspapers had claimed, the outbreak of a revolution was imminent. Even this sight aroused Shaw's mirth, and he said: "Oh, no, there's no previously-announced revolution. This is only the next instalment of the horror-play we have just been seeing."

When the Shaws had left Paris after the completion of Rodin's work, Rilke and I still had enough to talk about for several days, of which, however, only the evenings counted, for not only was the poet working on his book about Rodin, but the Master himself did not like to have the feeling that his secretary was not within reach, in the next room, during working hours. The end of this period was very sad for me, as a consequence of an accident that no one could foresee and no one, therefore, could prevent.

Catulle Mendès, who lived in one of the suburbs of Paris and always went home after the theatre in a suburban train, being overworked and tired, and, it must be admitted, already ageing, had fallen asleep in his compartment. As so often happened, the train suddenly stopped with a jerk, and Mendès, starting up out of his sleep, had the feeling that he had arrived and must get out. He tried to do so in great haste, rubbing the sleep out of his eyes, but he had not yet reached the bottom step when the train started off again at full speed. Losing his balance in the darkness, he plunged into the void. He fell between the wheels of the train and came to a quick, bloody, and unexpected end, which, as the tearful Courteline said, trying in vain to protest at this blow of fate, was not at all in keeping with the life of his friend Catulle.

I stayed long enough to take part in the funeral ceremonies, in company with Courteline, and had the feeling that after all these moving and so very different experiences it was only when I got home again that I would be able to return, more or less, to my daily routine.

It was in the nature of things that my wife could seldom accompany me, and that only on holiday travels and to pleasure resorts. In Paris and London I was almost always alone. Besides, she really had her hands full, looking after our house, and in my absence she considerably enlarged our circle. When the sculptor Josef Heu did a bust of me, he brought other sculptors and painters to our house, and when Gustinus Ambrosi did the same, ten years later, this circle was considerably enlarged once more. These two sculptors I have named were then regarded as revolutionaries, perhaps because they belonged to the Vienna Sezession, which had arisen as a modern counter-movement to the Künstlerhaus.

However, I cannot simply put the name Ambrosi on paper without dedicating words of remembrance to that great Austrian sculptor, who was, indeed, perhaps the greatest of them all. Above all, I must tell those who do not know it already that he was deaf and dumb, an afflicted man, whose creative power has raised him out of the lowest depths of despair into the light of a sculptural achievement hitherto practically unknown in our country. If he had not been so outstandingly important as a sculptor, many people would perhaps know that he was also an important poet. His poems were a cry of protest against his fate, a vain rebellion against the unheard-of fate of being from birth stricken with defects that were not in the least in keeping with the tumultuous nature of his fiery soul. His poetic outcry: 'O God, why hast Thou locked mine ears?' will not be forgotten by the few who came into the possession of his poems, of which only a tiny edition was published. Ambrosi was recognised, highly thought of, indeed, much praised both at home and abroad; this was a triumph that even his cruel fate could not deny him. And if today I do not even know what has become of him, whether he is alive or, suffering as he did, has perished, this remains my fault and the fault of this life, so full of dreadful happenings, to which our generation was doomed from the day of its maturity.*

About the time that I have been describing a great sensation was caused by a book, not because it was a literary masterpiece, but because of its amazing freshness, its faithful description of the local scene, and the knowledge it showed of the countryside, to which it was dedicated. This was *Zwölf aus der Steiermark* (*Twelve from Styria*), and its author was Rudolf Hans Bartsch, with whom I was soon linked by ties of close friendship as the result of a chance that caused him to move into the neighbourhood where we lived. Bartsch

* I hear this very hour that Ambrosi is still living and working in Vienna. What a relief!

was an Austrian through and through, and positively possessed by his great love of his native city, Graz. I have always thought that provincial capital beautiful and rich in tradition, but when I came to know it more intimately under Bartsch's guidance my eyes were literally opened for the first time to its loveliness and dream-like beauty.

Bartsch was one of the most charming writers of that time, and his great faith in life, his belief in the future, his indestructible optimism, although all these things are, of course, positive qualities, may have contributed to keeping him somewhat apart from those great figures that then set the tone in the criticism of literary works.

Bartsch twice left his fore-ordained path, which was that of a novelist: once in order to write a very original and significant book about Jesus Christ, which I felt an urge to review, and once again when in much later years he wrote his first and last drama, which was accepted at the Burgtheater, where it had a very remarkable success. He is today once more living in his native Styria, rather eccentric and slightly embittered, a little disappointed, too, trying to enjoy what is called the evening of life, which is so often life's nightfall.*

But now the time had come when the Austrian writers so often mentioned in these pages had reached the zenith of their creative activity. Both in the Deutsche Theater in Berlin and in the Vienna Burgtheater every new play by Arthur Schnitzler was hailed as an event and very joyfully accepted. Since *Der Einsame Weg (The Lonely Road)*, which had made a profound impression at the Deutsche Theater in Berlin, with Albert Bassermann, and since Arthur Schnitzler had been awarded the Grillparzer Prize for his *Zwischenspiel (Interlude)*, produced at the Burgtheater, he, who was now at the height of his powers and productivity, contributed to Austria's glory.

Karl Schönherr had also reached these proud heights in the drama, though in his case the emphasis falls rather more on his native Austria, since beyond its frontiers, in the Reich, he still met with but little appreciation. However, those great works *Der Weibsteufel (The She-Devil)*, *Glaube und Heimat (Faith and the Homeland)*, *Erde (Earth)*, *Ein Volk in Not (A Nation in Peril)* and *Judas von Tirol (A Judas of the Tyrol)* drew deep furrows in the fruitful plain of this author's success.

With Hermann Bahr it had not been very different. His comedies

* Author's note: He died about a year ago (1952).

Wienerinnen (*The Fair Viennese*), *Der Querulant* (*Crosspatch*), the already-mentioned play *Star* (*The Star*), *Der Meister* (*The Master*), which had also been produced for the first time by Brahm in Berlin, and above all *Das Konzert* (*The Concert*), were such great successes, both from the theatrical and from the literary point of view, that no one could any longer deny Hermann Bahr the recognition that had so long been refused him.

As so often happens, these successes overshadowed a dramatic work that almost makes Hermann Bahr appear more lovable than the achievements already listed. This work was his *Franzl*, an appealing comedy somewhat resembling a folk play, the hero of which was Franz Stelzhamer, an Upper Austrian national poet. Hermann Bahr would smile in conversation about this and say: "For once a man puts his whole heart into a play, giving it everything he has, and then the most he gets out of it is that it goes down with the flag flying."

Hugo von Hofmannsthal had now also reached the heights. His *Elektra* and *Der Schwierige* (*A Difficult Person*), which had, after all, sprung from quite a different world, quite a different kind of poetic inspiration, took care of worldly success, showing clearly enough that Hofmannsthal did not need Richard Strauss' collaboration in order to convince a large public of the greatness of his mission. Admittedly, the *Rosenkavalier*, which can also be regarded as a delightful poem by Hofmannsthal, *Die Frau ohne Schatten* (*The Woman Without a Shadow*), that wonderful work *Ariadne auf Naxos* (*Ariadne on Naxos*), *Die ægyptische Helena* (*Helen of Egypt*), saw to it that a name that for the elect had long been pre-eminent was now made known to the broad masses. The music of the greatest composer of opera in our time, the unparalleled tumults of enthusiasm that accompanied Richard Strauss' operas, also bore Hofmannsthal's name upward on their wings; yet he had already long been shining in his own imperishable splendour.

But even at this time there were others who could distinctly be heard knocking at the gates of fame. These were Max Mell, recognised and lauded by Hofmannsthal; Hermann Bahr's protégé, Rudolf Holzer, who is still working with undiminished vigour today; Stefan Zweig, mature and well used to success; Hans Müller, tumultuously storming ahead and so often frustrating his own efforts; Felix Braun; Oscar Maurus Fontana; Sil-Vara; and, the

G*

youngest of them all, Lernet-Holenia. Far in advance of all others and aloof from them, a law unto himself, stood that little-known genius, Robert Musil. Others who should be mentioned were the sparkling Roda-Roda, Emil Lucka, and Raoul Auernheimer.

Roda-Roda, Auernheimer, Stefan Zweig and I myself were impassioned chess players, but none of us could boast of the same mania as Jakob Wassermann, who could probably claim to be called the best amateur of that noble game among the writers of his time, reaching a level of excellence that almost qualified him as a championship player. This Austrian by choice, who had originally come from Bavaria, was the most zealous steward of his own fame. Nevertheless, he once nearly missed one of his own readings, he was so absorbed in a game of chess with that champion player, Artur Kaufmann, and could only just tear himself away in time by making a very great effort.

In those days two young Austrians, Anton Wildgans and Franz Theodor Csokor, were beginning to strike new and individual notes of great beauty that soon rang in the literary atmosphere of Vienna. And it is highly to the credit of Felix Salten, who was then the feuilleton editor of the former weekly, *Die Zeit*, which had now been transformed into a daily newspaper, that he was the first to publish poems by Wildgans, which he printed in the Sunday supplement of his paper, gladly yielding to my urgent requests that he should do so. Among these poems were the immortal verses: 'Bist du im Abendneigen denn allein?' ('When evening falls, are you indeed alone?')

Felix Salten had such an intense, overwhelmingly convincing poetic talent that—and this had to be said some time—he had no need at all of journalism, to which, after all, he sacrificed the prime of his life and most of his time, in order to attain recognition, indeed fame. His undeniable ability raised him high over most other literary journalists, and he only needed to find time and leisure, and to be able to concentrate on his so extremely fruitful subject-matter, in order to arrive with the greatest of ease at the success that his journalistic activities had not always yielded him, indeed had often barred to him. Scarcely had he got so far, in Vienna, that people were beginning to count on his fascinating stories, when he was summoned to take up a high position in a large German newspaper concern in Berlin. At that time he also took up very friendly relations with S. Fischer, who began to publish his stories. It was only

after some years that he returned to Vienna, in order to become one
of the most respected contributors of the *Neue Freie Presse*. After
Auernheimer's resignation he succeeded him as the Burgtheater
critic, in which position he remained long after the death of Moritz
Benedikt, down to the sad end of the *Neue Freie Presse*.

Felix Salten's remarkably stormy and variegated life was crowned
in his last years by the world-wide success of *Bambi*. The inner
secret of this extraordinary success was a passion Salten developed
in his maturity—hunting. He made use of every spare hour in
Vienna to hurry off to Stockerau, where he had a shooting-lodge,
and from there set out with his young son to shoot game. This queer
combination of love for animals and a passion for shooting made it
possible for him to study animal psychology in great detail, so
coming, incidentally, to a more acute understanding of human
nature as well.

Hugo von Hofmannsthal, who actually spent the whole year in the
country, in Rodaun, outside Vienna, was to be found every summer
in Alt-Aussee, where, in strict seclusion, he created many a miracle of
poetry. Few had the good fortune to be admitted to his society.
Among these were his boyhood friends Clemens and Georg von
Frankenstein, Leopold Andrian, Richard Beer-Hofmann, sometimes,
as a visitor, Arthur Schnitzler, and, keeping doggedly in the vicinity,
Jakob Wassermann, whose visions, and particularly the abundance
of them, greatly interested Hofmannsthal. He permitted this friend
many a glimpse into his own workshop, discussing the most important mysteries of poetic creation with the novelist, who held him
in high regard.

Since we owned a villa that was, in any case, more or less in
country surroundings, being opposite the Park of Schönbrunn and in
the quiet proximity of the Hietzing cemetery, we had no need to look
for a permanent holiday place in the country. However, we did often
make a summer journey to the sea or to the Swiss Alps and in this
way were able to compare the beauties of other countries with those
of our homeland.

In our garden, in which there stood ancient trees that one man
could not put his arms right round, there were white gravel paths
and, thanks to my wife's capacities as a gardener, many flowers and
also exotic plants that were tended in a hot-house. It was one of the
few gardens that provided plenty of coolness and shade even in

great heat, and in the hammock, the skittles alley, the little arbours we had built at the back, it was possible to work in comfort, quite undisturbed. Now that wonderful, unforgettable garden is a monument to the vandalism of Hitler's mercenaries. It is now a bare and miserable patch of meadow.

This garden in Hietzing, which belongs to memory and to the past, was often populated by our friends and visitors from all over the world, and voices both quiet and loud mingled with those inaudible sounds that some special grace sometimes made perceptible to my hearing. Then, when we were alone again, sometimes in the chords of evening we thought we heard a warning that these feelings, coming so near to human happiness, and all the greetings from endlessly far off, could not last for ever and that some day there would be a terrible awakening from the dream of this garden, a dream into which we often sank in silence. It was not long before this day came. Arthur Schnitzler and later Stefan Zweig, who came to see us more and more often, both felt something of this mood. I could see it in their faces.

In the course of the years, though I had not had triumphs like those of the writers I have been describing, who stamped upon their age the imprint of their sufferings and joys, a few valuable books had nevertheless come into being, such as *Der Tod und die Liebe* (*Death and Love*), *Die Last des Blutes* (*The Burden of the Blood*) and *Die Rache ist mein* (*Vengeance is Mine*). At the same time, I stood before difficult inner decisions. For the reasons already stated, I did not want to write any more plays, and tore up the notes I had made for future plays, destroying the material that had sometimes already reached the stage of a scenario. Now I had to devote all my energies to Bernard Shaw's monumental work, which was entitled *Back to Methuselah*, a dramatic pentateuch. It was impossible to think of a great work of my own at the same time.

Back to Methuselah is such a comprehensive, unusual work, so tremendous in every way, including its dimensions, that nothing could grow beside it and the German version of it. This work of Bernard Shaw's was called the work of a classic writer by those people in his native country who were in a position to pronounce judgments on literature. He himself later once said: "If that isn't the work of a classic writer, then it's nothing at all—then into the fire with it!"

I myself, and many others too, I am sure, may prefer works like

Saint Joan to this human comedy in five parts; but the very titles show that this is a drama embracing the whole of our existence. The first part begins with Adam and Eve and is entitled 'In the Beginning'; the second is 'The Gospel of the Brothers Barnabas'. Its theme is the belief in the possibility of reaching a far greater age than has hitherto been known. The third part, 'The Thing Happens', shows people who already live beyond the usual span of life. The fourth part is perhaps the most effective in the theatre, a delightful comedy, even though it is called 'The Tragedy of an Elderly Gentleman'. The fifth is called 'To the Limits of Thought' and might be considered Shaw's 'Faust.'

The theatrical director Viktor Barnowsky in Berlin daringly undertook to produce these five plays on three evenings, and it turned out that the work in its entirety is a unit of astonishingly dramatic effectiveness.

In theory Shaw had meant to come to Vienna some time to repay my many visits to London, but it never actually came about. The main reason was that he shrank, in a way that his wife encouraged, from the exertions that he would have to contend with. "Yes, if I were just a writer of plays," he said, "it might be managed all right. But after all, I would be in terrific demand as a man of politics and a social critic too. I simply wouldn't be able to cope with such a lot of very different expectations and demands, and we would see much less of each other than we do when you visit us here in London."

However, he came to meet me in Salzburg after a long motor-tour through Switzerland, and I had the pleasure of showing him not only that wonderful town but also its glorious surroundings. In the car, which he drove himself—and he was a remarkably good driver—we were able to make many interesting expeditions and be back in town again by dinner-time. If only because of Mozart, who had always been his great love in music and always remained so, he was unfailingly delighted by this town.

We went to Ischl too in his motor-car, and I showed him this scene of my youthful experiences. We even drove up the Ahorngasse where these dear friends of mine gazed in sincere sympathy at the silent house where my mother was slowly and uncomplainingly dying, in seclusion from the world.

On these trips through the most beautiful parts of my native country we got to know each other much better than in the many hours that I had spent with him in London and at his house in the

country. As the result of a slight accident she had had, my wife had
to keep to the house during those summer days, and we sent many a
nice picture-postcard to her in Vienna. She had never borne the
great man who was our friend any grudge for having been prejudiced
against her before he met her. This had been expressed in the letter
of congratulation he wrote in answer to the announcement of my
marriage. 'Good God!' he wrote, 'what have you gone and done?
Heaven knows whom you've married and what in the world is going
to happen to you now! Why at least didn't you show me your wife
first and get my verdict, advice and blessing?' We often laughed over
this half joking, half very seriously meant attitude to the event that I
had always treated as exclusively a private matter, and only much
later, when we were visiting Shaw and his charming wife at their
house in the country, spending a few weeks there, did he himself
come back to the subject of his former mistrust, which had actually
been directed at me and not at my wife. The liking that both the
Shaws had for my better half was considerable, and he did not
hesitate to give his somewhat tardy approval to my choice.

Among my wife's women friends who liked to come to our house a
great deal was Bertha von Suttner. She felt a touching maternal
affection for her, although my wife, not understanding anything
about the political situation and having no notion of the possibilities
ahead, was rather remote from the things that Bertha von Suttner
had so much at heart. I remember one very queer conversation that
Frau von Suttner had with Georg Brandes at our house, in which it
became apparent that the pacifist Brandes was not so unconditionally in favour of *Die Waffen nieder!* as that great woman
whom a Viennese wit had nicknamed the 'Fury of Peace'.

Among my friends at that time there was also an Austrian writer
of high quality, one, however, who never became entirely popular in
Vienna. His work appeared at the same time as mine in the S.
Fischer Verlag. Moritz Heimann had a very high opinion of him
and once called his talent 'Homeric'. This was Robert Michel, a
novelist of rare gifts, who had begun as an officer in the army. The
heroes of his books usually came from the Balkans, from Bosnia or
Herzegovina, precisely the countries that soon were to play such a
great and decisive part in the destiny of the Austrian monarchy.

A strange coincidence at that time gave me a foretaste of what was
to come. The doctors treating me, one of whom was now Professor

Otto Marburg, insisted that a cure at Gastein might again give me some relief, even if it did not do so permanently. The next summer we therefore went to the beautiful, quiet Kaiserhof Hotel, not far from the spa on the Ache, with its roaring waterfall. Among the illustrious guests at this famous hotel at that time there was A. J. (later Lord) Balfour, a member of the English House of Commons, who was there seeking to recuperate from the exertions of party leadership. In Gastein, moreover, he succeeded in doing so. It was a cheerful sight to behold the tall, grey-haired statesman climbing the steepest paths. He was besieged by journalists, who had come from all over the place to interview him, but who were not successful, because he inexorably waved aside all attempts in this direction.

We were just looking over towards his table, where he was lunching in the company of the French Rothschild, when a hotel page handed me a telegram bigger and heavier than any I had received before or have ever received since. I opened it eagerly, and the first thing I saw was that it was from the editor of the *Neue Freie Presse*, Moritz Benedikt. It was his opinion that I, backed up by my English contacts, would surely succeed in getting an interview with Balfour. There then followed a list of about eight points, elaborated in great detail, specifying the questions I was to put to the great English politician. I was to send the answers in the form of a comprehensive feuilleton.

I was rather taken aback. How embarrassing to bother the statesman who was there for the sake of his health! Apart from that, I was convinced of my incapacity as a journalist.

That extremely shrewd man Mortiz Benedikt had, however, correctly foreseen that Balfour might receive me simply because I was not a journalist. The great Viennese editor had also impressed it upon me in his long telegram that I was not to go and say that the answers to my questions were meant for a newspaper; I was to put them as though I wanted to hear Balfour's views on certain topical questions for my own edification.

What could I do, if I did not want to forfeit for ever my entry to that respected Viennese newspaper to which I was a frequent contributor, but at least show goodwill and ask this unapproachable man for an interview? So I wrote to him, introducing myself in my letter as a friend of Bernard Shaw, H. G. Wells and St. John Ervine. To our great surprise the answer came very quickly; A. J. Balfour

asked me to call on him in the afternoon of the following day.
When he had shaken hands with me and offered me a seat, he said,
smiling: "I already knew who you were—as a matter of fact, from
friends of Shaw's who are also friends of mine, who happened, quite
by chance, to be talking about you shortly before I set out on this
visit to your country. That is also the reason why I am treating you
as an exception and have asked you to come so that I may answer, in
so far as lies in my power, the questions you want to put to me."
Now the most difficult step had actually been taken. I had learnt
the eight questions by heart, in a way I usually only learn a poem,
and so did not need to betray myself by reading them from a manuscript. Lord Balfour listened attentively and answered, to the best of
his knowledge and belief, the questions for whose answers Moritz
Benedikt was waiting with such interest. I hammered them into my
brain with tense concentration in order not to lose the slightest
detail, so that I might arrange them then in the article I was planning
to write.

So I sat for a very long time—over an hour, I think—with this
somewhat tired and yet somehow passionately energetic man, who
became almost irritable and impatient when I spoke of Austria-
Hungary's annexation of Bosnia and Herzegovina, as I had been
instructed to. In order that I might be quite sure of remembering
the answer to this most important of all the questions put to the
ex-Premier, I had left this one to the last.

After a short pause, following his detailed answer, which was not
very flattering to the Empire, he nodded pleasantly and I rose to say
good-bye and thank him. Lord Balfour had also stood up, and now
he came a step nearer to me, looked into my eyes and said:

"Everything I have said to you, the frankness with which I have
answered your questions, is meant to show you that I know how
freely I can speak to you. You are a gentleman, and I definitely
count on not even *one* word of my views being made public. It was
meant only for you."

I held out my hand as though to confirm his confidence in me, and
he pressed it in the same spirit. The great coldness that was like an
aura about this tall man, keeping even the most pushing of people at
some distance from him, had given way to an exceedingly friendly
smile, which was still hovering about his lips when he had seen me
out and shut the door after me.

SIEGFRIED TREBITSCH
AS A LIEUTENANT OF THE DRAGOONS IN 1899

ANTOINETTE TREBITSCH
IN 1910

FELIX SALTEN
IN 1912

GEORGES COURTELINE
IN 1918

ARTHUR SCHNITZLER
IN 1920

STEFAN ZWEIG
IN 1940

BERNARD SHAW
IN 1945

My dear Tina

Siegfried arrived here yesterday in high spirits, none the worse for his journey; and we talked for two hours. I was very glad to see him, though I still think the money the journey cost should have been spent on new clothes and a holiday for you. However, our talk was most useful to me, as I have never had time to attend seriously to my foreign affairs. Siegfried has clarified them for me.

He is coming again on Thursday next, and yet again for a farewell visit before he leaves for Paris.

His visit is an outrageous extravagance in money, but a very enjoyable incident for both of us, and a healthy change and holiday for him. I wish you had come with him.

G. B. S.

LETTER FROM BERNARD SHAW TO THE AUTHOR'S WIFE

What was I to do now? I had to refuse the request of the man whose wish I would so gladly have fulfilled, and report the incident quite truthfully. I instantly did so, in a very detailed express letter in which I naturally kept to the extreme limit my promise to Balfour that I would confide to anyone else nothing—really nothing at all—of the answers he had given me. I assumed that my action would result in a break between myself and the *Neue Freie Presse*, but to Moritz Benedikt's credit I must now mention the much briefer telegram that soon came in answer to my letter. In it this great journalist said approximately this—though I could not swear to the exact wording at this late date: 'You must of course keep strictly to the promise you have given and say nothing to me, any more than to anyone else, and that until time has settled the questions so burning today. From now on converse with this great and cultured man about music and the theatre.'

It was a load off my mind. Now I could continue my cure without further worries, and after this, whenever I met Lord Balfour on the shady paths in the woods, he always glanced in my direction and acknowledged my greeting in a particularly friendly way.

In the course of the years of which I have been giving an account here the last manœuvres were held in which I took part. In accordance with regulations, after I had completed my period of service in the army I was transferred to the Landwehr (territorial army) and called up as a Landwehr Uhlan officer at Innsbruck. Now there were no Imperial manœuvres, no duties as an adjutant, for me any more. My new duties were much quieter and more modest, and sometimes, indeed, I had to spend a few hours sitting in an office, dealing with papers. The military exercises on horseback did arouse a longing in me for times now past and gone, and for the first time in my life it seemed to me as though my youth were now definitely left behind and as though this call-up as a Landwehr officer were the confirmation of it.

In order to anticipate the question whether my friends and colleagues did not also do military service, sharing my short army career, I should like at this point to mention that many rich men's sons had been 'bought out', as it was called, by their fathers at the appropriate time. In return for the payment of a certain sum, which had to be paid before the son reached the age of liability for military service—I think the price was two thousand guilders—he could be exempt from military service for ever. The fact that much use was made of this custom shows more than anything else how at that period an anxious father, thinking only of his children's welfare, either did not believe in the possibility of a war or imagined that such a purchased exemption would really free his son from any liability to military service in the event of war. We, however, lived to see how in the last resort even the unfit had to join up, and that no consideration was given, of course, to men whose fathers had once bought them out. They were merely deprived of the pleasures and the toughening-up they would have had from a year as cadets. But those who had been bought out were really exempt from doing any military service in peace-time. There were, of course, always some among them who had been looking forward to their year's service as volunteers and were somewhat disconcerted to discover that only a short time after their birth they had been deprived of what they perhaps wrongly expected to be the pleasures of that great change in their lives. Furthermore, they could not become officers. I, for one, was always grateful to my father for simply never having thought of that possibility. Nor, incidentally, had Hugo von Hofmannsthal's father; for Hofmannsthal also served in the cavalry, was a very successful horseman, and, as it is clear his letters to his father, he had quite a passion for the cavalry, even though it was only during the time of his actual service.

I spent a very pleasant time in Innsbruck and from there went to the near-by mountain resort, Fulpmes, to meet Fischer, with whom I had already once had a meeting in the Tyrol, in the summer after the appearance of my first book, *Convalescence*. The Fischers had spent that summer in Gossensass, accompanied by their little son and an infant daughter still in her cradle. While this child, whom I often dandled on my knee, later became the wife of the orthopædist, Doctor G. Bermann, the extremely gifted young Gerhart Fischer, of whose future as a musician not only his parents had great hopes, at an early age fell a victim to fish-poisoning in Venice. His early death, which his parents never really got over, altered many plans that Fischer had bound up with his promising son.

Later it was to be a bitter consolation to the severely shaken parents that this infinitely sensitive and easily wounded young man, a firm believer in humanity's noblest instincts, had been spared the tormenting and frightful experiences that he would not have escaped in his native country. His father lived to see the grim beginnings of a dreadful era, though his faculties were already impaired and had the good fortune soon to shut his eyes for ever. He remains linked for all time with the intellectual rise of the gifted literary generation in Germany at the beginning of the century, the pick of that generation being Gerhart Hauptmann, Thomas Mann, Hermann Hesse, Hugo von Hofmannsthal, Arthur Schnitzler and Jakob Wassermann.

One who died before Fischer was his faithful right-hand man in the discovery of many of his authors, Moritz Heimann, who had for years suffered from a disease of the kidney and heroically bore the grave sufferings to which his fate had doomed him. To his last breath he remained faithful to his ideas and stood up for what seemed to him great, beautiful, and right. But this is already anticipating; that time still lay far ahead, whereas in the days with which these pages are concerned those noble men were still alive and in the heartening vigour of creative activity.

Among the very finely-sifted and select talents to be found in the Fischer Verlag was that of an extremely competent employee by the name of Paul Eipper. He worked on the 'production' side, and the frequent expressions of satisfaction of which Fischer was not sparing with regard to his work long kept him tied to his job, although to me, who was already on very good terms with him at that time, he had long ago confided that he could not remain in that comfortable job for ever; he had another aim in life, since he had sworn allegiance to the animal world and knew more about animal psychology than other people did. He would, he said, not have the strength to go on suppressing his knowledge much longer and serving other writers instead of being one himself.

Paul Eipper did not overrate himself. When with a blessing from Fischer, to whom he had shown his first works, he finally left the firm, he soon followed that step with his first book *Tiere sehen dich an* (*There are Animals Looking at You*). It is today obvious to everyone that Paul Eipper had a vocation and that it would have been a crime against himself and his art if he had withheld his gifts from the world.

I still remember my last visit to Eipper's office at S. Fischer's in Berlin, when he said to me: "Well, now the step is taken. The next time you come, someone else will be sitting here, looking after your new book with the same interest as I have done. I'm beginning a new life now." I hailed this hour with great pleasure: it reminded me of a similar fateful hour in my own life.

Meanwhile Shaw's plays continued to be produced in Berlin. Productions that kept me there for some time were *Major Barbara* and *Fanny's First Play*, which I mention together because these two entirely different works both had a particularly great success. The first Barbara, if I am not mistaken, was Lucie Höflich, while Klöpfer was a very convincing Undershaft, dominating the stage. *Fanny's First Play*, the comedy of comedies in all Shaw's work, which he wrote expressly for the purpose of 'making money', as he liked to assert, was a great success in the production by Viktor Barnowsky, who gave that delightful actor Alfred Abel the part of the footman-duke, thereby assuring both Abel and himself of a quite outstanding success. Alfred Abel was one of the most remarkable and most reserved of German actors, but when he let himself go he could carry the theatre with him.

Together with Bernard Shaw, his fellow-countryman Oscar Wilde was having a great success in Berlin; but this was of an entirely different kind and more related to the theatrical experiences that the French dramatists were providing for the European public, so spoilt in matters of literary fare.

About this time, however, a foreign genius could not completely gain a hold on German emotions and the German mind. The German emotional world was too much under the spell of the great German dramatist Gerhart Hauptmann. His success was of an extent and a scope with which that of no modern best-seller can compare. For the theatre gets its effect both in breadth and in depth, and it sets an author who has achieved hitherto unheard-of successes in such a dazzling light that in comparison many considerable achievements in the realm of poetry and the novel are thrust into deep shadow. There is, furthermore, the additional factor that every novel, however great it is, must wait until it is discussed by the respected critics whose views count for so much with the public, while the voice of criticism is raised instantly, almost simultaneously, in the case of a play that has been produced on the stage. When an author is hailed unanimously and in such a way as Gerhart Hauptmann used to be, after every first night, until well into his old age, then he naturally becomes part and parcel of his contemporaries' picture of things.

Those important German literary critics, with Otto Brahm, Paul Schlenther, and Alfred Kerr at the head of those who wielded critical power by conviction, had lifted Gerhart Hauptmann as it were shoulder-high and, having adopted a consistent critical attitude, rejected almost everything that was not akin to the spirit to which they paid homage.

A Gerhart Hauptmann first night was a great event in Berlin, and I was among those who liked to arrange their visits in such a way as to be able to attend these performances. S. Fischer was Hauptmann's publisher, and every one of this writer's new works was published by Fischer on the same day as the play was first performed. Hauptmann was often to be met in Fischer's house, and it was there that I met that great writer. From the very beginning I enjoyed his benevolent interest in my work.

As a rule the path of a new play by Hauptmann was mapped out in advance. It began with a reading by the author, who was an impressive reciter, in the apartment of his director, Otto Brahm, where Fischer, Julius Elias, Hauptmann's brother-in-law Moritz Heimann, and sometimes Schlenther and Kerr, were also present. Afterwards the initiated knew what to expect, and usually the date of the first performance was fixed on that very evening.

When successes attain such a height, such an extent and such a far-reaching influence, an opposition forms almost automatically, keeping pace with the congregation of the faithful. This opposition tried to set up a counter-weight in Hermann Sudermann, and it is very characteristic and instructive to be able to note, after so many years, that the outward success of a work by Hermann Sudermann, to whom the Vienna Burgtheater was much more ready to open its doors, sometimes was no smaller than that of Gerhart Hauptmann. But Sudermann's successes could never shake Hauptmann's position or compete with his special quality as a writer, which was so obvious, so undeniably distinct, and so different from that of anyone else. For Sudermann, after all, was a brilliant playwright, a master of stage-craft, with all its pitfalls, and Hauptmann, by contrast, was a true poet, one to whom there was nothing of more moment than the representation of human suffering and human grief and the uncertainty of man's fate on earth, and an artist to whom the overcoming of technical difficulties was mere child's play. Hauptmann was as sovereign in his mastery of the dramatist's craft as Sudermann was in his best plays, but without building up his effects by that means and sacrificing the truthfulness of his characters for the sake of an effective curtain.

It was not only Brahm who paved the way for Hauptmann; Fischer also deserves great praise for what he did for Hauptmann's work and reputation. Fischer's idea of making Hauptmann's name known to the broad masses of the German people by means of an early, cheap collected edition of his most important and most successful plays was entirely successful. A father could hardly tend his child with more care and love and devotion than Fischer expended on each new work by Hauptmann, to whom he felt himself personally, too, more attracted than to most of those of his authors with whom he was on terms of friendship.

To my delight that old friend of my youth, Rainer Maria Rilke, constantly turned up at Fischer's house, without being one of the Fischer Verlag's authors. Fischer had unenviously left him to the Insel Verlag, to which it was not even artistic considerations that had drawn Rilke. Rilke had a great veneration for Hauptmann, and his naturalistic drama, *Das tägliche Brot* (*Our Daily Bread*), would perhaps never have been written without the unconscious influence that *Die Weber* (*The Weavers*) had exerted on him as on others.

I had the pleasure of making Gerhart Hauptmann's acquaintance in the company of Moritz Heimann and Gabriele Reuter in the Meineckestrasse, where Fischer lived before he moved to his villa in the Grunewald. It was only there, in those large and splendid rooms, that it was possible for him to entertain large numbers of guests. To this tastefully furnished villa Fischer used to invite his authors, young and old, and those who worked with him. Chief among them was always Gerhart Hauptmann, whose home was in Schreiberhau, but who liked to spend a lot of time in Berlin, both for professional and for temperamental reasons.

Another person who joined the steadily widening circle round Fischer was young Walter Rathenau. He first came with a very original work, *Zur Kritik der Zeit* (*Towards a Critical View of the Era*), which Fischer referred to as extremely promising, though he added with a smile: "But not in a literary respect." I believe he regarded young Rathenau as a follower of Werner Sombart and

Simmel, who were the *Neue Rundschau* specialists in sociology and economics; it was only later that Professor S. Saenger combined both these complex functions in himself, in his capacity as editor.

Gerhart Hauptmann at once took a great liking to Walter Rathenau, and the two of them soon struck up a lasting friendship. Rathenau's murder, many years later, made the most frightful and profound impression on his friend the writer, who expressed his horror of Rathenau's enemies in words of fury and despair. Rathenau had also once visited Shaw in London, and Shaw, who was delighted with him, said to me: "He's the most charming and cultured person I've ever met. He knows simply everything!"

Whenever the Hauptmanns were in Vienna, which happened more and more frequently—and he always travelled in the company of his fascinating wife, Grete, who was a virtuoso on the violin, but above all an artist, all sympathy down to her very finger-tips—we always had the pleasure of seeing them at our house. My wife, a Viennese by birth and not without local pride, then always made a point of having Viennese writers to meet him, either those whom he already knew from the circle round S. Fischer or those of whom he at least knew enough to take an interest in them.

The Hauptmanns were at that time also very close friends of the Werfels. The friendship had originated at the time when Hauptmann had become enthusiastic about *Das Lied von der Erde* (*The Song of the Earth*), and indeed all the work of Gustav Mahler, Alma Werfel's first husband, since when he had been on very cordial terms with Frau Alma. Hauptmann was also among the first admirers of her second husband, Franz Werfel. "There are great writers in Austria, and not a few of them!" he once exclaimed.

Richard Dehmel was another who belonged to Hauptmann's circle. Richard Dehmel was one whom the term 'bard' suited unusually well. Anyone who looked so striking was indeed under an obligation to be a great lyrical poet and to have the voice of a bell. This all applied to Richard Dehmel, and there was no disappointment. He had a way of disappearing as suddenly as he had come, and when one enquired after him one almost always heard that he had retired, grumbling and growling, to Blankenese, near Hamburg. This growling mood, gathering for reasons unknown, would then always discharge its fury in the thunder and lightning of his wonderful poetry.

Dehmel used to contribute poems to Fischer's *Neue Rundschau*, and his ballad 'Zwei Menschen' ('Two People') appeared in those immortal pages in those days. He was also among Fischer's frequent guests, and in spite of his seemingly gruff aloofness, his lingering on the poetic mountain-tops, he was a sociable person and was often to be found at Frau Hedwig Fischer's fascinating dinner-parties.

Hauptmann liked to make appointments with his friends to meet them at all sorts of places. Especially in later years, he used to spend the winter and the early spring at Rapallo, on the Italian Riviera, where his publisher and his admirers very often willingly followed him. Hauptmann not only found it easier to work in the south, but was also compelled, because of his delicate chest, to flee from the Nordic winter; indeed, until late in his manhood he had to struggle with a very frail and sensitive physical constitution. We all knew his way, which, after a late autumn in Berlin, used to take him to Rapallo for the winter, and then in the spring to the Ticino, and, long though the journey was, he would then often go to Baden-Baden for some weeks.

We once followed him there, and with this meeting is linked a memorable little incident that is worth recounting because it throws a characteristic light on the great unselfish benevolence that Hauptmann could show when he felt the need to express his liking for someone in practical form.

At the table around which we used to sit almost every evening in Baden-Baden there was always a friend of Hauptmann's youth, Professor Hermann G. Fiedler, Professor of German Language and Literature in the University of Oxford. Suddenly, after a pause in the conversation, Hauptmann turned to this very amiable man of learning, pointed to me, and said more or less the following: "Look, this man, with whom, as I have observed, you enjoy chatting, is more deserving than almost anyone else of receiving an honorary degree from Oxford. After all, he discovered Bernard Shaw, whom you all so long refused to acknowledge, for Central Europe. That is a merit, not only from the German point of view."

Professor Fiedler was of German descent, but had been British for many years and could therefore doubtless be included among those to whom Hauptmann referred. He at once eagerly agreed with Hauptmann's suggestion and said: "Yes, indeed you're right! As soon as I get home I'll put his name forward, and I hope I'll soon have some good news for you and for him."

Hauptmann was very pleased not to encounter any objections, but added, laughing: "You English can't say that gratitude is really one of your weaknesses, and perhaps you dislike Shaw all the more since you've been forced to acknowledge him."

Fiedler had meantime quietly noted down some particulars about me and now answered in his jolly way: "Well, well, we'll see if you're right in this case!"

I had already forgotten this little incident, being on my guard against reckoning with such a distinction, although it would have been the only one that would have really pleased me. But some months later I received from Professor Fiedler a very friendly letter in which he informed me, with unaffected annoyance, that I had been unlucky: an Oxford honorary degree had to be approved unanimously by twelve votes, and after eleven votes had been cast in my favour, the twelfth had been cast against me.

The reason for this seems to me interesting enough to deserve mention. The statement made by the twelfth member of this university body, a statement that Professor Fiedler quoted more or less verbatim, went approximately as follows:

"We are gathered together here in order to confer an honorary doctorate upon a Viennese writer for an achievement that in my view is far from deserving of our approval. He has made one of this island's playwrights famous beyond the frontiers of his native country, a playwright who has positively made it his life's work to expose and ridicule our manners and customs, our way of living, our way of thinking, in short, to ridicule and expose us English and all we stand for, at every opportunity. Your candidate," he said, turning to Fiedler, "has therefore only done us harm, even if that was certainly not his intention, and has done nothing for which we, as Englishmen, as Britons, can be under any obligation to him. If it had not been for what he has done, Bernard Shaw's attitude to his native country would perhaps have remained unknown much longer. It is therefore with all my heart that I say—no!"

In this letter, of which Gerhart Hauptmann received a copy, Professor Fiedler showed quite clearly how deeply this refusal had annoyed him and how much pleasure it would have given him if he had been able to inform us of his success and the acceptance of his proposal which nevertheless had been agreed to by eleven of his colleagues.

Gerhart Hauptmann, the son of a Silesian hotel-keeper, for all his unassuming manner and probably as a result of his unusual appearance, had something kingly about him, something that was not out of keeping with his resemblance to Goethe. I always had the feeling, wherever he might summon his adepts, whenever he settled down anywhere, that he was holding court. And of his castle, Agnetendorf, in the Giant Mountains, it might truly be said that it was as though built for a court to be held there. It had the atmosphere of some great lord's residence, even though it was a lord of the intellect and of achievement. Because of the interest I took in Hauptmann's native countryside, I took a journey into the Giant Mountains once in the early autumn, and I was greatly astonished by the beauty of all the castles and 'Bauden'. The goal of my journey was Agnetendorf, in response to an invitation of long standing.

In the shade of the park, which surrounded this palatial literary dwelling, I was many years later to have the pleasure, too, of reading aloud to Gerhart Hauptmann and his wife, at their urgent request, my story *Die Assistentin* (*The Female Assistant*), which I had just completed. I am glad to be able to say that I had a great success, which was followed by a long discussion of my work, in which Hauptmann once more proved to me what a creative listener he was and how he could see to the bottom of someone else's work, understanding its subtlest details and furthest implications. It was only natural that I should ask him to be allowed to dedicate this story to him, to which he agreed with cordial expressions of gratitude.

During my early stay in Berlin I had, so to speak incidentally, undergone a very grim metabolism cure under the supervision of an Italian doctor by the name of Buzzi. This man literally starved his patients, giving them, into the bargain—it made the impression almost of being deliberate sadism—appetisers such as pickled gherkins and herrings and, to round off such a stimulating meal, two apples. This diet prevailed on five days of the week. On the sixth day he insisted that one should eat a large and very good meal, if possible at the house of friends. He then made his patients give him a very exact description of the effect of this sudden change in their mode of life. From this he drew his conclusions—and so did his victims, who only discovered how painful hunger was and that to satisfy it with delicious food was of course a great pleasure.

I used regularly to celebrate this solemn day of eating at the home of my friends Julie and Julius Elias. To watch me eating was 'as good as a play' for my friends, and they would also invite other acquaintances we had in common, who would come and admire my appetite as much as they admired the audacity of Dr. Buzzi, who did not even feel called upon to provide his patients with such a meal himself and show them that he could offer other things apart from stimulating starvation fare. When I then returned home, after weeks that had been tormenting but, I must confess, free of migraines, my family was horrified at my appearance—my clothes were dropping off me—and the family doctor, who was at once called in, declared that if I continued with such a diet I would soon have no pains at all. The antidote that I now received was quite to my taste: it was plenty of strengthening food. When I had got back about six of the ten kilos I had lost, I had a visitation from my first migraine after this interval, and it seemed to me I could hear the far-off voice of Dr. Buzzi, with his Italian accent, asking me in mocking tones: "Well, which do you like better? Hunger or migraine?"

I could not resume this cure, if only because Dr. Buzzi, having married a German Countess Schwerin, had suddenly left Germany, for reasons I cannot now recall, and returned to his native Sicily. It is said that he later committed suicide there. However, I then several times went, accompanied by my wife, to Dr. Dapper's sanatorium in Kissingen, where the cure and the treatment, aided by the medicinal waters of the spa, did always give me great relief.

As a patient I was as long-suffering as I was obedient, having an unshakable trust, which was ever and again disappointed, in those who happened to be treating me at the time. There was only one order that I could not obey, and that was to do no work at all. Even if I did renounce all creative activity during the weeks when I was taking a cure, I simply could not neglect the correcting of proofs of my own books and above all of new plays of Shaw's, without running the risk of breaking a contract.

At this time I was engaged in translating the comedies *Misalliance* and *Getting Married* into German, as well as that drama, so moving in parts, *John Bull's Other Island*. This play about Shaw's native country, which was perhaps what first drew the attention of German audiences to Ireland, of which so little was known at that time, met with comparatively little interest in German-speaking territory, in spite of the promising first night.

Misalliance, on the other hand, had a happier fate, though much later. This comedy, the hero of which is the manufacturer of under-clothing, Tarleton, in which rôle Otto Walburg was unsurpassable, was very successful both in Vienna and in Berlin. The central figure of the Berlin production was Marlene Dietrich, whom the director, Robert Klein, had brought from Vienna, where she had been acting a small but very impressive part in the play *Broadway*. She was fascinating and compelling as Hypatia, Tarleton's daughter, and it was as such that she was discovered by the film producer, Josef von Sternberg, who was always in search of new talent. So it might be claimed that Shaw was partly answerable for the glittering career and dazzling success of one of the most fascinating of actresses, although doubtless nothing could long have delayed the rise of one of such talent and such charming personality.

Munich had long been one of my favourite cities, which was accounted for not least by the circumstance that Thomas Mann, whom I had got to know at Fischer's house, was at home there.

My acquaintance with that great writer followed a very remarkable course. Fischer and Heimann had made me very curious about *Buddenbrooks*, so that I did not want to read it at odd moments, like many another book that I took up after I had finished my day's work. I laid it aside and waited for the right moment.

When the urgent work on which I was engaged had been finished, I dedicated myself with double eagerness to this book, which had been so much lauded from the time of its first publication, and I remember having written to Moritz Heimann and having said to S. Fischer that even the expressions they had used in talking to me of this novel had not been enthusiastic enough; in my opinion it scarcely had its equal anywhere in German literature. Heimann at once replied on a post-card: 'You may be right. In another fifty years we'll know.' Fischer made a similar reply, immediately adding that he was enchanted with *Tonio Kröger*, as indeed I was myself. Shortly afterwards I read a review of *Buddenbrooks* by Rilke, which confirmed me in my opinion and pleased me even more for Rilke's sake than for Thomas Mann's.

In his beautiful house in the Poschingerstrasse in Munich in the family circle, with his delightful wife and charming children, I did not

quite dare to talk to Mann himself about his wonderful stories; but I
had the feeling that he knew exactly how I stood towards him and his
works, and so it has remained to the present day. I am silent, and he
knows.

We had the pleasure of repeatedly seeing the Manns at our house,
and I think he was even more frequently in Vienna than I was in
Munich. At that time he had a special fondness for Vienna, in
particular for Arthur Schnitzler. Hugo von Hofmannsthal was
another who very greatly interested him. I recall something Thomas
Mann said at that period, one day at our house. He said: "You
Viennese know more about death than other people. That knowledge of the final anguish hovers over all your writing, never letting it
slide all the way down into ordinariness."

Here I should like to make room for a poem that I dedicated to this
writer in celebration of his sixtieth birthday:

TO THOMAS MANN ON HIS SIXTIETH BIRTHDAY

You are the youngest, are the best of all
who, full of wonder, suffer such a birthday;
and if today we gratefully approach
to feast upon the plenitude of grace

that carried you so greatly, far, and high,
—that we presume to celebrate you now
and, with glad hearts, we dare proclaim to this our age
what you have long before this heard ring out from a
        thousand liars

—forgive us, for we love you, we who read you,
we who do ourselves this honour in your person on this day.
Remain for all what you have always been for all,
a writer giving form to what he knows, that he may teach.

We thank you for the works that you have given,
that with your grand, enormous sweep you brought into
        our day.
And may our greeting lend your hand new strength
in its great battle for a better world.

If today I have a specially clear memory of one visit to Thomas Mann in Munich—although of course I have forgotten none of those we had the privilege of enjoying at our house in Hietzing—the reason is partly that it was Mann's house where I met Bruno Frank and his charming wife, and likewise the writer Hans Reisiger, of whom Thomas Mann was especially fond.

I have known no writer since Thomas Mann whose way leads from work to work with such wonderful clarity and steadiness, reaching ever more luminous heights. He is the only writer in whose case I can recall no literary reverses, and I have often thought that the infinite care and devotion of his wife, Katja, was not quite without responsibility for this. As the daughter of the celebrated mathematician, Pringsheim, she evidently had the gift of calculating precisely how much of life's eventfulness she could let invade her husband's privacy and what, in the interest of his work, she should keep from him and deal with for him. The little things that we have to attend to and which nag at us and nibble away our time are, after all, often what prevents us from doing the great things.

The world events that had such a revolutionary effect on all our lives, destroying our peace of mind and the tranquillity we needed for work, did not leave Thomas Mann quite unscathed either. But perhaps he reacted to them creatively because he could not have dealt with them in any other way and because only by irradiating them and giving them artistic form could he master them to such an extent as to be able to keep them at the necessary distance from him on his path through life.

Hofmannsthal once said: "It is a poet's business to create forms, in fact to create poetry, and not to meddle in politics." Of course he would not have made that statement if he had had any premonition that politics in our time would cast a terrible net in which we would all flap like panic-stricken fish and that each of us would be forced to make some effort to return to something like his own element. What do we do when we are attached to some work, when we see its success as our highest aim in life? We strip ourselves of everything that hinders us from fulfilling that sublime task, and according to our temperament, talent, ability, and capacity for understanding, each of us tries, in a different way, to liberate himself from the terrible prison of everyday ordinariness to which we are all condemned.

When I was granted the pleasure of being with Thomas Mann

when he celebrated his seventy-fifth birthday, this became so clear to me, in the profound insight of retrospection, that I believe I am not mistaken. Thomas Mann's primary need to express himself with regard to the problems of the time was very slight; the secondary one, however, had become a vital necessity. And as the hero, the dragon-slayer that he always was, he had to take up the fight against misunderstandings and people, the elimination of which, by means of illumination, could be accomplished by no one more easily than by this mighty master of language.

In many a summer it was the same with me as with many another Viennese: we could not imagine slipping into autumn without having been to Salzburg—though that was before the time of the Festival—and to Munich. For me that was always as it were the crown of the recuperation that I sought, and usually found too, in the mountains . . or at the seaside. In Munich, where I would gladly have made longer stay, in the year of which I am here writing, because Rainer Maria Rilke, who was there, had introduced me to Franz Blei and those writers, like Max Halbe and Frank Wedekind, who frequented the Torggelstube, I received news that my mother was gravely ill, and I hastened home.

My wife at once gave me a clear picture of the situation, telling me that the danger was actually over. With a lighter heart, I went to see that lonely woman who had suffered in such an exemplary fashion all her life long. I found her now free of fever after the serious attack of bronchitis she had just got over, and sunk in thought, though very pleased to see me again, as was apparent in the smile that for a long time hovered on her face. She refused to talk about her illness, but wanted to hear more about me, my work, my travels and the people I had met, than she usually did; and in order to cheer her up and distract her, and also to prevent her from talking, I talked to her at great length, telling her about all that I had been doing.

When I took her hands, to say good-bye, I was struck by a remarkable trembling of her arms and fingers, which made me uneasy. I at once went to her doctor, a very well-known specialist. He told me that he did not think he ought to conceal from me how things really stood with the poor old woman. The acutely dangerous stage of her illness had been comparatively easy to treat, because her heart was quite strong, but another trouble had set in, which was called paralysis agitans or Parkinson's disease. We must be prepared, he said, to see her suffering from this malady in future.

I was very upset, and my wife told me that her own observations had for a long time prepared her to hear that it was this grave and almost incurable disease. My brothers, with the wives of such of them as were married, increased their visits from now on and were always in search of new doctors and new remedies, in the hope of finding a cure for this grave nervous ailment. However, all we could achieve was some alleviation of her condition, slowing up the process of nervous decay. Fortunately for our mother the progress of the disease was accompanied by increasing apathy. The poor woman was now practically without any desires of any kind, and although she was surrounded by servants who had been with her for many years and were very much attached to her, she scarcely showed any more interest in life. Her only wish, to which she constantly returned, was to go to Ischl in the hot season, for there her slowly fading memories still shone most brightly for her.

In Vienna itself everything was in full swing, as ever. But in spite of everything there was a noticeable tension in the atmosphere, something the Germans were later to refer to so often as 'dicke Luft'. Something was brewing in the darkness over the pitch-black banks of the never-blue Danube.

The never entirely settled struggles within the Empire, which had produced the expressions 'dualism', 'dynastic obligation', 'landowners loyal to the Constitution', had once again set Parliament in a roar, and now more than ever, and from all sides, one heard those disturbing words: "It can't go on like this!"

My lawyer had used them; so had our family doctor; so had the waiter who brought us our rolls in our Stammcafé; and, if I am not mistaken, so had Baron Burian, at that time Ministerpräsident, evidently expressing the mood he was in after receiving the telegrams sent by our Ambassador in Belgrade, Count Forgacz.

At this period Count Berchtold was the Austrian Foreign Minister, and the newspapers asserted that his constant visits to Budapest, to see the Hungarian Premier, Count Tisza, must indicate something alarming.

In our circles, both artistic and social, we were very disturbed by these ceaseless repetitions of the words "It can't go on like this". There was nothing we longed for more than that it should go on as it had been going, and that we might be able to accomplish our work in peace and quiet. But we had already been considerably agitated by the affair of Colonel Redl. A highly-gifted, seemingly unimpeachable, homosexual officer of such high rank had sold the Austrian strategic plans for use in the event of war with Russia to the Russian War Ministry. It was the expression 'strategic plans' that first made it clear to most Viennese that the perpetual peace in which they believed might turn out to be anything but perpetual. The bullet with which the traitor took his own life was the first one fired, ripping open the web of belief in our golden age.

In those days the name of Conrad von Hötzendorf was often to be heard. For most people it indicated not security but something like a menace, for the initiated knew that this brilliantly gifted patriot had been preaching preventive war against Italy, and had been doing so with the persistence of a Cato. For the first time now people talked of the possibility of war's breaking out, and there was a terrifying increase in the use of the expression "It can't go on like this".

Meanwhile relations between the aged Emperor Franz Joseph and the heir to the Throne had worsened alarmingly. It was known that in practically all matters relating to the Monarchy the heir to the Throne would have done the opposite of what official policy, under the Emperor's direction, thought right. It was hoped 'in high places' to clear the air in Vienna and give heated passions time to cool off by sending the Archduke Franz Ferdinand on a tour of inspection in Bosnia and Herzegovina, the province annexed under Aerenthal.

"Let's carry on as usual, we can't do anything about it, anyway," I had said to my wife, and she continued to keep house and cultivate her garden, which had been a wonderful show during the beautiful spring that had just passed.

I remember that Bertha von Suttner visited us once again toward the end of May and that my wife took leave of her in a particularly affectionate way, which she explained to me when the door had closed behind that noble old lady, saying: "The poor thing is mortally ill. However much she complains, fortunately she doesn't know how ill she is." Only a few weeks later Bertha von Suttner died of her grave illness.

The last memorable reception in our house, before the collapse of reason, was in honour of an old friend, August von Wassermann, who had just been made a Geheimrat (Privy Councillor) in recognition of his epoch-making discovery, known as the Wassermann

H

Reaction. We had specially invited, among others, the wife of that eminent painter, Viktor Krauss, who was in a nursing-home, slowly dying of the terrible disease that August von Wassermann was doing his best to combat. We succeeded in interesting the scientist in the case of this artist, who was at that time very popular, and he suggested to the painter's weeping wife that her husband should undergo Professor Wagner-Jauregg's new malaria treatment, promising that he himself would previously discuss the case with Wagner-Jauregg when he had confirmed the diagnosis by means of his 'reaction'.

Viktor Krauss had the good fortune to be completely cured. That great scientist, Wagner-Jauregg, was able to send him away restored to normal health, and Krauss is still alive and working today, in America.

Now, during this hot summer, so many rumours sprang up all over Vienna about trial mobilisations, large-scale preparations for manœuvres, and the like that it was best to pay little attention and keep one's mind on the problems of one's own life and work.

In the evenings of particularly hot days we used to motor out into the country and enjoy the coolness of Vienna's unique surroundings. And so came the fatal Sunday of the twenty-eighth of June, 1914. We had read the newspapers during the day, including the *Neue Freie Presse*, which gave a lengthy report of the archducal couple's reception in Bosnia. Everything seemed to be proceeding according to plan. The heat of the summer noonday lay heavy over our garden, and it was with renewed confidence that I went to the near-by swimming-pool to get relief for my headache, caused by the great heat, in the cool water of which I was so fond. After luncheon I attacked the as yet uncorrected proofs of Shaw's new play, which was to be produced in Vienna and likewise in Berlin in the autumn. The fact that it had not yet been read by the producers was now of no significance. That was the stage that we had reached at last.

About tea-time, then, we went for a drive in the Vienna Woods and walked along shady paths in the depths of the forest, listening to the chorus of bird-song, while the meadows beyond the trees exhaled the scent of many flowers. We intended to dine at that popular country inn, the Rote Stadl.

We had made a provisional appointment to meet Peter Altenberg there—provisional not because we were not sure of getting there, but because one could not arrange anything definitely with Peter

Altenberg. I once heard him say to someone: "Well, if it's to be a definite arrangement I won't be able to come."

When we had reached our destination and were just choosing a table in the open air, our chauffeur came running after us and, speechless with excitement, handed us the *Extraausgabe* (the 'late evening special'), which said: 'Assassination of Archduke Franz Ferdinand and his consort, the Duchess of Hohenberg. Shot at Sarajevo'.

We stood as though transfixed, and at first we were literally incapable of speaking. Then we saw Peter Altenberg coming towards us. Seeing from our faces that we had just read the news, he exclaimed: "We don't know yet that it's true. But if it is true, it won't have any great consequences. After all, it's not as though it had been the English heir to the Throne—that would have been quite a different matter—much worse." To this I retorted, as though to a challenge: "No, my dear fellow, this terrible crime, if it has really been committed—and I believe it has—means the doom of our world, the end of this era of peace!"

Turning to Altenberg, my wife said: "I'm afraid my husband is right. In any case, this event will have a far-reaching effect, and for us Viennese it is certainly a great shock."

Slowly we settled down at our table, and Peter Altenberg followed our example. Then we heard piano-music coming through the open door of the near-by restaurant. That was intolerable. Did the pianist not know what had happened? I hastened into the room and said: "For heaven's sake stop playing! Don't you know what has been announced in the special editions?" The young man, who had been absorbed in playing the piano, looked up and said: "Everyone's rushing about like mad. What's the matter?" I enlightened him. He turned pale and slammed the piano shut.

I went back to our table and told the others about the incident. Altenberg said: "One really doesn't know what to think."

In melancholy mood, our appetites quite gone, we ate the food that had been ordered, while the summer twilight sank peacefully over the scene as though nothing had happened. So far as eternal Nature was concerned nothing had happened, nothing could ever happen. Now we saw the other diners starting up with loud exclamations and hurrying to their motor-cars and carriages. After a while we did the same, for we were impatient to get more reliable news in town by buying the special editions of various newspapers. Peter Altenberg, however, wanted to stay where he was because he had appointments with other people.

During this time we were frequent visitors to the house of Frau Katharina Schratt, the Emperor's close friend, who had a great liking for my wife. She of course knew more than all the other people who thought themselves particularly well informed and who only passed on rumours, but she could maintain a discreet silence in a way that no one else could. Some days later we visited Frau Schratt, who lived only one street away from us, and heard from her and some well-informed visitors of hers of the whole horror of the tragedy that cast such great shadows ahead.

Shortly before the excursion I have just described we had reserved rooms in Ostend for the middle of July, and I remember that Frau Schratt, who was as kind as she was full of shrewd forethought, had said in warning when we told her about it: "Don't go so far away. In fact, it would be better not to go abroad at all until it is clear what the consequences of this calamity are going to be."

But my doctors, who did not take a very favourable view of my condition at that time, insisted that if I wanted to avoid much worse attacks of migraine I must leave Vienna, which was so hot, and go to the sea. Now, we had in any case reserved our rooms in Ostend, and, furthermore, arranged to meet Stefan Zweig there; we were particularly looking forward to this meeting, so that we did not want to change our plans now, and we began to prepare for the journey.

At the time of this terrible event Stefan Zweig was no longer in Vienna. He had gone to Belgium to visit his friends Verhaeren und Lemmonier, and then, before returning to Austria, intended to spend a few weeks resting in Ostend. He was looking forward to spending some time with me, discussing literary problems and important human affairs.

It was a glorious summer, and Ostend, whence I had so often set out for London, seemed to me more beautiful than ever before. Though there were high waves, the water of the sea was warm, for the ceaseless sunshine that was intolerable in town made the sea, with its healing influence, all the more pleasant for the sick and weary who sought recuperation on its shores.

We had been there about a week, without being very much disturbed by the ever-changing news in the papers, and were looking forward to seeing Stefan Zweig, when he telephoned to announce the fact that he had just arrived. This impassioned writer was remarkably well-informed on all spheres of life, and sometimes his feeling for things and states of affairs was unerring.

The managements of the big hotels were naturally very interested in making foreign visitors feel secure, and at the beginning of the catastrophe the Belgian newspapers and numerous posters on the walls tried to make one believe that a settlement of the dreadful crisis was possible by diplomatic means. Wherever one went, one heard people saying: *"Tout s'arrangera, tout s'arrangera."*

Stefan Zweig was of course very agitated about the terrible affair in Bosnia. At this period his play, *Das Haus am Meer* (*The House by the Sea*), had already been produced for the first time at the Burg-theater, and the success he had had on that stage, which had been his heart's desire, had done him good and given him inspiration. It was his intention to remain in Ostend about the same length of time as ourselves and, if all went well, to return to Vienna via Paris.

But one morning he came rushing into our hotel with the in-formation that he had booked himself a seat on the Ostend Express for the day after the next, and that he could hardly wait to get home. He implored us to do the same. He said he had had news from Brussels and Paris that made him fear the worst. Every day brought a new turn for the worse and now he was seriously afraid that a war was imminent, and, what was more, a world war, since England and Russia had already intervened in the futile negotiations that were going on. He positively pleaded with us to follow his example and, if possible, leave on the same train with him.

When he left us, without having convinced us, we did everything in our power to get reliable information; but it was our destiny to get only friendly and reassuring replies. The Rumanian Consul-General from Vienna, whose table was next to ours, assured us positively that he had the best of news from Bucharest.

I hurried off to the *wagon-lits* office and got reservations for us for a later date, about a week after the day on which Stefan Zweig had decided to leave. The clerk who took my booking, and whom I asked whether he was sure that the Ostend Express would definitely go on running, told me that there was not the slightest reason to expect anything else and that no one was thinking of leaving in a hurry.

With this reassuring news I went back to my wife, who had all the time been half-inclined to listen to Zweig's warnings. The information I had received reassured her, of course, and what settled the matter was that at table a brother of our friend August von Wassermann, who had just come from Brussels, where he was a banker, smilingly declared that an agreement with Serbia was to be expected at any moment. He himself, he told us, would not have come away on holiday, of course, if his own conviction had not been so pleasantly confirmed by information that he received in confidence.

On the afternoon of the next day Stefan Zweig came, in a state of still greater agitation, to say good-bye to us. He was profoundly upset by our refusing, in a grateful and friendly way, but quite resolutely, to follow his example that very instant.

He first said good-bye to my wife. Then he looked at me hard. I could not help thinking of the farewell scene between Oranien and Egmont when he exclaimed, with tears in his eyes: "You will regret it, my dear fellow, and I must go away without being able to do anything, because I did not manage to convince you that we are at the beginning of the end of the time that was our life."

Very touched, I assured him that I was greatly looking forward to our reunion and that we would at once get in touch with him on our return to Vienna and ask him to come and see us. Once again he said: "Well then, do come along! I'll give up my *wagon-lit* reservations to your both. I'll manage all right, being only one." Deeply moved, I shook his hand, and with the scarcely audible words *"Auf Wiedersehen!"* our disappointed friend left us, in good time— and very fortunately for him.

Only two days later I heard that the train on which he had left had been the last Ostend Express. The same clerk who was chiefly to blame for my refusal to accompany Stefan Zweig yelled at me when I went there again to pick up our tickets: "What do you take us for? In Liège there's fighting going on between us and the Germans, and you expect me to go on sitting here selling tickets to the foreigners who are to blame for everything? The office will be shut in two hours, and the last Ostend Express there's going to be for heaven knows how long went yesterday!"

I was stunned. It simply couldn't be true! Returning to the hotel, which was some distance away, I told my wife of the frightening things said by the clerk whom I had just left.

Then everything happened with a tremendous rush. Each item of news was followed by another that was even worse. It was as though as a result of Zweig's departure the whole panorama of the time had turned topsy-turvy, as though we were now caught in a trap the door of which our prudent friend had so long tried to hold open for us.

Naturally we now had only one thought: to get away, to start out home. And this indeed was what we finally succeeded in doing; but it was not without thoroughly and grimly paying for our mistake. It took us a fortnight to get from Ostend to Munich, where our motor-car was waiting for us, which we had had to put at the disposal of the Red Cross even from Ostend; and in the car we travelled on to Vienna. I do not feel justified in recounting the adventures and experiences of those strenuous two weeks, although we had to go through not only indescribable discomforts but real dangers—for what were they in comparison with the fates that had now befallen our fellow-countrymen, our friends and acquaintances? The bridge that had been blown up behind our train had, after all, yet carried us safely to the far side.

On the way, of course, we heard of the mobilisation of the Austrian Army as of the German, of the German invasion of Belgium, and of England's and Russia's declaration of war, so that when we entered our house we were shaken and profoundly distressed, although glad to be home again.

Declarations of war croaked all around us like evil ravens. Stefan Zweig, whom we immediately informed of our arrival and asked to come and see us, renounced the dismal satisfaction of telling us how right he had been. He only said: "How much I would give to have been mistaken in Ostend!" He was utterly desolate and threw himself with real fury into some work that was already under way, in order to keep his mind off things as much as possible.

My wife, who even on the journey had displayed unusual courage and confidence, which had often kept the little company with whom we were returning—and which included Professor Frankel, well-known for his cancer research—from frantic outbursts of emotion and anxiety, adjusted herself to the new state of affairs faster than I did.

The historic fact that now, after almost fifty years of peace, we were at war kept me sleepless for many nights, and I thought of the future in which I no longer believed. The gates of my youth had slammed behind me. I was now in the forty-fifth year of my life, my work seemed wasted, and the ways to my eminent friends abroad were blocked. All security was gone. The old era was dead.

III

THE END OF THE WORLD

AND so now we were at war, and people had to adjust themselves to it. Above all it has the new ideas and feelings to which people had to become accustomed, among them to the many anxieties about becoming involved sooner or later in some way oneself and that it might, after all, have 'gone on like that' and that actually none of the insoluble problems was any nearer a fortunate solution as a result of the new state of affairs.

Housewives began to hoard provisions; that is the way it always begins. And the younger generation, which had to put its strength at its country's service, anxiously studied the calendar and reckoned the date when the call-up to the armed forces would be inevitable, if the war was *not* over by Christmas, as at first most people had believed it would be.

I myself had time to reflect on my calling-up order, for I was no longer of an age to be liable for front-line service, if the regulations about military age-groups were to be believed. I was forty-five years of age and hence, in spite of my rank as an officer, I escaped all immediate danger. I was all the more interested in the cases of my younger friends and acquaintances from my army days.

One day I was shocked to read in the newspaper that the young writer, Oscar Maurus Fontana, had been killed on the Serbian front. Deeply grieved, I wrote a lengthy obituary notice for the Berlin *Vossische Zeitung*. And a short time later, when he was resurrected from the ranks of those reported missing or killed and came to my house, laughingly waving the *Vossische Zeitung*, our joy was great. From then dates our friendship, undimmed to the present day.

About this time the *Kriegsarchiv* (War Records Office) came into being under the direction of General von Höhn. This institution's function was to make the work of future historians easier by keeping a record of all the events of the war, describing every more important fight, to say nothing at all of the great battles, in a dignified and often thrilling manner. Those selected for this work were of course Austria's writers, and above all those who would otherwise, on account of their youth, have had to go to the front, but who, once they were called into the War Records Office and given a definite job to do, escaped the danger of being called up, at least temporarily. In this way the intelligentsia was to be saved. At the beginning the head of the literary department was Franz Karl Ginzkey. The liaison between literature and the army was represented by that man of subtle intellect, Colonel Veltzé, who carried out a censorship as skilful as it was mild, and who was responsible for the statements issued to the newspapers. Among the writers who were very soon gathered there were Hermann Bahr, Strobl, Erwin Reinalter, Alfred Polgar, Stefan Zweig and many others whose names I do not recall at the moment.

Rainer Maria Rilke, for whom the *Kriegsarchiv* would have had to have been invented if it had not already existed, after some détours at last arrived, in a rather peculiar way, at its offices. The poet, who had never had any military training, had suddenly been called up, evidently as a result of some administrative muddle—and, what was more, since he had never been in the army, he was called up as a ranker. It was his good fortune that he was ordered to report to the *Stiftskaserne* (Stift Barracks), in the upper storeys of which the Imperial and Royal War Records Office was housed—which would undoubtedly have applied for him with all speed if it had had the slightest notion that he was in any way liable to military service.

Now one morning there he stood in the barracks, a private soldier, without any idea of what to do, inwardly in despair. He would, however, certainly have got his bearings soon if there had not been an obstacle at first in the shape of a sergeant who, walking along the ranks with a list of the recruits' names in his hand, stopped in front of Rilke and barked at him:

"What's your name?" Pale and oppressed, the uniformed poet answered: "Rainer Maria Rilke." "What?" the sergeant shouted at him. "Who are you telling you're called Maria? Whoever heard of a man called Maria? People'd have to call you Mitzi for short! And that's what you look like, anyway." Rilke stammered in embarrassment: "Oh, I'm not the only one. Remember, after all, Karl Maria Weber, the composer of the *Free-Shooter*." "We don't go in for free-shooters here, we only shoot when we get orders. Take my advice and forget about that Maria of yours, Rainer Rilke." And with this the sergeant paced on.

The next morning—Rilke had spent the night sleepless on his palliasse—he was summoned by the harsh voice of his immediate superior who had been so displeased with his name and pruned it shorter: "Come on out of that, Mitzi! Rifle drill! Get a move on!" Bewildered and half stupefied, Rilke climbed down from his bunk and was being drilled, temporarily without a rifle, when the door to the men's quarters flew open and General von Höhn entered, accompanied by the Princess Thurm and Taxis. There was a deathly silence. "Is there a certain Rainer Maria Rilke here?" the General asked, walking up to the sergeant. Rilke had heard his name and seen the noble lady who took such an interest in his welfare. Ignorant as he was of discipline, he hastened to the side of his patroness and the General, who, stretching out his hand to him, exclaimed: "But what a mistake! How on earth do you come to be here? We need you in the Records Office more than I can tell you!"

So the military career of the poet Rainer Maria Rilke came to an inglorious end. The princess, who had evidently heard of the poet's 'delivery' to the Stift Barracks, had instantly hastened to the officer in charge of the *Kriegsarchiv*, in order that Rilke should not be exposed a minute longer to the kind of experiences just described. But the way had already been paved for this transfer by Franz Theodor Csokor and Major Binder, who had long ago taken steps intended to forestall the little scene described above. From this time on, Rilke performed valuable services in the *Kriegsarchiv* and, conscientious as he was, and being accustomed to clerkly occupations since his childhood, the work came easily to him. Many a readable report did he send out into the world, even though nobody dreamed what a lofty spirit had composed it.

We writers knew about the War Records Office, but the broad mass of the public was almost quite uninterested in this institution and only panted for news from the front.

Such news came soon enough. True, the Viennese, who cheered when they heard that the Austrian Army had taken Schabatz and imagined it already in Belgrade, pulled long faces when they read, as they soon did, of the furious courage with which the Serbs fought to defend the wrong that they had done the Empire. For the assassination of an exalted guest cannot be justified by pointing to unfavourable commercial agreements relating to the export of pigs, such as had been drawn up between Austria-Hungary and Serbia and had become a terrible apple of discord.

But what caused the Archduke Frederick, who was the Com-
mander-in-Chief of the Austro-Hungarian Army, much more
concern was the advance of the Russians into Galicia, those Crown
lands on the frontiers of Austria where in peace-time preparations
had been made in vain to repel the Russians whenever they should
come.

The Viennese, whose gay spirits were soon sunk in gloom, now
heard of the frightful losses that the Austrian Army had suffered at
Przemysl and, shortly afterwards, at Rawaruska. The battle of
Rawaruska can, in fact, be regarded as the turning-point in the
Empire's fate, for on the blood-soaked battle-fields around that place
the flower of the country's youth, which had so joyfully taken up
arms, soon lay beneath the ground. Many of my comrades of the
Seventh Dragoons were among them. Heroic gallantry, a reckless
risking of life and health, the tempestuous courage that these men
had by nature and by training, all this could not prevent the fate that
a greatly superior enemy inflicted on the Austrian troops, the
command of which was outstandingly good as often as it was very
bad indeed.

The war news that appeared in *Extraausgaben* and in the morning
newspapers was eagerly devoured, but it was to the German war
bulletins that the inhabitants of this sorely tried country owed most
of their optimism. It was not long before news came of the great
victory at Tannenberg. And how that propaganda department,
which for the most part remained anonymous, began its witches'
dance of high-flown language around Hindenburg, giving no rest
until that likeable general had become the German national hero!

From Austria there came a particularly striking piece of homage,
written by Franz Karl Ginzkey, which was an attempt to be sarcastic
about the fate of the Russians overrun at Tannenberg. This poem of
homage to Hindenburg was, however, very soon surpassed by the
verses of another poet, directed at another enemy—Ernst Lissauer's
'Hassgesang gegen England' ('Song of Hate against England').
Incidentally, it should be said to the honour of Viennese writers that,
apart from a few exceptions, they did not try to place their talent at
the service of the world war; particularly at the beginning, higher
authorities bore Austrian writers a severe grudge because they
thought it right to go on serving their country with their works

instead of by mocking enemies whom but few of them felt to be
enemies, for which reason they profoundly deplored the conflict that
had led to this confusion between the concepts 'friend' and 'foe'.

Many of us, after all, had our best friends abroad and could never
be got to see them as suddenly metamorphosed into damnable
enemies. In my own case, I speak from the heart. I was in great
anxiety about Georges Courteline and René Puaux, as well as my
childhood friends Edmond and Paul Gillet; and as for Shaw, his last
postcard, which reached me on the last day of peace, said: 'You and
I at war, and enemies? What nonsense!'

In our cellar we still had the crate that had contained Rodin's
bust of Shaw—his splendid gift to me—and since he was the only
foreign writer whose plays anyone still tried to perform, I could not
drop the habit of writing to him, the last time being, I believe,
through a member of the British Consulate, which was still in
existence. Then suddenly I received a summons to the Ministry of
Foreign Affairs, which I instantly obeyed, only to learn that I was
under strict orders to abandon all attempts at correspondence with
an 'enemy alien', whoever it might be, until the conclusion of
hostilities, if I did not want to expose myself to consequences quite as
unpleasant as anything I would be causing the recipient of my
letters.

Now, more than in those days of peace to which we looked back
so yearningly, there was a general desire to talk freely and exchange
with others all that was in one's mind. Sociability, with all its
consolations, increased, taking up many hours of one's time, until
those who were willing and keen on their work came to the conclusion that the best thing they could do would be to stick to their
last and put all their energies into their usual jobs, perhaps indeed
facing things more conscientiously than before, and producing the
best of which they were capable. For who could tell how much time
he would be granted for the perfecting of his essential being?

And then, besides, there was nothing that took one's mind off the
disagreeable events of the time as effectively as work did. The
theatres continued to function without a break; and, be it said to
their honour, only a few war plays altered the programmes, at least
at the great theatres.

In the city itself there were varying moods and outbursts of
emotion to be observed at all times. Every occasion for loud

rejoicing was made an opportunity for personal exaltation and, if one was among those who were in positions of responsibility, an opportunity also for whipping up the optimism of those who were very quickly losing it. The volatile Viennese temperament doubtless accounted for the fact that the population reacted to bad news or even rumours of catastrophe by becoming profoundly depressed, even despairing. The city was soon overflowing with the wounded, the sick, and invalids, who were either coming from the front on their way to hospital or were already out of it again. But when one saw the ladies of one's own circle got up as canteen and welfare workers at the railway station, zealously playing their Good Samaritan rôles, one was often overtaken by a peculiar sense of amusement and wondered what sort of event it would take to stop the people of certain circles from trying to impress others. At the same time, the government authorities and others concerned did all that was in their power to draw the widest possible middle-class circles into the service of the country, encouraging, even in fact publicly lauding, those all too eager ladies who got themselves so much into the lime-light.

As Bernard Shaw, in contradistinction to other foreign writers, had never said or written a single hostile word about the Central Powers, his most successful plays, such as *Candida* and *Pygmalion*, were allowed to remain in the repertoire of the theatres, until those who were now in a position to dictate succeeded in declaring him an 'enemy alien', even while acknowledging his silence.

The première of my play, *Gefährliche Jahre* (*Dangerous Years*), of which mention has already been made, took place toward the end of 1914. Its success was at any rate so great that Direktor Stolberg of the Munich Schauspielhaus, who was present, that very first evening took me aside behind the scenes and expressed his intention of producing the play in Munich. This next production in fact took place in 1915, and since I had not yet been called up, I was able to be present as a civilian. Because a young Viennese actress was taking the important main part, I went to the Bavarian capital beforehand, to the rehearsals. I think I ought to mention that the producer was the Swiss writer Doktor Bernhard Diebold. He was at that time the dramaturgist and producer at this theatre.

Bernhard Diebold, whose shrewd individuality and determination as a producer had struck me even at the first rehearsal, did not long remain in that position, but was appointed to the position of first critic on the *Frankfurter Zeitung*, where he remained for many years, even after the end of the war, doing an extremely successful job. He then returned to his native Switzerland, to Zurich, where he also held a high position as a critic. He wrote a very distinguished novel, *Das Reich ohne Mitte* (*The Empire Without a Centre*), in which he portrayed the Germany of his day in glaring colours. His sudden and all too early death was deeply lamented by all his colleagues.

About a year after the Munich production, my play *Dangerous Years*, which had been performed during the war, was also produced in Hamburg. This was at the Thalia Theater, which was at that time under the direction of the same Röbbeling who later became the director of the Vienna Burgtheater, in which position he remained up to Hitler's occupation of Austria.

It is not, of course, for the purpose of describing this play's glorious career—for it did not have anything of the kind—but again for the sake of speaking of a man, one who is today a respected writer in Zurich, that I should like to mention that the most successful production of *Dangerous Years* was that done by N. O. Scarpi (Fritz Bondy) at the Deutsche Landestheater in Prague. Scarpi excelled through the fact that he always knew a play he was producing down to its smallest detail and deepest implication, which meant that he was able to bring out effects that were not immediately obvious to others and to provide the audience with the guidance that it so often does not get, especially in modern plays. Furthermore, Martha Newes, a sister-in-law of Frank Wedekind, was admirable in the leading rôle.

Inwardly, however, I was by this time at a considerable remove from these 'Dangerous Times'. Apart from my journeys to Munich and Hamburg, which were the only trips I had taken abroad (for Prague was at that time still part of the Austrian Empire), except for a journey on duty of which I shall write in due course, I remained at my desk as much as possible, if only in order to make good use of the years in which no work for Bernard Shaw could deprive me of many hours of my time. I worked away at my verse-drama, *Emperor Diocletian*, the action of which takes place in Rome at the time of the persecution of the Christians. It kept me fully occupied for a long while. After I had finished the first two acts I laid it aside again for many years, and only completed it much later. As it was published by Kiepenheuer, I was able to give myself the pleasure of dedicating it to my friends S. Fischer and his wife.

The year 1915 also brought Italy's tragic decision to declare war on her Austrian ally, after which very few well-informed observers of the trend of Austria's destinies could still bring themselves to believe in a victory for the Empire.

After this catastrophe had occurred many of us who nearly jumped out of our skins with rage whenever we heard that frivolous expression 'preventive war' did begin to respect and admire the Cato-like doggedness of that great general, Conrad von Hötzendorf. He had over and over again declared that war against Italy was essential for the survival of the Empire, and he had kept on demanding it, with iron determination. Many people today believe that the fate of Europe would have been quite different if Hötzendorf's seemingly so cruel proposal had been accepted.

So the time passed swiftly, and toward the end of the summer, when I was at Gastein, I was informed that I would be called up in the autumn. My age-group was now being called up, not in order to be sent to the front, but in order to replace those who would be sent to the front from the Ministries and hospitals and other administrative positions.

I should have reported on April 5th, 1916, but shortly before that I fell ill, with a serious inflammation of the middle ear, which kept me in bed for weeks and delayed my taking up my duties. I had to undergo a perforation of the ear drum, which was carried out quite admirably by the celebrated Professor Heinrich Neumann. It was not until April 25th, twenty days late, that I took up my duties as orderly officer at a very fine hospital, the Meidling Convalescent Home for Disabled Soldiers.

Now, as an Oberleutnant on duty, once again, day in, day out, I wore the uniform I had worn in my youth. I was still a cavalry officer, but I never set eyes on a horse. The hospital was under the command of Colonel Zeller von Lukashort. I and two brother-officers of the same rank as myself shared out the work and duties assigned to us.

My job was rather monotonous. I did proper office work, apart from inspecting stores, and at first the days dragged somewhat, with just enough work to make them pass. All I remember of these first weeks is one episode, the central point of which was a man's death, but which nevertheless made us laugh against our will.

There was a non-commissioned officer on permanent night duty, of course in rotation with other N.C.O.s of the same rank, and it was my duty to send for him every morning and have him report whatever had happened in the night, so that I, in my turn, might report to my superior officer. Now, there was a notorious inmate of this hospital, a man with a slight wound, of whom it was generally said that he was one of the cleverest malingerers, being able to simulate all possible diseases in the most convincing way, in order to be excused work of any kind and to be able to go out as often as he liked.

And now there came a morning when, in reply to my question: "Anything happened?" the N.C.O. on duty answered: "Everything as usual, sir. Except that the malingerer died in the night." I passed on the report in the same form, feeling somewhat thoughtful at the fact the latter end of malingerers was no different from that of humanity in general and that they really did not need to simulate diseases, because they were sure to have one or the other anyway.

Our commanding officer, Colonel von Zeller, was an impassioned, though not a good, speaker, and he would deliver a farewell speech to each of the disabled men when he was discharged from hospital and went home, now resigned to his lot and in a slightly better condition than when he had come. In such cases the commandant always made a particular point of his affection for these disabled soldiers and would invite them to come and visit him on his estates in Herzogsdorf, near Linz, if they were ever in that part of Upper Austria.

I could never understand how anyone could make the same speech almost every day, and on some days more than once, always stressing his own patriotism and his own love of his native country, which was not diminished by any blow of fate.

The monotony of the weeks and the cheap and facile interpretation of the daily war news were gradually beginning to have a depressing influence on me when a little incident took place that bothered me greatly until it was completely explained.

The losses at the front were continually increasing, and whether the military authorities liked it or not, they were in fact compelled to resort to calling up older age-groups, and also those exempt from and those unfit for front-line service, in order to throw them in against the enemy. The Empire had no such inexhaustible reserves of manpower as Russia had, and the gaps in the trenches began to make themselves increasingly felt. There was nothing for it; a break had to be made with tradition, and the pledges that had been given, which in any case had not been unconditional, could not be kept.

Now all government offices, hospitals and institutions were combed for soldiers, N.C.O.s and officers whose physical condition, regardless of their age—which was, however, never that of really old men—made them capable of greater exertions than any they had had to make hitherto. One read and heard about a great many of one's acquaintances and former comrades-in-arms being all at once declared fit for front-line service and being sent into the field. Of course, selection boards had to be set up to carry out these measures. They were set up overnight, so to speak; they sprang up like mushrooms. The work of these new boards was as interesting as it was responsible and meritorious, and it was for the most part entrusted only to men of merit and rank. In charge of this campaign, for which one newspaper coined the slogan: 'All fit for the front-line belong in the front-line!', was General von Teisinger, who was very soon dreaded on account of his merciless severity. It was known far and wide that he could track down the hiding-places of those who had as yet saved their skins, as a hunter could track down the game, and pitilessly sent to the front all those whom his equally dreaded right-hand man, Chief Staff Medical Officer Pospischil, passed as 'fit for active service'.

'Some day the day will come', was the title of a song that was very popular at that time, and it was often hummed in our hospital, although we might be lucky enough to be overlooked or passed over. But things were to turn out differently.

One morning when I had got ready to make my early morning report, the bugle-signal resounded that heralded the arrival of a high-ranking military visitor. We hurried outside on parade, while our commandant, Colonel von Zeller, also hastened up to face whatever might be about to happen.

Hardly had we fallen in when the familiar bugle-note rang out. The gate of the courtyard flew open and His Excellency Feldmarschalleutnant von Teisinger crossed our threshold in his dazzling uniform, that of an Austrian general. Directly behind him appeared his adjutant, together with Chief Staff Medical Officer Pospischil. Now here it was. We were rather heavy of heart, and my two brother officers fell back a pace behind me as though they wished to give precedence to me as a cavalry officer.

General von Teisinger glanced about him with swift, searching gaze, then came up to me and said in an unexpectedly friendly voice: "Well, well, Lieutenant, and what are you doing here? You look the very picture of youthful health. You must be perfectly miserable surrounded by all these ailing people. You must be longing to get away into the fresh air of the battle-field and the interesting life that awaits you there."

I was speechless. I was only just capable of springing to attention and clicking my heels. The General now pointed to a near-by door and said: "Simply in order to comply with regulations, will you please follow the Chief Staff Medical officer in there and answer his questions?"

A moment later the doctor was telling me to take off my tunic. He then came up to me and began tapping and listening to my chest.

"Is there anything wrong with you?" he asked me. "Or are you as healthy as you look?"

I thereupon answered frankly and truthfully: "I am not ill, but from my childhood I have suffered from severe migraines and neuralgia."

At this moment he laid his ear against my chest and told me to draw a deep breath. Then he looked at me, shaking his head, and said: "Queer. You don't look a bit like that. I didn't expect that. And your nervous complaint, on top of it." He shrugged his shoulders.

But the General had already become impatient and came into the room in order to be told the result of this formal examination and to have his adjutant register my name and grade of fitness. The Chief Staff Medical Officer, however, turned to his superior officer and whispered something into his ear. Thereupon the General looked at me with an expression of extreme astonishment, while I, having put my tunic on again, was just about to button it up. And since now my commanding officer, the Colonel, had also joined the group, as he was expected to do, the General said to us both: "Well, it isn't necessarily fatal. At your age that can still be dealt with. But I wouldn't have thought it. No one would think it to look at you. Still, for the present you must take things easy and have things made easy for you."

I was so dumbfounded by the unexpected outcome of this examination that I could not think what to say. All I could take in was that my commandant was making a note, on a writing-pad in front of him, that the Chief Staff Medical Officer was dictating to him in a low voice. My two brother officers were then quickly examined also and passed as fit for front-line service, as I guessed from their pallor when they came out of the room in which I had been examined a few minutes earlier.

Once more the General, even more amiable now, turned to me and said: "Cheer up, Lieutenant. We shall meet again, and next time you'll come along with us." He then turned his back on all of us and, accompanied by his small suite, vanished from our gaze. All of them were swept away by the motor-cars that had been waiting for them, and our high-ranking visitor, somewhat disappointed, passed on to deliver new death sentences. . . .

But now my self-control was at an end. I rushed away from my brother officers, who were congratulating me, and up to our Colonel. Much more aghast than if I had been declared fit for front-line service, I asked: "For God's sake tell me what's the matter with me! Am I, without knowing it, doomed to die?"

Colonel von Zeller was very embarrassed. "It's official and confidential," he said. But when the two others had moved away, he beckoned to me, indicating that I should follow him into his office. When I was sitting opposite him, he said: "The matter is particularly awkward for me, my dear Lieutenant, as a friend and a frequent guest at your house and because I am anxious, above all, that you should not alarm your wife. I myself had exactly the same trouble years ago and even received Extreme Unction once, in the middle of the night—and look at me now, you can see for yourself how well I am! At your age all that can be dealt with. And of course we're all doomed to die, come to think of it—from the time when we're born."

"But for heaven's sake what's the matter with me?" I almost groaned.

"If you give me your word of honour that it remains between the two of us I'll show you what the Chief Staff Medical Officer wrote." And he showed me the form, which bore the words: 'Heart enlarged to an extreme degree. Total destruction of the central nervous system. Only fit for the very lightest of duties in the rear.'

I was almost stunned. It was as though the ground had been pulled away from under my feet. It was surely not possible to be in such a state of physical misery without at the same time being in agony. I quite literally could not speak. But I then gave my word of honour, as had been required of me, and took the fleshy hand held out to me.

"Well, that puts my mind at rest," Colonel von Zeller said. He rose and added more or less in his 'duty' voice: "Owing to your illness, Lieutenant, I exempt you from afternoon duty, and in the morning too you can come later than is demanded by regulations. And whenever you feel ill, you may ask your brother officers to relieve you of some of your duties."

How splendid all this might have been if only I had been well! But it was horrible to receive it as a favour done to a dying man. Once again my kindly superior officer tried to comfort and encourage me, in the most touching way, continually begging me not to say anything to my wife. "Look at me! I'm walking proof of how much alive people can be long after the doctors have given them up!" If this plump, almost stout man had had a fatty heart, who could wonder at it who, like us, had seen the huge platefuls of food he devoured at meal-times with the greatest of ease and at top speed? While I was thinking of that, this friendly man at once shook my hand and said: "Now go along home, Lieutenant. You've had enough excitement, you need a rest. Then," he added a little absent-mindedly, "everything may yet turn out all right."

Of course I kept my word when I got home, only telling my wife that to my surprise I had been declared unfit for front-line service by the notorious General von Teisinger and his equally dreaded aide, Chief Staff Medical Officer Pospischil, when I spoke of my nervous trouble. As a result of the excitement caused by this visit, with its malevolent purpose, I had also had palpitations, which had likewise made quite an impression on the doctor. I at once said to my wife: "But I must find out definitely what's the matter with me, for those two man-hunters must have considered it pretty serious or else they wouldn't have exempted me."

I also told her about how nice our commanding officer had been, giving me the afternoons off, as a result of which I should again be able to devote myself to my work much more than had been possible recently.

"Yes," my wife said, "you must certainly go and see a leading specialist." And so on that point we were in agreement. But I wanted to go only to a man who did not know who I was, who did not know me personally, and that was not so easy, all the more since I could hardly wait to hear what such a man would say and then to adjust my life accordingly.

I was on terms of personal friendship with the best-known specialists. It was difficult to find anyone whom I could visit in his consulting-room and ask for a diagnosis just like anyone else.

Leafing through the telephone directory, I came across the name, hitherto unknown to me, of Professor Josef Wiesel, who was a heart specialist. That was the man for me. We had never met face to face, as was the case with so many of his colleagues with whom my wife and I were on social terms.

The next day I put on civilian clothes and at the appointed time for consultations drove to the Piaristengasse, whence it was only a few steps to the house where Professor Josef Wiesel had his consulting-room. I had to cool my heels in the waiting-room for about an hour, but then the door opened and Professor Wiesel received me personally and invited me to sit down. I very quickly told him why I had come to him. I asked him to examine me and above all to be quite frank with me about the state of my heart.

Professor Wiesel nodded. I undressed, and he examined me with as much thoroughness as though it were *he*, and not Chief Staff Medical Officer Pospischil, whose business it was to decide my fate. Then he said: "Your heart is as sound as a bell. At the moment it's affected by a fairly marked upward displacement of the diaphragm, that's all. We can get rid of that very easily. Incidentally, if you were being called up," he added, laughing, "it might well turn out to be very lucky for you. My colleagues in the army are often deceived by heart sounds caused by a displaced diaphragm, because it's the same sort of sound as one gets from a valvular defect or enlargement of the heart. So they sometimes diagnose accordingly and exempt the happy man who has nothing at all the matter with him. It's frightful."

And now, when I told Professor Wiesel that I had suffered from severe migraine and still had constant attacks of it, which had caused the Chief Staff Medical Officer to make the diagnosis 'destruction of the central nervous system', he said jovially: "I must confess I don't know what that is. You see, there's no such thing."

Only after this discussion, which made me indescribably happy, did I introduce myself to Professor Wiesel, and from that memorable day onwards we were very good friends and remained so till his all too early death. It was a happy evening when I recounted this queer adventure, in all its details, to my wife.

That great, tranquil happiness that filled my being for days was soon extinguished by a tragic event of which I must, I think, give an account, since it was a sign of the confusion and dangerous pedantry of that time. It was an event that cost a human life, the life of one near and dear to me.

A step-brother of mine, who was about six years my junior, had studied medicine in his youth; he had in fact qualified and even for some time made a special study of skin diseases. However, he had never practised as a physician, having very soon begun to take such an interest in exploration that he completely abandoned medicine. Thorough as he was, however, he did not simply make the change without more ado, but spent another three years reading philosophy, in which he then took his degree. It was only then (I believe I am right in saying) that he went to see the Director of the Vienna Natural History Museum, Professor Haberland, in order to expound a long-cherished plan of his for an expedition to Greenland. He wanted to make the trip especially in order to make a study of Eskimo dialects. He undertook the greatest of exertions, spending more than a year in Greenland. The fruit of these endeavours was a book on Greenland, one of such great scientific value that it was published by the Vienna Natural History Museum.

Now, when the war broke out, Dr. Rudolf Trebitsch was called up as a medical officer and to his unspeakable horror was ordered to treat the sick and, if necessary, of course, also perform operations. The poor man was almost desperate. He moved heaven and earth in his attempts to escape this fate, which for him was nothing less than frightful. However, the authorities failed to appreciate his desperate objections and his outcry of: "I won't let myself be made a murderer!" They stuck to their point of view: "You're a doctor of medicine, hence you are under an obligation to serve as a doctor. If you refuse to do your duty, you will be degraded and will be sent to the front as a private soldier. The highest rank you will be able to rise to there will be that of stretcher-bearer."

At the same time he was informed that he was being transferred to

the Serbian border and must take up his medical duties in the field-
hospital at Karansebes. In that miserable frontier town he had the
good fortune to come across a friendly and understanding dispenser,
who realised what impossible things were being demanded of the
doctor of medicine who had never treated a patient.

This man so tragically caught in the meshes managed as best he
could, being helped by two other doctors who did for him what he
could not do himself, while he did a medical orderly's work for them
and compensated them in other ways. The unfortunate man was
haunted by one single thought: 'For heaven's sake, I mustn't
become the murderer of a human being, I must not incur guilt for the
possibility that a slightly wounded man, who, if properly treated,
would have been saved, by my intervention might be injured for life
or even die'. This man who was the prisoner of his medical degree
grew mortally weary in these silent struggles against an, as it seemed,
inexorable destiny, and it was no wonder that he became fairly
seriously ill, which he hailed as nothing less than salvation, for now
he himself needed doctors to help him. The doctors, however, soon
realised that he must be nursed in a way that was quite impossible
in the field. And so, after the necessary reports had to be sent in to
the higher authorities, he was given four weeks sick-leave at home,
which meant that the unfortunate man could return temporarily to
Vienna.

At that time he struck me as being not physically ill but rather
more like someone in a state of acute depression. The doctors who
gathered around his sick-bed insisted that he should spend the
remaining three weeks of his leave in a sanatorium. And so,
exceedingly glad about this turn of events, he moved to the Juden-
dorf Sanatorium near Graz.

In this splendid institution, staffed by conscientious doctors and
self-sacrificing nurses, this poor man, who was inwardly much more
gravely wrecked than we dreamt, sought and found his death. The
time was drawing ever nearer when he would have to return to the
life he had only just left, and the thought of it drove him to his doom.

On his last day of liberty he said to one of the nurses: "You
know, it's quite impossible for me to take up my duties again. I
simply can't do it." The high-minded answer he received was: "One
can always do what one has got to do." Obviously it was there and
then that it became apparent to him how impossible it was for him,

in his position, to make other people understand his point of view. They all harped on the fact of his medical degree and went on regarding him as a doctor of medicine, who was obliged to do his duty like all the other men of his profession. The war was a bad time to choose for having complicated psychological conditions and being super-sensitive.

On the morning of the day when, having recovered from his physical ailments, he was due to leave the sanatorium, he asked the nurse, who was anxious about him and slightly suspicious, for a glass of really cold water. He made use of the minutes during which he was left alone to throw himself out of the window, which might not even have resulted in his death if his head had not grazed a lamp-post, so that his skull was fractured. When the nurse came back, he was already lying in his blood among the fallen yellow leaves in the beautiful park. Death seemed to have been instantaneous, doubtless also as a result of internal injuries, and so this misunderstood man, who had been driven to the brink of despair, had found eternal peace before his time.

Afterwards, when the relatives came hurrying along, the medical officer in charge said: "The patient could not have been saved. He was suffering from acute melancholia. That is a form of mental illness that makes those who suffer from it go on and on trying to commit suicide, resorting to the most incredibly cunning tricks, until in the end they succeed."

But who, at that period, had the time—and perhaps, for that matter, the right—to linger for long over *one* sorrow? I told the whole story to my understanding friend, Stefan Zweig, with whom I at that time had the chance of talking almost every day, and he was profoundly shocked and grieved.

Stefan Zweig, who was just about to get married to Maria von Winternitz, was at that time living in a little hotel on the Hietzinger Platz, a few minutes' walk from my own house. We used to meet regularly in the morning, in the Café Gröppl, which was so pleasantly situated opposite the Kaiser Maximilian monument, and we used to pour out our hearts to each other. Then for weeks on end we used to take the walk from there through the Hietzing Gate of the Park to the Meidling Gate, where I turned right to go to my hospital, while Stefan Zweig walked to the left, to the tram stop, in order to go to the War Records Office.

It was at this time that Stefan Zweig told me the plot and setting of his play, *Jeremias*; and even after the successful première I still remembered the vivid impression I had received from the passionate emotion with which he had spoken.

I did not see much of other colleagues from the War Records Office. I did not even know how it came about that Rilke was suddenly no longer there, but back in his native city, Prague. But even after he had gone, one saying of his was never again forgotten by those of us who were there at the time it was coined: "Who speaks of victory?" Rainer Maria Rilke had exclaimed. "Survival is all."

It was only many years later that we realised how utterly unjustifiably and undeservedly we had led what was actually a pretty comfortable life during those first years of the war. The war bulletins, becoming steadily more and more unfavourable, had blunted our sensibilities a little by this time.

A very remarkable, amusing, and bizarre episode still remains to be recounted; it deserves mention because of its oddity and the consequences it had. My Colonel one day sent for me and, when the orderly who had announced me had gone, ceremoniously asked me to sit down, looked at me hard for a moment, scrutinising me, and then, pointing to a bundle of files in front of him, said: "I have just seen from your papers, Lieutenant, which I have to prepare, together with those of the others, for a control commission I have been warned to expect, that you belong to no religious denomination. I find this very awkward. It interferes with my prospect of receiving a decoration from His Majesty, quite apart from other difficulties it is likely to cause both of us. Just look at it! 'No religious denomination!' And the husband, into the bargain, of a good Catholic woman whom I have repeatedly had the pleasure of meeting in the Hietzing church! What do you mean by it? The officers under my command are not 'of no religious denomination'! The officers under my command have a religion! Really, I ask you!"

I really did not know what to say in reply to this. Nor did the Colonel give me a chance to say anything. He went on, speaking, for the first time since I had known him, in a rather grave, severe tone: "No, my dear fellow, you're not going to remain 'of no religious denomination' as an officer in this detachment! I give you a fortnight. But——" and he leafed through the calendar to fix the date, "—but then I expect you back here in this very room with documents proving that you have a religion. I don't want to impose anything on you. You have a free choice. According to the Constitution of our country, I shall accept any religion. But officers under my command are not 'of no religious denomination'!"

What could I do but say "Very good, sir!"? Before I had even got to the door I had begun thinking how I could carry out this order. But then Colonel von Zeller called after me: "You know my personal liking for you, Lieutenant. So I should just like to warn you: don't rush off and become a Jew because it might turn out to be the quickest and easiest thing!"

"Very good, sir," I replied, disconcerted. Then I could not stop myself from adding: "But Judaism isn't exactly an 'easy thing'."

Well, I certainly had a job in hand if I was to report back in a fortnight with the necessary papers. During this period we naturally saw each other quite often in the course of duty, but as though by agreement neither of us uttered a word about this awkward affair. I consulted my wife, but all she knew was that it was impossible to become a Catholic inside a fortnight. As it happened, in Vienna there lived a theologian of repute, the head of the Protestant community in Austria, that well-known pastor, Professor Zimmermann. It was to him that I resorted; and indeed this man lived up to what was said of him. Hardly ever have I liked anyone as much as, after the very first few words, I liked Professor Zimmermann.

Gratifyingly enough, I was able to answer to his satisfaction the questions he put to me, in particular those regarding my attitude to the profound, eternal verities of the Christian religion. Then, in the kindliest way, he put me on the right track with regard to all the formalities that had to be fulfilled, and in fact scarcely twelve days had passed when I became a member of the Augsburg Confession of the Protestant Church. Armed with the necessary documents I then reported to my superior officer who did not stand any nonsense in matters of religion, even some days earlier than the fixed date, if only to demonstrate my keenness. He received me very amiably indeed, glanced at the papers, nodded, and said: "Augsburg Confession—ah, yes, excellent!"

Then we both gave a sigh of relief. I grasped the fleshy hand held out to me and thanked him for his words: "Now you will be doubly welcome on my estates after the end of the war! And I'm sure it's a load off your good lady's mind."

"Very good, sir," I answered.

My wife and I often went to a house only a few doors from our own, where we knew we would be comforted and cheered up by our hostess, Frau Katharina Schratt, the Emperor's intimate friend, who was better able to remain silent, better able to keep a secret, than anyone I have ever known. But this superb actress was nevertheless not so adept in control of her expression that one could not tell by looking at her face, and by patching together various things she said, how everything stood; which interested us, of course not out of curiosity, but because it was what would soon decide our destiny.

Frau Schratt, who was very fond of my wife and, in fact, after the Archduke's assassination in 1914 had without offering any reason for it tried to prevent her from going abroad, because she herself knew very well what storm-clouds were gathering, naturally had the most reliable news about the course of the war from her exalted friend. It was at her house that the Emperor Franz Joseph had one evening with profound sorrow said to her, who was also the human being to whom he was most attached: "The Empire is lost, Madam. All I can do is to see that it comes to an honourable end."

Frau Schratt did not repeat these words in our presence, but they must have been repeated at some time. One of her most intimate woman friends repeated them again, and so they circulated in the little circle around that wonderful woman, Katharina Schratt, and reached our ears too. When the Emperor relieved his heavy heart by uttering this confession, admitting the tragedy of his life, those who read the newspapers carefully already knew that all was lost, since Austria's great German ally, in spite of overwhelming successes at first, was slowly but steadily going down the road to disaster.

I myself was involved in an incident that showed me all too clearly how over-sensitive people had now become and how Austria was trying, though perhaps too late, to rally its own moral resources. I had suddenly been entrusted with a mission that it was a privilege to undertake and which was as simple as it was responsible. My Colonel informed me of it, congratulating me in exaggerated terms and making the not entirely comprehensible remark: "See that you carry out this job in exemplary fashion, so that you do credit to the detachment, to me, and to yourself."

My mission consisted in fetching from the Ministry of War in Vienna a sealed envelope that I was to take to Berlin, travelling overnight by sleeping-car, and the next morning, on arrival in Berlin, delivering it to a certain department (which had been described to me exactly) in the German War Ministry, at a certain grille, the number of which was written on the envelope. My orders were, further, that after receiving the receipt I was to return to Vienna the next night and deliver the receipt at the place where I had received the letter the day before. I was then to report to my detachment again and resume my duties without speaking to anyone about the incident, of which only my detachment commandant knew.

This official journey passed off without incident, and I would not mention it here if I had not had a rather characteristic experience on the way to Berlin. The other man in my compartment was a North German, who was very talkative and recognised me as an Austrian officer by my uniform. This was reason enough for him to begin haranguing me about the glories and advantages of a united supreme command, while my eyelids drooped with sleepiness. In order to make this lively gesticulating man stop talking—and not because I was of his opinion, for in fact I had no opinion on the matter at all— I agreed with him. "Of course, naturally, I'm sure that would be best," was probably what I said. And the man did in fact quiet down and leave me in peace.

I was about to lie down, without removing the official envelope from my breast pocket, when there was a knock at the door of the compartment. I opened the door, and there was the guard, who said in a remarkably soldierly tone: "His Highness wishes to see you in his compartment, sir." I quickly tidied myself up, without quite understanding what this curious summons could mean, for I did not even know who was in the neighbouring compartment. A moment later I knocked at the door of that compartment. And then I found myself standing before General Prince Gottfried Hohenlohe, the son-in-law of the Supreme Commander of the Austrian forces, Archduke Frederick. I saluted and told him my name.

"Lieutenant, I could not help overhearing a conversation that you and your travelling companion have been having, from which I cannot but conclude that you do not approve of Austria's conduct of the war, but, like your companion, wish to see a joint command under German leadership. Is that really your opinion?"

This sudden and entirely unexpected question came as a shock. I was greatly embarrassed and stammered: "All I wanted was to be left alone by that tiresome talkative man. I only wanted him to stop talking. That's why I agreed."

At this His Highness smiled and said: "The leader of Austria's Army is called Conrad von Hötzendorf, and surely the name of this man of such great intellect and eminence must mean something to you."

"That is indeed the case, Your Excellency," I immediately concurred, in my subconscious mind greatly astonished that he ignored the existence of his father-in-law, the official Supreme Commander, Archduke Frederick.

"Well then, I should like to ask you to express that opinion in very clear terms to this conceited ally of ours before you leave your compartment tomorrow morning."

"Very good, Your Excellency, I shall see that there is no shadow of doubt about my opinion," I replied.

Prince Hohenlohe held out his hand to me, smiling, and said: "Yes, one can't be careful enough these days. One never knows what may come of a casual remark. One must consider every word, and that applies even to the highest ranks," he added, smiling. I was thereupon graciously dismissed.

I recounted this little incident to friends I could trust, among them Stefan Zweig, on our walk through the Schönbrunn Park, and he commented: "Just imagine if you had been a Prussian officer, being overheard by a Prussian prince. Where and what would you be today? *O du mein Oesterreich!*" he exclaimed laughingly. But never again did Stefan Zweig quote that well-known marching song.

For the year 1916 brought with it an event so tremendous that it was enough to make one forget much of one's own past for ever: the Emperor Franz Joseph I, on his camp-bed in the Palace of Schönbrunn, had closed his eyes for ever.

What the Viennese felt really had nothing to do with an historical appreciation, nothing to do with an attempt to honour a man who —whatever anyone might say—had carried the time in which he lived with him and had influenced it. No, that universal mourning, which came from the very bottom of people's hearts, can be explained only by the fact that everyone aged between twenty and sixty was in some way or other also lamenting his own life, which had now more or less lost its meaning, and somehow, for good or for evil, laid the responsibility for his own fate upon the late Emperor.

We watched the funeral, which was an unprecedented sensation, from the apartment of friends in the Babenbergerstrasse, where we stood shivering at one of the windows. There was something singularly gloomy about it, and the ancient Spanish splendour dating back to the days when the sun never set on the Hapsburg Empire seemed to blaze away across the centuries, once more glorifying the last great prince of this truly doom-laden dynasty. The senior line had died out with the passing of the Emperor Franz Joseph.

Six horses drew the gold-studded hearse, and as they paced slowly and solemnly through the broad Mariahilferstrasse, ceaselessly lifting and dipping their plumed heads, it seemed as though they felt that they were beings apart and as though by this long journey they would remain linked for ever with a rare human destiny. They drew the coffin, invisible under wreaths and flowers, to the Kapuzinergruft (the burial vault of the Imperial family, under the Capuchin church), where the Emperor Franz Joseph was awaited by so many ancestors and also by those Hapsburgs who in recent years had died before their time.

The whole population, already depressed by the war situation, was suddenly united in one great common sorrow. And even though everyone, dismay in his heart, as is inevitable in such cases, was deeply shaken by this event, which somehow touched him as though with evil forebodings, outwardly he related his feelings to the passing of a man who certainly had always meant everything for the best and seldom had been able to achieve even the good.

In order that this long-expected death should not cause any disturbing changes where the alliance of the Central Powers was concerned, the succession to the Throne had to be settled with all speed. Hence a great many formalities arising out of the Spanish ceremonial of the Hapsburg Court were dispensed with.

In a twinkling we had all taken our oath of loyalty to the Emperor Franz Joseph's successor (about whom there was no doubt of any kind), the Emperor Karl, a great-nephew of the old Emperor's; and the Emperor Karl himself did his utmost to fill the vacant place, and fulfil the duties that he had now assumed, as quickly as possible. He had a hard time from the beginning, for he had to let everything go on in the old way, and it was difficult enough, indeed now almost impossible, to discuss with his wavering ally each of the problems that arose every day. Surrounded by advisers who were not always as wise as they might have been, he finally contented himself with doing whatever the fairly hopeless majority expected of him.

It is not the object of this book to linger much over events that now belong to history and have been discussed from every point of view by those who are qualified to discuss them.

In those sombre days Arthur Schnitzler and Stefan Zweig in particular often came to see us, and the opportunity to have thorough talks about what we must now expect did us all good. None of us and the like of us doubted that difficult days were ahead for every worker, whether it was as an artist or as a labourer that he worked. House-wives began to hoard provisions even more eagerly than before, and writers began to worry about sales-possibilities in connection with their new books. They hoped that at least from the publishing point of view there would not be any sort of change.

Meanwhile everything that mattered to us had become visibly and tangibly worse. Vienna was beginning to wear the unmistakable appearance of a doomed city. The gloriously beautiful Vienna Woods, the joy of everyone who lived there, had to a large extent been felled and the timber used for fuel. People had little to eat, and what they had was of poor quality; they had no clothes, and there was doubtless no one, however great his means and his connections might be, who had not discovered what it was to be cold. The icy cold in places of entertainment, in the bravely struggling theatres, was unendurable.

People who had never dreamt of carrying a rucksack were forced to shoulder that kind of receptacle and travel out into the country, in order at least to provide their children with a few drops of milk.

But things were now happening at a tremendous pace. There was no time for prolonged lamentations and the brooding fantasies of the bereaved. And everything pointed clearly to the greatest event of all, Germany's capitulation.

Now, at a blow, everything was different. There was no longer a trace of military discipline. Officers returning home had their distinctions torn off their uniform, as a sign of gratitude for their vain courage at the front and without regard for the scars and wounds that were all they had to show for having tried to save their ruined country. The demonstrators were, of course, precisely those elements that had the least justification for committing such excesses, but had been waiting all the time for these critical hours in order to emerge from the underworld and if possible seize power themselves.

The hospital detachment with which I had been serving had been disbanded without much ado by Colonel von Zeller, who had received his decoration, the Franz-Joseph Order, in time; he acted on instructions from the War Ministry. All of us, officers, non-commissioned officers, and the poor war-wounded men, soon lost sight of each other. Colonel von Zeller had taken leave of us very quietly, to return to his home in Herzogsdorf, in Upper Austria. The outcome of the war had literally broken his heart, and he was a gravely-ill man when he left us. The only thing that kept the poor disappointed old soldier going was the news that his son, who had been a prisoner-of-war in Russia almost since the beginning of the war, was on his way home and in moderately good health.

And indeed hardly six weeks had passed since I had hung up my uniform in the darkest and furthest corner of the wardrobe, when this much-sorrowed-for son of the man who had so frequently been our guest, young Lieutenant Hans von Zeller, paid a call on us, evidently at his father's wish, still tattered and torn and looking extremely exhausted. We quickly made tea for him, and it was a real pleasure to spend an hour chatting with this cultivated young man, who had just had time to qualify as an engineer before being called up and whose eyes flashed with personality, which he had evidently inherited from his beautiful mother, who had died young. His father must have told him many pleasant and gratifying things about us, for he talked with remarkable frankness, and when my wife said to him: "Well, Lieutenant, after you have had a rest and got your strength up again —which I dare say will be much easier in the country around Linz than here in Vienna—I suppose you will take up the job of looking after your father's estates. Your father looked rather as though he needed a long rest when we saw him last," young von Zeller jumped up in great embarrassment and burst out: "Please, please, *gnädige Frau*, permit me to correct this misunderstanding. It's all quite terrible! My father has no estates! I could never manage to make him drop these pretensions. As a matter of fact, he has a cottage with an orchard. That's all, and such 'estates' really don't need anyone to look after them. I shall have to look around for myself to start a sensible life on my own."

We could ill conceal our amazement. Afterwards we felt sorry for

I

that boastful man, whom we would, after all, not have grudged all the landed estates that he had pretended he owned.

In that one hour he spent with us that nice young man almost became more of a friend than his progenitor, who had liked us so well and always been so amusing. We never saw him again. He sent us word of his father's death, after which we exchanged a few letters. May our good wishes for him have been fulfilled.

Now, truly, we had other things to worry about than the past and its consequences.

Inflation came overnight, with all the frightful misery it meant, for us as well as for others. My step-father's firm, which had been neglected during the war as a result of the managing-director's having been called up, was now on the way to ruin, if for no other reason than that of having recently considerably overstrained its credit at the bank. Social life all around us, high and low, had become insalubrious and joyless, as a result of harsh restrictions and laws sanctioned overnight without being properly thought out. Vienna had become a city of almost unimaginable misery. Government officials, clerks, respectable small tradesmen, all could tell the same story.

Those who were worst off, as always in this world, of course, were the most innocent, the children, and no praise can be loud enough or repeated often enough—and hence in this book space must be found too—for the fact that Switzerland was the first country to help, sending food for the children of Vienna through the Red Cross, even before taking these unfortunate little ones on to its own soil. And there was much else that Switzerland did for the future of those, stricken by destiny, who had suffered so much want and misery.

Simultaneously with the arrival of the first food-trains there came to Vienna two noble Swiss who were in charge of the distribution of the precious cargo. They were Colonel Frey-Vigier, from Solothurn, who sixteen years later was to play a quite especially tragic part in my life, and Dr. Louis Ferrière, from Geneva, whose father and uncle had held high positions in the Red Cross. We made the acquaintance of these two Swiss emissaries at the house of the Burgtheater actress Lili Marberg, and when Dr. Ferrière told us that he must now pitch his tent in Vienna for at least a year and was in search of a small hotel apartment for himself and his young wife, who was a virtuoso on the violin, and that he was dreading the prospect of such an apartment, my wife spontaneously suggested to this elegant young man that his wife and he should for the period of their stay occupy the guest-rooms in our villa in Hietzing. Dr. Ferrière was obviously enchanted with this proposal, but my wife said laughingly: "I shouldn't like you to buy a pig in a poke. Bring your wife to tea with us next Sunday afternoon and have a look at your prospective home before you decide."

This tea-party, which included not only Docteur and Madame Ferrière, but also Colonel Frey and Lili Marberg, with her husband Karl Hans Jaray, was followed by an inspection of the rooms that we were able to put at Dr. Ferrière's disposal. He was so charmed with the situation and quietness of these rooms, and with the furnishing, which, as it happened, really left nothing to be desired, that he asked if he and his wife—who even outdid him in expressions of approval and gratitude—might move in during the next few days.

He stayed in our house for over a year, and between us and that highly cultured neurologist, Dr. Ferrière, there developed a cordial friendship that has continued right down to the present day. As he was in Vienna in what was, after all, a semi-official capacity and he made a point of letting this become apparent, our front door was soon adorned with the badge of the Swiss Red Cross, the result of which was that before and after every official journey he took Dr. Ferrière was overwhelmed with applications and petitions of all kinds and had enough work to justify his presence a hundred times over.

But however great the help was that came from abroad, especially from Switzerland, it could not be more than a very slight alleviation of the endless misery that spread like a conflagration and which it seemed nothing could bring to an end. A walk through the streets of Vienna on the far side of the First District presented one with a vivid picture of what it meant to have lost a war and then have to knuckle under to a peace that resulted in the break-up of a great Empire.

It was not easy to shake off all these things and prevent politics from invading one's private life. One only had to leave the house or board a tram in order to know all that had happened to us, to hear that our money was now worthless and that the new republic would inevitably be a wretched pygmy state against which nobody would be able to make any claims; and yet there was no one who did not make some sort of claim on some government office or, rather, on life itself.

I should like now to be permitted to speak for a few minutes of the house next door to ours. We lived at number twenty in the Maxingstrasse. In number eighteen Johann Strauss had written his world-famous, immortal operetta, *Die Fledermaus*, a fact that was recorded on a small bronze plaque. In our time there was again a very distinguished musician living there; this was Professor Karl Prochaska, of the Vienna Conservatory.

But he was not the only inmate of the house. It also harboured the widow of the former Austrian Ambassador to Japan, Countess Mitsou Coudenhove-Kalergi, and her two sons. One of these sons was Richard Coudenhove-Kalergi, later the originator of the Pan-Europe movement, an idea that he had had early in his life, suppressing it while he was still a youth, but from the time of his maturity, right down to the present day, sacrificing much to publicise it.

My wife had got to know Coudenhove's mother on strolls in the Schönbrunn Park, and before long the Coudenhove family and ourselves were on extremely cordial terms. The young Count Richard was then, I should think, in his early twenties, and it was in our company that he came to know that great actress Ida Roland, whom I do not hesitate to call the German Sarah Bernardt. It was only a few years later that she became Richard Coudenhove's wife, which she remained until her sudden death; she likewise always remained an admirable artist in the medium of life itself. This marriage began, as so often happens, with a sincere enthusiasm for an enchanting actress' great art, and ended with a great love between two people who seemed to be separated by a certain difference in age, but who were very intensely drawn to one another by an unusual mutual understanding, which finally, as we know today, united them for ever. Ida Roland-Coudenhove renounced her great art all too early in order to follow her chosen husband wherever he went, to fight his battles with him and be at his side to help him, above all to guard him from disappointments as far as was in her power, which was certainly not to be under-estimated.

But now a profound personal grief was my lot, and first among the losses of friends and values is the great sorrow of my mother's death.

She had passed the last years of her life literally in the twilight of semi-consciousness. I think the cause was mainly the large doses of heroin that she had to take continually in order to combat the terrible paralysis agitans from which she was suffering. Sometimes her

interest in her sons would flare up into vivid life; and then she would
send for whichever of them had been in her thoughts at the time and
overwhelm him with questions, which, whether they were difficult or
easy to answer, left in the poor woman's mind only a faint residue of
knowledge of what was going on in the lives of those near and dear
to her. Only when summer came for the last time for her did she ask
to be taken to Ischl, to that blessed valley where, although her health
was now irrevocably lost, her maternal heart was still warmed and
rejoiced by memories of happy hours, of the early days of her second
marriage, and her children playing at her feet.

In those last years of her life we many and many a time visited this
lonely woman in Ischl, staying at her side as long as her doctors
would let us. Sometimes we could not help feeling that some
invisible hand reached far back into her life and brought her before
us as she had once been when we could still count on her encouragement, her pronouncements on life, and her advice. And then, when
we said good-bye, to make way for another two of her children—for
she was not allowed ever to have more than two visitors at once—she
would drag herself through the french windows on to the balcony
and wave good-bye to us with her tremulous right hand, while the
light that had flashed for a while in her still beautiful eyes slowly died
out again, as though some ghostly hand had taken the memories
away, putting them back again in an invisible treasure-chest woven of
mists.

We went on visiting her in the autumn, as often as it could be
managed, when she was back in her apartment in Vienna. On such
occasions we always avoided—and it was agreed with other visitors
that it should be so—telling her anything about the end of the war
and the new age that we did our best to keep from her in so far as was
possible. One sombre winter's morning she passed, as the doctors
and nurses assured us, without any pain.

During those hard times, of which I have just spoken, of course I
was not idle. My drama *Frau Gitta's Sühne* (*Jitta's Atonement*) was
practically finished. A volume of stories, *Die Last des Blutes* (*The
Burden of the Blood*), was ready for the press, and a gratifying
commission had arrived from S. Fischer in Berlin, a city to which
I felt myself strongly attracted. 'I should like to publish a new
novel by you,' he wrote to me and repeated it in person a short while
later, 'on the occasion of your fiftieth birthday. If it could also

contain some allusions to your own life, that would be doubly acceptable.'

This remark, behind which there may have been more than the inscrutable Fischer expressed in words, accounts for the fact that in *Spätes Licht* (*The Late Light*), the novel of a marriage, which was the outcome of this commission, some names actually appear that have been of importance at the beginning of this present book. My fiftieth birthday was not yet immediately impending, but a book, after all, has a much longer period of gestation than a human being, and so of course I set about the work even then in the autumn of 1917. I interrupted this work repeatedly in order to make journeys to Germany, especially to Berlin, where I found my friends S. Fischer and Moritz Heimann utterly unchanged in their attitude to me. But we were all changed, as a result of the scarcely endurable experiences that we had nevertheless endured, changed, if not in our feelings for each other, certainly in our attitude to the world, in our view of human life and in the demands each of us was still justified in making.

Fischer was very worried about the incredible German inflation, in comparison with which the Austrian inflation was nothing worth mentioning. It was more or less as though in a country ravaged by a cholera epidemic one were to speak of an outbreak of measles at home. S. Fischer, who not only bore a responsibility towards his authors but really felt that responsibility and never in any way tried to dodge it, was simply desperate when he collected royalties that were due from a theatre at eleven o'clock in the morning and then at three in the afternoon realised that the sum had again shrunk by a third. There was no time for either investment or sending money abroad, and like all eminent foreign authors Bernard Shaw too lost almost the whole of his not inconsiderable German property as a result of the German inflation.

I shared this fate without, however, complaining to him about it. But of course it was hard to see the fruits of years of endeavour and sometimes strenuous work evaporate into nothing.

The only way to deal with these material catastrophes was to do without any performances of the plays. Fischer in fact did this at first in Shaw's interest. For he was not a little proud, and rightly so, that this man was the only foreign writer whose work had time and again been performed, here and there, during the war, chiefly, however, under the direction of Viktor Barnowsky in the Lessingtheater. It was there, during the time when the British were pressing the Germans hardest, that the comedy, *John Bull's Other Island*, one of Shaw's few genuinely poetic works, was produced with a particularly fine cast. The delightful part of the girl, Norah Reilly, was fascinatingly played by Traute Carlsen. She shared the great success of the evening with, among others, Fritz Kayssler.

At that time the general public still knew very little about Ireland, and Barnowsky was able to justify his audacity by pointing out that this was so, accounting for having undertaken this production during the war by saying that in this play Ireland, which was ready to secede from England, was for the first time shown in all its misery and suffering and disappointment. It was in a certain sense Shaw's *Hassgesang* (hymn of hate) against the oppression of his native country. The great European encountered a great deal of ill-feeling as a result of this production in enemy territory, although he had had absolutely nothing to do with it and had not lifted a finger to have precisely this play performed during the war. It was we, and we alone, who bore the responsibility for it. Perhaps for the very reason of its anti-English tendency, this play has since that time never again been performed in any German city, and Shaw himself, having accomplished far greater dramatic feats, thrust it back into a twilight in which we have all let it remain, although of course it could not be omitted from a complete edition of Shaw's works, which was begun by S. Fischer and only a short time ago finished by the Artemis Verlag.

Stefan Zweig was in Switzerland about this time. From there he could at last resume his correspondence with his dearly loved foreign friends. It was only at the beginning of 1919 that I received a memorable and unforgettable letter from the foreign world that during all these years had not been foreign to my way of feeling. This letter came from Georges Courteline and was written on the day that the Treaty of Versailles was signed. It went as follows:

My dear Friend,

I feel that you share my sentiments and that there has been no hour in these terrible four years in which we ceased to be the friends that we have always been. Let me, as the elder, take the first step towards you and hold out the hand of friendship to you. What have we to do with the frightfulness of history, under which we

have suffered and, I dare say, shall go on suffering for a long time
to come, because the stupidity of the great ones of the world has
at last concentrated on the task of beating the little people of the
world and making them unhappy? Come as fast as ever you can
and try to console an inconsolable friend who has missed you
more than you can imagine, and convince him that you are still
of the same mind as ever, as he takes it for granted that you are.
I long to read something from you, I long to see you, just as I hope
that you and your wife are more or less as well as we ourselves
have somehow managed to remain in spite of all the catastrophes
and hardships we have been through.

Ever,

GEORGES COURTELINE.

I was not long in answering, and truly my letter did not disappoint
this dear old friend of my youth; but a journey to Paris could not be
thought of for a long time yet.

I believe I wrote my first letter to Bernard Shaw after the war even
before the end of 1918, from Berlin, from where even then it was
possible to get letters abroad.

Life in Vienna was overshadowed by a great physical and
psychological depression. Of course one relatively quickly became
used to no longer being a citizen of a country that was a Great Power;
but the exhausting little day-to-day worries and anxieties so much
depressed this 'nation of dancers and fiddlers', as Anton Wildgans
had called the Austrians at the beginning of the war, that people
gradually forgot what real life was like, slowly groping their way
along the invisible railing of their trade or profession, towards an
uncertain future which, whether one looked at it with optimistic or
with pessimistic eyes, was equally unattractive.

We had always had a great taste for travel, and for four years this
taste had been unsatisfied, except by journeys inside Austria itself.
But at last, in the summer of 1919, we bestirred ourselves and went a
journey to Switzerland, a journey that took us through more or less
all the chief towns and districts of that wonderful country, which had
been utterly untouched by the war.

It was only there, after we had found our feet to some extent in
Zurich, our first stopping-place, that we became fully conscious of
the feeling of the difference between the city from which we had

come and the happy city in which we were now staying. Here we felt more strongly than at home that we had been captives for four years and now for the first time were free and could breathe in freedom. Captivity changes man, as freedom also changes him, and never since then have I felt the difference between two peoples as deeply as during that transition from Vienna to Zurich, that gracious city on one of the most beautiful Swiss lakes.

Very soon one met many acquaintances from Vienna. But we also had the pleasure of being reunited, in Zurich, with many old friends from France and Switzerland itself. We stayed as long as our means and the situation at home permitted. From Zurich we went on to Lucerne, to the happy shores of Lake Lucerne, of which we had sometimes dreamed in the constriction of Vienna and its surroundings. In Engelberg it only took us a few weeks to recover from some minor ailments that we had been suffering from when we came, and for the first time had the opportunity to admire the skill of Swiss doctors. Then we made a somewhat longer stay in Caux, where at last we began to recuperate properly and we gradually began to feel better, physically and mentally. Relapses, of course, were to occur later when we were at home again, but it was splendid, all the same, to set out on the homeward journey with new hopes and an entirely new faith in a still immaculate future, come what might.

It was Zurich from where I frequently wrote to Bernard Shaw and it was there, too, that I had many letters from him. I learned that he had finished a great drama, *Heartbreak House*, during the war, together with a long preface, and had also written a considerable number of one-act plays.

Heartbreak House was soon sent to me, and I hailed it as a drama that I reckoned among his finest. From the literary point of view it belongs to his greatest works, and if one must make comparisons, then one can find a structural resemblance to Tchekov's *Cherry Orchard*. The whole work, from the beginning to the end, is filled with a faint tremor of melancholy leave-taking. People and things that are dear to one vanish away in it, and the extremely interesting action, which rapidly works up toward a climax, makes *Heartbreak House* a really great work for the theatre.

In the one-act plays, on the other hand, there were high-spirited allusions arising out of the war, which were more interesting for Great Britain than for an international public. It was for this reason

I*

that I did not include all of these amusing little works in the German complete edition that was published later.

We had begun to exchange views in our letters, but Shaw had written a little book, *Common Sense and the War*, in which he had clearly stated his attitude to the world disaster, and he sent a copy of it to me. I translated it into German for S. Fischer as quickly as I could.

When we had returned to Vienna after our wonderfully carefree stay in Switzerland (carefree because my wife had sacrificed some very beautiful pieces of her jewellery), I set about finishing my novel, *Spätes Licht*, and translating *Heartbreak House*. To my delight I was kept so busy with these two jobs and had to work so hard that the altered conditions and the ever more noticeable signs that the world I had known in my youth had disappeared for ever could not distress me as deeply as it would have been only natural that they should.

I delivered my novel on time, and it was in fact published shortly before my fiftieth birthday. I looked upon it as a beautiful present from S. Fischer.

Heartbreak House was a disappointment to many theatrical directors because it was so entirely different from everything that was expected of Bernard Shaw in theatrical circles. In my eyes it was, above all, the Burgtheater play *par excellence*, and I had the pleasure of discovering that Albert Heine, who was then temporarily in charge of the Burgtheater, was completely of my opinion. He did in fact present a production of it very quickly.

The first night came more swiftly than usual, and Max Paulsen, in the part of the ninety-year-old Captain Shotover, was particularly good. The play ends with a German air-raid on London, one that costs the lives of several inhabitants of the old and much-loved house that is actually the silent main protagonist. In this way Shaw was the first to bring the war into a play and to show on the stage something of the warfare in which the lives of innocent men and women behind the lines were lost.

The event that this production was and the deep impression that the work made on me from the first moment when I became acquainted with it thrust into the background the little events that were connected with my birthday. The present that meant most to me was my novel, *Spätes Licht*, but in those days I had once again come to feel intensely and painfully that birthdays, or at least the annual reference to them, ought to be abolished.

I had always held this view, which became stronger and stronger in the course of the years. I had noticed that Arthur Schnitzler, too, and even Stefan Zweig, who was much younger, also felt the same. And I once saw Hermann Bahr on his birthday irritably pushing away a pile of letters and telegrams that he had received.

Vienna was now ravaged by socialism—of a kind that was not wholly understood by its leaders, some of whom had fought at the front and whose feelings of resentment were the chief driving-force of the new life that they wanted to help to bring about—socialism that was not yet communism but was groping its way forward towards it with pretty rough hands. The way in which the Emperor Karl had been treated at Schönbrunn and ejected from Schönbrunn was something that non-party and impartial spectators could not find pleasing. Lernet-Holenia, in his finest novel, *Die Standarte (The Standard)*, gave a very moving picture of this leave-taking of the last of the Hapsburgs.

The aristocracy had been abolished, but it had deserved its fate, for nobody had heard anything of its fighting for its existence. Nor did it do what would have been expected of it and gather round the figure of the hard-pressed poor young Emperor, as it is, after all, the duty of Paladins to do. He disappeared without much stir and without putting up any resistance.

The law regarding the abolition of the nobility in the new Austrian Republic was of course for a time the talk of the day and was yet another piece of material on which Viennese humour, which perhaps had helped to prevent a complete breakdown, could get to work. For instance, Count Adalbert Sternberg, an exceedingly witty and dashing man, had new visiting-cards printed, saying:

Adalbert Sternberg
of that family which was ennobled by Charlemagne in
800 and deprived of its nobility by Karl Renner in 1918

And Egon Friedell, who had for the most part remained fairly calm, announced at the top of his voice: "So long as the Burgtheater actor Max Devrient walks through the streets of Vienna, the nobility has not been abolished!"

But what was abolished was something that mattered to us much more—the nobility that is greatness of heart, and everything that is connected with that rare grace which lights up only at select hours and in a few beings.

It was great good luck for the Viennese that at that time they had in their Burgomaster, Karl Seitz, one who held the scales of justice evenly balanced, when justice was becoming ever more questionable, and who was able to maintain it so for many years. In personality and character he towered over his colleagues and co-workers, radiating the secret magical charm that makes a man in a leading position popular.

Now, however, an event occurred that suddenly lightened the gloomy sky for poets and writers and their satellites, making tired literary hearts beat more strongly again after the terrible experiences of the war. This was the founding of the great international Pen Club in London by Mrs. Dawson-Scott, who, recognising with subtle shrewdness that her name had not quite sufficient weight, at once turned to that great and widely-celebrated novelist, John Galsworthy, who was delighted to accept the offer of the presidency of this new-born organisation and who applied all the energy of his leisure hours, in a positively model fashion, to this foundation, the ideas and aims of which could not but fill every human heart, every writer's mind, with confidence, courage, and the resolve to do intellectual humanity those services for which Mrs. Dawson-Scott campaigned.

This great and modest woman had an admirable gift for keeping in the background, which she did more and more, leaving the popular and respected Nobel Prize winner, John Galsworthy, who had just finished that world-wide success, *The Forsyte Saga*, to hold the foreground and take the lead, in such a way that for the general reading public and the circles that gradually began to take an interest in the objects of the Pen Club the founding of it appeared to be entirely his doing. High-minded and modest as he was, Galsworthy nevertheless always declined to let this honour be foisted on him and gave all due credit to Mrs. Dawson-Scott. The initials of this new club stood for 'Playwrights, Essayists, Novelists', and Galsworthy was a master of all three arts.

I do not feel justified in expounding in detail what the aims of the Pen Club were, because in the meantime, of course, those aims have become known throughout the world. Galsworthy and those of a like mind never missed a chance of emphasising: "We are non-political. We fight for freedom of thought, but political views must not be either put forward or argued against at our gatherings."

In the course of the years it sometimes turned out to be very difficult indeed to hold these things strictly apart, and it needed all the tact and authority that the Pen Club Presidents could display— for in a few years every nation had its own Pen Club—to see that this rule was kept and that there was no sliding into the morasses of party-political strife. That fiery spirit, Ernst Toller, for instance, was always kicking over the traces at congresses.

There was one person who was always admirably deft in steering clear of these menacing controversies, and that was Galsworthy's right-hand man, the Club's secretary, Hermon Ould. I must not omit to mention that Bernard Shaw, who had an aversion to clubs and was perhaps the only person who did not believe in the Pen Club's great possibilities from the very beginning, did however become a member when his friend Galsworthy asked him to.

Only a short time passed and Paris was the centre of a French, Rome of an Italian, Berlin of a German Pen Club; Vienna was likewise the centre of an Austrian Pen Club. But this last came about in a peculiar way.

One day Raoul Auernheimer, Arthur Schnitzler, the publisher Ernst Peter Tal, and I were asked to take part in a meeting called by the writer Grete von Urbanitzky at a certain place, of which we were given the exact address. In her first letter she indicated that the founder of an English literary association, known as the Pen Club, had entrusted her with the task of founding such a club in Vienna, on the pattern of the English one.

We were immediately interested, recognising that here was a movement from which Austrian writers must not hold aloof. At the same time we could not help wondering why Mrs. Dawson-Scott had not got in touch with our country's leading writers. Hugo von Hofmannsthal or Arthur Schnitzler, for instance, would have been a suitable choice for the first president. Instead, at this memorable first meeting, which was actually only a preliminary discussion, Raoul Auernheimer, who was present, was elected president, and the rest of us—I think the writer Moritz Scheyer was also there—immediately and automatically became members of the committee.

Naturally we tried to do everything on the English pattern, but what will serve in one place will not necessarily do in another, and we soon had to produce ideas of our own. The first happy idea was undoubtedly that of making Arthur Schnitzler honorary president. After anxiously making sure that this would not interfere with his work, he very charmingly accepted. Of course Hugo von Hofmannsthal also became a member, and together with him all those whose names made it necessary for us to invite them to become members.

John Galsworthy succeeded in bringing about world congresses of the international Pen Club. The first took place, as was to be expected, in London. Its success, which was doubtless due in the main to the unexpectedly large number of those taking part, encouraged all the other centres to follow London's example. So it came about that a world congress took place every year in one of the other capitals. In Vienna, and elsewhere too, there was furthermore the opportunity to make something like a celebration one evening, generally on the occasion of a visit from some eminent writer from home or abroad.

The leading men in the government and in the chief theatres were very soon to be found among the guests on such evenings. Galsworthy himself was many times the centre of a Pen Club celebration in Vienna, where of course his publisher Paul Zsolnay lived. Special mention must, I think, be made of an evening when, among several outstanding French writers, Edouard Herriot was the Pen Club's guest and Hofmannsthal made a dazzling, rapturous speech, in French, in praise of international goodwill, which he declared was essential for the future happiness of mankind.

Now came stirring times for me, which carried me over all the disturbances in my work and the material worries with which I had had to deal. For now rehearsals of my drama, *Jitta's Atonement*, began at the Burgtheater. Although it was the second play of mine that was presented at the Burgtheater, the rehearsal period and the first night remain particularly vivid in my memory, perhaps all the more vivid because this work enjoyed a greater and more widespread success. The production was by Albert Heine. Tressler was amazing in the great scene of his life and death in the first act, overwhelming in his realism and in the sense he gave of the closeness of death—clearly something that he had learnt at some sick-bed. The part of his colleague and opposite number was played with enchanting nonchalance by Max Paulsen, while Lili Marberg made Frau Gitta one of her greatest triumphs. But Maria Mayer and Maria Bard were also so extremely good that they could not be acted off the stage.

After the dress rehearsal, which provided many a sign of what way the wind was blowing, Arthur Schnitzler said very charmingly and approvingly: "Well, here at last is a play of yours that I can say 'yes' to without a qualm. It sets out to please, and it will please. But there, that's poaching on the critics' preserves!" Other authoritative voices also reached my ears, heightening my confidence.

At that time, for the reasons I have already stated and explained, I had resolved not to write any more plays. But the comedy *Der Geliebte* (*The Man She loved*) was almost finished and the performing rights had been acquired by Director Bernau for the Deutsche Volkstheater. So I had to be patient a while longer before putting the irrevocable and necessary period to the dramatic side of my work. The first night of *Jitta's Atonement* at the Burgtheater was a great success, as was also the Berlin first night. Since S. Fischer, furthermore, considered the play worthy of being published in book form, it appeared under his imprint, and in fact on the very day of the Burgtheater première. This made it possible for me to send a copy to my friend Bernard Shaw, who was particularly interested in this work of mine after reading my letters about it, before he knew the work itself.

He wrote to tell me that *Jitta's Atonement* had made a deep impression on him and struck him as very characteristic both of the atmosphere of Vienna and of the author. Of course, he said, he had not been able to read it himself, but a secretary who read German fluently had given him a vivid picture of it, half reading it in English, half telling him about it. He asked me whether I would give my approval to his paying me back, for once, in small coin, for the tremendous amount of time and energy I had expended on his account. After having a careful draft translation made, which he intended going over very painstakingly with a dictionary, he meant to translate *Jitta's Atonement* into English and have it performed in England and America.

Mention must here be made only of the fact that Shaw, overwhelmingly self-confident as he was and sure of his diabolical skill as a dramatist, in handling this work, which had, after all, been entrusted to his care, took liberties that he himself would scarcely have forgiven his translator. He was convinced that it was quite essential to brighten up my play for Anglo-Saxon audiences. In his version the last two acts are more like a comedy than a drama. He wrote to me about this in the following words: 'I had to brighten your heroine up a bit. I couldn't let her walk right through the whole play being as tragic and irreconcilable as a modern Lady Macbeth. The English will only put up with that in a classic. What they expect of a modern comedy is mirror reflections of all the highlights of life, and you must take my word for it that what I have done has only been for the good of your play and has increased its chances of success in this country.'

What could I do but agree? The drama as I had written it existed in print, as evidence of what I had set out to do.

And as so often happens in life, once again Shaw turned out to be right. The play was indeed a success, in London with Violet Vanbrugh and in New York with Berta Kalisch, a success that—to judge only by the number of performances—was even greater than that at the Vienna Burgtheater and that at the Berlin Residenztheater and in other German cities. Only the English dramatist and critic, St. John Ervine, wrote that Shaw had done something 'very naughty' where I was concerned. From a purely emotional point of view I could not even agree, perhaps because Bernard Shaw had already read me the first scenes of his *Saint Joan* on the visit I paid him soon after all this happened.

It was doubtless my desire to see my friend again that caused me to make a vow that in spite of all difficulties and all qualms I would receive the master's new work only from his own hand. The work was there; *Saint Joan* summoned me, and I had to go and receive her. So it was my destiny and privilege, after a long separation of more than seven years, once more to meet the man who constituted the great human, intellectual, and artistic experience, indeed the great intellectual event of my youth. Discussion as to the time of our meeting went on through many weeks of correspondence, until at last the day and the hour could be settled.

Arrangements for the journey were easier to make than I had feared. However, the British Embassy warned me against trusting only in my visa, because I might nevertheless be turned back across the Channel from Dover if I had no letter from a British citizen to show, stating that my presence in England was necessary or at least important to him. For this reason Shaw wrote me an amusing letter that I could show at the frontier. This letter did in fact fulfil its function and caused considerable merriment among the austere passport control officials.

How much had happened since the last time when I had got into the Pullman carriage in which one travels, so comfortably and at such a tremendous speed, from the chalk cliffs of the English coast to the colossal city of London! A whole world of certainties, which had seemed guaranteed for a short human lifetime, had been overturned; yet here the unreliable earth seemed to be still the same old planet. Anyone who by some miracle might have had the experience of awakening out of an enchanted sleep that had lasted almost ten years would have noticed no changes here; he would have seen no sign to make him guess at what a hell the paradise had turned into in which we had all once unsuspectingly and dully failed to enjoy our carefree happiness.

How dark the railway stations were at home compared with the light-streaked station at Victoria, into which my train came thundering, punctual to the very minute! The shining, radiantly sparkling streets told of peace where all was stern and hard at work, told of the assured existence of all the things that in our own country had long begun to totter and fall.

And now the heart experienced the sensation to which it had many and many a time looked forward with so much yearning. Coming with long strides along the platform, which was actually part of a street covered with people and vehicles, was a laughing giant who advanced to meet me, and when I grasped the hand this long-missed man held out to me and looked into his eyes, which were as kindly as they were bright with the sublime light of intellect, I saw that though the years had covered the hair of his head with snow, they had failed to take away anything of his youthful energy. Affectionate joy for an instant made all the usual phrases of greeting impossible, and it was only when we were in his motor-car, driving beyond the limits of London out to his place in the country, that we began to talk freely, launching out into a lively exchange of question and answer. But it was only a quick running of the fingers over the immediate surface of life, a rapid panoramic glance over the years of silence, for even the most intensive correspondence cannot make up for the spoken word and the communication received with swift sympathy. I felt rather as though some doctor who was also a friend of mine had merely made preliminary enquiries as to my general state of health before proceeding to examine the various organs.

Shaw gave his attention to driving his motor-car, which, now that the suburbs of London were left behind, dashed on into the darkness of the splendid highway, already speeding out beyond Hatfield. From here to Ayot, our journey's destination, was only an hour's walk. Ten minutes later we pulled up outside Shaw's delightful country house, at the wide-open doors of which his wonderful wife greeted me not only with a cordiality that at once made me feel at home, but as familiarly as if I had been his guest only a week before.

Now we began to go thoroughly over the ground of all we had experienced in the intervening time. We reached far back into the past. We evoked the dreadful war years; bitterest experiences, moods, and impressions were described; and finally explanations were given and opinions confessed to that could not have been put into writing and sent through the mail. But we both hastened as quickly as possible over happenings that were painful and incomprehensible, in order not to spoil these good hours together with memories of evil.

Shaw was in high spirits, and had every reason to be so. His monumental work, *Back to Methuselah*, which had remained unperformed and almost unknown in England as on the Continent, even after the great and lasting effect it had had with the Guild people in New York, had just now had an entirely surprising success in the sober industrial city of Birmingham. This colossus of a drama, which was as though it had been written for theatrical festivals of a kind and in a setting that still had to be found, took three long evenings to perform. Hitherto it had frightened off all theatrical managers, although they might have learned a lesson from serialised films with as many as eight successive parts and might have realised that plays could be performed in instalments too, so long as each part was so effective, so interesting, and so much worth seeing that the audience would be eager to discover what was going to happen next.

A new man, Barry Jackson by name, had realised this and acted accordingly, so making a name for himself and furthering the cause of a world-famous writer's greatest work in such a way as to earn the gratitude of us all. Shaw, who had been positively delighted by his new apostle's productions, had obviously been surprised by this success, for he had not thought it possible in England; at the same time, he was rightly amazed that we, who had always shown so much understanding for and interest in his plays, had not yet set about staging his *Ring*, as he jokingly liked to call this pentateuch, which needed three evenings before the footlights that were to illuminate a far-reaching complex of ideas that might have the function, far beyond the scope of the drama itself, of creating a new view and evaluation of life.

"It is not happiness I want, but to complete my work," Shaw has, I think, said somewhere, freely adapting Nietzsche's words. Nevertheless, satisfaction at the success of such an unusual achievement could not fail to bring the writer near to happiness; at any rate, a gleam of lofty contentment lit up his face all through the period of my stay. The great experiment that for years kept the creator of *Methuselah* chained to his tremendous task had ended in triumph. But meanwhile the utterly inexhaustible and untiring creative power of this restless genius had led him to new shores. The German *Methuselah* was still awaiting its birth, while *Saint Joan*, a clear German version of which had recently been completed, was very soon to begin its triumphal progress through the German theatres.

For the modest herald of a unique genius' great achievements, it was of no little interest, and extremely illuminating, for the first time to hear Shaw read one of his own works aloud. Every author whose visions rise up out of the depths of the soul, and who is at the same time a creator of form, reads or recites his own work in the same way in which he created it, which means more or less that the inner voice that hitherto only he himself has been able to hear now becomes audible to others, so leading the understanding listener close to the gates of origin, to the primal spring of poetic creativeness.

So it was with closed eyes and listening intently that I experienced the first act of the new work. Shaw read with tremendous intensity, bringing every word to life, brilliantly illuminating every smallest scene with the light of its own inevitability. All at once I understood why he was more obstinately opposed to shortening of his work than many other authors, who would and do permit important cuts for the sake of theatrical effect, even at the price of destroying beautiful passages. The organic nature of each of the many sentences, the density of the stylistic texture of Shaw's writing, became apparent. These opening scenes of a serious play, shot through with but a little of Shaw's usual humour, revealed both the fact that he had made the most thorough historical studies and the faithfulness with which he insisted on upholding historical truth. This was what the Maid of Orleans was like, the straightforward soldier-girl, the simple peasant lass, whom our own great Schiller raised to tragic heights in his poetical play, through which she storms as a divine heroine.

This singularly effective play, which was to be produced for the first time in England that same year, contains fascinating scenes, such as that between the Maid and the Bastard of Orleans, the scene in Warwick's tent, the whole of the strange coronation of the King of France, and above all the deeply moving trial scene, in which Joan is to be condemned to be burnt at the stake if she does not repent and confess her heresies and dæmonic possession and recant her previous errors.

Incapable of understanding the distinction between God and the Church, but filled with an infinite hunger for life, Joan is prepared to buy her liberty with a formality that cannot destroy her soul. So she consents to sign a document that contains her recantation and her confession of heresy, together with a vow not to put any trust in her inner voices from now on, but to see the Church and the Pope as being in rightful spiritual authority over her. She cannot write, but she agrees to let her hand be guided, as usual, in order to make her signature on the parchment.

What follows now is one of the most moving scenes in modern dramatic writing. Joan is jubilantly looking forward to her freedom, which she, entirely at peace with herself and sure in her unshakable faith in her inner voice, believes she has not bought too dearly. Then to her horror she is informed by the Inquisition that although she will escape with her life, in order to do penance for her sins she is to be condemned to life-long imprisonment. In despair she flings herself on the deceptive document and tears it to pieces. In heart-rending words she declares that a quick death is a much milder punishment than what her treacherous rescuers have in mind. In an overwhelming outburst of emotion the Maid, now finally condemned to be burnt at the stake, describes the importance of personal freedom and abandons herself to her judges with the wild cry: "Now I know that your word is from the Devil, but mine is from God!"

There is perhaps scarcely any work of Shaw's that contains so many unforgettable sayings and phrases as his *Saint Joan*. From many scenes there rise undertones of a vainly combated despair of humanity's goodwill.

The few days spent uninterruptedly in the company of two rare human beings passed all too quickly. And when I exchanged with that great European those heartfelt words *Auf Wiedersehen!* ('Until we meet again!') it was no mere formality, and the additional phrase 'in a better world', which we suppressed, would by no means have meant the Beyond, but only a better Here and Now, something that one could not despair of after having just had the privilege of enjoying the happiness of this most noble companionship.

The temptation to return home via Paris was great, and I could not resist it. The journey to the capital of one of the victorious countries was instructive enough, but to the honour of the French and of the government they had at that time, which was still in a belligerent state of mind, it must be said that they showed no signs of boastfulness, over-weeningness, or exaggerated self-confidence.

My reunion with Courteline this time took place not in a café but at his house, and his dear wife Marie-Jeanne opened the door and embraced me. But our sincere pleasure in being together again at last was to some extent muted by the fact that my friend appeared, alas, to have aged terribly. To my sorrow I learned that the unfortunate writer of comedies was the victim of a tragic fate. He was now suffering from a severe diabetic condition which was progressing at an alarming rate, something that he himself, to divert attention from his illness, glossed over with the words: "Old age has suddenly descended upon me and is getting me down, and the name of the disease that it uses to beat me and rob me is a matter of complete indifference."

During a short interval when Courteline was called away to the telephone, Madame Courteline told me that the doctors were even talking of the possibility of an operation's becoming necessary, since the malignant disease had set up a gangrenous condition in his right leg. My poor friend came back to his chair in quite a gay mood and said: "All the things I was told about insulin, so long as it was only the others who had diabetes! I get injections every day. But what good does it do me? I'm hoping it *will* do some good, if only so that I can return your visits some day at long last and descend upon you in Vienna."

Then he began talking about the war and the little happenings that it had brought about in his own life, and he talked so un-wearyingly that I did not try to interrupt him. He was greatly embittered against the vanquished, but equally so against the victors. He had not a single good word to say for anyone, not even for those who had, after all, saved France in her hour of need. All he wanted was the impossible, all that was irrevocably lost: a return to the old days and his own glorious youth, which he mourned every day.

Yes, in the days of his youth we would not have remained in his house, beautiful and comfortable even though it was. We would have rushed off to the Café Napolitain, and thence, if the weather had been fine, have gone to the Bois, to admire the little blondes strolling about there, as he had been accustomed to do in those by-gone times.

We were rather heavy-hearted when we took leave of each other. But Courteline knew that Paris was not as far away for me as Vienna was for him.

René Puaux had in the meantime become a leader-writer on *Le Temps*, while his brother was the French Ambassador in Bucharest and had perhaps got ahead of him in the race up the ladder of life. But Puaux was as pleased as if he had been privileged to represent not only the views of his newspaper, but, like his brother, his country as well. His rise on the staff of this newspaper, on which he had been working even at the time when he translated my *Convalescence*, had been slow and difficult, but from a number of things he said I gathered that he had made himself indispensable there.

After my return to Vienna the first interesting encounter I had was with the young actress Elisabeth Bergner, about whom I had already heard many good things said on my travels in Switzerland. We talked on the telephone and met several times in the lounge of her hotel. I remember that I promised her the first fair copy of the typescript of the German version of *Saint Joan*. But she was only passing through Vienna, and it was not until the very day she left that I was able to keep my word and hand her the play. She was very deeply moved and suddenly said, pressing the manuscript to her bosom: "With this Saint Joan, which I don't even know yet, I shall stand or fall." During this tiny scene I had the feeling that she might well be the right actress for the part, even though her appearance had little in common with that of the original and with that of the Joan that Shaw had in mind.

But the case of *Saint Joan* was quite different from that of, for instance, *Pygmalion*. The world première took place in London, with Sybil Thorndike in the title-rôle, and was an amazing success, the greatest that Shaw had ever had with a play. But this only increased my responsibility, and since there were at that time not yet any great bonds of friendship between me and Elisabeth Bergner, I did not go any further than suggesting her for the title-rôle to Max Reinhardt, who had at once acquired the rights of the play for his Deutsches Theater. I also mentioned the name of Käthe Dorsch; but Reinhardt, who would have liked to see Helene Thimig as Saint Joan in Vienna, at once and with the greatest of confidence decided on Elisabeth Bergner for the Berlin production, a choice that demanded as much of her as it helped her on.

He demanded and received the rights of the first German production of this extremely important masterpiece, with which Bernard Shaw had continued his incredibly high flights of achievement to which all the most outstanding intellects of that time looked up with admiration and approval.

Elisabeth Bergner and Max Reinhardt insisted that I should be present from the first rehearsal to the first night of this noble work, accompanying it in all its remarkable peripeteias, and in those days of hard work I saw the proof of the genius not only of Shaw but of Max Reinhardt and Elisabeth Bergner too. The première of this play was the greatest theatrical success that I have ever known. Overnight, as it were, it transformed a young actress, who was feverish with doubts, into the most sensational figure of a production with which nothing on the German stage could stand comparison. The iron curtain had to be raised again and again, because the enthusiastic audience simply refused to leave the theatre.

I remember that then, after the first night in Berlin, I wrote Shaw the longest letter I ever wrote to him, to reconcile him to the casting of his Joan in Germany. For what he envisaged was nothing like a sensitive being, filled to the last fibre of her soul with a sense of her mission, but a robust girl, much less spiritual, but physically all the graver, a view in which he was confirmed not only by history but also by Sybil Thorndike's triumph.

It caused me some slight malicious satisfaction that a few years later, in Paris, Shaw had to accept a Joan in comparison with whom Elisabeth Bergner was a Sybil Thorndike. This was Ludmilla Pitoeff, whom Shaw did not want to consider even for a moment. Elisabeth Bergner stood halfway between the English tragedienne and the little saint, the child of anguish, that Ludmilla Pitoeff so touchingly made of this heroic figure, not without likewise considerably increasing the fame that she already enjoyed at that period.

Some months after the Berlin première, which in my opinion had in itself made Shaw a candidate for the Nobel Prize, the play had to be produced at the Deutsche Volkstheater in Vienna, because the Burgtheater could not make up its mind to become involved in the religious and political controversies that are so wonderfully associated with the tragedy of the purity and innocence of heaven-sent being.

Beer, the director of the Deutsche Volkstheater, and his producer, Karl Heins Martin, had of course been present at the Berlin première and wanted to engage a famous actress for the title-rôle, even if it could not be Elisabeth Bergner, who had already been playing Joan every night for months in Berlin. But in the Volkstheater's own company there was the unusually beautiful, ambitious, and very gifted Annemarie Steinsieck, who was a friend of mine. It would simply have broken her heart if she, whom nobody in the company could compete with in this part, had been thrust on one side to make way for an outsider.

Now, admittedly, the secret of this part is that scarcely any gifted actress can fail to do brilliantly in it. Up to this day I have not heard of any failure in the part, and it is Bernard Shaw who must be given the credit for having brought many a German actress to the forefront simply by the fact that she had the good fortune of being allowed to act this part.

From the moment of this unusual event onward it had become impossible for me to expect any interest or sympathy for a dramatic work of my own or to think of its making any impact. I was badly cornered.

It had now become much harder to interest the great mass of the public, especially of the theatre-going public—and, after all, most educated readers go to the theatre—in the translator of *Saint Joan* and his own works. A horrible expression was coined for referring to me publicly, one that the reviewers cannot bring themselves to drop even to this day. And this expression is 'Shaw's translator'.

To the best of my knowledge there has never been a parallel case where any other writer was concerned.

A novel by me was henceforth by 'Shaw's translator'. A volume of poems had been published by 'Shaw's translator', and I saw myself literally driven into a corner from which I found it very difficult to escape. All that I had published up to then, not entirely unsuccessfully, quietly flickered out. There was no longer any demand for it, only for Shaw's next works. My name as a writer in my own right faded away; the public and its spokesmen became impatient when I spoke on my own account.

Shaw himself was one of the first to notice this change, with the uneasiness of friendly sympathy. He thought that the success of *Frau Gitta's Sühne* in England and America would counterbalance the failure that I myself thought I would be at least for the next few years—a fate like any other fate with which one has to come to terms for the time being. For me this undeserved state of affairs was a blow, even though others, above all S. Fischer and Moritz Heimann, would not admit that I was justified in being depressed. At that time they both tried, each in very different words, to put my mind at rest about this odd depreciation. Fischer said: "There are a few stories of yours that cannot be thrust into oblivion by any success anyone else may have, and I shall do my utmost to see that no attempt is made to do so, either."

Heimann took the same attitude where several poems were concerned, though as a friend he shared my opinion, shaking his head over what he also had observed and feeling with me more deeply than my publisher, who made light of the whole thing. But down to the present day nothing much has changed in the situation, if only because the theatre is stronger than books are and a dramatic author always has more success with his plays than with his narrative works—something that Gerhart Hauptmann too, for instance, was distressed to find.

I thought that with my endeavours for Shaw I was adding a plus to my own work, but, alas, it was a minus. It was incomprehensible! It was not long since my play, *The Man She Loved*, had had a pleasing success at the Deutsche Volkstheater. But of what play could one say as much if one thought of *Saint Joan*, which, admittedly, *The Man She Loved* had preceded in point of time? After the première at the Deutsche Volkstheater it was not long before Director Arthur

Hellmer put the play on for the first time in Frankfurt-am-Main, where it was perhaps even more successful than in Vienna, although this production came about in a very strange manner.

I received a peculiar telegram from Hellmer, saying more or less this: 'We have begun rehearsing *The Man She Loved*, but the leading actress strikes me as inadequate. Come at once and bring a suitable actress with you.'

At first I was rather taken aback, almost bewildered, but I accepted the challenge, quickly remembering that Helene Landing, the unusually talented and good-looking wife of that well-known *jeune premier*, Ernst Dumke, and a famous Lulu in Wedekind's *Erdgeist* (*Earth Spirit*), had a short time ago come to live in Vienna and was only waiting to continue the great success with which she had begun her career in Germany. I hurried along to her with my play and showed her Hellmer's telegram. She was all agog to do it, asked for twenty-four hours in which to read the play and give her decision, and, when the time was up and I went to see her again, she agreed with the utmost enthusiasm, deplored the fact that as a result of her divorce she had missed the première in Vienna, and set about packing her trunks in order to travel to Frankfurt with me.

I wired to Director Hellmer to inform him of this turn of events He answered with great satisfaction that he was expecting us both for rehearsals within three days. We then arrived punctually, though rather worn out from studying parts during our railway journey, but Frau Landing displayed an enthusiasm and zeal that was linked up with her magnificent talent and which perhaps also had some bearing on the tragic end that she unexpectedly met with only a few weeks after the première, at which her personal success was greater and more convincing than that of the play itself. As became apparent later, she had taken a risk in accepting the part at all. Like so many women, this remarkable actress, who was probably also trying to deaden her feelings of disappointment and grief over her broken marriage, had taken too much on herself; after about five performances she collapsed as the result of a sudden inflammation of the gall-bladder. I had the opportunity of visiting her in hospital, and confidently said *Au revoir*, because she was positively looking forward to the operation that she was about to undergo and was in thoroughly good spirits. It was therefore a great shock to hear, about ten days later, that the operation, which she had not merely agreed to have but insisted on having, had been too much for her heart and she had died.

Now there was only one play of mine left unproduced, that is to say, if I except *Kaiser Diokletian*. This was *Das Land der Treue* (*The Land of Constancy*), the rights of which were some years later acquired by Reinhardt for the repertoire of the Deutsche Theater, where it was staged by that excellent producer Mittler.

Meanwhile, however, my wife and I had been invited by Bernard Shaw to come and stay with him at his country place at Ayot. This happened at a time when I was feeling a great deal of mental and emotional strain, and I hoped that I would soon be restored by his company, perhaps even more by that of his incomparable wife.

I had come to know what English hospitality meant even as a young man, in the houses of families with whom we were on terms of friendship. But this case was entirely different. After so many successful endeavours in the cause of his fame, the Shaws wanted to get to know me—but above all my wife, too—better, by means of spending some time together informally; and since they were admirably considerate in leaving us alone when we needed rest and making the time pass entertainingly when we joined them, the few weeks that were granted us in the company of these good hosts were in every way stimulating and delightful, without any trace of disharmony.

We went with our host and hostess on their regular walks and came to know the pretty, hilly surroundings of Ayot and St. Albans very well. Bernard Shaw was, as I have already mentioned, an excellent motorist and also drove us about the district a good deal. He showed us the wonderful old church of St. Albans, and on that occasion displayed unexpectedly great historical knowledge, such as I had, however, always admired in him.

Whenever we did not find Shaw waiting for us at the usual hour, we knew that he was working in his tent at the bottom of the garden. Mrs. Shaw then liked to have us with her, so that we did not disturb him until he came out of his tent and looked around for us. The evenings were particularly stimulating, because Shaw was very musical and remained very fond of music into his extreme old age. After dinner he would sit down at the piano and play. He insisted that my wife, who had quite a good voice, though not a very highly trained one, should sing to his accompaniment. That always went off quite well and entirely satisfied the audience's modest demands, until Shaw suddenly launched into *Tristan* and my wife vainly tried to hold her own as Isolde. In order to set her a good example—as though that could have helped—he himself began to shriek in the highest and loudest of voices, without succeeding in convincing us that this was a satisfactory cast for *Tristan*.

In Ayot I was once again to meet with the blessings of vegetarian cookery. There, more than in his London home, I had the opportunity of observing the strange division of diet that this couple had instituted. I was no longer sorry for Shaw as a vegetarian, for he used to get two extra helpings of macaroni au gratin, twice as many potatoes as anyone else, a large piece of Emmenthal cheese afterwards, three oranges instead of one—and I could go on in this way for a long time—while Mrs. Shaw served her guests and herself with the choicest of dishes but not with so much of them. Even at breakfast there was tea and coffee, ham, cold partridge, and masses of all kinds of cheese and butter. We, who were naturally not used to such luxurious breakfasts, had to our great regret, feasting our eyes more than our stomachs on these delicacies, to renounce most of this delicious fare. Mrs. Shaw herself did not eat much of any of these many titbits, but there they were, after all, and it seemed to be a point of pride with her that all these things were to be had in her house in the country. When I consider what quantities of food Shaw devoured instead of the small slice of meat that we ate, I rather doubt whether the vegetarian way of living is to be regarded as particularly abstemious or ascetic.

It was only when we had to begin to think about our journey home that we realised how incredibly fast the stimulating days had passed, and we parted from this noble couple less light-heartedly than we would have done if everything had been as cool and formal as one involuntarily expects a British household to be.

Mrs. Shaw accompanied us to London, while Shaw remained in Ayot in order to deal with correspondence that had been somewhat neglected as a result of our presence. It was doubtless also in order to get on with his new work, *The Intelligent Woman's Guide to Socialism and Capitalism*; for he had temporarily turned his back on the drama and given his attention to a work that fulfilled the hopes that had been set on him in his youth as a Fabian, as a campaigner for the just distribution of property, and as one who would help to solve the difficult problems of life.

Far from presuming to pass a qualified judgment on this work, which I translated into German with the help of a political writer by the name of Freissler, I must nevertheless state that it caused a great sensation in Germany, though it did not meet with the boundless admiration that was accorded it by prominent public figures and statesmen especially in England; among them I should like to mention Ramsay MacDonald. At a casual meeting we had on the Orient Express, the Prime Minister said to me: "After the Bible this is in my eyes the most important book that humanity possesses."

I had scarcely returned home when I realised that with this visit to Shaw providence had given me great moral strength for the future. I soon needed it, for only a few months later, and much sooner than we had expected, Moritz Heimann closed his eyes for ever. As long as he lived he was so lively that only a few weeks before his death, when I visited him, even his wife and his most intimate friends, who saw him daily, did not believe that he would have such an early end. They were most grievously surprised.

It is not given to all to praise admired persons and friends in the hour of death's visitation in such a way that they succeed in collecting all knowledge about the deceased, in giving form to their sincere grief and, as it were, firing a salute out across freshly-filled graves. How firmly and dreamlessly one must be rooted in the ground of one's own life in order to be able to survey another's life so swiftly and be so ready with words to speak of it! It is such people who comfort the bereaved, who give them consolation and strength with their incontestable words and their correct evaluation of the great gifts that the friend now dead called his own. And if he who has passed over was one who gave from among the noblest of possessions, they are able to settle the debt they once incurred and speak aloud of what they received from him. These, such as are reliable beyond the limits of the grave itself, can prove themselves and depart in an exalted mood, full of comfort for others, from the place where they have cast the first sods of earth upon the gradually lowered coffin.

But those oppressed people who are poor in words, those people whom sorrow makes dumb, whom no god has endowed with the fortunate gift of fluent speech and swift summarising statement—

they creep away like ingrates who cannot but feel ashamed. Yet among these too there are true friends. Shy-eyed, they glance up at those who are astonished at their silence. Comfortless and unable to give comfort, they hasten away, bowed under their burden, as though they were superfluous and uninvited guests whom no emotional need, but only the apparent wish to join in with others in their mourning, had brought among the select throng of eloquent friends who have been doing the dead man the last honour they can do him.

And Moritz Heimann's friends, too, were divided into these two groups, into the eloquent, who had long ago declared what man he was, and the silent, who had for a long time been groping for words— for words to draw the portrait of the man now passed into eternity and to hold it fast for ever, more sharply, more vividly, more irrevocably even than it had already been alive in their hearts. I myself went through this struggle for weeks on end. I dreamed of him, heard his voice, felt his familiar gaze bent on me. It was no vision from the realm of shades that visited my soul. Alive, as in the years of his most robust strength and energy, he stood before me, talking and expounding as it had been his way, taking away my doubts and anxieties, distributing the light and shade that my sun cast more rightly than my own feelings could do it, seeking to put me in the place that was, after all, the place my destiny had allotted me, and showering me with tokens of his kindness as in the days of our long friendship. Many a night was animated, for me, by the sound of that voice. How could I speak *about* him so long as I was still speaking *with* him?

Only when the certainty of his death in the body, the irrefutable fact of his non-existence, had inexorably stamped itself on my brain did I find my way back to clarity. At last I could associate myself with those who had already uttered what things about a man can be comprehended in words.

They had done justice to his mind, as to his model character, and yet I could not help feeling as though the great masters who had gone a good distance along the road with him had unintentionally and almost imperceptibly adapted him for the purpose of general admiration, as it were turning him into a statue for later generations to admire, and as though without their noticing it the peculiar and elusive being that Moritz Heimann had been had somehow slipped between their fingers. I missed the reproduction of the shadowy being that he had been, a man who was lonely in the furthest depths of his soul—traits that, sharpened by a strange bitterness, shifted him into the twilight of those to whom no salvation has come. His fate, which was to be incapable of either opening up or communicating himself to others, and a quiet desperation about being so walled up in himself—these were things that very often spoke in his eyes, his melancholy eyes, always reaching out along the horizon for inaccessible distances. The joy of being completely recognised for what he was by those, such as Oscar Loerke, who had a profound gift of understanding and were his intimates, doubtless was some comfort to him; but he wavered in many a direction, yearning for the embrace of unattainable and perhaps never present things. His great heart, which so few understood, was less the heart of a lover than it was a father's heart, such was his kindness and his warmth of affection for his own son as for the son, of man everywhere—who, indeed, for the most part wanders fatherless through his errors and his sins.

Moritz Heimann had tasted moments of success and had felt the intoxication of sheer ability in his brain; but, above and beyond that, what he enjoyed, perhaps, with ever deeper pleasure, with still richer pride, was the success of those whom he had helped in their career, whom he had guided and whose powers he had heightened to their limit. He loved all the blossoms of the tree with equal love and suffered under the cruel, irrevocable fate that causes many to drop to the ground, never developing towards that day when the successful fruits shine out all the more radiantly. And how he cherished and tended the little tree that had already suffered its first blow! How he always tried to heal it and give it its place among the undamaged and more fortunate tree-trunks already growing tall! His busy gardener's hand gave many a plant the chance to bloom that without him would have withered and died away.

Moritz Heimann, his brothers' keeper, was not the man who could keep and look after himself. He squandered himself on others, in endless, fruitful conversations, to the point of exhaustion. And this ever-recurring exhaustion, which some strange dæmonism drove him to seek, was surely what contained the mortal seeds of that long illness of which he perished all too early, not yet old in years.

His life had confronted him with many problems, which he was too wise to settle but which he ever and again tried in vain to weigh up and balance against others. A fateful series of circumstances, misunderstandings, chance happenings, queer turns of destiny, loaded him with indescribably heavy burdens, which were often within an ace of crushing this erect and courageous fighter to the ground. He knew himself for what he was; he saw right through himself and his environment; and anyone, whoever it might be, who believed he could open Moritz Heimann's eyes soon came to realise how much wider they were already open than those of the apostles of truth who sometimes jostled around him. The protective covering of an affected naïvety lay side by side with a penetrating recognition of the bitterest truth. And he also knew everything that he did not want to know. Moritz Heimann probably never made a mistake about a human being. But his fine sense of fairness sometimes made him take up the defence of lost positions; he could not be an enemy, because he loved goodness too much to be anything but the friend of his foes. His striving and endeavour was for perfection, to which he sought to bring—as nearly as possible—every talent that confided itself to him in its need of help. And in so doing what he most contributed to was often the perfection of his own soul; and so he went from us long before his time, one who had early reached perfection. The solitaries and eccentrics who struggle for utterance, the self-absorbed dreamers and visionaries, the stammerers and fumblers—it was his words, his illumination and encouragement, that thawed them and drew forth their eloquence, while he himself, a man of infinite silences, never ceased to work at the improvement of his own treasures of mind and heart. Since the many who owed him a debt of gratitude, who can bear witness for him and stand up for him, must perish or have already perished, everything that is today known of Moritz Heimann to the few of us who are still alive will some day be buried and forgotten.

What will remain is his work, and that is pure and great enough to banish every doubt of his mission. Yet it is at the same time work that does not offer itself easily to one and all, which has not the gift of appealing, pleasingly and complacently, to anyone who approaches it lightly, turning the pages with a casual hand, wishing to absorb it as rapidly as possible in order to be able to join in the conversation when this teacher of mankind is the subject. Only those who can really provide themselves with leisure, those who are capable of seeking hours for edification and finding them, will find in Moritz

Heimann's writings the illumination and redemption that the devout reader does ultimately seek when he is alone with his book as with his God.

After these experiences in the spirit and in the world and this long absence from Vienna, I was no little astonished to find, on my return, that my native city was really quite altered. The era of the new-rich had come, and they gave tormented Vienna a peculiar imprint, creating contrasts such as are not often seen. While Deutsch, Bauer and Breitner, the Socialist leaders, did all they could to save the working-class population from the worst extremities of want and to impose on the rich as much as possible in the way of burdens, and while these unresting men did in fact succeed in alleviating the misery and in suffocating the ever and again up-flaring flames of a revolution of the discontented by means of the wise measures that they took, the newly acquired wealth of the war profiteers and racketeers spread out recklessly and for all to see, with its dubious camp-following of debauches and the barefaced mania for gambling, speculation and every sort of adventuring.

But it was also the time of the great operetta successes, which resounded far beyond the frontiers of our native country. The triumvirate Lehár, Fall, and Oscar Straus had their triumphs everywhere in the world and did, in spite of everything, restore to fame and reputation a Vienna that was different from the Vienna of the gamblers and the newly rich. Nor was it long before Emmerich Kalman appeared, another brilliant light beside that constellation of three.

From the artistic point of view, too, Vienna had greatly changed, and in one particular case for the good. Max Reinhardt had always wanted to have a theatre in Vienna and had repeatedly spoken of how much easier it would be to put plays on in Berlin and Vienna simultaneously than in only one of these cities, because each would be able to help the other out, and, with all the artists gathered together under one leadership, alternating productions by visiting companies under a single producer would be much easier. Now as a result of the death of Joseph Jarno, the husband of that celebrated actress from the Volkstheater, Hansi Niese, the Theater in der Josefstadt was left without a director. There did not seem to be anyone of ability prepared to take it over and make something of it, pretty much without tradition as it was, for not everyone had Jarno's

K

flair and, above all, the chance to have Hansi Niese acting in the plays presented.

And now this orphaned little theatre was available—this Theater in der Josefstadt, which Max Reinhardt knew pretty well from his early days, from the time when he had brought his little company of chosen actors there on visits and had had his first sensational successes.

And now Max Reinhardt sought a Mæcenas, whom he found in Camillo Castiglioni, a financier who glowed with passion for the theatre and who was at that time tremendously rich. Castiglioni, the husband of Iphigenie Buchmann, a man who was ambitious in every sphere of life, who later learnt to know life's heights and depths, and today, an aged man, after another world war lives on in Rome and seems at the end of his life to be rising to prominence and reputation once again—this man, who was at that time a millionaire, granted Max Reinhardt his dream's fulfilment and made him a present of a theatre. For that reason, even though he cannot be thought of in the same terms as Reinhardt and cannot be crowned with an artist's laurels, his name is inseparable from that of Max Reinhardt and his rise in Vienna.

Nor did he content himself with simply buying the theatre for the producer whom he so much admired, because after all he had money to spare for the purchase of it; he went further and completely rebuilt it, transforming it into one of the sights of Europe. Down to the present day it remains the jewel among German theatres. Providence saw to it that it was spared during the war; this delightful building with the chandelier that goes up and down was saved from all the bombs and other forms of destruction. And today, after the bombing of the Burgtheater, after the collapse, after the terrible 'liberation', it is the most beautiful theatre in Vienna, a memorial to bygone carefree days with all their *joie de vivre*.

It was here that the Thimigs, two brothers and a sister, Paula Wessely, Attila Hörbiger, Lily Darvas, Gustav Waldau, Anton Edthofer, Adrienne Gessner, and many others who are today still the delight of theatre-goers celebrated their first triumphs. Max Reinhardt, who had reserved the management for himself, was naturally kept far too busy by his theatres in Berlin to be able to direct theatrical affairs in Vienna regularly; but it must be said that at the Theater in der Josefstadt nothing was done that had not first been agreed to and approved by Max Reinhardt.

The chief managers of this theatre, moreover, were touchingly and enthusiastically devoted to their great exemplar, to whose ideals they were utterly loyal in their work, none more so than Ernst Lothar and Max Preminger, both most energetically and efficiently supported by Emil Geyer, who much earlier on had been in independent control of the Neue Wiener Bühne.

It must be said to the eternal credit of that temperamental Mæcenas, Camillo Castiglioni, that he gave Max Reinhardt and his directors a completely free hand and did not keep any check on them even in a material respect. The Theater in der Josefstadt was his hobby, not his business. On the other hand, Castiglioni had a more noble, though perhaps also more snobbish, ambition of a social kind. When this extremely busy man was in Vienna, he always insisted that Reinhardt and his most prominent colleagues—authors, producers, actors and actresses—must be present at the receptions he gave. At these large and splendid entertainments 'his' theatre must be well represented, with all that went with it.

Iphigenie Buchmann, the wife of the man who created Vienna's most beautiful theatre, was a woman of such grace, tact and charm that she made Castiglioni's house a point of great attraction; and so, with the exception of a few personal antagonists, the guests he wished to have were glad to come thronging to his receptions.

Never before had Professor Max Reinhardt taken so much interest in still unwritten plays of Bernard Shaw's as he did after the success— which was still far from having come to an end—of *Saint Joan*. He begged me in the most pressing terms to come to Berlin, asking me to put it to Shaw in his name that he should follow up *Saint Joan* with a drama about Christ, which in his view nobody except Bernard Shaw was capable of writing. I conveyed to him the exact wording of the detailed answer I received from my friend, who had found this suggestion highly interesting.

Shaw explained to this great magician of the theatre that Christ was quite impossible as a dramatic hero because he was always silent just when he ought to speak and because his story was undramatic from the beginning to the end. Christ was less the hero of a drama than the creator of innumerable dramas that were the result of his magnificent influence and his noble silence. It would, according to Shaw, have meant falsifying the imperishable image of a great human figure to set it forth as that of a dramatic hero, reducing it to a mere 'rôle'.

By the same mail Shaw sent me his new play, which he had written after completing the *Intelligent Woman's Guide to Socialism and Capitalism*, although everyone in the theatrical world—those initiated and qualified to speak, those uninitiated and unqualified, all alike—urged him in the strongest terms never again to write a play after that overwhelming success, because another play must infallibly fall far below the heights on which *Saint Joan* towered—heights that every dramatist reaches only once in his life, if he ever reaches them at all. But Shaw did not have any qualms in this direction; he simply set straight about writing and giving form to whatever was closest to his heart, turning to the subject that happened to be preoccupying him at the time.

The new play was called *The Apple Cart*, an expression that in English has a figurative meaning too, namely *Verkehrshindernis* (a barricade or road-block). In German a literal translation of the title would have been almost nonsensical, because an apple cart in German is no different from, say, a bread cart. I was of course under uncommonly great pressure in the case of this new play and very quickly got to work, not budging from my desk until I had finished it.

Reinhardt's Mæcenas had his eye on this new work of Shaw's and demanded that Reinhardt should get me—of course long before there was any question of its being produced—to come and read this play, for which everyone was waiting with such tremendous eagerness, to a select audience of writers and artists at his house. Max Reinhardt told me of this wish, and since I was never a spoil-sport, I at once agreed to the proposal. So it came about, only a few weeks after I had made the first draft of my German version, that the memorable reading was held at Castiglioni's house.

The play had meanwhile been entitled by me *Der Kaiser von Amerika* (*The Emperor of America*), a title that, however remotely it was drawn from a passage in the dialogue, to my delight pleased everyone very much and was said to be very effective. The reading itself went off extraordinarily successfully. Not only did it meet with the singular approval of the connoisseurs present, some of whom were destined to act the play; it also turned out quite unexpectedly that our host, Camillo Castiglioni, had an unusually great understanding of things theatrical, perhaps as a result of living together with the artist his wife was, or as the result of an inborn gift, which he had, admittedly, diverted into quite different and much more lucrative channels.

Castiglioni was the first person who began to speak after the conclusion of the reading, while the others remained silent with approval. We looked at each other in astonishment, for we had seldom heard anyone, immediately after hearing a dramatic work for the first time, speak words so shrewd and so decisive with regard to the impending production.

To our amazement this ambitious man demanded a cast that was precisely that which Max Reinhardt had had in mind: Werner Krauss for the title-rôle in Berlin, and Gustav Waldau for the title-rôle in Vienna. This financier, whose reputation had such ups and downs in the day-to-day history of Vienna, was the first to utter these two names; he also suggested various others for the cast. Among them was the lovely young Nora Gregor.

I hope I may be forgiven this historical reminiscence, because this scene was, as it happens, fairly characteristic of that period, and also because honour should be paid to the memory of a man who quite unselfishly—even if perhaps out of vanity—gave a city a beautiful theatre, if for no other reason than to get himself publicity and to stimulate possible emulation.

However, this was a rather shy beginning to the career that *The Apple Cart* had in German-speaking territory. Soon afterwards the memorable German première took place in Berlin, with Werner Krauss, Maria Bard and Hans Albers in the leading parts. And as almost every play of Shaw's has some little story that goes with it, a story that I do not, however, always feel justified in repeating, because each of them does, after all, already belong to the traditional stock of theatrical anecdotes and does not seem interesting enough for a larger public, here I will for once permit myself to speak of a dress-rehearsal that aroused many very different reactions at the Deutsche Theater in Berlin.

It was particularly with regard to prophecies of possible success that fundamentally different views were held by various dramaturgists, actors, theatrical agents and others present, including all those visitors who never fail to appear on such an occasion. Some at once foretold a roaring success, while others, obviously still thinking of the wild enthusiasm set up in the same audience at the dress-rehearsal of *Saint Joan*, took a much more sober view of the play's prospects. My wife, who was sitting beside me, during the long interlude somewhat damped my expectations, and I was just going to try to convert her to another opinion when Director Herzberg, at that time Reinhardt's treasurer, came up to me and sat down beside me. He began by saying quite frankly: "Do you really think this play will be a great success? I mean a success that can compare even remotely with that of *Saint Joan*? Even at the dress-rehearsal the audience isn't really keen!"

I nodded in agreement, seeing this comment as a continuation of the views my wife had been expressing. Herzberg however now became very lively and said: "Well, I'm a gambler by nature and I'd be prepared to buy the royalties of this play from you, from the première on, for all time." He mentioned the considerable sum of twenty-five thousand marks. At this moment he was called to the telephone. Exclaiming: "I'll be back in a moment!" he rushed away.

Now my wife began trying to talk me over, saying: "You should jump at it! The man's out of his senses. The play will never bring in as much money as that. Take what he offers you and let's go straight home after the first night, which we must stay for, however painful it will be."

Meanwhile Herzberg had returned. "Now," he said, "we can draw up the agreement at once. You do agree? Are you glad I'm so reckless?"

Having rapidly considered all the consequences, above all the annoyance that my agreement would arouse in Bernard Shaw, who would never in any circumstances have agreed to such a thing and had many and many a time rejected similar suggestions, I replied: "You know, my dear Director, why, after all, should I have less confidence in this play than you have? Why shouldn't I take the same risk myself? It would not be any satisfaction to me to see you lose a lot of money if the failure you foresee should in fact eventuate, but, being the kind of person I am, I should be frightfully annoyed if in the end I had to look on while you reaped the profit from my lack of confidence. I'm no business man and I don't see any sort of business deal in the production of this strange experiment here, with which I seem to have been successful. Whether in the end it turns out to be good business or is a financial failure interests me much less than the effect that is to be created by these scenes, in which the clash between feudalism and socialism is presented on the stage for the first time."

Director Herzberg only laughed, turned to my wife and said: "You have my sympathy, *gnädige Frau*!" and held out his hand to me with the words: "Well, no harm done!" As the curtain rose at that moment he slipped away as quickly as he had come.

I was then very richly rewarded for my valiant trust in the play. The first night turned out to be one of the greatest successes I have ever known. It was hardly any less than that of *Saint Joan*. But the two first nights could scarcely be compared. *The Apple Cart* did not, after all, create any such tremendous emotional upheavals. On the other hand, it gave one the feeling that it was the most progressive and modern play of our time, and in due course I learned that the takings had far exceeded the sum that Director Herzberg had offered me.

The fact is that in the theatre one can never be sure of anything. Nor did I then see in this anything more than the confirmation of that axiom—for who knows what the fate of the play would have been if Max Reinhardt had not been the producer of it, if Werner Krauss and Hans Albers had not excelled themselves, and if Maria Bard had not made such a charming effect with her little piece at the piano, with which her part opened, working the audience up to a frenzy of applause that did not diminish all through the evening?

And so Castiglioni's prophecy had been fulfilled in Berlin. But how would it be now in Vienna, at that wonderful Theater in der Josefstadt?

Having been treated with such princely generosity by his Mæcenas, Max Reinhardt naturally exerted himself to the utmost in order to repay him with supremely good productions. This brilliant artist had never been good at arithmetic, and if his incredible artistic successes did in the end, as it happened, also turn out to be financially profitable, he owed that exclusively to his brother Edmund, who was a model of what a business man should be and, pencil in hand, checked his brother's all too audacious plans and schemes for the casts he would engage, which were always drawn up without the slightest thought of expense.

Edmund Reinhardt had come to Vienna when the time arrived to make a final decision about the cast of the Viennese production of

The Apple Cart. Max Reinhardt had, indeed, the wildest notions about what he would lavish on this play. He would really have liked to have had every part, down to the very smallest, taken by a 'star'— an expression for a famous actor or actress that was not yet current at that time.

I remember the great conference to discuss casting and production, for the sake of which Edmund Reinhardt had rushed post-haste to be at his brother's side. While Max Reinhardt recited the list of all his wishes, Edmund sat beside his brother, looking very grave and not saying a word, but busily working out sums. When Max Reinhardt had finished and all that remained to be decided was the date of the première, Edmund Reinhardt commented rather drily, addressing the ever-rapturous, intimate circle that surrounded Max: "If with this wonderful cast of actors and actresses brought from all over the world, which in many ways is beyond even what the Berlin production was, you sell every seat in the theatre every night for a hundred nights, then, my dear Max, I will certainly agree to your doing it, for then it will not cost you more than about a hundred marks a night."

There was a mildly horrified pause, and then everyone burst into roars of laughter. Max Reinhardt, who attached great importance to his brother's opinion, instantly agreed to revise his plans for the casting, and accordingly watered his wine, which however still turned out to be a wonderful drink.

If it had not been for the news of 'house full' boards going up every night in Berlin we would doubtless have been quite content, for Gustav Waldau, as King Magnus, was in his way perhaps even more convincing than Werner Krauss, and above all he was more kingly. But the Viennese public was less developed politically, and accordingly a social comedy could not be such a resounding success in Vienna as in the German capital.

Now it seemed to me that Bernard Shaw had reached the highest limits of what was possible in the German language, and it was not surprising that now, when the year 1926 was just looming up, the expectations of this remarkable man and artist should be fulfilled, expectations that had been as bold as they were justifiable, expectations, indeed, that I had had for him perhaps even to a greater extent when we were still fighting our way ahead and he had cared so little for worldly honour and evidence of public approval.

What could have been foreseen, and doubtless had been bound to come, now came about. One year before his seventieth birthday, Bernard Shaw was awarded the Nobel Prize. So far as I could observe, this distinction did not leave him entirely unmoved, if only because at that time he was the first writer in the English language to be distinguished with the award. Although I know that the Nobel Prize is always given for a writer's work as a whole and for the influence it has had throughout the world, at that time I could not shake off the feeling that in his case the international success of *Saint Joan* had been decisive in winning him this highest of all distinctions that a writer can gain.

Shaw, who was at this time deeply absorbed in his work, did not travel to Stockholm to receive the prize and attend the ceremonies associated with the awarding of it. But he informed the committee of a remarkable arrangement that he wished to make. Instead of accepting the large sum of money that goes with the award, he asked that it should be used to form a fund for the translation of Swedish masterpieces into English. This generous gift was greeted with the greatest of enthusiasm in Sweden, and now once again it was Shaw's turn to be thanked instead of his gratitude's being conveyed to others.

I am afraid what I have said about the German-language productions of *The Apple Cart* may create the impression that this play, like *Pygmalion*, was first produced in the German language. This is not so. The English première preceded that in Germany.

Sir Barry Jackson, the English Reinhardt, whose means had enabled him to create a theatre in Birmingham comparable to the Deutsche Theater and who was, as has already been mentioned, one of the earliest and most enthusiastic champions of Shaw's work, now took an extraordinary step for the sake of the master he venerated. On Shaw's seventieth birthday, which occurred in 1926, he created a kind of Bayreuth for him, organising the Shaw Festival at Malvern.

Only some few miles away from Shakespeare's birthplace, Stratford-on-Avon, halfway to Oxford, in the glorious Worcestershire countryside, is the picturesquely rambling, pretty little town of Great Malvern, an English summer resort very popular on account of its climate. In this little place among the hills, endowed with all kinds of natural beauties, there is even a spring the waters of which are reputed to be mysteriously health-giving and therefore, because *after*

K*

all one never knows, are credulously drunk, without its being easy to find out the name and nature of the salts to which the healing action might be ascribed.

Scarcely more than one hour's journey by express train from Birmingham and Oxford, less than three hours' journey from London, still more easily reached from the much-visited cathedral towns of Tewkesbury, Worcester and Gloucester, this famous old town among the hills is as though it had been made to lend a festive character to productions of an artistic kind.

Here it was possible to provide an English version of the German Bayreuth and, if there a home was created for a daring innovator and master among composers, here the same could be done for a master of the art of words, one who had had an equally hard fight to earn the recognition that was his due.

Sir Barry Jackson, the creator and organiser of the Shaw Festival at Malvern, was born in Birmingham and had known the charm of the district that he had chosen for the scene of his labours since his boyhood every bit as well as the Berliner knows, say, Wannsee and the Harz, or as most Viennese know the Semmering district. It may be that he had early felt that artistic festivals, centred in Great Malvern, would interest the whole English-speaking world and other nations as well. Bayreuth's advantages were all united here, heightened by the additional pleasure of pilgrimage.

After Sir Barry's incomparable success with the Birmingham Repertory Theatre, which he had founded, and after he had with his wonderful productions gained a large public for the favourite writer of his youth, Bernard Shaw, who was misunderstood and far too little recognised in his own country, he doubtless thought the time had come to set the crown on a life-work that he had seen growing and extending, by elevating it beyond the general theatrical routine and presenting it in such a way as to make a festival of it.

Jackson was one of those campaigners in the world of art whose voices can never fail, because he was a very marked personality, taken seriously by all who knew his achievements, one therefore who could be sure of getting a following whenever he came forward with new proposals. And what in fact happened was that not only the members of his Birmingham Repertory Company, but also eminent figures in the London theatrical world, came to serve the great cause, and, under the direction of that highly gifted producer H. K. Ayliff, offered the public stylistically rounded productions of important dramas by the master.

Sir Barry Jackson was far from wanting to make things easy for himself or to pick easy laurels. Those of his friend's works that he chose were the most dry and difficult, though at the same time, admittedly, the most profound and imperishable. He presented that noble poetic work *Heartbreak House* in a way that made it glow with an entirely new, unsuspectedly mystical radiance. He presented that profound intellectual work, *Back to Methuselah*, on three successive evenings, with such successful intellectual fireworks and with such a simple stressing of the main lines of this pentateuch that nothing of the feared brittleness of the material became apparent; even the naïvest among the audience were convinced and carried away by the sheer theatrical effectiveness of a great, new, and inspiring idea. By the exquisite simplicity with which he produced the fifth part, he achieved miracles of stagecraft and made the most of such effective material as the birth of human beings of the future out of the egg, the dance of the laboratory automata, and the deeply searching, plastic conversations of the Ancients.

These great weeks began with one of the early works, that well-known historical fantasy, *Cæsar and Cleopatra*. The main interest was, however, as was only natural, concentrated on Bernard Shaw's recently completed drama, *The Apple Cart*, the German success of which has already been described.

This world première was, of course, the centre of public interest and of the most intense discussion, all the more since, to the astonishment of Bernard Shaw's German and English friends, a performance had already been given in Polish, at the Polski Theatre in Warsaw, a production concerning which the most contradictory reports and rumours were abroad. What was undeniable was that the play had drawn huge audiences in the Polish capital, while of course the announcement that Pilsudski had asked for the première to take place in Warsaw on account of the similarity to Polish conditions was to be relegated to the realm of fairy tale.

Shaw had been inspired to write this unique comedy by his old friend Sidney Webb, who had again and again suggested that it was high time he wrote a political play, bringing politics on to the stage as the theme and substance of a drama and lifting the veil from those backstairs machinations of which the general public often knows nothing at all, but which are nevertheless the cause of so many important decisions. Shaw soon recognised that a political comedy, if it was to fulfil the profounder purpose of teaching people something and was not merely to be a casual entertainment presenting contrasting views, must above all show that there is no ruling class, that the rulers are not a class in themselves but members of all classes.

The mixed reception that this work was given by the English critics is, I am sure, partly to be explained by the fact that many people's party-political feelings were injured and even Bernard Shaw's socialist friends were not very edified by his glorification of a king and kingly gifts, because they believed the writer's standpoint was fixed once and for all as a result of his past and his great work on socialism, while, on the other hand, his dazzling intellect continually soared beyond the limits of present knowledge and did justice to all the possibilities that manifested themselves to his prophetic gaze.

The leading English critic, St. John Ervine, attacked Shaw's old enemies in an article entitled 'Shaw's Glorious Pantomime'. He called the play a spendid mixture of a kind of *Everyman* with *Ali Baba and the Forty Thieves*, and pointed out that thousands of people from all parts of Great Britain and numerous visitors from abroad had followed the play with delight and interest. If, however, they happened to have read that the work they found so fascinating had nothing to do with life, as one of its hostile critics had asserted, they might well ask in amazement: "Nothing to do with what sort of life? With whose life?" For 'our' life, Ervine declared, was indeed affected by such processes.

When the last word had faded into silence on the last evening with the voice speaking from the Beyond in *Back to Methuselah*, the applause that broke out seemed as if it would never come to an end. The audience wanted to show its gratitude to all who had helped to make the Festival weeks a success. Above all, there were repeated shouts of 'Author!' from the auditorium. The author finally yielded to the mood of this solemn moment and appeared on the stage, yet not in order to thank the audience, but to make a sparkling extempore speech about Shakespeare and to refer to all that had been done to make it possible for this difficult project to be realised. Refusing to speak at all of himself, he referred to his debt to Sir Barry Jackson, to H. K. Ayliff, modestly effacing himself behind his handiwork, to Paul Shelving, the designer of the excellent stage-sets, and to the self-sacrificing actors and actresses, most of all to Cedric Hardwicke, who had not only been a really excellent King Magnus, but had also created the noblest of Cæsars, also proving his unusual gift for characterisation in the difficult rôle of Captain Shotover in *Heartbreak House*.

Then there were many further exchanges of compliments and congratulations, with speeches by Sir Barry Jackson and others, until the curtain sank in front of the stage for the last time. When he rose once more before the now almost empty theatre, the hero of these many evenings crossed the stage slowly and thoughtfully, walking towards the exit where I was waiting for him.

As he strode up to me I thought of our first meeting so long before, and it seemed to me that the great adventure of my youth was now finally stamped with the seal of triumph, nay more, was crowned.

Bernard Shaw had never before appeared on the stage to thank the audience that was applauding and shouting for him. Sitting very inconspicuously at one side of the front row of the stalls, with his German harbinger beside him, he enjoyed the effect of his accomplished work. During the day we used to go out for walks or drives together. Shaw never ceased to recommend Stratford-on-Avon, that near-by place of pilgrimage where his immortal predecessor in the drama, William Shakespeare, was likewise having homage paid to him, as the most beautiful and worthy of goals for an expedition.

In Malvern we all had the opportunity of observing the inexhaustible energy of this Irish playwright who was still as youthful in body as he was in mind. On hot days this tireless man would seek refreshment and recreation in Malvern's crystal-clear swimming-pool. The sloping lawns around this beautiful pool framed in green were besieged by the curious, and many a sly camera snapped a gay picture of those summery water-sports in which a creative master was the central figure. In contrast with his wife, of whom no photograph exists that was taken with her consent, Bernard Shaw was at that time sympathetically inclined to his eager snapshot-taking contemporaries, and since he himself was a skilful amateur photographer, he could often be seen hastening to some dilettante's aid. He would place the camera correctly for him and focus it correctly, and in general help an admirer—a stranger to him and quite unimportant as a person— to attain his secret wish.

Many distinguished persons had gathered in that wonderfully beautiful little country resort to celebrate the master's birthday with him and congratulate this youthful, whimsical celebrity on his jubilee. It goes without saying that Bernard Shaw's intimate friends were also there, among them H. G. Wells and Sidney Webb, together with his wife. Nor was I the only one from German lands who had come for the occasion of the Festival's inauguration and the birthday celebrations on July 26th. Together with me there came Shaw's German publisher, S. Fischer, with his wife and daughter and his daughter's husband, Dr. Bermann. Some of the other German admirers who played their part in Shaw's life, preparing his way for him, were prevented from coming, but saw to it that there was no lack of thoroughly impressive messages by letter and telegram.

Although S. Fischer, unlike his wife and daughter, did not speak English, Shaw's interest was chiefly focused on his German publisher, and to him, as was his habit, he constantly addressed the expressions: 'Ausgezeichnet!' ('Excellent!') and 'Hand aufs Herz!' (approximately: 'Cross my heart!'). These were the two expressions that he always used, heaven knows why, when he wanted to give proof of his interest to people who were talking away to him in German. Later that evening, when I was alone at table with him and his wife, he told me that he had liked Fischer immensely; this was the first occasion that he had met him personally.

Unfortunately while I was in Malvern I received rather sad news of the state in which that poor friend of my youth, Georges Courteline, now was—news that caused me to hurry to Paris as soon as possible. His wife, whose generally happy face was shadowed with profound sorrow, now opening the door to me on my arrival told me what she had not wanted to write, namely that the unfortunate writer of comedies, who had always been so good at making the most of the gay side of life, had now been overtaken by a tragic fate. He had had to have his right leg amputated.

She especially prepared me for this before taking me into his study, where Courteline was sitting at his desk with his back to the door. His intelligent and much-enduring wife had intended that by telling me this beforehand she would prevent Courteline from seeing the shock and horror in my eyes. And indeed I tried to control myself as much as possible and held out my hand to him, which he took as cordially as ever, saying at the same time: "Well, my dear fellow, the

things that can happen to us!" I could not find the right words, but
he must nevertheless have seen how deeply moved I was, for he
suddenly burst out laughing and exclaimed: "It's not as bad as all
that, my dear friend! Let us be thankful to fate that I am not a
dancer. One can write even with *one* leg. Only I haven't much
inclination for it."

Three years later I received the news of the amputation of the other
leg, shortly after which I was informed of Courteline's decease.

In the meantime I had had the opportunity of seeing him once or
twice again and—to my joyful dismay, I should almost like to say—
noticed how quickly he, who had been the most mobile of people, had
adjusted himself to being immobile and made a successful attempt
still to get some pleasure out of life, which was now worth so very
much less.

These impressions, resulting from the great misfortune that had
overtaken one who was not only one of my dearest friends but such a
wonderful artist too, made it impossible for me to settle down when
I returned home. They had burrowed deeply into my mind, and for a
time I could not get over them and regain that normal cheerfulness
without which one can scarcely get along in life at all. It was therefore lucky for me that at this period I could not find the time to
immerse myself in my sorrow and quarrel with destiny on behalf of
another sorely afflicted being.

I still had not produced my personal birthday present for Shaw. It
consisted in a long prepared lecture tour (which an agent had already
organised) that was to take me through the largest cities in Germany.
The subject was: 'Bernard Shaw's Rise to Fame in Germany. A
retrospective survey on the occasion of his seventieth birthday'.

I was bound by the obligations I had incurred with my contract
and could not risk breaking it by indulging in paralysing sadness and
unproductive melancholy. My work was not yet quite finished,
either, and I had to get down to it in earnest. Then, when everything
seemed to have been included and the material presented in a
successful form, the time came for me to set out on the tour.

The subject—certainly not any gifts of mine as a lecturer—
guaranteed full houses on many evenings and a great success. Even
when I left Vienna, I had heard from my manager that I would find
halls with all the seats sold out and an audience agog with interest.
Now, however, for the first time I was not free, but tied; and, looking

at the list of the many very large German towns that were expecting me, I realised that I had undertaken a thoroughly strenuous tour.

It began in Breslau, where the first lecture was so successful that I felt entitled to look forward to the approaching evenings. Most nights I spent in a railway sleeping-compartment, and sometimes I had to hurry away to the station immediately after the lecture. Everything went off without any incident worth recounting, excepting one intermezzo, which I shall now describe.

It was in Bremen, on a terribly foggy morning, that I noticed, on leaving my compartment, that I had lost my voice overnight. I was horrified, not because of the slight illness, which I would have put up with all right, but because in this condition I should not be able to deliver my evening's lecture, which lasted for not less than an hour and a quarter.

I arrived at Hillmann's splendid hotel in a very gloomy state of mind and at once noticed two large posters in the hall. One announced that my lecture would be held that evening, and the other announced a performance of *Saint Joan*—this was however not the première, but simply one of many performances. In any case, it gave me the idea of ringing up the director of the Bremen Stadttheater—I think his name was Wiegand—and bemoaning my dismal fate to him in a whisper.

"If I were the actor you were expecting to act Dunois tonight," I said to him, "what would you do on hearing a voice like this, in order not to have to cancel the performance?"

His answer was: "Exactly what I will arrange for you this minute. Please come straight round to me."

Ten minutes later I was received by this charming man of the theatre, whom I had once met before.

"We must of course always be prepared for such things to happen," he said to me. "And so I have already rung up the doctor who once transformed my Hamlet, who had been reduced to whispering, into the possessor of a silvery clear speaking voice. He is expecting you in half an hour."

This man who had so much presence of mind had offered me a seat and now talked to me about *Saint Joan*, which I would of course not be able to see that evening, any more than he would himself, since he too had taken tickets for my lecture. He showed me a few newspaper-cuttings containing exceedingly kindly reviews of my previous lectures, and sent me away with the words: "Till tonight, then! If you are not too tired, we might meet again afterwards."

As I went downstairs, covering my mouth, I saw that there was already a taxi waiting for me outside. A short while later it brought me to the house of the doctor whose card Director Wiegand had pressed into my hand. I rang the bell and the doctor himself opened the door. He obviously wanted to prevent any display on my part of what I was suffering from, for he waved his hand for silence when I began to speak and himself said: "I know all about it. Director Wiegand has explained the whole thing."

He first took me into his consulting-room, where he examined my throat very thoroughly and tested the degree of my hoarseness. Then he asked me to come into another room, which was a kind of laboratory. Here he told me to take off my jacket and lie down on a couch, while he went to a little cupboard and took out a fairly large ampoule containing some brown fluid.

Without waiting for me to agree, he pushed up my shirt-sleeve and gave me an intravenous injection—so far as I remember, quite painlessly. My curiosity being aroused, I asked him what the fluid was. At this the little man said, with his characteristic North German accent: "Oh no, my dear fellow—just so that you can go and tell my colleagues when it's done the job? Those gentry can find out for themselves instead of prescribing worthless medicaments!"

I was slightly surprised, but at the same time also I felt rather numb. However, I already heard the little man's voice saying commandingly: "You will now drive back to your hotel and go to bed. By then it'll be about twelve. You are to stay in bed till half-past four, without speaking a word or eating a bite of anything. Then drink a glass of Russian tea, as hot as you can drink it, and stay in bed for another hour. About twenty to six ring me up. Then we shall both know whether you can do your stuff tonight."

It was quite a good thing that I had kept the taxi waiting, in order to waste no time at all. I must have stammered something about a fee, whereupon the little doctor replied: "You don't have to bother about that. The director tells me he's seeing to it."

I was in fact in bed shortly after twelve, and being in such a state of mingled excitement and exhaustion, instantly dropped off and slept the sleep of the just. About four o'clock I woke up, rang, and ordered tea as I had been told to, bravely fighting down a sudden

marked desire for food. Speechless—but this time with astonishment—I gave this order in a voice that was already quite altered, no
longer hoarse, but half clear. When I had taken the little drink, I lay
down once more, amazed at the sense of well-being that now came
over me. What on earth had that magician injected into my system?

The hour that I now spent, still lying in bed, was particularly
pleasant. In my mind I read out whole passages of my lecture, which
I had not got handy, being still far too frightened to make any
attempts to speak. Then when it was nearly six o'cock and I rang up
my saviour, I was astonished to find that my voice was completely
restored to normal clarity, which, when I had overcome my astonishment, caused the doctor to burst out into loud laughter.

He prescribed further rest in my room until immediately before
my lecture, which he declared was now a complete certainty. I had
long felt that he was right and began to do elocution exercises,
which, however, I quickly stopped, for my obedience had doubtless
been the unknown doctor's greatest helper.

All seats were sold out for the lecture. There were many students,
including girls, standing along the walls of the hall. In the front row I
saw—when I had finished—the amiable director frantically applauding, and beside him the miracle-working doctor, who had not wanted
to miss the opportunity of enjoying his triumph.

Down to this day I have never ceased to ask myself and many
doctors what the elixir can possibly have been. Like so many other
questions, this is one to which life still owes me the answer.

My contract was fulfilled when I had delivered a last lecture in
Berlin, and I was already looking forward to returning home. In
Vienna I then gave a rapidly improvised lecture on 'Bernard Shaw's
Rise to Fame in Germany' in addition to those I had given within
the framework of the tour. At various points on the journey I
had sent off postcards to Shaw, assuring him that Saint Joan had
made him at the moment the most popular theatrical author of our
time.

However, I was not fated to reach the end of this eventful year,
1926, without losing the best-loved of all my friends, the Ariel of my
youth, Rainer Maria Rilke, whom I had ever and again hoped to
visit in Muzot, all the more since he wrote me very mournful cards
from there, though without saying much about his illness.

That reunion, for which I had so devoutly wished, was not to be.

Rilke slowly vanished from sight on his floating, silent flight into eternity.

I felt as though I had suddenly been deprived of a spiritual possession that I had never tended and watched over sufficiently, and all at once that experience in our early youth took on an aspect of unreality, even of something legendary. Rilke was the only person whose death depressed me so much that I was incapable even of writing a single word about him and dwelling in words on those remote days of our youth. Such blows do we suffer, and such heart-ache. And because for all that we must go on living our own life, we hide them from the world, like a soldier who, seeing his dearest comrades around him falling on the battlefield, yet goes marching on until the bullet strikes him too. But let no one believe that these wounds heal without leaving any trace. They scar over and grow old, stigmatising us, reminding us not to cling overmuch to anything that is earthly.

What would I not give today if that wan boy, René, with his great starry eyes, could once again come and take me on the long drive to that brightly-lighted castle and that exalted lady who, like a fairy, knew everything about us and left us to each other so that in her enchanted garden we might consult the stars concerning our destiny? What would I not give!

It was a long time before I could adjust myself to my everyday routine again, but I was quick to clutch at the only consolation we have if we would not plunge headlong into the void after the dear ones we have lost—and that was work.

This time the work was in keeping with my mood. The story that soon kept me occupied in every leisure hour and was closer to my heart than anything else was called *Der Geheilte* (*The Man who was Healed*). It was published by S. Fischer the following summer in a little volume that also contained a second story, *Die Assistentin* (*The Female Assistant*), which was the work that I had read aloud to Gerhart Hauptmann many years ago at Agnetendorf. But for me the one that counted was *Der Geheilte*, in which, taking a particular case to exemplify my theme, I had tried to give artistic form to one of the human body's most important problems, with its reaction on the mind.

Apart from my work, I was at that time fascinated by a figure of an unusual kind, the figure of one who justified my hopes, though not in the artistic sphere. This was the Chancellor, Doctor Ignaz Seipel, whose significance I, as a completely unpolitically-minded person, naturally cannot presume to describe.

But the fact of the matter is that one always feels some radiation from such a superior mind, even if it is that of someone active in fields other than one's own, so that one pauses to read everything about him and by him that is printed in the newspapers, and expects that an era sunken in misery will be improved by the man whose importance one has recognised so joyfully.

This was what I and many of my friends felt about this prelate, Dr. Ignaz Seipel, who fell victim to an assassin's attack as a result of which he lost not his life but his health. Some years then passed during which, as the result of being physically enfeebled, he ceased to be the vehement and dazzling orator of old, and was already, even though almost imperceptibly, sinking toward death. But in the short period during which he held office and wielded his influence he did, in spite of all, do something to pull Austria out of the misery into which she had sunk after the break-up of the Empire.

Meanwhile I had published another little novel, *Renate Aldringen*, and in connection with this book I had an experience so remarkable that I want to recount it here.

The 'Renate Aldringen' of my novel was an enchanting figure of fantasy whom I had tricked out with all the charms that a living heroine, I am sure, rarely possesses. Since the story was set on the Wörthersee in Carinthia, I had made my heroine live and languish in Klagenfurt, the capital of that province. The fateful events that take place on the shores of that beautiful Carinthian lake occur for the most part in a place that, being within easy reach of Klagenfurt, serves as a holiday resort not only for tourists but also for the inhabitants of this town.

Now, one day in Vienna I was on my way to a bookshop to see whether *Renate Aldringen*, which had just been published, was in the window yet, when I passed a hat-shop where my wife often bought her hats. The proprietress of this shop, who had evidently seen me passing, rushed out and intercepted me, exclaiming excitedly: "Renate Aldringen is in there, in the shop! Do please come in, quick!"

I was struck dumb and so disconcerted, but likewise so incredulously curious to know what this might mean, that I followed her as she hastened back into the shop.

In the salon, which was as it were fenced in with hats, stood a tall, bony, fair young woman with rather coarse features, more or less the opposite of the Renate I had pictured. "Yes, yes," she began instantly, "I am really your Renate Aldringen!" That was too much for me, and I sank into the chair that the obsequious modiste had pushed towards me. "Neighbour, your smelling salts," was my first reaction.

"What?" I finally gasped out. "So your name is Renate Aldringen?"

To this she replied rather haughtily, as though the name were a slur:

"Oh no, I'm Gerda Passegger, and I was your model! It all fits me absolutely, so it's no use your making excuses. After all, I ought to know best! I'm the daughter of a jeweller. I often used to go to the Wörthersee to visit a friend of mine who came from Vienna, and he committed suicide for my sake, too!" she added, proudly tossing her little head, which was not so very small either.

These were harsh blows, for to some extent what she said corresponded to the contents of my novel. I merely stammered: "But for heaven's sake, in my book it's the young man's girl friend who chooses death, and not he himself! And since here you stand, so full of health and strength, positively demanding satisfaction from me, you seem to be pretty much alive—if I may still presume to have any opinion about anything at all!"

"Oh yes," she said, "you've turned the story round quite neatly so that I won't be recognised, but it's me all right, because the locality is exactly the same, you see, and described as exactly as can only be done by someone who has been there. The whole of Klagenfurt is set by the ears about it all. And I'm frightfully compromised!" she added challengingly, but—obviously because I reached out to the wall in search of support—she at once added soothingly: "It's lucky for you that people know quite well what I'm like, anyway, and that I always have gentlemen friends at the Wörthersee in the summer."

What could I do but apologise to Fräulein Passegger for my knowledge of the invented places and events? And I therefore did so.

"How do you come to know all these things, anyway?" she asked. "Because I must admit this is the first time in my life I've ever seen you."

Yes, there was the rub, indeed! How gladly I would have answered this question quite truthfully! I tried to do so, saying: "I invented it all, and it's just a coincidence that it fits the case."

She shook her head. "But that's impossible, if you don't know the place!"

"Oh, Fräulein Passegger," I groaned, "you've no idea about all the things that are possible in my profession! Forgive me and forget me."

She looked at me rather scornfully and then exclaimed: "The only thing that's free is death, and that costs a person their life!" She then took a copy of my book out of her bag, saying: "If I get a really nice dedication written in, I shall be appeased and call off the steps I actually had in mind!"

I was glad to escape on payment of such a light ransom, and what I wrote in the little book for this heartless creature, who did not seem at all grieved by the suicide that she certainly was to some extent to blame for, was: 'For Fräulein Gerda Passegger, the invented original of Renate Aldringen, with best thanks for an instructive experience', and underneath that, of course, my full name and the date of this memorable day.

It did indeed take me a little time to recover from the emotional confusion caused by this little incident and reach the stage when I could laugh about it as heartily as it deserved.

This year, 1929, was in many respects a very important one for me. I remember that I was just having a discussion with my wife about our summer holiday trip, which was to give me rest and recuperation from work, when I received the sad news of the death of my old friend Georges Courteline. His second leg had been amputated, because the doctors saw this as the only chance of saving his life. The unfortunate writer instantly proved them wrong, for although he survived the operation itself, he did not get over its after-effects, and while still in the nursing home he passed away—which was a kindness on the part of providence, for I cannot imagine (and his wife says I am quite right) that he would have been able to bear living in that entirely crippled condition. It was difficult for us to get over this news, and the funeral took place so soon after his death that I could not have the privilege of attending it and of paying him the last honours, as the irresponsible expression goes, and of showing his inconsolable widow the sympathy that she certainly never for an instant doubted.

It was in the autumn, then, on my way to London, that together with her I visited the still fresh grave of that great French writer. And it was long before I could tear myself away from that celebrated cemetery where, not very far away, Heinrich Heine also found his eternal rest.

But it was life, and not death, that had the further authority over my destiny. After some days spent together with common friends I hurried on to London, where I was drawn by Shaw's news of his newly begun play.

I have not yet mentioned that Bernard Shaw, yielding less to any wish he himself felt than to a little passion of his wife's, used to make very long journeys all round the world, always starting out in a different direction and always returning to some different point in Europe. On one of these later journeys he wrote that delightful little play *A Village Wooing*. He said little about these travels, and oddly enough he as good as never gave any public account of them. It was only his most intimate friends whom he happened to tell that he had flown over the Great Wall of China in an aeroplane, which was, after all, rather a feat. At the same time, I could not help having the feeling that the tremendous distances he had covered and the strange people and places he had seen had nevertheless made a great impression on him and had been very inspiring to him. That fantastic play, *The Simpleton of the Unexpected Isles*, would probably never have been written if it had not been for his travels round the world.

Even before he went on his really long journeys he had once told me of the beauty of Jamaica, although to my great regret I had not received as much as a picture postcard from him while he was there. He must obviously have felt some awkwardness about talking much of such enterprises, which did, after all, cost a very great deal of money and would arouse the envy of many people who could never permit themselves even to dream of enjoying visits to those far-off countries.

In the old days, when I had come on visits to Shaw, I had always made the acquaintance of interesting friends, or met them again— such people as Granville Barker, Shaw's first Eugene Marchbanks and also his first Tanner. That was all over now, but meanwhile I myself had become friends with H. G. Wells and John Galsworthy and always made use of my visits to London to see something of these writers. I particularly associated with Galsworthy as a result of our common interest in the Pen Club.

One day, after luncheon, which I took punctually at half-past one with Bernard Shaw as almost every day, he asked me what I was doing in the afternoon and whether we should not take advantage of the fine weather and go for a walk together. I replied that I was expected to tea with Galsworthy and his charming wife at five o'clock, because as the delegate of the Vienna Pen Club I had important questions to discuss with our President, which were all the more urgent since there was a world congress approaching.

I had scarcely finished my answer to Shaw, when he exclaimed: "That's splendid, I'll come along with you. It's simply years since I've seen Galsworthy and his wife. You'll do very well as the excuse for a visit that will come as a surprise, just as I like things to be."

At the time agreed on I called for Shaw and we set out. From the very beginning of our acquaintance I always found it particularly difficult to keep in step with Bernard Shaw, and with the passing of the years this had become worse, if anything, because I walked more slowly, while he rushed along with tremendous strides that I could hardly follow. At first we chatted during our walk, which as a matter of fact began only after approximately ten minutes' journey by Underground; but then Shaw had to keep stopping and turning round to wait until I caught up with him. I did my best to stay at his side, and I did in fact succeed in keeping up a far greater speed than I was accustomed to.

I panted along after him, and when he reached the top of the steps and stood outside the door of the house, he turned round, laughing, to see where I was, and had to wait for quite a while until I, doing my utmost to avoid causing any damage either to my nerves or to my clothes, which had by now lost their pristine freshness, at last arrived beside him. Then we rang the bell, and when the maid opened the door I handed her my card, while Shaw, with a casual wave of the hand peculiar to himself said: "And say I've come too." To my surprise the maid did not ask him his name, but hastily disappeared behind a curtain that concealed a door. Before we had followed her as far as the threshold, she returned and threw wide the door to another room. At this moment John Galsworthy rushed towards us in joyful excitement, exchanged a fleeting handshake with me, and immediately put his arm through Shaw's and drew Shaw into his study, where the two of them, taking no more notice of me, sat down side by side on a comfortable sofa, immersed in eager talk.

The lady of the house had also turned to the famous native guest, but after a moment turned her back on him in order to start a conversation with me.

I was quite charmed by this amiability, and when she offered me a seat some distance from the men and sat down beside me, I felt particularly flattered, until I realised that what this intelligent lady was concerned with, obviously much more than with me, was not disturbing the great antipodes at any price, but leaving them to their talk, which was already in full swing. She kept me, as it were, at a distance from them, which was no trouble at all to one of her charm and her conversational skill. She was, besides, so well informed that I was able to tell her everything that I had come to tell her husband, and since I had to resort to my notebook for help, I dare say we sat together for a good half-hour, which was apparently quite agreeable to her. My observation was confirmed by the contented smile with which she turned her head to the other two, who did indeed seem to have a vast amount to tell each other. When eminent Britons have a chance meeting, let no man put them asunder.

Suddenly Shaw raised his voice and called out to me: "You know, the thing is we haven't had a talk together for thirty years! You came to London just at the right moment." I now approached shyly, to the accompaniment of significant nods from our hostess. At tea, which now followed, there was the usual conversation about current affairs, talk in which Bernard Shaw laid down the law in his witty way, while the Galsworthys and I listened to him admiringly, an arrangement G. B. S. was not disinclined to regard as his privilege.

When we left the Galsworthys about an hour later, after they had both come to the front door with us, I had not spoken a word to the World President of all the Pen Clubs about the object of my visit, departing with the hope, however, that his wife would tell him all about it.

The way back was downhill, and I was able to keep up with Shaw's long joyful strides. "That was a brilliant idea of yours," he said to me when we parted, not without arranging to meet the next day. However, Galsworthy rang me up at my hotel only a moment after I arrived back, and was completely transformed into the thoughtful guardian of the Pen Club and its destinies, laughingly apologising as he made an appointment for another meeting with me—one that I kept a secret from Bernard Shaw so that it too should not be spoilt in so delightful a manner.

After this visit it happened that I once again had occasion to talk to Shaw about his novel, *Cashel Byron's Profession,* and once again told him how amazing I found it that he should be so familiar with all the technical details and indeed the whole world of boxing. By way of answer and explanation he told me that particularly when he was younger he had been in the habit of going to big fights, such as world-championship matches, as a regular thing, and that this minor passion of his, which was so entirely out of keeping with his own creative work, was one that he kept secret from his wife as far as was possible, because she would not have anything at all to do with it.

.It was only on this occasion that I learned that a properly directed blow on the chin is quite painless, because it instantly causes complete unconsciousness, and that this is also the reason why the man so hit at once drops to the ground. It was regrettable, Shaw went on to say smilingly, that this state did not last long enough to be made use of for surgical purposes instead of anæsthetics. The person who suffered the blow came back to his senses only some instants later, which was why such a blow did not necessarily mean that a boxer would be counted out, since he might, after all, be on his feet again and once more joyfully ready to fight before the referee had counted up to ten, as he had to.

And so I was not in the least surprised that Shaw, when spending a holiday on the island of Brioni on the Adriatic, should have become friends with the world-champion boxer G. Tunney. At that time Shaw's interest was evenly divided between Richard Strauss, the greatest living composer, who was also on Brioni, and Tunney, the greatest living boxer.

Dempsey's famous vanquisher, who defended his world-championship title for years, was, incidentally, married to a very cultured young lady and was himself very well-informed and well-read in many spheres, a connoisseur of Bernard Shaw's work and one of his greatest admirers. So far as I can remember, this relationship continued later in England, which was all the more easily possible since Tunney, who was a very shrewd man, did not wait until his time was up, but withdrew into private life while still at the height of his success.

Doubtless every artist has something in common with a boxer: there is the struggle to remain at the height of achievement, which makes it possible to forget the brutality of this sport. And it was doubtless the symbolic quality of it that aroused Shaw's liking for this inexorable contest with an equally inexorable opponent.

About that time Shaw, who had no confidence in posterity and wanted to do everything himself, began editing his great Standard Edition, which he continued doing up to his death. This complete edition of his collected works finally, if I am not mistaken, contained more than twenty-five volumes. Like everything that Shaw had done it was published by Constable, in London. These handsome volumes, bound in red linen, Shaw sent to me in Vienna, and I held them in high honour as one of the most precious of gifts, until Hitler's highwaymen stole or destroyed them. This English edition gave me the basis for a German complete edition, which I was much later able to bring about and indeed carry to its conclusion, in which matter it was clear to me from the beginning that so far as German readers were concerned it was above all, and almost exclusively, Shaw's dramatic works, together with the incredibly interesting prefaces, that must be included.

Now, however, a fairly disagreeable autumn set in, making me impatient to return to Vienna, whither my wife was also summoning me with a certain urgency, because she had heard from our friend Felix Salten of the great preparations that the Pen Club was intending to make in connection with my approaching sixtieth birthday.

Shaw, whom I told about this when I was saying good-bye to him, said, laughing: "You mustn't expect to find me among the people who congratulate you, after I've at last managed to make you leave off this nonsensical business of good wishes on birthdays. I would gladly wish you many happy returns of your twentieth or thirtieth birthday. But to go and draw your attention to the fact that you are on the miserable road to old age is something you really haven't deserved from me! How much happier we would all be if we ourselves didn't know when our birthdays were and how old we had become!" Oh, how heartily we agreed about this!

The day came, and the evening came, when the Pen Club committee and some other close friends assembled in the banqueting-room at the Hotel Imperial in Vienna in order to honour their colleague and friend, who was for the first time the centre of such an official celebration, feeling the eyes of his friends on him.

To my delight the younger writers were also there, among whom I had the privilege of shaking hands with Friedrich Schreyvogel, Oscar Maurus Fontana, Franz Theodor Csokor, Gisela von Berger, Guido Zernatto, Robert Musil, Grete von Urbanitzky, and many others who were friends of mine. In conclusion, to my particular delight, Anton Wildgans came hurrying over from the Burgtheater, of which he was at that time the director, in order to say a few pleasant words to me and about me. But the person I particularly missed was Stefan Zweig, who was in a far country; he had nevertheless seen to it that on the morning of this day a long essay about me, written by him, should appear in the *Neue Freie Presse*.

The main speech at the banquet was delivered by Felix Salten, who was at that time the President of the Pen Club, and he spoke not only in this capacity but also in that of one of the oldest friends of my youth. Then I too had to make a short speech of thanks for everybody's good opinion of me and all the kind things they had said about me.

I had also received an official honour that I must record here for the sake of completeness. The Austrian Government on the occasion of my sixtieth birthday bestowed on me the title of professor *honoris causa*, for my 'services to Austrian literature'.

However happy all this made me, it was nevertheless difficult for me to bear suddenly finding myself in the midst of all these honours, and when we got home, fairly tired, after that great evening, I was glad to have all the sufferings and joys of that day behind me.

On the next Sunday there now followed—and I must confess that it was a very great pleasure to me—a matinée, at which the actor Wilhelm Klitsch gave a very effective reading of my drama, *Kaiser Diokletian*, which had been 'cut' with incredible skill. This was preceded by an introductory speech by one of my oldest friends Richard Specht. This celebration took place in the Theater in der Josefstadt. I do not any longer recall exactly whether it was Otto Preminger or Ernst Lothar, in collaboration with Emil Geyer, who had organised this birthday matinée, naturally at the instance and wish of Max Reinhardt, who however could not be in Vienna that Sunday and sent his apologies in a telegram that moved me deeply.

The reading, which I attended, sitting well back in a box, at my wife's side, left me with a beautiful memory. The Intendant of the Burgtheater, Schneiderhan, who was present—a highly cultured man of artistic tastes, whose original field of activity had been music and who took his position very seriously and was always in the centre of any literary controversies that were going on, which he always settled with as much kindliness as high-mindedness—hurried up to me in the interval and congratulated me on this work. The exact words of his exclamation were: "So there are such things, and the author is a Viennese, and the Burgtheater knows nothing of it and does nothing about it!"

To this I said laughingly: "That surprises me too, Herr Intendant, but since luck will have it that you have now made the acquaintance of this work, nothing will prevent you from presenting it on the Burgtheater stage, which seems to be the one and only stage that is capable of producing it. The Burgtheater is, after all, the place for a verse drama."

Schneiderhan, whom my wife now drew into conversation, remained in our box during the reading of the next act, and we did not doubt that *Kaiser Diokletian* would now soon appear at the Burgtheater. But since that moment I have never heard anything more about plans for the production of this play, which, thanks to the dramatic art of Wilhelm Klitsch at that birthday matinée, was a greatly applauded success.

In spite of all the pleasure that these overwhelming, to some extent entirely unexpected, honours had given me, the mood I was in was not entirely a happy one. I had been too expressly reminded of my age, which I myself did not really feel at all. It must be said frankly for once that people are tormented by an hereditary affliction, a convention that is hundreds of years old and is unquestioningly handed on from generation to generation although it makes life bitterly, almost unendurably, more difficult. This is nothing other than the convention of counting and the official establishment of our birthdays. The year and the day, which in sober truth concern none but ourselves, are inexorably entered into records by all the authorities with which we have anything to do in the course of our life, and are set at the head of all documents.

And yet there is nothing more unimportant and trivial, nothing says less about our nature, than our birthday. So long as one is young one gladly puts up with the reckoning of birthdays, and likewise with the good wishes that are offered one on the day. Later, however, when the age of maturity comes and one begins to grow old, as they say, this all too conscientious checking of our years becomes unbearable, to say nothing of being a danger. It causes us to lose our easy naturalness, our confidence in ourselves. Indeed, our youth seems to flee more swiftly under the urgings of the evil rhythm into which it is pressed. On the other hand, if we, together with our contemporaries, had forgotten when we were born, if we were not ceaselessly and regularly reminded of it, we would in fact be precisely as old as we look, as we feel, and as we are in our behaviour.

In later years this disagreeable reminder affects us like a push in the direction where our grave will be, and we are thankful for every forgetting of it and are glad not to see those oddly admonishing looks in the eyes of many who come with good wishes, which seem to be telling us: 'Well, now it'll soon be time to take leave of life and make way for us, won't it?' We must show particular amiability in meeting the reproachful glances that patiently allow us to begin yet another year of life, although we have actually forfeited our right to walk this earth.

Great men, whose fame drags their birthday into the glare of publicity, suffer quite especially under the lash of the birthday. Bernard Shaw, for instance, strictly forbade his friends, and me too, to remind him regularly of his and annoy him with good wishes. And my dear friend Georges Courteline, who had rebelled against each new birthday and all mention of its occurrence even from the age of forty, caused the most moving of protests against this wretched custom to be inscribed on his tombstone. The words of it are:

> 'J'étais né pour rester jeune
> et j'avais l'avantage de m'en apercevoir
> le jour même où j'ai cessé de l'être'.

Yet I do not want to be ungrateful. I will confess that those many proofs of friendship also gave me much pleasure, although I would of course gladly have done without all I have described, since the bitter reminder that did, after all, lie behind every token of friendship ceaselessly poured drops of wormwood into the cup of gratitude. But the word 'gratitude' reminds me that among many others I must mention two letters that I had the good fortune to receive in the tranquillity of my own study, letters that I have not forgotten to this day.

One was from Arthur Schnitzler, whose subtle hand unrolled the years of my past life before me, and the second was from our Burgomaster, Karl Seitz, whose letter was most touchingly beautiful. This former teacher seemed in these lines for a few moments to return to his old vocation, and I believed myself justified in thinking that if his destiny had only permitted it Karl Seitz would perhaps have been just as great a poet as he was a leader in Vienna's most difficult days.

Of Max Mell, who was already at work, extolled by Hofmannsthal, I can tell little, because I only met him a few times and all too fleetingly. Berthold Viertel, who early went off to Hollywood and then settled down in London, was another Viennese writer of high standing, who earned a great reputation as a producer and here in Zurich presented a masterly staging of Shaw's last play, *Buoyant Billions*.

About the time of which I am speaking there was also a woman who caused a justifiable stir in Viennese circles by her talent and the fact that she was the daughter of that well-known friend and biographer of the Crown Prince Rudolf, Julius Szeps. This was Berta Zuckerkandl, the wife of that world-famous anatomist, Professor Emil Zuckerkandl. As a result of her sister's having married Paul Clemenceau, the brother of that tremendous figure, Georges Clemenceau, and although literature and painting were in the forefront of her interest, she also had excellent connections with those who were then the leading figures in the political world. She seldom failed to appear at a Pen Club evening, and once she brought Painlevé, the French Prime Minister, along with her. This distinguished woman, who as 'Hofrätin Zuckerkandl' was well-known in the whole of Vienna, entertained on a large scale, giving many literary parties, to which I too enjoyed going. She was furthermore the early herald of many a reputation, particularly with regard to those who were later to be the leading painters of the *Sezession*. Her greatest hero was Gustav Klimt, for whom she took up the cudgels together with Hermann Bahr, until even those who were least inclined to recognise the fact had to admit that Vienna had reason to be proud of this artist. Somewhat later it was similar in the case of Kokoschka.

Because of her husband's profession, Berta Zuckerkandl was of course also well acquainted with the great Viennese doctors, whose reputation was known throughout the world. Frequent visitors to her house were Professors Eiselsberg, Wenckebach, Hochenegg, Julius Schnitzler (the writer's brother), and Halban, to mention only the names that are most familiar to the general public.

It is difficult to linger over the name of Halban without recalling his wife, who under her maiden name, Selma Kurz, was one of the greatest and most celebrated coloratura singers, and probably not only of her own time.

At that period Vienna possessed a wealth of talents and artists of every kind, of whom posterity, too, may well be proud. At the opera triumphs of the rarest kind were achieved by Selma Kurz, who has just been mentioned, Maria Jeritza, Elisabeth Schumann, Maria Renard, Maria Gutheil-Schoder, Piccaver, Demuth, Leo Slezak and Eric Schmedes. At that time there was still a young Erich Korngold who justified our having the greatest hopes of him, being only a little hampered by his father, who, as the music critic of the *Neue Freie Presse*, carried on somewhat too intense propaganda for his son and so failed to notice that he could not question the supremacy of Richard Strauss' sublime genius without in fact damaging the very cause he wanted to further.

Vienna was doubtless *the* city that in fact allowed itself to be influenced by its leading critics, something that never applied, and does not now apply, to the same extent either in Paris or in London, and which is of course far from being the case in Switzerland.

When the First World War and the break-up of the Empire had plunged Vienna into what seemed, when regarded from outside, the lowest depths of misery, it was of course of the utmost importance that its intellectual, artistic and ethical values should be upheld by every means.

But before I leave the year 1929, which, toward its end, brought my sixtieth birthday with it, I must recall the great and irreparable loss that this year brought not only to us but to the whole civilised world: Hofmannsthal was no longer among the living. I have elsewhere recounted that I owed this immortal poet a great debt of personal gratitude, and it was not only the fact of his passing on that shocked and grieved me, and indeed all of us, but above all the cause and the manner of his death.

The immediate cause was a scene with his son, which took on a form as violent as the clash of opposing emotional and artistic forces in any drama by Hofmannsthal himself, the father who was here rejecting his son's demands. After a violent argument the hot-tempered young man rushed into the next room and there shot himself; an instant later he lay dead upon the floor. Hofmannsthal's paternal heart, violently agitated by the scene that had just taken place and indeed already an afflicted and failing heart, could not stand up to this terrible and utterly unexpected blow of fate and broke almost at the same instant.

What a good thing it was that in this evil hour the Salzburg Festival, which Hugo von Hofmannsthal had brought into existence, was already on a sure basis and that he himself had lived long enough to enjoy the sublime satisfaction of seeing his *Jedermann* (*Everyman*) produced by Max Reinhardt and acted by Alexander Moissi, and likewise *Das Kleine Welttheater* (*The Little Theatre of the World*), which was, however, not so close to his heart, and the high soaring of which he himself had not foreseen as clearly as that of *Jedermann*, which will yet long ennoble the summer days in Salzburg and make the whole world tremulous with awe and admiration.

Hofmannsthal was a festive personality through and through. His works are festivals that he held for himself, and those who appear in them are guests that this *grand seigneur* admitted there by the grace of poetry. And here again mention must be made of Max Reinhardt, who instantly agreed to Hofmannsthal's plans and schemes and stood by this sensitive but strong-willed poet, never disappointing him, until Salzburg was transformed and perfected as a festival town, as which it is today famous throughout the world; he did this in association with such men as the Austrian Ambassador in London, Baron Frankenstein, a friend of Hofmannstahl's youth, and the chief men in the Austrian Government.

Among the men who turned Hofmannsthal's great ideas for the organisation of this festival into a reality and caused the name of Mozart to ascend like a rocket beside that of Hofmannsthal, one who should also be mentioned is Franz Schalk, who at the time when Hofmannsthal was campaigning for the realisation of his ideal was the director of the Vienna State Opera and one of Austria's most eminent conductors. Like Bruno Walter, he occasionally exchanged

L

the conductor's baton for the pen, and not without success. He was for many years a close friend of Hugo von Hofmannsthal.

Few people know that Franz Schalk was all his life possessed by yet another passion—for the noble game of chess. It was positively a mania with him, and a wit whose own addiction was to wine once called him a '*Quartalspieler*' (the equivalent, in chess terms, of a 'periodic drinker'). Schalk's sense of his artistic duty naturally always triumphed over his longing for the chequered board, which he often had to pine for during many months. Only in the summer, in Salzburg, at the time of the great Festival, could he indulge himself in this frustrated passion, sitting down at the chess board more or less regularly; for there he escaped from his arduous activities as a director—to make up for which, of course, he had to be in the full glare of publicity while conducting the masterpieces to which he had dedicated his love and his life.

The scene of Franz Schalk's chess matches was the Café Bazar, in the centre of Salzburg. There this excellent amateur fought his witty battles, beating many a tough opponent. In the furthest corner of this popular, crowded café he would be watched by admirers with similar tastes as he sat, his head resting on his hand, meditating on complicated moves. And except for the rustling of newspapers all was hushed round about Schalk.

One afternoon his harsh voice suddenly rang out: "I wish I knew as little about anything in the world as you know about chess!" There were roars of laughter from the near-by tables. Schalk's opponent, attacked thus fiercely, joined in the laughter and—won the game in the presence of the many onlookers who now gathered around these two inexorable players. Slowly Schalk rose, smiled soothingly and cordially shook the hand his opponent held out to him. Then he hurried to the cloakroom at the theatre—and away to work.

I was myself among his regular opponents in the summer. Lost to the world, absorbed in thought, we would sit opposite each other for many an hour, given over to the battle of will against will. Late one afternoon we had once again met over the all-important board and were soon silently immersed in this strangest of all intellectual disciplines. Any reference—before the game began, that is to say— to *Fidelio*, which the maestro would have to conduct in a few hours, would have been felt as an impertinence and, purely for reasons of tact, had to be suppressed. Solemn hours passed. Suddenly Franz Schalk started up, as though awakening from profound dreams, and exclaimed in dismay: "For heaven's sake, the curtain goes up in five minutes, I ought to have changed ages ago and to be sitting over the score!" With these words he grabbed his hat and coat and rushed away.

Since I had reserved a seat for this memorable performance, I hastened after the maestro. Aghast and genuinely worried, I finally reached the Festival Theatre. When I slipped quietly into my seat, the auditorium was already in darkness and the orchestra was playing the first bars of the Leonora Overture. Franz Schalk, for whom the orchestra had been waiting impatiently, was conducting in a lounge suit, and it seemed to me he was vainly trying to disappear behind his ivory baton as he lifted it on high. At last the lights went up and the enthusiastically applauding audience sought the master with its grateful gaze. However, he had become invisible. In the main interval I remained in my seat, worn out with sympathetic anxiety, and enjoyed the soothing emptiness of the festive auditorium. And behold—long before the end of the interval the Herr Kapellmeister came into the orchestra pit, tall and dignified in immaculate evening dress, calmly striding up to his music desk, where he began to arrange the piles of music that lay before him. Then he turned round and surveyed the beautiful auditorium which would soon begin to fill up again with Franz Schalk's numerous admirers male and female, who this time would not cause him any embarrassment. Suddenly his sharp eyes, peering through the half-darkness, recognised me where I sat in the orchestra stalls. He turned briskly towards me and waved his magic wand in laughing menace. Only now did I heave a sigh of relief. Shortly afterwards, behind the conductor's back, I sank into the immortal music of *Fidelio* that was here being conjured up, becoming far more profoundly absorbed than I had ever been absorbed in a game of chess. The game that had been broken off so hastily, that still stood untouched, awaiting the fugitives' return, in the Café Bazar, had been won in grand style by Beethoven.

My feelings about this beloved town of my youth, which Salzburg has remained from the time when I first set foot in it down to the present day, had now become somewhat ambiguous. In one respect the town had been dearer to me, more intimate, more my own, when it was not yet the site of a festival; on the other hand I could not help feeling proud and happy that it had now become so, magically transformed by those two great Austrians, Hugo von Hofmannsthal and Max Reinhardt, who had been so effectively and loyally supported by their friends in bringing the great project into being.

What, I suppose, most bothered and disturbed me was the many strangers and foreigners, with everything that was associated with them, whose presence there was, however, of course, the very object and intention of those who had founded the Festival that now made this city an imperishable artistic centre.

On the other hand, Salzburg now possessed an extra attraction so far as I was concerned. Stefan Zweig had settled down permanently on the Kapuzinerberg, where he had made himself an exquisitely beautiful home—for his work, his comprehensive autograph-collection, his many books, and his friends from all over the world, who always found his house open to them. The not over-accessible situation of his house, on the steep hillside, was really indescribably beautiful, and the whole atmosphere, particularly on spring days, must have done much to inspire and delight him.

His wife was at that time a brave ally at his side whenever help was needed in dealing with the tremendous amount of work that was involved in keeping up such a household. She entirely gave herself up to Zweig's work, and her loyal devotion to such a furious intellectual worker ought to receive recognition.

Another person who now came to live in Salzburg for some months, Max Reinhardt, was almost the counterpart of Stefan Zweig, living as he did in princely style in Leopoldskron, a magnificent castle that had once belonged to a member of the Austrian Imperial family and had been altered and refurnished by this great man of the theatre for his own purposes. It is by no means an exaggeration to say that those who bore the greatest names in the realm of art and the smaller territories adjoining used to come there as the guests of this most superb of all producers. I had the great pleasure of frequently being a guest at Leopoldskron, with and without my wife, incidentally having the opportunity of admiring the virtuosity and graciousness of Helene Thimig, who was a fascinating hostess.

Since Max Reinhardt had at that time already taken his company more than once to America, enjoying a particularly sensational success with Vollmöller's *Miracle,* Leopoldskron in the summer months was overrun with Americans who had got to know him. Theatre men, film magnates, Hollywood celebrities male and female, all were to be met with at Reinhardt's charming round-table entertainments. Yet there was one man who never sat at his table in the season, and never received a visit from him either, although summer after summer they were both living in Salzburg. This one man was Stefan Zweig.

I had a long struggle with myself before I decided, in the end, to make this fact known, because, after all, I was a close friend of each of them and had heard Stefan Zweig utter words of hurt astonishment on this score, although when I tried to go further into the subject of their curious alienation he swiftly began to speak of something else, and I had the feeling: 'Hands off!' However, I believe I know the reason for Max Reinhardt's reserve, and in order to anticipate all possible and impossible interpretations I should like after all to declare openly that Reinhardt would have cast a shadow on, perhaps even risked losing, his great lifelong friendship with Hofmannsthal, which dated back to their youth, if he had entered on to a friendlier footing with Zweig. I do not know the reasons and have not the right to indulge in conjectures, but it is established— and it was indeed too well known in the circles around Reinhardt and Hofmannsthal for me to be able to hush it up in this book—that Hofmannsthal had a scarcely explicable dislike of Zweig, an allergy that compelled him to reject this exceedingly successful writer, who produced his work perhaps far too quickly for Hofmannsthal's critical standards.

However painful and regrettable it may be that such psychological resistances should exist between a man of rare intellect and another creative artist, they are in themselves entirely justified, having all the legitimacy of, say, an uncontrollable irritability of the skin, against which one cannot put up a fight any more than against nettle-rash, which one of the most glorious and fragrant of the fruits of the earth, the strawberry, does actually cause to break out in many people. It is something one must put up with, passing on to the day's business; and this was what Max Reinhardt did. So it was that Stefan Zweig was never to be found among the guests of honour who received invitations from Max Reinhardt in Salzburg.

Meanwhile I was very busy working on my new novel, *Mord im*

Nebel (*Murder in the Fog*), which I had begun long before. For my hero I had deliberately chosen a young German who, in contrast with the popular notion, was tormented by such a tender conscience that he felt he could not go on living unless it was proved how entirely innocent he was of causing an accident that had brought about the death of a human being.

In Vienna at that time we were all kept slightly breathless by the rise of a new Viennese publisher, whose name was Paul von Zsolnay and who, supported by good advice from Felix Salten, who was a friend of his, opened his list with Arthur Schnitzler's latest work, or rather, inaugurated his undertaking with that wonderful story, *Fräulein Else*.

When I made Fischer's acquaintance he was already a large and prominent German publisher who had made his way. In Zsolnay's rise to eminence, however, I saw what it means to be gifted for the occupation that one has chosen and what such a gift can enable one to achieve. Within a few years Paul Zsolnay was the largest and most interesting publisher in Austria. If anyone helped him, it was perhaps his sensitive and sympathetic mother. With his own unique temperament and his captivating charm he was successful in gaining Franz Werfel, above all, for his list, and keeping him, which was doubtless made easier by the fact that he was married to a daughter of Alma Werfel-Mahler. It was, above all, the younger generation that rallied to Zsolnay's banner, and his firm began by publishing books by Frank Thiess, Robert Neumann, Broch, Colerus, Ernst Lothar, Schreyvogel, Fontana, Albert von Trentini, Torberg, and many others. Felix Salten, in so far as he was not tied to S. Fischer, then also became a Zsolnay author. Apart from *Fräulein Else*, Zsolnay made a lucky hit at the very beginning of his career as a publisher with Werfel's novel, *Verdi*, and the subsequent incredible success of one of the most deeply moving books in world literature, Werfel's *Forty days of Musa Dagh*, stamped the name of Zsolnay deep into the cultural history of those years.

His greatest achievement, however, really lay in his acquiring the rights of the works of John Galsworthy and making them widely read and very popular in Austria, in which task he was admirably supported by this great English writer's hard-working translator, Leon Schalit. True, Galsworthy was no longer unknown, but what Zsolnay made of his work, where Central Europe was concerned, cannot be valued too highly. It was thanks to this circumstance that Galsworthy became such a frequent visitor to Vienna. He did not wait for the Pen Club World Congress before coming repeatedly to Schnitzler's and Hofmannsthal's native city; every time a German first edition of one of his books was published, or there was a première of one of his plays, he made use of the opportunity to increase his already great popularity by giving lectures and delivering wonderful speeches and to gain ever larger audiences and larger circles of readers as a result of his appearance at performances of his very striking and effective plays. In this he was no little helped by the delightful charm of his wife, the most unassuming great lady I ever met.

Zsolnay and Galsworthy had become real friends, and the great man more than once came accompanied by the secretary-general of his English Pen Club, Hermon Ould, who had a weakness for Vienna and Viennese authors and in his admirably diplomatic and tactful way saw that his great fellow-countryman's journeys had the proper repercussions in England.

Paul Zsolnay also became a member of the Viennese—or, more precisely, of the Austrian—Pen Club, and there too was of much use to us, with his shrewdness, foresight and the great tact that was characteristic of him, as of his mother, who was his tremendously active co-worker.

If I, who was after all permanently tied to S. Fischer, both for myself and where Shaw was concerned, took a greater interest in Zsolnay and his circle than might otherwise have been the case with a publisher who was not my own, this was partly accounted for by the fact that in 1930 he became a neighbour of ours. He had bought the spacious villa next to ours, which fell vacant, and there entertained on such a large scale that, as regards the standing of the people who frequented his house regularly, comparison could very well be made with S. Fischer's villa in Grunewald and the guests entertained there.

We ourselves were often guests of our new next-door neighbour's and spent pleasant hours there with the Werfels and others who also often visited at our own house. Zsolnay, however, did not exclusively entertain writers, painters, sculptors and great musicians such as Bruno Walter; members of the government also enjoyed his hospitality.

Paul von Zsolnay has to this very day not disappointed the

expectations that we felt entitled to have of him. He bore himself very valiantly in Vienna's most difficult years, and when he was compelled to leave, he gave admirable proof of the excellent work he could do: robbed and deprived of everything, like the rest of us, he succeeded in making a fine position for himself as a director of Heinemann's and also in keeping his Viennese firm from being completely ruined. It continues in honour to this day, doubtless the largest publishing house in Austria.

But in the years of which I am now speaking none of us yet knew what lay in store for us. Nor did the Chancellor, Dollfuss, whom we often encountered in eager conversation with artists from the Burgtheater at Zsolnay's house, dream of the tragic fate that was about to befall him.

Arthur Schnitzler's death was a severe blow to all the intelligentsia of Vienna, and particularly to us, his friends. All at once we realised that something that could never be recaptured had disappeared with his passing and that a great era had gone to its grave with this writer.

Inconsolable as we were, we sought comfort and refuge in his work. And when we measured it against Schnitzler's own movingly beautiful, painless death, that deeply touching collapse at his writing-desk which had been of a suddenness such as is the lot only of the greatest on this earth, those who are nearest to the stars, we comprehended that it embraced a love and selfless devotion that seemed to have no end and emphasised nothing more intensely than the cry of rebellion against the immutable passing away of love, as of life, into nothingness, into the unfathomable abyss of death.

Arthur Schnitzler's great secret, which elevated all his creative work to sublime heights, was his unique knowledge of the sorrow that walks beside all happiness, the bitterness that lies in all that is sweet, the hidden tears behind all the jubilation of the soaring human heart. He had drunk of the dangerous waters from an unknown well. In him there was no oblivion as there was in other men and in those exalted ones among them who are the artists.

A permanent state of preparedness, which no happiness and no rise to fame could ever lull into indifference, distinguished him from all the other creative artists of all times, and this too explains the unmistakable individuality of his writings. In them the atmosphere of Austrian life—which resounds in the immortal melodies of

Schubert and Strauss, and in Grillparzer, after he had wasted himself on the world, finally became the hiss of a bitterness that would not let go—found its complete interpretation and fully rounded effect. The lover by the grace of God is not converted to any transformation of his attitude to life either by disappointment or by age. He does not lose the gift of ever and again illumining the figures of his imaginative world—for such they remain, even if he takes them from the worst of realities—though he never forgets the shadows that darken them. Such an artist was Arthur Schnitzler, and that is why all his characters are kept alive by his super-abundantly flowing sentiment, and ever and again, whatever lonely roads they may go into whatever abysses he may cause them to plunge, somehow find their way back into the open country of the soul—the soul, of which Schnitzler never quite deprived them. Never in Arthur Schnitzler's work is there what one finds in, say, that elective Austrian, Friedrich Hebbel—figures that have lost their souls through the cares and profoundly bitter experiences of life, figures that have become beast-like, that can only be given the name of men and women because they still have the physical functions of human beings. Even his sombre 'Therese' does not utterly lose her humanity in her despair; her wounds never cease to bleed. Whatever the destruction, whatever the unbearable suffering that their creator imposes on them and that he does not let us off experiencing with them, Schnitzler's characters never lose something that might be called the melody of their life, which hopefully rings out time and again. And this is the reason why they cannot perish and ever and again will win our sympathy when we meet them again after a year and a day or at the cross-roads of new generations.

Much emphasis was often given to the fact that Arthur Schnitzler always approached his characters both as a doctor and as a writer. And he himself once said: "What I write is diagnoses." But must not every writer, after all, also have the qualities of a physician, even if he has not studied medicine? In his inexorable insight into human emotions Schnitzler the writer was undoubtedly stronger than Schnitzler the doctor, and the beings on whom he inflicted pain when he had them under the scalpel of his analytical art could look forward to a certain cure or to a death that was preceded by the most ecstatic of all human sensations—a transfiguring euphoria or, to put it in poetic terms, the music of the spheres.

Arthur Schnitzler once said to me, when I asked him about the development of a new comedy, the plot of which he had told me: "I'm no longer sure whether it's going to be a comedy at all. I have the greatest trouble in keeping the characters of this play alive." This was a revealing remark, which betrayed the melancholic; and that was what Arthur Schnitzler was in his hours of greatest intensity. But it may be left to later literary historians to prove whether the deepest springs of his poetry had their origin in the melancholic or in the gay and cheerful, musingly epicurean aspect of his personality. Apart from this, something that literary research must not overlook is the profoundly musical quality of his prose, as of his diction. For Arthur Schnitzler was a musician to his finger-tips. He once confessed to me half-jokingly, when asked which he would choose: "I would find it easier to do without Goethe than without Beethoven."

It has often been written that Arthur Schnitzler was the writer *par excellence* of the 'eighties of the last century and that his work is inseparable from that happy epoch of Viennese history in which he spent his youth. But if one reads his works, causing his characters to spring to life again before one's eyes, or meets them again in successful stage-productions, one quickly recognises that they have an intrinsic vitality that is timeless and limitless and will always find its way to the heart of new generations, because the long and the short of it is that a great writer gives form to figures and essential traits of character that consist not of their outer guise and their time, but have their existence in their inwardness, the down-to-earth sincerity of their joys and sorrows.

Schnitzler was one who had a contempt for fame. The happiness that is only to be found in work, and in succeeding in his work, meant more to him; but personal happiness meant everything. After a heart-warming hour that I had once spent chatting with him at his house, he walked along to the tram stop with me. I can still hear the inspired words he spoke, which, it seemed to me, were full of the echoes of his own grievous experience. "Believe me," he said as we took leave of each other, "fame and success don't count if there's no one at home who fears for us, no one who waits impatiently for the sound of our footsteps and the ring of our voice." Schnitzler's books are peopled by those, both men and women, who are filled with nostalgia and disappointed, those for whom there is now nobody waiting.

In uttering these wise words, he did not dream, I am sure, for such was his great modesty, how many hearts at that time in all the quarters of our city, in the palaces of the rich as in the cottages of the poor, were filled with affection for the best-loved of all Viennese writers. But solitude was his house, and when he left it he stood as in a strange country; and perhaps it was only in his best moments that he knew that his destiny, with which he often quarrelled, had given him this wandering soul as the price of his greatness and his undying youth—that and the blood restlessly beating for a happiness that is granted only to those whose kindly gifts nevertheless direct them into life's valleys, while Schnitzler's work—as will some day be recognised—although it apparently revolves only round those two great urges, death and love, towers up into those heights where the air is already far too rarefied to permit the human beings who are near and dear to us to stand at our side and breathe it easily and cheerfully—heights upon which, all through his long youth, Arthur Schnitzler paced serenely and tranquilly, at once highly conscious and lost in dreams.

And we, who were the chief eye-witnesses of Arthur Schnitzler's life, must assert it again and again, must urge the contemporary world, and posterity too, to understand that this much loved and often misunderstood, even bitterly attacked, writer was never inspired by common ambition and never wrote a single line for the sake of any 'movement', never a single line that was not dictated to him by his mission.

However deeply affected my wife and I were by Schnitzler's death, and however upset we were by the manner of it, although at the same time we were comforted by the fact that he had suffered no pain—for he was just opening his letters when he suddenly crumpled up in his chair, closing his eyes for ever—I was egotistical enough also to mourn the fact that he would now never read my new novel, *Murder in the Fog*, which I had just completed. He had taken a particular interest in this book, and I had often had the privilege of telling him about it.

So that book of mine is sombrely enveloped in a tragic atmosphere far beyond anything in its contents, which can scarcely be called tragic. After all, I had only just turned sixty and did not know that this meant I too had entered into the years when, if oneself remains alive, one is bound to lose people whom one loves, partly because they are older and partly because they are the victims of diseases that they, being self-sufficient and reserved and dealing with their difficulties all on their own, conceal if for no other reason than from friendship.

My first novel of some length, *Mord im Nebel* (*Murder in the Fog*), had been born in the shadow of sincere grief over such deaths. For was it not in the last few years that I had lost three of my oldest and greatest friends, Courteline, Hugo von Hofmannsthal, and Arthur Schnitzler? Now, however, I hurried back to the very oldest of them all, who was more alive than ever, to Bernard Shaw; I did so in order to regain my strength, of course, yet above all because he summoned me.

At that period, after Shaw had spent a long time sifting and arranging his Standard Edition, a work for the stage, that highly topical play, *Too True to be Good*, had just sprung into existence, and to my delight I was able to arrange to be present at its première in London, in spite of the amount of work of my own that had accumulated. Shaw had invited me to join him in his box on the first night. He seemed pleased in the letter he wrote acknowledging my acceptance, which he regarded as a good omen.

Then, when I arrived in London on the morning of that significant day, what I found waiting for me was an invitation to dinner at his house, whence we would all set out together to undergo the highly sensational experience of a Shaw first night in England. With this invitation Shaw had anticipated my habitual question as to how he was, which was of course always the first question I asked on my arrival in London.

It took him an hour-and-three-quarters' driving to reach his London home from his house in the country, and this was a considerable exertion for him and his wife, that very wise and understanding woman who kept much too modestly in the background. It seemed rather too much after the stirring day, with the nervous strain that the evening would be. But these anxious considerations in his drawing-room were quickly set at nought by the appearance of those tall, familiar figures. They came towards me smiling and obviously in the pink of health, and Shaw amazed me by at once continuing a conversation where we had to break it off a year earlier, as though the earth had not, after all, travelled once around the sun since we had last been face to face with each other.

We went in to dinner punctually and the conversation was at first concerned with the vagaries of the dramatist's fate, which he had experienced in the rather cool reception that the public had accorded this new play at the Malvern Festival—a fate that was far from being continued when, to his delight, the public flocked to see the play in London. All the same we were full of confidence and looking forward to the first night, which was nevertheless to turn out a very pleasant surprise.

At its first performance in London, which we attended, the new play was an unusual success. There was not the slightest sign of hostility or boredom to diminish the salvos of applause and laughter with which the beautiful New Theatre resounded all that evening. As fresh as when he had arrived, and inexorably deaf to tempestuous shouts of 'Author!', after the continually delayed conclusion of the performance, to which Sir Barry Jackson once again gave a touch of ceremony by delivering a speech, Bernard Shaw went off in the best of spirits, accompanied by his wife and myself, to take his well-earned rest. He was extremely interested in the fact, to which he kept on referring, that Doktor Robert Klein, a well-known theatrical director from Berlin, whom I had summoned to London, had come specially in order to get to know his new play. "When I began," Shaw remarked, smiling, "any German producer would have run away from such an event as fast as his legs could carry him!"

The next few days, which I spent for the most part with my old friend and master, were dedicated to detailed discussion of many questions of an artistic nature.

In the leisure of the week-end, which I spent, as always, in the deep tranquillity of Shaw's country place, I had the privilege of being the witness of a minor incident that was extremely characteristic of the modest and kindly personality of the great Irish playwright.

On the way home from our Sunday walk, when we were already quite near his house, outside the beautiful old church in Ayot St. Lawrence we encountered a little throng of young people being shown round the sights of the place by a guide. The trippers were just beginning to look round the ivy-clad building and the ruin that adjoins it when they caught sight of Bernard Shaw and paused, gazing at him in admiration. Then he walked unassumingly into their midst and said: "Come along, I can tell you all about it." And

now it was he who took over the professional guide's job and showed
the little crowd round the interior of the old church. With great
thoroughness and expert knowledge he showed the attentive young
people round the fourteenth-century building and gave a detailed
explanation of this ancient and beautiful part of the English countryside. I was amazed by his deep knowledge of the history and legends
of the place. His grateful listeners undoubtedly learned more that
afternoon than their ordinary guide could have managed to show
and explain to them. Shaw, however, slipped away before they could
thank him, vanishing with long strides from the crowd of young
people that had surrounded him.

But the crowning moment of those summer hours was when
Bernard Shaw handed over his two new plays to his Viennese friend.
Conceived and shaped while he was on a journey round the world
and then completed during the fruitful summer months in Malvern,
the acting copies had just arrived from the printer's. I at once eagerly
began to read them. The little play, *A Village Wooing*, a graceful
idyll, paled, however, when contrasted with the world that opened
up before me when I came to read that important drama, that great
comedy, *On the Rocks*.

When I described my impressions to Bernard Shaw, his wife's
usual remote expression gave way, as she listened attentively, to a
bright look of pleasure, and I had the satisfaction of hearing this
unswerving and sternly critical woman express the same opinion as
her guest had just uttered not without enthusiasm. Shaw himself
remarked with a smile that one must, after all, sooner or later reach
the point of having learnt one's trade, and there was no one for whom
it was so necessary to keep in practice as the dramatist who was as yet
far from having finished his life's work.

I now confessed to Bernard Shaw that I had already made a
German translation of the play the première of which we had just
attended, and that I had already read it to Max Reinhardt in Berlin.
As Reinhardt at that time owned not only the Deutsche Theater but
also the Theater am Kurfürstendamm, we agreed, in consideration of
the heavy commitments already undertaken by the Deutsche Theater
and the Kammerspiele, that this work should be staged at the
Kurfürstendamm Theatre, which Director Robert Klein was
managing for Reinhardt. Fortunately Alexander Moissi was free to
play the main part, that of |the burglar, and, with him playing

the lead, the comedy, the other parts in which were also splendidly cast, had a great success, which was in every respect satisfactory.

This success, as it happens, was not a certainty from the very beginning. The first criticisms were confusing, since they made contradictory statements. Some reported that the first night was a roaring success, which, however, might be undone by empty houses to follow, since the play was written with an audience of philosophers in mind; others asserted that the real rush for seats would only begin when the word had gone round concerning all the audacities in the work; and others, again, took the view expressed in the old joke and said that *Too True to be Good* was no play for a first night. I had of course gone to Berlin for the rehearsals and I can definitely state that the dress-rehearsal went off splendidly, with such vociferous approval from all present that I myself, trusting in an old superstition, no longer quite dared to hope for an equally successful first night. In the long interval after the second act the Generalintendant of the Dresden Staatstheater came up to me and congratulated me, expressing his intense delight at having acquired the performing rights of the work in good time.

The première, which took place the following evening, in fact did not seem to be under a very lucky star. Several of the props failed to work; in the last act, indeed, a siren, to which specific reference is made in the dialogue and which plays an important part in the course of grotesque and startling happenings, refused to go off. Further, the actors were over-rehearsed and tired and did not live up to the heights they had attained at the dress rehearsal. When, at a passage that was a challenge to the emotions of the majority, someone hissed, I began to fear for the first time for the fate of the play. Soon, however, it became apparent that this expression of disapproval was a solitary one, and at the end of the act there were gales of applause to make up for it. The first night was saved, and the play was given many more performances and with great success.

In Vienna, whither I returned after this première, the performing-rights had been acquired by Director Jahn of the Deutsche Volks-theater, where it could not, however, be produced so quickly, because Alexander Moissi, whom Jahn wanted for the leading part, was for the present not available. When things did eventually reach that stage, the production had a special character, because Luise Rainer, the young actress who was at that time so much talked of and so highly admired, took the part of the 'patient', while Rita Georg, originally an operetta star, had an unexpected triumph in her first speaking part, as the 'nurse'. The important part of the soldier was brilliantly characterised by that dry comedian, Schafheitlin.

However, in creating this figure Shaw had not aimed merely at writing a rewarding part but had also wanted to set up a memorial to a namesake whom he greatly admired. This was Colonel T. E. Lawrence, who after the war enlisted in the Air Force and was known as Aircraftsman Shaw. He was not even remotely related to Bernard Shaw. Colonel Lawrence played a great part in Arabia's revolt and liberation from the Turkish empire. He also did much to unify the Arabian tribes.

These tasks, which he had carried out during the world war to the admiration of all those who knew what he was doing, remained, as did his mission, veiled in mystical obscurity. The man as a whole was nothing less than adventure itself in human form, celebrated far and wide, with a halo of awe around him—one who refused the highest decorations and promotion.

I had met him at Malvern with the Shaws, but I had quickly realised that he did not wish to divert the conversation from the Festival itself. Bernard Shaw and his wife were very fond of this great and modest man, and he in his turn was one of the Irish writer's greatest admirers and one who had a deep understanding of his work. This strange man was also the author of that book, so widely read in England, *The Seven Pillars of Wisdom*, which was written with a masterly skill that did all honour to his eminent friend Bernard Shaw.

After the stir that had been caused in my life by the German productions of *Too True to be Good*, I yearned for a chance to settle down once more in peace to my own ideas, which happened to be harassing me with particular intensity at that very time; but life was making everything difficult for me. *Murder in the Fog*, the novel that I had been working at for several years, had now reached the happy stage of being published in Berlin by S. Fischer, who prophesied that it would be a success.

Above all, I now set about translating Shaw's strange fable, *The Black Girl in Search of God*, which my friend had handed to me together with his last play. This profound little book was, however, not published by S. Fischer, because by that time it would have been banned by the German censorship; it was only many years later that it was published, by the Artemis Verlag in Zurich.

About that time I received the joyful news, which was published in the newspapers throughout the world, that John Galsworthy had been awarded the Nobel Prize. Unfortunately this happy event was very soon followed by the writer's death, which happened quite unexpectedly, snatching away a man who was still in his prime and at the height of his creative energy. Since this death coincided with the beginning of the most appalling period that Germany has ever experienced and hence took on a somewhat ghostly symbolic character, I felt it as something like a terrible warning that with this great writer's death the civilisation that meant so much to all of us had also entered on the road to its doom.

It was long before we could get over this, and I could not shake off the feeling that now there was some danger to the existence of the Pen Club, which had lost its most enthusiastic president in Galsworthy.

The Viennese Pen Club had also lost a valuable member of its committee in the last year through the death of Richard Specht. This highly gifted writer on music passed on only after terrible sufferings. What inevitably caused the bitterest regret in those who mourned him as his friends and intimates, in particular his oldest friend, Felix Salten, was the tragedy of a life that had here ended all too early, in all the horrors of deepest misery.

Richard Specht had been ill since the age of six—a condition that, however decisive it was, can be understood in all its grimness, in its fatal influence, only by those who are ill themselves or at least by those who are ailing, that is to say, not by the generality of people for whom an artist must live and die.

Just like Marcel Proust, with whom Richard Specht seemed to be linked by a peculiar though remote resemblance—he was always his German double—without himself ever in the least having realised that it was so, he himself never had the chance to know what it meant to be free from pain. Chronic asthma made his youth a hell, and this artistic man could not but seek to escape into the deceptive relief provided by drugs, and indeed often under the direction of his doctor. The beauties of the world, which he drank in so greedily, were as though under a haze. The lucidity of feeling and of perception, and the luminous sense of happiness that are the right of an aspiring youth, were something he never knew; he always had to fight his way through physical agonies to every enjoyment—and all he cared for was the most sublime of intellectual pleasures, the soul's exaltations; he had to pay for all he ever enjoyed, purchasing it at the price of the unimaginable anguish that a neuropath suffers. This *danse macabre* that his daemon led him was controlled, as it were tamed, in the more fortunate moments that his strange fate permitted him, and sometimes, though only for a few months, brought to a standstill, by a strong, unswerving, upward-striving will to live.

Then this young man, a born master of words both written and spoken, would plunge headlong and with insatiable hunger upon his self-chosen poetic medium, in the waves of which he would immerse himself in the blissful oblivion of endless nocturnal hours.

Fame meant much less to him than did the happiness of his work, wrested from the calamities of his physical constitution, work that often helped this pain-intoxicated man to achieve a blissful sobriety. He confronted the doubters with work after work; and since his unfortunate condition time and again tore to shreds the fine meshes of his poetic achievement, time and again diminishing and paralysing this artist's creative powers, he turned with true devotion to the characterisation and representation of those artists who for him represented all that was most sublime. And it was no accident that the majority of them sat on undisputed thrones in the realm of music.

In Richard Specht's parental home—he came of a family that had been in trade for generations—the musical grand masters of the era were daily guests. And his books on Brahms, Mahler, and Richard Strauss would not have the permanent value that is intrinsic to them if he had not known these masters personally, seeing them face to face and soul to soul, and if he had not had a deep insight into their aims and abilities such as was scarcely equalled by any other music critics of our time.

Nevertheless it was only his work on Beethoven that gained Richard Specht lasting fame, for it towers high over all his other biographical writings. For in Beethoven Specht felt the presence not only of the inimitable artist to whom he looked up in worship, but also the fellow human being tormented by the devils of all pain. Beethoven's heroic destiny deeply moved the writer of this great musical biography and by its example enabled him to liberate himself.

Richard Specht, stigmatised from childhood, was filled with a love as unenvious as any love could be for the healthy and strong, for those who squander the superabundance of their being, and he was always among the very first to recognise and hail each new note that was sounded, each new form in which a unique genius proved himself. His books on Arthur Schnitzler and Franz Werfel bear witness to this, as do also his countless masterly criticisms of poetic works in journals and newspapers. To him it was given, as to few, to distinguish the genuine from the false, without his having to enter into learned examinations of what had been intended and what had been achieved. For together with all the catastrophes and despairs of his life, which had been disastrous from the beginning, he possessed the gift of the divining-rod. His heart leaped up without fail whenever a genuine feeling which had been given a new form and had been experienced for the first time was wafted to his ear. And if a god had only grudgingly given him the gift of expressing in tremendous terms what he himself suffered, the sufferings of the great who surrounded him were something he could represent, explain and expound on their behalf.

His work is extant, and it is the task and duty of those who will come after him to preserve it for the future. For Richard Specht, so little esteemed, so often hurt and often pushed aside, will sooner or later be recognised for what he was: a leader with only a small following, one crowned with thorns who went towards his Calvary determined not to shorten his sufferings but to savour them to the last bitter dregs, as one who loved his cup of hemlock because the council of the gods had allotted him no more delicious drink.

I have the feeling—and the further I press on as I write, the more I have it—that what I am doing in these pages, I am glad to say, is mainly recounting the story of the heroes of my youth as my own story. But there would be no end to it, after all, if I were to accompany all these beloved figures all the way until they closed their eyes for ever. So, for instance, in the years that I have just been describing, I lost the intimate contact with Hermann Bahr. We wrote to each other, of course, but he had moved with his wife, Anna von Mildenburg, to Munich, where this great singer became one of the most prominent teachers of singing, even at a time when her magnificent voice would still have entitled her to continue performing at great theatrical events.

When Hermann Bahr had written a new play, which happened ever more infrequently, the whole world learned of it when I did. But in the last period of his life he was concerned with something else, which I have already hinted at in these pages: his religious devoutness increased with the years, years in which he withdrew further and further from his friends, though not without waving and smiling to us. After his seventieth birthday this man, who had become more and more wrapped up in himself and who, unlike others who had returned to the bosom of the Church, had never denied or, worse, poured scorn upon a single act committed in his wild youth, became so silent that his death, which occurred only a few years later, was taken almost for granted as something that was long overdue, honour being paid to his memory, it is true, but by no means in exaggerated terms. The Burgtheater, which up to this day has never ceased to perform his brilliant, timeless plays, most movingly paid particular homage to his memory under the direction of Erhard Buschbeck.

I often wonder what would have become of that magnificent and historic theatre, which meant so much to all cultured Viennese, if it had not been for its guardian, the keeper of its tradition, its good angel, the poet Erhard Buschbeck. Happily this state of affairs has not changed down to the present day. Directors come and go, but Erhard Buschbeck remains, because the first thing every new director of this theatre, which imposes such heavy responsibilities on those in charge of it, does is to ask for him, since everyone primarily seeks his invaluable co-operation.

I had now become more or less accustomed to losing the irreplaceable companions of my youth; but I tried to console myself as well as possible for these grievous losses by giving recognition to a rising younger generation. Anton Wildgans, that wonderful lyric poet, should be mentioned before anyone else. There were also those writers who had in the meantime reached maturity, Franz Theodor Csokor, Oscar Maurus Fontana, Ernst Lothar and many others whom I have already named or, wrongly perhaps, failed to name.

Among those who particularly mourned Hermann Bahr there was also Stefan Zweig, who was just about to give up his delightfully beautiful home in Salzburg and leave his native Austria for ever, only to return now and then as a fleeting visitor to Vienna, where besides his old friends a brother dear to him and an old sick mother still lived.

For me, however, there was one great and genuine sorrow yet to come. This came to me when my dear publisher, S. Fischer, closed his eyes in eternal sleep.

The departure of this faithful friend, who had been almost a father to me, at first sealed my lips. It is not everyone who can instantly find little words for a great sorrow. In a dream-like state, which was, however, much more desolate and dreary than dreams are, I had time and again to go back over the thirty years of a tried fellowship before I could enter into and find repose in the phantom house of memories. I wanted to savour them all once again, once again testing them and lingering over each. But even that was not fated to succeed. They withdrew from me, fleeing from me and returning once more, even giving me the lie in this wearisome play; and only those that were inextinguishable stirred again and again, always producing that dim tranquillity that comes with all mourning for what is irrevocably lost.

It was long before I could speak of the man with whom I had talked so much, with whom I had felt such a deep need to discuss things in all the years of our meetings, even if it was only in order to get to know myself and my aims better. What an alert listener he had been! How keenly he waited, full of kindly understanding, for the word that would give him the chance to intervene with contradiction or agreement! And how he helped one—true paver that he was of other people's way—to find the truth and where it was to lead!

And so it was in silence that the first and hardest weeks passed, so far as I was concerned, those weeks during which one cannot believe that he who has passed on is really mute for ever, will really remain absent for ever, and is really dissolved in the vastness of the universe, weeks in which he who is no more is still followed by a wavering hope that is utterly groundless, pitiable, and refuted by ordinary experience and which wanders after him along a joyless path without a goal and in the end must die.

Everyone knows the helplessness with which one asks all those questions, never asked before, that fly towards one who has ceased to be and whom one has loved, as though perhaps after all the miracle of an answer might still be expected. An unyielding silence confirms what we already know, and before the words that would wildly burst out in grateful appreciation of one who is now vanished can be summoned up, a strange whispering and murmuring begins, which once more commands silence. These are the torrents of a new and vehement grief. They flow and flow, they fall and fall, until the night-dark waves pour ever more quietly and brightly. When at last they begin to trickle crystal-clear, the nocturnally mourning mind lifts its battered pinions, and he who has received this grace is then enabled to behold a pure image and, speaking of the monument into which love and a great hope transform that image, is able to say how it is with the symbol and the living reality for which it stands. Only then can memories become vocal, and then indeed they are really the genuine and immutable memories of which that is for ever made up which mankind calls immortality.

Fischer asked little, but what he asked went deep. On various occasions when we met, as happened at short intervals, I had to tell him about my beginnings, my boyhood, and my youth wasted in a bad dream. In those hours of frequent meetings I did not keep back much for myself, scarcely even what was shameful.

The fact that this little man with the blue eyes and the wonderful gaze full of wisdom and goodness—such as I have never seen in anyone else, and the mystery of which that great German painter Max Liebermann caught, glimmering, on his canvas—together with many other excellent qualities possessed that of heroism, too, was something that I learned when he suffered the first grievous blow, that unique sorrow that comes to all of us, casting us down, transforming us and suddenly making us years older. I am thinking of the death of his son Gerhardt, whom he loved more than anything in the world and with whom his fairest hopes in life were bound up. I have never seen such controlled despair, such an inconsolable acceptance of suffering and sorrow, as in those moments of overwhelming distress when there was nothing to be done but to accept the crushing loss and endure it. I have already related in this book how, much later, when the terrible war years overwhelmed the deepest private sorrow by the horror they caused in all truly human hearts, this sorely tried man clung to the thought, as strange as it was natural, that this son would have been lost to him even if it had not been for the sudden illness that had wrested him away. "Oh yes, he would have been killed in the war," declared this father who had never ceased to mourn, and he said it to tranquillise and strengthen himself, to make his heavy lot easier to bear and in order that he might be capable of continuing to hold up his head and so serve his mission to the end. He believed in destiny. That, I think, was why Fischer's spirit was a match for all the blows of that time as of the time that was to come later; but his strong heart suffered as a result of it, and began to fail.

The man who was accustomed to be influential and a central figure among the most eminent German intellectuals of his days, counting among his best friends such men as Gerhart Hauptmann, Thomas Mann, Peter Nansen, Hermann Bang, Arthur Schnitzler, Hugo von Hofmannsthal, Rainer Maria Rilke, and Walter Rathenau, to mention only some names belonging to the great period when his publishing house flourished, nevertheless possessed the divine gift of being infallibly able to sense the true value of quite different talents, so long as they were of full integrity and developed to the height of their creative powers. He missed no one, either young or old, who rallied to his flag, if he deserved to be singled out from amid the throng and discovered. And so it was that very many writers of all degrees and all movements had Fischer to thank for it if—guided by his paternal hand—they had the privilege of enjoying their rise to fame while they were still in their prime, and not only after soul-destroying struggles and going the long way round.

Fischer was mistrustful, not out of petty-mindedness or selfishness, but out of a very alert sense of responsibility; yet in any case where he saw himself confronted with misery or want that was not the sufferer's own fault or only produced for the sake of effect, he was ever a philanthropist, and he kept many a man with his head above water, shrinking from no sacrifices if he could enable a genuine talent to develop. Gratitude was something he never craved, but all the more tempestuously did he insist on work that should reward him for his sympathetic care and aid, and it is not the worst books that owe their existence to Fischer's secret patronage.

Since this little man had a strong and stern will and was not afraid of creating the impression that he was inexorable, which he may sometimes have created when the situation seemed to him to make such an attitude necessary, of course he did not go through life without being attacked.

"We do not always reach the age we are destined to reach," he once said to me. "Everything depends on the attendant circumstances and unforeseen events." And this saying of his seems to me to reveal the depth of his inner life. He liked to hearken, as it were, inwards; and yet he kept to himself many an answer that he was given by his blood and his deeply searching mind. He knew all about himself, and he was not taken by surprise when illness and death came. The pain of dying with the feeling that he ought to go on serving his created work, which still had need of him, was something he could not be spared. But anyone who can be comforted at all is perhaps entitled to tell himself that S. Fischer, as a result of his great and imperishable achievements, without which the history of German culture is now unthinkable, has entered into the throng of those redeemed spirits who have had the well-deserved happiness of enriching their time and fulfilling themselves.

In dying when he did Fischer was spared much, for in the last years of his life it had become apparent that neither was he capable of recognising the menaces that crowded upon Germany when Hitler seized power nor had he the strength to protect himself and his firm from these things in any way and take steps in good time in order to save his handiwork.

Indeed, shortly before his death his power of reasoning had become impaired, and so the magnificent bequest that he left behind him was more or less a ship without a helm. It was less so because Fischer did, after all, have a successor who had the right to make decisions. This was his son-in-law, Dr. Gottfried Bermann, an orthopædist from Kattowitz, who, if one could credit the reputation that preceded him to Berlin, was a good and capable doctor. It must be said in his favour that there could not have been a time in which anyone in control of the Fischer Verlag would have encountered graver difficulties. Under normal conditions Gottfried Bermann would certainly have been a very capable, sound publisher. Dr. Bermann had nothing in common with his father-in-law. In addition, there was the uncertainty of his taste, which again had the consequence that he made wavering and fumbling decisions. He had the good fortune to find an unusually capable right-hand man of S. Fischer's in Peter Suhrkamp, an adviser and pillar of strength to whom he might well have entrusted the management of the firm, in which Suhrkamp had, so to speak, grown up. And indeed he did so, though only at the last minute when the situation in Germany was becoming critical and he decided to seek his fortune as a publisher in Vienna, which he did hesitantly and somewhat reluctantly. His wife, who had, of course, breathed the air of the old Fischer Verlag and grown up in its atmosphere, began only somewhat late, when her days in Berlin were already numbered, to influence her husband in publishing matters too, and I am sure not unfavourably. Old Frau Hedwig Fischer, who in her youth had for years been something like her husband's partner, as a result of the terrible events that were breaking ever more stormily over cultural Germany had now begun to suffer from heart trouble and was incapable of doing more than give her daughter and her daughter's husband *carte blanche* and put herself under their protection.

The terrible burnings of the books, which were such a disgrace to the German world, were something that the Fischer family was still in Berlin to experience, bewildered and disillusioned as they were by all the horrors of the time. This world-famous 'non-Aryan' publishing house, which was of course a thorn in the flesh of the Nazis, but which they did not wish to remove without seizing the business for themselves, was in spite of all for a long time saved from being 'Aryanised', through the courage and resourcefulness of Peter Suhrkamp, until he too in the end partly fell a victim to the threats and the pressure exerted by the gangsters in power. In so doing Suhrkamp sacrificed his health and was near to losing his life, and came to know the horrors of the concentration camp.

Gradually now almost all the representatives of German culture left their native country, and those who remained fell into one or the other of two groups: there were those who thought they would run with the hounds, and there were those, dreamers and unworldly simpletons, who imagined they would be able to continue living their own lives apart from any demands the Nazis might make. Most of these were taught their lesson in the most appalling way, especially if they were 'non-Aryans' and for that reason alone already doomed to perish.

So far as I was concerned, Berlin's main attraction disappeared with the death of Fischer, and for the time being I remained in Vienna, getting on with my work, all the more since I was deeply immersed in a new novel that lay closer to my heart than any previous book of mine, and in this I began to find distraction and consolation. This was the novel, *Heimkehr zum Ich* (*Return Home to*

Myself), which I was working away at, making very swift progress, when I was interrupted by a frightful event that all at once lit up the future of my native country as though in the glare of flames: this was the murder of our Chancellor, Dr. Engelbert Dollfuss.

Stefan Zweig, who had the uncanny gift of foreknowledge, was at this time no longer in Austria; but when I gently reproached him for his all too speedy abandonment of his magnificent home at Salzburg, he said in a tone of intense conviction: "The thing is, you can't imagine what is coming to Austria and what we shall all go through, if we remain where we are not wanted."

This Nazi outrage, the assassination of the Austrian Chancellor, at once caused me to think of Stefan Zweig's words, and if we were deeply affected by this crime, which had been planned so long in advance, it was because we had grown fond of Dr. Dollfuss and his enchanting wife, who had on several occasions been our guests in Hietzing, and whom we had got to know at innumerable Pen Club meetings, which he scarcely ever failed to attend. We knew him for a lovable man who was always guided by the best of intentions, one who had made his way up in the world through his far from usual gifts. He would have liked to help everyone who came to him for help. Whether it was an actor, a writer, a musician, or a politician, Dollfuss would give him his attention, and his eyes reflected the good will of a sympathetic heart and the feelings of one who was always ready to do what he could. The manner of his murder and the treachery of which he was the victim naturally aroused not only our sympathy but that of all whose expectations had been linked with his great abilities and his gift for mediation.

The monstrous character of these events, the long-term conspiracy on the part of Austria's so much stronger neighbour and its sad consequences, caused us, however, to hope that now at last strong measures would be taken and above all that the ordinary Austrian would now come to his senses.

In order to allay the unrest that was seething in my mind with alarming intensity, making all work impossible for the time being, I hurried away to a distant part of the world that I had always had a longing to visit, setting out on a journey from a land of little promise to that called The Promised Land.

It was then that I remembered a promise I had given my dentist, an impassioned Zionist, to visit him in his new home country, and so, encouraged by the praise I had heard of the new ocean-going steamer *Rex*, of which reliable acquaintances had told me very many very pleasant things, I embarked at Genoa. This ship was to take us to Palestine, to the country that was the goal of the journey we had planned.

The *Piroscafo Rex* was anchored at Genoa for a day and a night, and I made use of this opportunity to visit Gerhart Hauptmann at Rapallo, where he had pitched his tent as he did every spring. There it was that my last meeting with this poet took place, and I remember that he came to meet me with the words: "My friends, you know, are all very cross with me, most of all Emil Ludwig, who can't forgive me for staying in Germany, which he has been saved the trouble of doing in any case, because, of course, he, as a Swiss citizen, has been settled in a wonderful new home of his own in Ascona for years."

Gerhart Hauptmann made use of my visit to explain to me what his position was and how impossible it was to improve it by, say, emigrating to America. "I have two sons," he said, "in big German firms, who would be dismissed as a matter of course if I were to try to make my way out. But that would be the least disagreeable thing they would have to expect. They would doubtless scarcely be left at liberty, but would come to know the delights of a concentration camp. And what would they live on? As to that my friends have unfortunately made no suggestions. If you ask me whether I still feel comfortable in my native Germany, after all that has been done to my friends, of course that is quite a different matter."

After this sudden outpouring, with which he burst out after we had been sitting together for only a moment, I steered the conversation away from this delicate subject, telling Hauptmann first of all what chance it was that had brought me to Genoa and how I had to be on board again that evening, in the ship that was to take me on a holiday trip to Palestine.

The time that I was able to spend with him passed in more or less trivial conversation, and when we took leave of each other we avoided uttering the words *Auf Wiedersehen!* precisely because it was improbable that we would see each other again but was nevertheless what we hoped for.

Overwhelming are the impressions that, even as they take possession of us, rob us of all words and, sinking deep into our minds, would make the silence of such emotion last for ever. This happens for the most part at those places that themselves radiate a powerful and impenetrable silence, which would not be broken by judgments and cheap ecstasies of astonishment and admiration. Our intrusive words are suppressed, and he who seeks such words in order to give an account of the experience is convinced of the superfluity of his attempt as soon as he recognises that in fact everything that is great has always lain enclosed in silence.

In that stormy, wild, and frosty spring I fared much like this when I took as my goal the place for which the Crusaders had yearned, the Holy Sepulchre in Jerusalem. I am incapable of describing anything. Only I would quietly admit that I stood at the eternal tomb, I was privileged to shudder in awe on that sacred ground to which ever new pilgrimages have been undertaken all through the centuries by mortals of every kind, yearningly and vengefully, death-drunken and faith-illumined, salvation-thirsty and shaken by doubts. With poor human eyes I stared amazed at the four pillars of the mighty Mosque of Omar, which King Solomon had the strength and wisdom to erect; besides the burden of the vault that they help to support they must bear the weight of many centuries and ineradicable traditions. I stood at the Wailing Wall, which had absorbed seas of tears and devoured myriads of wafted sighs, and I saluted in astonishment those who had come to hammer in a nail on the spot under which they wished to be buried.

But the wonders began when the sun broke through the morning mist that hung over the harbour at Haifa, and the town suddenly arose in unexpected brilliance, glimmering alluringly out of a sea now calm, before the late sleeper's gaze. This town, which extends up the sides of all the hills around it, was the point of departure for a journey on which the legendary land of Palestine became reality for me. A vast and, as it seemed, unceasing bustle reigned in the ancient Arab settlement, which even then was being startled out of its dreams by countless immigrants who were here beginning to build a new present and a new future for themselves. This meant that things were not particularly quiet, and the noise produced by hammer, pick, and shovel was a not always pleasing accompaniment, and one that mercifully was not to be heard in the centre of Palestine, in Jerusalem. There all belonged to the past, here all to the future. Those who so eagerly and impatiently wielded their spades all paid homage to their patron saint, my never forgotten friend Herzl, who had originated the great idea that was now setting thousands on the move. His name cropped up ever and again, everywhere, painted in large letters on the signboards of chemists' shops, of squares, parks, and archways.

This city contained a very large number of magnificent and luxurious motor-cars, for the most part American, all of which were for hire and their praises sung by industrious natives and immigrants, who also suggested to the harassed traveller what sights he should see, what places he should drive out to explore. So then—almost too quickly—it came that we were driving via Nazareth and the Sea of Galilee to the sacred city.

It is natural that the names of such places should have an electrifying effect, in however oddly matter-of-fact and routine a manner they often fall from the lips of the guides whose ambition it is to show one round the splendours one is in search of. But when we walked through Nazareth's narrow winding streets and everywhere, as it were, were standing on Biblical ground, the explanations that we were given fell on our ears almost like faint recollections of our earliest schooldays. It was as if we were now granted the opportunity of finding out for certain whether all that had been impressed on us then was really true—all those things that had had to be repeated, sometimes like a burdensome litany. So then this journey was at the same time a journey through the long-forgotten country of our childhood, and the terrace outside the restaurant on the Sea of Galilee suddenly, when we turned our eyes away from so many wonders, became the forgotten schoolroom in which those words, those revelations, had for the first time been uttered by the voices of devout teachers. It was doubtless also in order to reinforce these feelings of ours that our driver stopped at Rachel's tomb, before he took the winding uphill road to the city that had been the goal of so many dreams—Jerusalem.

Who could have dreamed, in those hot plains over which we had just been racing, that now we would reach cool mountain air and for some days be able to enjoy the refreshing atmosphere of a mountain resort? Outside the magnificent King David Hotel the best and most reliable guides to this sublime city stood beside the inevitable motor-cars. The Arab who took charge of me showed me everything there was to be seen and explained it all in faultless French. He took me to the Holy Sepulchre, where he uttered his explanations in a low, hesitant voice in order not to startle me disagreeably out of the profound emotion that overwhelmed me here where I was face to face with so much proven tradition, and that I long could not shake off. At his side I saw the wonders of Zion, the Mount of Olives, and the Garden of Gethsemane, the sacred precincts of which were in the charge of a Swiss monk. My dragoman motored me to Bethlehem, to Jericho, to the Dead Sea and to the Jordan, which slid lazily through the yellow countryside, nothing about it revealing anything of what a world-shaking holy event had once occurred between its banks.

These expeditions were fairly tiring, but the evening always brought us back to Jerusalem, that eternal city with the best climate in the Near East, and the refreshing coolness there restored us after all the hardships and ponderous reflections of the day.

But it would be an ungrateful leave-taking from a land that gave me so much that was overpowering and strange, and with the rapidity of visions flashing past, if I failed to mention that cheek by jowl with the monuments of vanished epochs I had the privilege of seeing, indeed almost of experiencing, something of the tremendous contrast of the new age that was springing into life. Not far from Jerusalem, an everlasting peak that seems to crown the whole landscape of Palestine, I saw a new world, one that was utterly without tradition, growing out of this ancient soil. To me it was astonishing and almost incomprehensible, this daily observed growth of the sea-washed capital of the immigrant realm, Tel-Aviv.

But now I must not pass in silence over a remarkably fateful personal adventure, which, after it had come to an undeservedly fortunate conclusion, caused me to shudder with more emotion than any other experience had ever done.

Our ship was anchored in Port Said and had given the travellers about a week in order to see something of Palestine and even to make a trip to Cairo. I knew exactly which evening it was when I had to go on board at Port Said, and all my arrangements were made with reference to this date. The final goal of my expedition had been Jerusalem, and now there was only one more night separating me from the day when I must make my way to Port Said.

Transport conditions were at that time certainly not nearly as comfortable as I am sure they are today. At Cook's I had discovered that I would have to take a desert train at eight o'clock in the morning in order to arrive at Port Said about eight in the evening, which made it perfectly possible for me to go aboard my ship there at eleven that night. Cook's had furthermore told me that there was also an air-line from Jerusalem to Port Said, a very convenient connection that took only two or three hours. I was of course instantly all agog to go by plane, since this would have made it possible for me to spend several hours of daylight in Port Said, getting to know that interesting sea-port. Hence it was with no small disappointment that I heard the assurances given me in the crowded travel agency that there were no reservations to be had on the plane for several days and that I would be wise not to hope for an improbable and unexpected chance, but rather to make sure of my railway ticket. I was somewhat depressed, for the twelve-hour journey through the desert held no charms for me.

I therefore applied to the porter at the hotel, who had previously attracted my attention through his politeness and eagerness to help in every way, as well as by the shrewd answers he had given to many a stupid question. I bewailed my lot to him. He listened attentively and said: "Yes, I know, in the normal way there is no plane reservation to be had for tomorrow, at least not from the travel agency. But staying here in the hotel we have a Swiss gentleman, Colonel Frey, with his wife and daughter. He has a seat on the plane. And it happens to be lucky for you," he added, smiling, "that his ladies keep on telling him he shouldn't leave them to go alone by train, but should give up his air ticket and go with them. Up to now the Colonel wouldn't hear of it, he's firmly resolved to make use of being the fortunate owner of a plane reservation. But you never can tell. Perhaps the ladies will succeed after all in making him change his mind. Then I shall see to it that nobody but you gets the seat."

Here now was a gleam of hope. Naturally I at once said to myself: "Colonel Frey from Solothurn is surely the same man I met through my friend Ferrière in Vienna almost twenty years ago now. But perhaps he won't remember me," I reflected. "And then, after all, I can't simply speak or write to a man who is, however one may look at it, barely an acquaintance, and ask him to make such a sacrifice for me, one that I myself would doubtless hardly have made for anyone else. There's nothing to be done but wait and see."

Then, after dinner, when I went to get the key of my room in order to go to bed early, my protector, who seemed to have no little sympathy with my disappointment, said to me: "I'll have to call you at seven o'clock in the morning anyway, because your train goes at eight. And that's the last minute when anything could have changed. So when I come into your room, either I'll have Colonel Frey's plane ticket in my hand or I shall ask you not to keep our car waiting which is to take you to the station."

I thanked this obliging porter cordially and went to bed, sighing.

I had been awake for an hour when the mediator between me and my destiny knocked at the door of my room. I wrenched the door open, and the man stood before me, looking at me gravely and shaking his head. "I am sorry to say nothing could be done. The ladies are going by train, and the Colonel is flying to Port Said two hours later, to wait for his family there."

I clenched my teeth, gulped down the breakfast that was very shortly afterwards brought to me by the room-waiter, and was soon in the train by which it was my fate to travel.

I thought I knew the two Frey ladies by sight, and would have liked to get into a conversation with them concerning this incident; however, it was not their compartment in which I found myself sitting. Every coach of the train was very crowded, and the number of the coaches was very considerable indeed. But the thing about time is that it does pass, and so this long hot day in the train, tormented by the dust of the desert, passed away too, and the shadows of evening had fallen long before the time when I left my compartment and made it my first object to seek refreshment in the station restaurant. The whole time I had been thinking enviously of Colonel Frey, and even now, just as I was leaving the train and my two suitcases were being torn from me by a pretty unsavoury-looking, dark-skinned individual, the envy that I had scarcely been able to assuage rose up in me again.

I had taken only a few steps when I was struck by the uproar that suddenly surrounded me. People went hastily running past me, shouts rang out in all languages, and when I entered the restaurant, I saw that there were large posters on the walls and that there were in addition a number of announcers in front of these posters. The noise around me increased in volume, and the crowd became ever more and more excited, so that I went up close to my porter in order to remain in the proximity of my luggage, while everything around me seemed to be revolving as though in a nightmare. I felt as though

I had suddenly been stunned, and was startled out of that condition by hearing my own words: "What has happened? What's the matter?"

Now I heard the explanation of this truly Oriental tumult, given in English and in French. The aeroplane, which was expected to arrive from Jerusalem, had crashed in flames some five kilometres away from the airport, for reasons unknown. There were no survivors.

A moment later a list of the passengers who had been killed was posted up on the besmeared walls, and, speechless with horror, I read at the head of the list the name: 'Colonel Frey, Solothurn'.

Motor-cars were racing past me obviously bearing away people who had been expecting their friends and relatives and who were now rushing to the scene of the disaster. I was still feeling quite stunned.

It was only about an hour later that I came to myself properly, when I was lying in my cabin on board the *Rex*, in a state of utter exhaustion. The unsuspecting steward came in and informed me that at the request of a number of passengers who wished to make a somewhat longer stay in Cairo, the captain had agreed to postpone sailing for one day longer, so that the *Rex* would begin its return journey to Italy only on the next day. I would thus have time to go to Cairo too.

I myself only realised what a state I was in when it became clear to me that I could not seize this opportunity to see Cairo once again in such an easy way. I was as though paralysed, not, however, by sorrow and regret for a man whom I had known so slightly, but simply overwhelmed by my own destiny, so incomprehensible to myself. I had passionately stretched out a greedy hand, desiring to bring my own destruction on myself by force, and providence had withheld it from me. Having been, as it were, snatched back out of the plane that I had wished to board, it seemed to me as though a voice that I had never heard before had called out to me: "You are to remain here!" Was there then such a thing as predestination?

Even today it is not possible for me to say any more about this adventure than is implicit in it for those to whom I recount it, even though some among them are people who believe in predestination. I racked my brains about this experience for a long time, posing questions that got me no further, and the mystery behind this strange incident was naturally never revealed to me.

On my return home, I thoroughly terrified my wife by telling her of this catastrophe. What she said did me good, even if among her various comments there were such as the question: "Well, can you be allowed to go off travelling on your own?" All in all what she said brought me back quickly to my ordinary life, the daily round, and my writing-desk.

But in order to get rid of my contradictory feelings I was glad to answer a fairly impatient summons from Shaw, to whom I had written, briefly and casually informing him of the inexplicable incident.

Later, then, when I was sitting opposite him, he would not even let me speak, but, the moment I tried to begin, exclaimed: "Don't go and think that this lucky escape is the result of a weighty pronouncement on the part of *your* destiny! It's entirely mine. Destiny wanted to save *me* the trouble that your sudden death would have caused *me*. Busy though I am, I would instantly have had to look after your poor wife, and apart from that, I would have had to look for a new German translator for my works. It doesn't bear thinking of, the amount of work and trouble it would have caused me! Oh how thankful I am to *my* destiny that you are here again, sitting face to face with me. Besides, this time there is a great deal to discuss. The first thing I want you to do is to interview me, so that I can get rid of the journalists who try to do it every day. What I want is a standard interview that will do once and for all. The thing is, they ask me the most wildly impossible questions, which I either can't or won't answer. Here are some questions that I have prepared for you, which you are to put to me, because I myself am interested in having them answered."

I was equally taken aback by this reception and this interpretation of my adventure and by Shaw's peculiar idea that I should suddenly interview him, when, after all, I had imagined that our abundant correspondence and our frequent meetings had already made me acquainted with his attitude to the prescribed questions. However, I laughingly agreed to do as he wanted, and the questions and answers on the political events of the day, which are now of course long out of date, I published in Berlin, in the *Vossische Zeitung*.

That was the first time the name of Hitler was uttered between us, and Bernard Shaw, who always found it much more difficult than the world in general imagines to judge a non-English person, especially if that person was in a high position, took me no little aback with his view of the terrible upheaval in Germany. However much he had been upset by Rathenau's assassination, because he had met him personally on the occasion of a visit, he was very far from taking a sufficiently serious view of the events that had occurred since the Nazi seizure of power in Germany and even refused to see that the murder of Dollfuss was a sure sign that Austria's independence was now very gravely threatened.

We then also discussed the German possibilities of his new play, *On the Rocks*, which in my translation had been given the title *Festgefahren*, and which to me seemed—for all its theatrical effectiveness and in spite of its great originality, which sometimes produced startling effects—nevertheless in its style and intention to be something like a pendant to *The Apple Cart*.

But we had a still more important theatrical event to discuss. About this time that keen film man, Gabriel Pascal, had already come into Bernard Shaw's life and had, oddly enough, quickly won over to his side this mistrustful writer who had rejected one after another of the offers, with which he was all the time being bombarded, to produce films of his plays. The first consequence of this was the English version of *Pygmalion*, with Leslie Howard and Wendy Hiller in the leading rôles. But Shaw had given me permission to film the play in German without any reference to the English version. This was the first and last time that a film appeared in two versions.

At this late date I cannot definitely remember how this double film production came about with Bernard Shaw's complete agreement. I only recall that I was one day summoned to see that well-known copyright lawyer, Dr. Paul Koretz, who was also among Shaw's trustees, and received from him a German film-script of *Pygmalion*, which he declared was a complete failure. The German rights had been acquired by the Klagemann Film Company, I believe in conjunction with the Fox company in America.

The part of Eliza was to be played in Berlin by that delightfully pretty and highly-gifted actress, Jenny Jugo, while that brilliant actor, Gustaf Gründgens, was intended for the part of Professor Higgins. I now set about the work of preparing a new script, with the blessing of many guardian angels, chief among them Bernard Shaw himself. I am sure I should not have succeeded so well as I was at that time appreciatively told that I had, if I had not had the rejected script as a basis. I had only just got back to Vienna from London when I received a visit from Klagemann and Jenny Jugo, who discussed all the details with me and made me promise that I would begin my work in Berlin some weeks later.

The première of *On the Rocks* took place at approximately the same time in Berlin, and this play, produced at the Volksbühne in the Bülowplatz, was a very great success. The interesting part of the English Prime Minister was taken by the actor Grunwald, who had been discovered a few years previously in the leading part in Gerhart Hauptmann's *Gabriel Schilling's Flucht* (*The Flight of Gabriel Schilling*).

But in saying so much I have slightly anticipated events. An account remains to be given of how I came to Berlin for the last time in the menacing political conditions that prevailed in the year 1936. At first nothing would induce me to leave Vienna, where I had to look for a new publisher after Fischer's demise, and had indeed found him in Herbert Reichner. I knew, of course, that for the time being it would not be possible for my new book to be published in Germany and that it would therefore be useless to offer it to S. Fischer's successor.

Apart from this, Shaw's new play, *The Millionairess*, had followed me to Vienna, suddenly appearing on my desk and insistently demanding to be provided with its German guise.

If I had not sunk in a little sea of work at that time, I really do not know what would have become of me. There was far too much crowding in upon me. Now the new age, to whose coming we had so long shut our eyes in self-defence, was hammering and battering at our only seemingly solid door.

My family's firm began to creak in all its joints. The last head of the firm had long ago lost grip, having devoted all his attention to horse-racing, and from the neighbouring country, which had been the great love of my youth, terrible notes of menace sounded across the frontier.

Our country's leader was that brave and highly-cultured man of honour, Dr. Kurt von Schuschnigg, who, precisely because of those qualities, which made it impossible for him even to comprehend the criminal thought-processes of his enemy at Berchtesgaden, was perhaps not the right man for this period of looming danger. In order to fight the menace of the time he would have needed to be more robust and adaptable in a rather worse sense. His wife, Herma, was frequently a guest of ours in Hietzing; she would then sometimes go over with us to the Zsolnays, where her husband would later appear, as charming as he was careworn, and visibly breathing more freely in the company of artists. He was a cousin of the writer Albert von Trentini and, as he told me, in their youth they had often chatted about which of them was to become a statesman and which a poet. Then all at once I knew how it was that Schuschnigg wrote in such a good style, quite different from the usual Austrian civil service style. And when Trentini, who lived a rather withdrawn life and worked in solitude, once appeared at the same time as he did at a reception, Schuschnigg pointed at him and said: "He's better off. He chose the better part compared with me."

Now, the fact was that Schuschnigg, the idealist, had an ideal for the sake of which he had taken up the unequal struggle with his neighbour, and this was the salvation of Austria. If this aim was scarcely attainable, in view of the incomprehensible swing-over of opinion among the population of Austria, what made things even harder for Chancellor Schuschnigg was a terrible blow of fate. His wife, who was deeply devoted to him and was at his side, full of the most touching confidence, throughout all his struggles, was snatched from him through a motor accident. The other occupants of the motor-car were Kurt von Schuschnigg, his little son, and the child's nurse, but fate stretched out its hand to take what was most dear to him, his wife, and thus deprived him of his greatest and most reliable support.

At that time it was as though the city were holding its breath, and once again the stillness that precedes the storm was forcing people to come to their senses. But it was only a short breathing-space, and the country's deeply afflicted leader could not even abandon himself to his sorrow.

I fared similarly in many ways now where many a loss was concerned, even though in my own life none caused such frightful havoc as that I have just described. It was with mixed feelings that I saw my new book, *Heimkehr zum Ich*, appear under the imprint of that exceedingly charming and efficient man, Herbert Reichner, after I had all my life long had my own and Shaw's works published by S. Fischer, apart, that is, from little diversions that were never of my own choosing. This first of my books to be published by a Viennese firm caused me to indulge in strange reminiscences. For my little story, *Das verkaufte Lächeln* (*The Smile that was Sold*), had been published twenty-five years earlier in the Wiener Verlag, which was under the direction of that gifted man, Fritz Freund.

Heimkehr zum Ich began by having a very marked success, although the book was published at a far from fortunate time, because people were already much too restless to lose themselves in the reading of a work in which the main concern was the dissection of the most strange and peculiar of human feelings.

This book was translated into French almost at the same time. The translation was done by Hélène Chaudoir, who occasionally devoted herself to such work of literary mediation and whom I had known since her childhood. She seemed to be very taken with this novel, and she said it must definitely be published in France. And now, as luck would have it, I showed her translation to my old friend René Puaux, who immediately offered to write a biographical introduction to this novel, by which he was deeply moved. I was of course highly delighted and at once sent the manuscript, with the introduction, to the publisher Fernand Sorlot, who had long ago been recommended to me. The answer I received was certainly the quickest I have ever had from a publisher. He instantly declared himself prepared to publish the book, which he wished to have in the series *Les maîtres étrangers*; this however, he said, was the reason why he must insist on cuts, with which I must give him a free hand. I was all too quick to agree, for the French edition that is now extant strikes me as far too severely abbreviated; things that are really essential have been removed, and the translation is not very successful either. But there was something of the hand of fate in it, it seemed to me, in that René Puaux, the friend of my youth, had once again, in my old age, played an important part in the publication of one of my books in a French translation.

Once again it was Shaw who was able to distract me from taking an interest in the fate of my own work, this time with the fantastic and charming comedy, *The Simpleton of the Unexpected Isles*.

Like *A Village Wooing*, this play is the fruit of one of his journeys round the world, and I think that in the many hours of his leisure he must have become retrospectively absorbed in revelling in the beauty of the South Sea Islands that he had come to know. That seemed very like him. For he had once written: 'Poor as I was, I only needed to shut my eyes in order to be Sardanapalus, revelling in incredible and paradisical beauties.'

This play, was furthermore, the last that I was to translate into German while still living in my native country, and the last the German première of which (at the Leipzig Stadttheater) I was able to attend, during the very time when I was in Berlin, hammering away at the script of the German film-version of *Pygmalion*, while staying at Jenny Jugo's wonderful villa on the Wannsee.

This work had the great charm of novelty for me, and later, when I was present at the shooting of the first scenes in Klagemann's studio and there made some small changes and improvements, it seemed to me a very enviable thing to be busy in such a place with all the unforeseen surprises that are part and parcel of such work. I was also present at the première of this film in Berlin. As a foreigner, I was still more or less safe in Germany and could take leave of this so much loved city for ever at least unmolested and, fortunately, also without dreaming of what the future was to bring.

At this time we frequented the houses of foreign diplomats a very great deal. My wife was on very good terms with several ladies from those circles. Above all there was at that time one diplomat in Vienna who took an unusually great interest in writers and artists. This was the American Ambassador, G. Messersmith. He had just come from Berlin, where he had been the only one to tell those in power what he thought of them, without mincing his words. He was on especially strained terms with Dr. Goebbels, because in his capacity as American Consul-General he had, regardless of the consequences, charged him with making statements that were lies. I believe that was the reason why Messersmith was transferred from Berlin to Vienna, though of course it was to a higher position.

With this man, who had from our very first meeting shown a lively interest in me, we were soon on terms not only of social intimacy but of sincere friendship. We were often in his company, at his house and at ours, and it was he who urged me so insistently to visit America that I did actually make the journey in 1937. Ambassador Messersmith rewarded me for my willingness in the most handsome fashion, using his excellent connections in New York in order to arrange both radio talks and a lecture tour through a number of large cities. This then finally put an end to my ever-recurring hesitation. I had suddenly taken on obligations, and so I did in fact set out on the journey in the second half of March.

I had reserved a cabin on board the French ship *Ile de France*, an ocean giant that was among the fastest ships at that time linking America with France. The journey itself was, I am sorry to say, a great disappointment. Handsome as my cabin was, panelled right up to the ceiling in the most beautiful wood, it was precisely this luxurious décor that was to blame for the fact that during this unusually long crossing—it took seven days—I hardly closed my eyes at all, for in storms and high seas the wood creaked and squeaked at every joint. It was the worst voyage I have ever experienced, even worse than the long-forgotten crossing from Algiers to Marseilles, when the captain himself believed his far from seaworthy old ship would never get to port.

Although I was never seasick, I arrived in a wretched state, worn out by headaches. It was the lack of sleep, more than anything else, that had made a wreck of me. Now I had the misfortune, which I admit I then hailed as great good fortune, to be received by such dear friends as Rudolf Kommer and Tilly Losch.

Rudolf Kommer played a great part in Max Reinhardt's life. It was he who had built up his American connections and who not only paved the way for his later life in America, but also organised all his theatrical tours there before the Nazis came to power; he was a devoted and unselfish friend to the great producer, one who scarcely had his equal in all Max Reinhardt's career, which was truly rich in friendships. One got the impression that Kommer was everywhere at once. His permanent residence had for a long time been the Hotel Ambassador in New York, where he also got a room for me; but he never failed to turn up for a Reinhardt première in Vienna or Berlin, and in the summer he was something like a butler and major domo at Leopoldskron. Wherever he was, Kommer was in fact a stroke of luck and a real blessing to Reinhardt, who was always besieged by people, always extremely busy, and yet always devoted, with all his soul, only to one work of literature and the task it set him as a producer.

Kommer first accompanied me to the hotel, took me up to my nice room and told me—it was about twelve o'clock—that I just had time to tidy up a bit, because he had arranged a luncheon for me at the Colony Restaurant, at which, among other celebrities of the film world, Gary Cooper would be present. However unwell I felt, I could not very well refuse my friend's kind offer, especially as he gave me no chance to do so, for he remained in my room until I had tidied up as well as I could and then hurried along with me to the enchanting restaurant in which, apart from celebrities I did not yet know, I discovered the great singer Lotte Lehmann, whom it was a particular pleasure for me to see again.

After luncheon Kommer announced to me that I was to spend the evening with him and Tilly Losch at a performance of Franz Werfel's *The Eternal Road*. My objections, with reference to the appalling crossing I had just had and also to my age, which was beginning to make me have to take a little care of myself, produced no results. Rudolf Kommer said, laughing: "Our friend Werfel's wonderful play is bound to make up for everything, no matter how tired you feel, and tomorrow, after a good night's rest, you'll have forgotten all about the bad trip."

I knew Kommer well enough to realise that no amount of protesting would help me and that he had the stronger will. Besides, I was in any case, of course, looking forward to the performance with singular interest, for I had heard and read about this production. So I pulled myself together and was glad to be the victim of this seduction.

The Eternal Road (called *Der Weg der Verheissung* in the original German) was a wonderful poetic work that had been performed well over a hundred times in Max Reinhardt's production at the Manhattan Opera House, which had been specially altered for the purpose; it won new friends and admirers daily, although this out-of-the-way theatre was in general not particularly popular. Anyone who has not heard and seen this Biblical play, anyone who has not been profoundly stirred by its force and grandeur, can scarcely imagine what heights Max Reinhardt—who seemed to have excelled himself—reached in this production, in combination with Kurt Weil's bewitching music. I would not know when this great producer ever succeeded in producing anything better.

When we left the theatre together, I could scarcely keep on my feet any longer. Even Kommer realised what a state I was in and quickly dropped the suggestion that we should go on somewhere else. He took me to my hotel, and I was soon in bed, in a terrible condition. Sleep, into which in the end my leaden weariness caused me to sink, brought me no relief; and in the morning the sea voyage seemed to be

M*

continuing in my room. Everything danced before my eyes, and I began to be afraid that I was seriously ill.

It was only with the greatest of efforts that I succeeded in not merely gloating over the magnificent breakfast that was brought to me, the *pièce de resistance* of which was a gigantic grapefruit, but even gulping down a few bites of food. By the time I was at last dressed, it had become quite clear to me that my life in New York and the plans that I now had to carry out could not be got under way until I obtained medical advice.

In Vienna I had been prudent enough to get my family doctor there to give me a very cordial recommendation to a New York doctor, who was, incidentally, also a Viennese and who, to my delight, lived only a few streets away from my hotel. I decided to consult this man, whose name was Dr. Adelsberg, and to get him to prescribe a regime that would, I hoped, quickly transform me back into the person I had been before my voyage.

When I set out on my way to the lift, I noticed that my pulse, racing at an incredible speed, made it almost impossible for me to walk. I felt as if invisible hands were all the time pushing me back and preventing me from moving forward. At last I sat in a taxi, and a short time later I was in the consulting-room of the doctor on whom—though admittedly I did not know it yet at that moment— my fate depended. Dr. Adelsberg, who had studied under the celebrated Professor Scherf, received me very kindly indeed and began a thorough examination. When he had finished, he said: "I am sorry that I must destroy your plans." (I had told him what I was intending to do.) "If you had gone to bed yesterday straight after your arrival and spent about three days in bed, you would then have been ready for all the demands made on you, and I could only have given you my blessing on your way. But now you have a cardiac neurosis, which I hope, however, I shall soon be able to get rid of for you, but which will keep you in bed for at least five days. And when you get up after that, there can be no question of your undergoing any exertion or strain for the next few weeks. You must, I am afraid, give up your elaborate plans."

Two hours later this doctor, who had a very soothing effect on me through the sureness with which he pronounced his diagnosis, stood beside my bed and gave me the first digitalis injection. This he continued to do once or twice a day. The states of agitation gave way to peace and quiet; but when my heart was once more beating normally and I was allowed to dispose freely of my time, I could tell by my general condition, which compelled me to observe precautions such as I had never had to take previously, that Dr. Adelsberg had unfortunately been right in his prognosis. I found too that I suddenly lacked the inner *élan* and confident courage to carry out all that I had intended to do.

I now wrote to my friend, Ambassador Messersmith, telling him all about my misfortune, and set about cancelling all the arrangements to which I had pledged myself. Then, however, there was no longer much sense in wasting time and money in this most expensive of cities. The long and the short of it was that I was not destined to immerse myself in the New World as thoroughly and as long as I had planned, and I only thanked my stars in secret that I had nevertheless been granted the privilege of travelling through almost the whole of America decades earlier, getting to know its amazingly beautiful scenery. Now all depended on memory and the power of recollection; and indeed I did succeed in once again travelling in spirit over the endlessly long distances I had once roamed. In doing so I could at least obey the doctor's orders and keep quiet, yearning for the unattainable. It was painful to have to pass over so many pleasures offered me by my friends, who were full of the most touching sympathy, and to have to adopt a fairly modest regime of enjoyment. At least at the end of my stay I was able to see several uncommonly interesting plays, some of which have since attained world fame.

Rudolf Kommer, who was innocently partly to blame for this little débacle, had told me that he was going to London in about a fortnight, on the *Queen Mary*, in order to give financial advice to Raimund von Hofmannsthal and his wife; and so I also reserved a cabin on the same ship. In the end, with dear friends accompanying me, I departed, quite glad to be returning home. This colossal British steamer was thoroughly in keeping with the tremendous dimensions of all the things I had seen, dimensions to which I was just beginning to become accustomed.

Now I was grateful to this colossus of the ocean for the swiftness with which we drove through the waves, this time calm. And when Europe's shores loomed up and I had to make preparations for imminent disembarkation, I felt as though the whole enterprise, which had drawn me to such far distances, had been nothing but an unsuccessful attempt to travel into the land of now vanished youth; and what had been gained—in spite of many a new professional experience—was the recognition that the simple folk-song tells us truly: 'The road I travel on grows longer every day, Yet never takes me back to years when I was young'.

I was very glad to enter our house again, which had been so well cared-for by my wife, and at that time did not dream how short a span remained to us for this happiness of being at home. The artistic success—if one may so describe the detailed and highly favourable reviews—of *Heimkehr zum Ich* had grown even greater during my absence, and I heard and read many very pleasant things about this woe-begotten child of mine. Both my zealous publisher, Herbert Reichner, and I myself were looking forward to a new work, which, I am glad to say, had already been begun. This was the little novel, *Die Dritte (The Third Woman)*, which I now completed in the weeks of hard work that followed. Previous to its publication in book form this story was printed in a large newspaper; Reichner meanwhile set about arranging for a new edition in book form of the novel, *Heimkehr zum Ich*, of which he had a very high opinion.

It was not long since our friends Clauzel, those greatly beloved representatives of France in Vienna, had been succeeded by a diplomat who was associated, for me, with stirring memories of my youth. This was Gabriel Puaux, the brother of my friend René, with whom I had, of course, never ceased to keep up a correspondence. In recent years his translation of my first book had tended to fade out, being somewhat displaced by the eventfulness of the times and the vividness of experience; but now everything revived again and seemed to be as fresh as ever when René Puaux came to Vienna for some weeks on a visit to his brother. In this short time he was often our guest too, and we were at a large dinner that the French Ambassador gave in his brother's honour. René Puaux confessed to me then that he was suffering from grave heart trouble, which one would not have supposed from his appearance and which I took for hypochondriac exaggeration. It was all the more overwhelmingly grievous a shock to me when, only a year later, the news came of his sudden death.

His life had not been easy, not only because of the high aims he set himself, but also because of the entirely divergent fields in which he worked. From early in the morning until some time in the afternoon this busy and responsible man was occupied with political journalism. It was primarily foreign policy to which he had to give that very sensitive intuitive understanding he possessed and to which he devoted himself for the good of his country. Then he used to go home, take an all too short rest, which he managed to fit into his daily programme, and then, not in the least tired or exhausted, but with heightened powers, he set about the work of a poet and philosopher. Of the books that placed him in the front rank of contemporary French writers, it is the novels *La grande vague, La femme du rêve* and *Le jardin de Candide* that must be particularly mentioned. Apart from this, however, René Puaux was also a travel-writer of unusual brilliance, one to whom we owe books on Greece and Finland, such works as *Pour rencontrer Lord Savander, Silhouettes anglaises, Découvertes des Americains* and *Sappho-Paraphrases*.

René Puaux served all through the world war as a front-line officer, always where the battle was hottest, and came out of the war with his health unimpaired, with new plans for work and ready to take on new responsibilities. Some months before his sudden death he had gone to Scandinavia on a lecture tour, and it was at that time that I saw him again, in high spirits, buoyed up by his success in Copenhagen, Helsingfors and Stockholm. It was to be the last time that we grasped each other's hands in farewell after happy hours spent together and looking forward, as we thought, to yet more glad meetings in the future.

At that time he wanted to begin writing his memoirs, for there was scarcely any great man in the last thirty years whom René Puaux had not met, either privately or in the course of his work.

Now an inscrutable and incomprehensible fate had not only made us all poorer by a delightful book, but had robbed us of a rare human being, whose words, whether spoken or written, would always have spread love and warmth throughout a world that was becoming ever colder. His philosophy of life, which was religious and optimistic, his profound conviction that no misfortune, no catastrophe, could fail to have kindly consequences as well, had rewarded him with a cheerfulness that nothing could shake and with an inexhaustible patience. It helped him to endure the difficult hours of his illness and illumined his sudden end, which he had not expected. So, borne to his all too early rest, he passed away in wisdom and kindliness that were exemplary, as his life had been exemplary.

The eventful year 1937, which should surely have opened all Austrians' eyes, had, remarkably enough, closed them even more tightly. But that is the way it always is when an irresistible and fore-ordained fate is on the march. The Germans had long known how things stood, and it had indeed been a clear sign to us of the way things were going over there that, among many others, Dr. Bermann-Fischer, together with his wife and his publishing house, had moved to Vienna more than two years ago. He was very skilful in his manipulations and managed to secure the necessary connections for himself and his business, a matter in which we all helped him according to our ability. He tried partly to continue the business that he had inherited, partly to build up a new one here in this neighbouring country, a task that was certainly not particularly difficult for him, as the representative of the greatest name in German publishing, because of the wave of talented writers who were just beginning to rise in the world.

The last book that I wrote in my native city was called *Der Verjüngte* (*Rejuvenated*); it was published by Bermann-Fischer in the second half of 1937. It was about this time that Dr. Doppler had a great success with his rejuvenation method, which for a time even bore away the palm from Professor Steinach's great discovery. The subject was one that attracted me very much indeed, if for no other reason than that every ageing man doubtless pricks up his ears when he hears praises sung of methods of restoring the energies of years now lost, promising a revival of youth. I was therefore intensely taken with the idea of making the fate of an overworked and worn-out captain of industry the central point of a story giving credibility to his transformation through rejuvenation, in order then to show the consequences, which I had for the time being freely invented, only to hear much later, to my delight, that the reality very often in fact corresponded to my portrayal of it.

Clouds of anxiety at that time lay heavy on the spirits of the Viennese, and today it is almost incomprehensible to me how it was that the shrewdest and most prudent of people ever and again raised their voices in the pronouncement that the atrocities of National Socialism could never gain a hold in our native city and that in our beloved country even the worst of terrors would before long give

way to the harmless and easy-going characteristics it had had of old.
Today we know that the bloodiest orgies that Hitler's bestial
supporters carried out during the period of his initial successes must
be recorded as having taken place in Vienna and throughout the
whole of Austria.

Only the truly wise, among whom Stefan Zweig was one, left their
country in good time, with the intention of not returning in any
circumstances until National Socialism had been completely
destroyed. With that dear friend's departure abroad I had also
lost an adviser who had already once shown me how accurately he
could recognise the face of his time; and his advice was of course
something we sorely missed.

In those days we were often with the Bermann-Fischers, who
had rented an apartment in our neighbourhood, and we found
that he and his wife were resolved to hold on in Vienna so long as it
was in any way possible at all. They had not yet shaken off the
horror of their experiences in Berlin—horrors that they had escaped
from only by chance and a series of lucky accidents—and they were
determined to regard Vienna not merely as a new stopping-place on
their way into further and less familiar lands, but as their new home.
As people had earlier dreamed and talked of happiness and riches, of
fame and success, now people talked and dreamed of safety. It was at
this time that I learned how difficult it is for people to free themselves from deeply-rooted illusions and above all from conditions
that they refer to as 'acknowledged rights'.

In a merely external sense Viennese life went on its graceful, light-
hearted way. The Opera produced festivals of song; the Burgtheater
shone in all its accustomed glory; and the other theatres, too, were
always crowded. But for those of particularly acute sensibility it was
now sometimes possible to feel that people were trying to grab what
they could of pleasure while there was still such a thing at all, and
many a festive occasion, many a reception at foreign embassies,
seemed to be directed at distracting the guests from their all too
justifiable sense of a world coming to an end. People wanted to
enjoy life so long as the lamp was still alight, deliberately ignoring
the fact that the flame had flickered out long ago.

These sorely tried people had a foreboding that their time of
direst need had not yet begun, and the government did all that was in
its power to prevent the atmosphere from becoming one of despair,

to reinforce the wavering confidence of the banks and of industry, and to make clear to those who only wanted to be comforted that an attack on Austria, a violation of its independence, which so many people had feared after the terrible Dollfuss affair, was utterly impossible.

And indeed the untiring spokesmen and optimists did almost wholly succeed in raising the people's drooping spirits, naturally to the misfortune of all who would have done better to expect the worst and save in time whatever could be saved, instead of so clumsily running into the traps that had so obviously been set.

What came now I relate with a heart that is all the heavier because it is easy for all who experienced these things to check whether what I say is correct. Our Chancellor Schuschnigg was asked—it would doubtless be more accurate to say, ordered—to Berchtesgaden by Hitler, and had set great hopes on his visit to that vile and illiterate dictator, hopes that were all the greater because the German Ambassador, von Papen, had arranged this meeting and, doubtless against his better knowledge, had strongly advised the Chancellor to bring about the desired discussions as quickly as possible. Every newspaper reader knows what the result of that meeting was, how brutally the power-drunk Hitler behaved to Kurt von Schuschnigg, that loyal-hearted and courageous man, a general's son, and how the listening world rejoiced to know that the loser, whose most modest requests had been refused, had at least returned to Vienna safe and sound.

When Schuschnigg came home he first had a talk with his Secretary of State, the poet Guido Zernatto, who after their conversation at once wisely began making preparations to leave the country. According to the report of what had happened, which was followed by a brilliant speech by Schuschnigg, calling on everyone to stand united and defend the country, a plebiscite was to be held throughout Austria, which, if one could believe those who were at that time in the know, would have ended in an overwhelming refusal to unite with Germany. At that time Schuschnigg did not know that one whom he held to be his friend, the minister Seyss-Inquart, was a traitor who had long been in the pay of the German Government and whose rôle was to take over the leadership of the new Austrian Government.

None of us knew how many of our acquaintances, friends, and the people with whom we had to do every day were members of 'the Party', desiring nothing more intensely than an invasion by Hitler, which would bring about the feared, and several times averted, union of Austria with Germany. Those were exciting and distressing last days in a country that thousands credulously and erroneously had thought of as their own while they had long been surrounded by foreigners who infested it, thousands who now saw this turn of events, after all that had irrevocably befallen Austria, as the only hope for a rebirth of their country, so small and now so maimed. But those who thought like this were still the better sort. The rest, the masses, who were ready to desert to the other side, had simply let wild promises rob them of the little reasoning power they still possessed.

The slogan 'It can't go on like this', which had first fallen from the lips of the Viennese in 1914, was now once again to be heard uttered by many who, for the most part for private reasons and because they had grudges of the vilest kind, were rejoicing in the prospect of the Germans' coming and beckoning them on into the much lauded country of 'dancers and fiddlers'.

Almost at the same time as Schuschnigg went to Berchtesgaden, my wife went to the Semmering, in the attempt to get rid of a very severe and persistent cold. She had forebodings of the future, although her foreign women friends assured her that if it should ever come to the hour of need they would be prepared to help her with all the means in their power. To the honour of those great ladies it must be said that they very soon kept this promise in a movingly unselfish way. My wife came home two days before the collapse, which she had not expected, because men who ought to have known all about it had managed to allay her grave fears. She had scarcely arrived when I explained to her in detail all that I considered it my duty to tell her, and she listened to me with remarkable composure and calm, as though I were saying nothing new and as though she had long been expecting the worst. In those days we also went to see the Bermanns, whom we found now resolved to leave Vienna, once more dissolving the publishing firm they had only just established, in order to go to Switzerland, at any rate for the time being, and that as quickly as possible.

We then spent many an hour in our house, having a last long look at all the things we were so fond of in the rooms and on the walls.

We said good-bye to each object that we could not take with us and that had grown dear to our hearts—good-bye in case a parting should become inevitable.

We also had long discussions with Guido Zernatto and his charming wife in those last few days and recognised that he in particular, in consideration of his official position, refrained from saying openly what he thought was really likely to happen; but what we could infer from his words and the atmosphere while we were drinking the tea that was offered us—these things were for us signs that we neither could nor should have overlooked or failed to hear.

Without our having asked each other what we would do if . . . we both seemed inclined to leave it to destiny to point out the way to us. For now things happened thick and fast. The plebiscite that was to have taken place was forbidden by Hitler, and his invasion, which he had allegedly been asked to make in order to save the Austrians from the danger threatening them, had been more or less announced. Schuschnigg, who, in spite of having the army behind him and knowing it was reliable, wanted to avoid all bloodshed, preferred to deliver a speech. It was a memorable one. It was announced for an hour in the afternoon when I had an appointment with Oscar Maurus Fontana in the Café Vindobona. We sat together, pale, silent, and thoroughly disturbed, close to the radio, which the obliging head-waiter had set up for us. And now, all too distinctly, we heard the unforgettably moving speech that Schuschnigg delivered before laying down his office. It concluded with the words: "God save Austria!" And when at these words Fontana and I glanced up at each other, each saw that the other's eyes were full of tears.

This was on March 10th. That evening I returned home rather a wreck, but both my wife and I were still incapable of imagining all that was in store for us in the immediate future.

An evil chance waked us out of our last trustful illusions. The next day Hitler marched into Austria, surrounded by his flying columns, his mercenaries and ministers. Late on the evening of March 11th he crossed the boundaries of the city of Vienna.

It is doubtless implicit in human nature that in hours of crisis, when we are threatened by dangers, none of us can suppress the faint hope that perhaps he, of all people, may be spared, overlooked, forgotten, when the tide of disaster descends upon his native country.

On Friday and Saturday evening we again went, as we had so often done before, to have dinner at the Park Hotel, which was so convenient to our house. We were struck by the fact that almost all the tables were occupied by German soldiers and officers, and the waiter, who knew us, hastened to warn us that the civilians among the uniformed men all around us were members of the Gestapo. Since no one took any particular notice of us, and when, as it happened, an actor who had come with the Germans, and who knew me well, hailed me very cordially, we lost the immediate sense of great danger for a few hours. The next day, however, we meant to go to see our lawyer, in order to have a thorough talk about the situation and what attitude we should adopt. On my desk lay two plane reservations, dated March 16th, for Prague, where I was to give a lecture at the Masaryk University. So we had to leave Vienna on that day in any case; but this was only the thirteenth. The Ides of March.

On the way to see our lawyer we were stopped by an S.A. man, armed to the teeth, and at a place where the chauffeur had to stop the car in any case because German military columns were marching past. In a flash the door of the car was wrenched open and we were being yelled at: "Where are your papers?" I retorted: "We are going to see a friend who lives only ten minutes' drive from us, and naturally we have not brought papers for the purpose of visiting him." "Why isn't there a swastika on your car?" the intruder asked in a loud and disagreeable voice. "Because we are utterly non-political and are not visiting a politician," was my answer. The questioner shook his head angrily, jumped in next to the chauffeur with the words: "The car is commandeered!" and told the chauffeur the address he was to drive to. However, since the marching column had not yet passed, I made use of the last moment to get out and pull my wife out of the car, which was certainly the luckiest imaginable reaction to the behaviour of the man who had so suddenly descended upon us.

To this day I do not know whether the infuriated S.A. man noticed our disappearance. He was too busy attending to the answers that our chauffeur was just giving to his questions and which he was noting down. My wife at first did not want to get out, but to drive on in order to make a complaint to some higher authority about this outrageous behaviour. Fortunately I prevented this, my words being, if I recollect rightly: "A new age has dawned. This is only a little fiery beacon, yet one that is meant to show us our road." By then our motor-car had disappeared. We never saw it again.

We had not far to go, since the incident took place quite close to our house. Having arrived there, we suddenly realised that we could no longer remain in Vienna without risking our liberty, even our lives. True, we must wait patiently until the sixteenth. Meanwhile, of course, anything might happen, and whenever the door-bell rang we looked at each other with questioning eyes. However, the decision lay with our destiny.

The days that now followed were more than full of work of every kind. Such an extensive house, filled with so many things that really belong to one, is naturally not easy to leave. Like myself, my wife had her hands full, above all with finding a place of safety for her jewellery, which was taken care of for her by a touchingly kind friend, the wife of an ambassador. To this day we do not know how it was that we remained completely unmolested down to the date of our departure, which was, after all, three whole days and four nights. Our chauffeur, an honest fellow and most touchingly loyal, came back, some hours after the episode I have described, with one eye blackened and swollen, and told us indignantly what had happened to him when he had demanded to have the commandeered car restored to him.

I packed my most important documents, endeavouring to get into my wardrobe trunk everything that was precious to me, before we set out on our journey into the unknown; for it was clear to us that Prague could only be a temporary stopping-place on our way. The house and everything we were attached to, with the things that *we* called treasures, even if they were perhaps nothing of the kind, the handsome library with its five thousand volumes, the pictures, the countless souvenirs, all this we could gaze at every day, grieving over it, but we could never take it with us. My wife endured those days with remarkable calm and a tranquillity that was perhaps to some extent pretended.

Punctually on March 16th we flew to Prague, but not without my wife first of all at the air-port having to undergo the indignity of being searched, as the result of a telephone message from the Gestapo, who had meanwhile arrived at our villa. Our very intelligent maid had pointed to the invitation to the Prague lecture that was lying on my desk and said that we would probably be back in a week at the latest. Our kindly visitors instantly demanded to be given the keys, whereupon the maid assured them that she had none.

My pen has become much too feeble to describe the feeling that overcame us when we were at last high in the air, knowing that now we had won freedom, possession of which was worth the greatest losses. But we had lost our country. Our world, the security in which we had believed much too long and until the last moment, had collapsed. What we had possessed was gone for ever. A new and dubious life was to begin.

IV

SWITZERLAND

BUT now it is necessary, to my way of feeling, that I should do justice to my wife, of whom I have in these pages hitherto said only what was most essential. Her praises must now be sung. She surprised me, indeed reduced me to speechlessness, by the complete change that came over her. The wise and prudent helpmate who had gone through life at my side had now all at once become a comrade-in-arms. Suddenly she could do things I would never have imagined her capable of, standing in queues outside passport offices, waiting in government offices to the point of exhaustion, beginning to work early in the morning in order to get everything ready for our imminent departure, which, without wasting a word on the subject, she had decided was inevitable from the moment we had had the adventure I have described, with the loss of our motor-car, and in general organising many things that were to turn out to be for our benefit only much later. She saw important personages who were helpfully inclined, doing it instead of me, and never forgot anything so that I had to go and put it right afterwards.

Working, thinking, arranging, fighting down her most painful feelings, from morning to night she was a tower of strength, and without her our departure might perhaps not have been managed so smoothly. It was evident that, in the course of the very sheltered life that we had led in spite of all its variety, she had been able to accumulate resources of strength, which she was now able to apply with amazing ease, when this our gravest hour came. Even when we were already in Prague, she wrote to give important instructions to our touchingly faithful and devoted servants. Until our landing in Strassburg, of which I shall have to speak later, she had her energies under control. Then, admittedly, she had a sort of breakdown, because the events with which she had had to contend and the strain of facing them out did after all demand too much on a sometimes superhuman presence of mind.

Our plane tickets did not at once take us into a new life. They took us via Prague to Paris, where we intended to start all over again.

We stayed in Prague for about two weeks, surrounded by many friends, as well as by acquaintances from Vienna who shared our fate. There our thoughts were distracted by splendid theatrical performances under the direction of Paul Eger, the Swiss. Then we boarded a plane that had come from Bucharest and was to take us to Paris, where we were of course expected, and by some of our friends, indeed, quite impatiently. We were still in Prague when my wife one morning exclaimed: "We shall not be able to get through the time that is coming with our passports. I've just read that Oscar Straus and Bruno Walter have got French nationality. You must see about getting it too, at once."

I smiled, remembering Georges Courteline, who had constantly uttered the wish that he might some day hail me as a French citizen, whereupon I had ever and again had to explain to him that I should then be treated as a deserter in my native country, since I was still liable for military service. Grumbling, he had each time accepted this excuse.

I was now immediately very much in favour of posthumously fulfilling my dead friend's wish. How much he would have welcomed my decision now, and how he would have helped!

On our stormy flight to Paris I noticed that my wife felt very unwell and kept on pressing her hand to her side. This surprised me less than it alarmed me, since I knew that she suffered from bilious attacks. Now on this trip from Prague to Paris there was a stop at Strassburg, with an hour's wait. I began to try to cheer my wife up, saying that we would soon be in our hotel room in Paris, where she would be able to rest as long as she liked, if necessary for days, and have all the care she needed. However, she shook her head and said: "It is completely impossible for me to continue this journey, I can't endure any more of the frightful way this rather miserable plane rocks up and down in this storm. And now, when all the strain I have been through is just beginning to tell, I can't face the noise of a big city. I must without fail have quiet country surroundings, wherever it may be."

In a very gloomy mood I now accompanied the sick woman to the station buffet at Strassburg, and on the way it occurred to me that I had once travelled in a train that had borne the charming name of 'Edelweiss Express' and had reached Zurich three hours after leaving Strassburg. And I went on to remember a hotel, pleasantly situated on the edge of the forest, which I had once noted as having the name Dolder, and so I telephoned through to Zurich and reserved rooms in this establishment for the night. I then returned to my wife, who was deeply sunk in the pain she was suffering. She heard my news with very great delight.

I now hastened to the telephone in order, before all else, to get in touch with Bernard Shaw, who was ailing and who had sent me impatient postcards and letters when I was in Prague, being for the first time concerned about our domicile, and to inform him of the change in our plans and give him our new address.

The plan of acquiring French nationality had by no means been abandoned, but instead of being in Paris on the evening of that fateful day we were now in the Hotel Dolder in Zurich. Here it was that our new life now began, which was, it must be admitted, at first interrupted by frequent journeys to France.

We did perhaps feel that we were in exile; but oddly enough we did not feel in the least like refugees, and for me it was as though I were only now enjoying the fruits of my many travels abroad, my months of staying in foreign countries and cities like London and Paris, and as though it were utterly impossible for me to become entirely homeless. There was certainly no question of it in Switzerland, a country I had often visited and dearly loved.

It was the same with my wife. Even though our means were very slight and we were in spite of everything, in a profound sense of the word, refugees, this first stopping-place was too beautiful for us to be able to feel the misery that is implicit in the words 'homeless', 'refugee', or 'emigrant'.

Among the first Viennese whom we met in Zurich were Richard Beer-Hofmann and his wife; but he had never thought of settling down here and was actually on his way to America. He was kept here longer than he had planned as a result of the sudden death of his dearly-loved wife, whose weak heart had been overstrained as a consequence of the great anxiety she had been through in Vienna; she had in fact sacrificed her life in order to get away in time. Beer-Hofmann himself, whom we saw a few times more before he left, seemed broken by sorrow but was surrounded by very faithful patrons, who took him to New York and there saw to it that he did not know any kind of hardship until the end of his life, which came all too soon.

The meeting with this *doyen* of Viennese writers was all too brief and overshadowed by too much gloom for it to have done anything at all to strengthen or weaken our former relationship in any way. On the other hand, in the course of the next few years two great composers with whom we had been on very good terms in Vienna, without however actually being friends of theirs, became particularly intimate with us in Switzerland. These two men were Franz Lehár and Richard Strauss, the latter of whom we visited repeatedly in Montreux. Later, when we were saddened by the death of these two men, great as artists and highly out of the ordinary as personalities, the egoism of the human heart caused us almost to regret that we had found each other so late and in a foreign country, only to lose each other again so soon. Even now I cannot bring myself to part with Lehár's farewell postcard, which he wrote me two days before his death, when he felt his end approaching.

Now, however, I find it difficult to continue with this chronicle. I do not feel justified in mentioning, far less in describing, the many trifling—and sometimes not so trifling—unpleasantnesses and mortifications of all kinds and the difficulties that we too, after all, were not spared, while friends, comrades, relatives, and acquaintances perished miserably in concentration camps, were burnt in Auschwitz or, at best, arrived in some foreign country worn out and wretched after going through endless torments, in comparison with which everything that happened to us is simply not worth mentioning at all. We also had been driven abroad, but into a paradise. Chance and good fortune had made that possible where we were concerned, and I suppose we shall never find out whether it was all really just chance.

Bernard Shaw maintained over and over again that he had saved my life, or at least my liberty. I cannot judge this, but where one has the obligation to say 'thank you' I suppose one should not argue. He was, besides, the last person to tell a fib.

We spent very little time in Switzerland in those years, 1938 and 1939. The plan of acquiring French nationality inevitably took us to France. We spent months living in Nice and months in Paris. The authorities did not make things easy for us, although French writers and the former Ambassador in Vienna, Count Clauzel, together with his wife, who was a close friend of my wife's, most unselfishly took our part.

I had of course a dossier. This important bundle of documents, which everyone who sets out to acquire another nationality must have, quite soon attracted attention in high quarters as a result of the urgency of the documents bearing testimony on my behalf, which continued to swell it. Madame Marie-Jeanne Courteline even wrote a personal letter to the minister who was concerned with my application, referring to me in high-flown words of praise and alluding to her husband's friendship for me. The writers Roland Dorgelès, Gaston Riou, and Jules Romain also found so much that was good to say about me that I am sure merits that I seemed to have gained gradually, without noticing it myself, were exaggerated in my favour. Incidentally, I first went to Paris by way of London, for we had been only a few days at the Dolder Hotel when I was handed a registered letter from Bernard Shaw, which contained rather a large sum of money and a frantic summons to come to London instantly and report to him. I answered this summons all the faster since I knew that he had become really seriously ill a short time earlier, for the first time since I knew him—he was suffering from leukæmia.

On this occasion—and now hard it must have been for him!—he had had to put himself into the hands of specialists, one of whom remarked with a smile that Shaw was now having to absorb large doses, by injection, of the substances that he had obstinately refused, as a vegetarian, to enjoy in the form of food. These life-saving injections consisted for the most part of liver preparations. The gravity of this more-than-eighty-year-old man's condition at the beginning of his illness was only equalled by the speed with which he recovered. In the words of his friend, the producer Ayliff, he had 'mysterious powers of resistance'.

Although Shaw still looked rather the worse for what he had been through, he was remarkably lively when I appeared, obviously because he had now received his doctors' assurance that he was on the way to recovery. He himself joked about his fate, which was giving his friends the chance to indulge in all sorts of teasing remarks, and said that, after all, meat-eaters too had often fallen ill of leukæmia and probably then the doctors did not know what else to do but inject liver-extract into them too, in addition to all the meat they ate.

Now, however, he wanted to hear from me about our escape— which was in fact nothing of the kind, because we had, after all, not been pursued, about experiences with the Nazis, which I had not had, and in short, a great deal more than I could tell. He asked me how I pictured our new life, and at once emphasised that he wanted to help me, in so far as was in his power, to make good all that I had lost. He then advised me to remain in Switzerland at all costs, if I did not want to move to London—because of the climate, and also approved of my plan to acquire French nationality and to spend the necessary time in France. I could of course also become British, but only after five years' domicile. Finally he stopped his voluble flow of persuasive talk, during which I had really not been able to get a word in edgeways, with the good-humoured remark that I had now drawn much nearer to him and that he hoped that I would risk taking these refreshing plane flights to London fairly often.

We then began to talk of his last play, *The Simpleton of the Unexpected Isles,* and he exclaimed: "Yes, if only Reinhardt were in Vienna now instead of in Hollywood! The whole work cries out for a producer like him." He also told me about the work he was doing at that time on a play that he called *Geneva,* which was concerned with the League of Nations at Geneva. Only his illness had prevented him from finishing it; but he meant to make up for that soon now.

Shaw had written me several postcards, when I was still in Vienna, with 'Heil Hitler' and expressions of admiration for National Socialism, which had irritated me very much, as indeed they still did in retrospect. I made no bones about it, but complained bitterly. At this he assured me very seriously: "Whether you believe it or not, if you were quite unmolested for four whole days, and could fly to your lecture in Prague without anyone's stopping you, it's owing to nothing but those postcards—it's all my doing! Are you really stupid enough to believe that I'm pro-Hitler?" I did not want to contradict him and also refrained from saying much about all I had lost, because Shaw would have thought it 'sentimental'—the expression he had ready to hand for practically all the feelings that he himself refused to have anything to do with, if only out of complacency.

I told his wife, who enquired in detail about my wife, about my landing in Croydon and the disappointment of the reporters who had thronged around me, clamouring for detailed descriptions of my experiences with the Gestapo. Luckily for myself, I could only disappoint them, truthfully informing them that I had experienced nothing apart from the theft of our motor-car, which, regarded from the point of view of another scale of criminality, and according to the now prevailing conception of law, was a quite insignificant trifle. Some days after my return to the Dolder the manuscript of *Geneva* arrived, and I at once set about translating it. This work made it easier for me to do what seemed the most important thing at the moment—to forget. Above all to forget that my family's firm was now finally destroyed, only a memory now, and that as a result I was now penniless.

My wife had in the meantime recovered sufficiently—incidentally also from the very annoying visits of some highly disagreeable Viennese lawyers—to be able to accompany me to France. We now spent some months in Paris, where the necessary steps were taken to arrange for our naturalisation, and then went to Nice, whence I was repeatedly summoned to Paris in order to make statements, produce documents, sign things, and in general conscientiously carry out all the formalities that were to bring us to our goal. In Paris, of course, I could not get down to any work, but I had finished the translation of *Geneva* while I was in Nice. This was then polished up in Zurich, as was only fitting, and there given its finishing touches. It soon became quite evident to me, in working on this play, that although it must not be omitted from a German complete edition—something of which I was already dreaming—it had no prospect of being produced on any stage in German-speaking territory.

In Paris, shortly after this, I felt the gathering storm-clouds of war, which, however, still seemed remote. On August 31st I became a French citizen, and when, after this event had been publicly announced in the *Journal Officiel*, I received my passport and my wife's, I went to London, while my wife remained on the Riviera. Some days later I was with Shaw, with the justifiable premonition that this would have to be my last visit for a long time, for the *drôle de guerre* had already begun. Besides, my dear friend Stefan Zweig, whom I had already visited in London on a former occasion, was again there, and, understandably enough, we felt the need of a long talk together about many things.

I found Shaw completely restored to health and had the pleasure of receiving from him a very noble, easily actable and accomplished play, which was called *Good King Charles*. More than this, however, it was once more to be granted to me to be at the first night of this comedy in Shaw's box. The performance took place at the theatre in Golder's Green, a London suburb; for the West End theatres, reverting to a now long-forgotten tradition, had once again shown they were afraid of their great dramatist's new work. The first night went off very noisily, as the audience was determined to do everything it could to make it quite clear that this comedy was a great success. We left the theatre fairly soon after the last curtain, and when the three of us were sitting in Shaw's car, it was surrounded by a crowd of young people cheering and shouting. Shaw laughed, waved them off in a friendly way, and said: "I can be seen every night on the stage, from the seats you've just been sitting in. But now I must go home quickly, because I'm an old man."

It is now high time to mention a very touching and charming gesture on the part of Mrs. Shaw, who for years, when I had come on my earlier visits, had always told me I should bring along to luncheon any friends of mine who I thought might interest her husband. This I did, many and many a time. I now accepted this suggestion once again, all the more gladly since at this time there were so many distinguished refugee writers living in London. I well knew, of course, what pleasure I should give many a dear old friend and colleague—and his wife, if he had one—with such an invitation. But Mrs. Shaw would not let herself be saved any trouble; nobody must be allowed to feel he had been 'brought along too', she said with her kindly smile. She asked for the exact address of each person I suggested and then wrote inviting him for the day I had proposed— on which I had already agreed previously, in secret discussion with the favoured person.

So the Shaws came to know Stefan Zweig, that knowledgeable and widely-read man, that rapid and voluble talker, who was well able to make the most of the hour, not only in order to receive great impressions, but also in such a way as not to be forgotten the moment he had left. There were also Carl Zuckmayer, who was at that time engaged in film work, of which he gave a humorous description, in Korda's studios, Bruno Frank and his pretty wife, who were just about to leave Europe, and Professor Johann Plesch, the celebrated doctor, the inventor of a new hæmodynamometer and a sedative called theominal, which Shaw, in spite of all extolling of it, would never try in order to be sure of going to sleep. When asked about this, he explained to me: "You ought to know that a cat that's been washed, even if only once, will never wash itself again." Professor Plesch turned out to be a brilliant conversationalist, but what I would so gladly have seen happen did not eventuate: the Shaws remained faithful to their English doctors.

Others who were summoned at my request were: the Austrian Ambassador in London, the friend of Hugo von Hofmannsthal's youth, Baron Georg Frankenstein, who proved his charming powers of diplomacy and persuasion by getting the Shaws, who refused all invitations on principle, to fall in with his insistent proposal that they should accept his invitation to lunch with him some time. So a delicious luncheon came about, with Shaw at his most sparkling. Shaw had a particularly warm liking for the Czech Ambassador, Jan Masaryk, whose parents he had come to know and admire in America. The Minister's excellent English, his fluent conversational powers, and his obviously immense brilliance made that a singularly stimulating luncheon-party at Whitehall Court, which soon led to another invitation's being sent to this particularly agreeable visitor, who had grown up in the same beliefs as the great Fabian himself.

There was also a Swiss writer and actor whom I had invited to lunch: this was Curt Götz, together with his highly gifted, enchanting wife. He had points of contact in plenty, for he had repeatedly taken leading rôles in the master's plays and his own writing had shown Shaw's influence on style and dialogue construction.

Curt Götz could, however, boast of yet another point of contact with his host: he was distantly related to him, in a way that he tried to explain to me on our way there. If I am not mistaken, Curt Götz had a great-aunt who was Bernard Shaw's second cousin. We had jokingly agreed that I should therefore introduce him as Shaw's long-lost cousin. I must have done this not very skilfully, with Götz's challenging gaze fixed on me, and have set about it rather too seriously, for both were at first startled to hear of the blood-relationship thus revealed. Then, however, I had the satisfaction of hearing Bernard Shaw quickly and unconditionally accept the kinship, explained to him wonderfully clearly by Curt Götz, and laughingly express his delight at this belated discovery.

Even long after consuming the black coffee that the good-for-nothing 'cousin' enjoyed far more heartily than was to the taste of his abstemious host, the charming Swiss couple were still fascinating their good-humoured hosts by their skill in dialogue, which was of rare quality even in English.

Now once again in the prospect of imminent war I had to take leave of Shaw; but even more insistently than ever before he refused to believe that the whole world would soon be in flames again. He hoped that the *drôle de guerre* would turn out to be a way of avoiding the outbreak of a real war, with all its horrors. However, we did ask each other whether we were sure we had not forgotten anything, for it was always possible that it might be years before we could correspond with each other again.

My leave-taking from Stefan Zweig, very soon after this, was much harder and more depressing. Zweig indulged in the gloomiest of prophecies, and he reminded me of Ostend, where it had after all turned out to our great misfortune that he was right. Although he had a very comfortable home in Portland Place and the distraction of his work, which he loved and which did somewhat cheer him in his depression, I had the feeling that I was saying good-bye to a profoundly unhappy man. During our last conversation—for such it turned out to be—he declared his very definite conviction that it would really be the best thing for us to turn our backs on this world and put an end to a life that had become completely senseless. His intelligent secretary, who was probably suffering from melancholia and shortly afterwards became his wife, did all she could to strengthen him in this conviction. I pointed to the invitations to give lectures in North and South America lying on his desk, and said: "I don't want to—indeed, I can't—regard what you say otherwise than as the residue of terrible moods and depressions you are subject to, for you are not one of the outcasts who are abandoned to their lonely lot. On the contrary, you are surrounded by tokens, indeed by proofs, of how life is calling to you, how much people need you and your voice, and I hope sooner or later to see you again in a somewhat more cheerful state of mind."

Stefan Zweig did not give me any answer to this. He accompanied me to the door, shaking his head, only mentioning a strangely intense fear of growing old.

As I was about to board the plane that was to take me back to Paris, where I had arranged to meet my wife the next day on her arrival from Nice, I heard an English stewardess saying: "Have a good trip—and watch out for the Messerschmitts!" When we arrived in Le Bourget, after a smooth trip through the peaceful spring sky, the pilot told us that he had had to make a détour because a German Messerschmitt had followed the plane.

When I met my wife, she had already experienced one grim warning. Her train had been very late, as Lyons had suddenly been bombed by the Germans, in spite of the *drôle de guerre*; luckily for her, the railway-station was not hit, only because the Germans knew they would need it for their troops and supplies. We now discussed what we should do. We both agreed that we owed it to our French friends to make a serious attempt now, being French citizens, to live in France, if it was in any way possible. I was well acquainted with one of the chief clerks at the *wagons-lits* company, and we now went to see him, after several exciting nights in Paris, which most of the occupants of our hotel spent in the cellar because of the air-raid warnings. Everyone advised us not to stay in Paris, and no one was more insistent that we should leave than our old friend Dr. Ferrière, whom we had met in Paris and who was leaving that same evening to return to his home in Switzerland.

The shrewd man whom we now consulted, who knew the French provinces well, was also of the opinion that we should not expose ourselves to danger in Paris, but should go to Biarritz, where he was sure the Germans would never come. But then, when he saw how mournful my wife looked, he said: "You have come from Switzerland and you don't feel comfortable unless you are close to the Swiss frontier. Your husband has already told me that. So there is only one thing for you, and it is also the most convenient thing for you to do—namely to go to Vichy. Incidentally, that's where almost all our clients are going who want to be safe." And so we decided to go to Vichy, which was only about five hours' drive from Geneva.

My wife had always been attracted toward Switzerland, which may be partly due to the fact that Fritz von Marquart, of Berne, who was her guardian, had taken her to Beatenberg from Vienna when she was a girl of fifteen; in Beatenberg she had had the good fortune to be completely cured of a catarrh in the apex of the lung. It was then that she had come to know the beauties of that wonderful country. Her first words when we entered our pleasant hotel in Vichy were uttered with sighs: "What wouldn't I give to be in Switzerland!"

And now the inevitable thing happened, exceeding even the forebodings of all our friends and advisers: the Germans were in Paris. I must now be on my guard against drifting into historical reminiscences. They also came to Vichy all too soon, although according to all the assurances they had given they should never have come there. One morning the chambermaid rushed into my wife's room, deadly pale, exclaiming: *"Ils sont là! 'Qui?' Les Allemands!"*

In Vichy, before the Germans came, we had the pleasure of meeting our friends Franz and Alma Werfel, Oscar Straus and his wife, and astonishingly many other Viennese. This at least gave us a chance to talk about our worries to our hearts' content, pouring out our woes to one another in our native language.

But everything did not go off as smoothly as I make it sound here. The terrifying stream of refugees, the incredible scramble at the railway-stations, the frightful screaming and shouting and loud scenes of lamentation—all this went with us on all our ways through France. But I cannot linger over these psychological shocks, for the same reason that I have already noted, because at the same time people near and dear to us were starving and suffering in concentration camps, indeed were being tormented and tortured and done to death. When one thinks of that, every complaint must cease, and every adventure that in normal times would have counted as an adventure, with all its terrors and the sleepless nights that were the consequence, simply shrinks to nothing in comparison.

And then came the day when our friends had to leave Vichy, that little town that we had known in earlier times, and had to do so in great haste and menaced by vague dangers. Oscar Straus and ourselves were the only people who had French passports. The others had to get away. The government's orders had been placarded up on the walls everywhere and had to be obeyed. Oscar Straus, who had received a call to America, therefore joined this fleeing throng, together with his wife, and soon we were following the hired cars with very dismal gaze as they disappeared into the distance; suddenly we found it difficult to believe in the possibility of ever meeting again. What now?

Now to Switzerland, of course! But it was no easy matter to get a visa on a French passport to go abroad during a war, and although we had only one thought—to get away, only to get away from it all! —if only in order to escape from those nights when there was a knocking at so many doors, which almost always meant something dreadful—we nevertheless had to possess ourselves in patience, sitting in the dining-room evening after evening in the proximity of German military and seeing the uncanny figures of the Gestapo, which a waiter always pointed out to us, go stamping past. And our friends, of whom we of course never forgot to think—what would become of them in Biarritz, which was their first destination? Would they succeed in getting away from a near-by port and escaping to America? Oh, all the things that went through one's mind at that time!

If anything kept us going at that period, it was the unconditional and touching reliability of our friends, who proved their friendship for us in the most deeply moving way. It must be said here that there was not one, whether French or German or American or English, who caused us even the slightest disappointment. They were all on the spot, ready to help, whether they were actually there in person or did so by letter, and the eagerness with which they showed their willingness to help was really touching, something that is unforgotten to this very hour.

Without that resolution to help us we would not have got out of the mouse-trap in which we suddenly found ourselves. However it may be, the fact is that here, as in Vienna, the Gestapo left us unmolested and that I was very lucky indeed on the afternoon when I went to make a last attempt to get the department concerned with our passports to give us permission to go to Switzerland. Through a strange series of improbable-seeming coincidences I really came into possession of the necessary visas. Deeply moved and happy, I hastened back to the hotel to my wife, who was by now somewhat gloomy, and showed her the incredible tokens of our liberation. The next thing I did was to hire a car, the driver of which had already told me that his papers, oddly enough, entitled him to cross the frontier if he returned the same day, and the following morning we set out with our entire luggage and reached Geneva after six hours' motoring.

My wife's condition had become so alarming that we took the advice of the hotel doctor, whom we had summoned, and the next day went to the Sanatorium Valmont near Glion, where she was nursed and kept under treatment for six weeks, after which she was more or less restored to the state she had been in when we left Zurich. I spent this time in Glion polishing up the rough translation of *Good King Charles*, which I had already finished in Zurich. At last we returned to Zurich, to exactly the same hotel that we had left almost two years ago—always to return for some weeks—and from that hour our new life in Switzerland began. We were now resolved not to change again, all the more since in a round-about way we had received the depressing information from Vienna that the contents of our villa had been auctioned and carried away in all directions, loaded upon lorry after lorry.

The house was taken over by a military court, which occupied all the rooms with its large staff. Many a death sentence was pronounced there, and our *concierge*, who, strangely enough, was allotted a tiny little room for himself and his wife, there learnt 'to know what shuddering meant'.

In Zurich I had the great pleasure of meeting again with those friends of my Viennese youth, Felix Salten and his wife. They had stayed on in their native country until the spring of 1939. They had been helped to leave the country by their daughter, who was married to that distinguished Swiss actor, Hans Rehmann. As a Swiss she could of course always travel to see her parents and return, and with her diplomacy and the respected name she bore she finally succeeded in getting her parents to Switzerland.

Felix Salten, who died in Zurich only some years later, after long and severe suffering, and after his wife had preceded him to the grave, to our delight experienced one last great happiness: even at that late date, at what was, all in all, a fairly advanced age, he was brushed by the wings of world-wide fame, which came to him as the author of that delicious animal book, *Bambi*. But that was not the only great satisfaction that came to him and to us. Above all there was the fact that now he could spend the last years of his life completely untrammelled by cares of any kind, for the great success the film of *Bambi* had throughout the world naturally earned him enough to keep all worries away from the happy author of that enchanting story. Salten was still alive to be present at the première in Zurich, and we were all able to admire Walt Disney's sympathetic insight and the *bravura* with which he made it possible for this poetic work to become an international success.

We spent as much time as possible with our old friends, and before and after every journey I sat with him, as in the old days, plucking the flowers of memory.

We also made several stays with another writer, in this case one whom we had to seek out in the place like an eagle's eyrie that he had chosen as his quarters to work in. This was Emil Ludwig. He was one of those who in the bygone days of the beginnings of their career had been presented to the public by the S. Fischer Verlag. Fischer had, however, very soon dissociated himself from this always very quarrelsome and aggressive author. About thirty-five years earlier Emil Ludwig had acquired Swiss nationality, out of passionate admiration for the Ticino, and had settled down in Moscia near Ascona for ever, or so he had hoped.

Then came the Second World War and Emil Ludwig felt himself to be in danger, in spite of his Swiss passport, because he was the German writer who was best-hated and most sought-after by the Nazis. Even before Hitler had come to Berlin he had raised his voice in warning in the *Berliner Tagebuch* and the *Weltbühne*. 'Hitler means war, Hitler means war,' he kept on crying out to deaf ears. This shrill litany called forth very loud threats in reply. Emil Ludwig's works were burnt to ashes in the Party's bonfires, but this honour fell also to my own books, as to most others. If I had been on the spot they would have taken me to Dachau for all eventualities, like that harmless man, Raoul Auernheimer. But, like him, I had never been a political writer, not even with one single line, and hence remained completely uninteresting and anonymous so far as 'the Party' was concerned. Emil Ludwig, on the other hand, was to them as a red rag to a bull.

When Czechoslovakia had still been just as independent as Switzerland, members of the Gestapo had murdered Professor Theodor Lessing, who was not nearly as much hated as Emil Ludwig, in Marienbad. Emil Ludwig was quite aware of this. He even believed himself to be surrounded by political assassins on Swiss territory, had nightmares about ambushes and kidnappings, and, as reluctantly as anyone well could, he left his elective land.

When he returned to Switzerland from America after the war, he found that he had to meet bitter reproaches, which he thought unjust, and lost his head as a result. He was awkward in his attempts to justify himself against attacks and, doubtless as a result of his heart trouble, which now dominated everything, was inclined to have outbursts of fury. So he made enemies of the public and his colleagues, instead of calmly and carefully explaining the situation and proving how he had always taken the part of his elective country while in America.

Although he was then indeed once more back in his peaceful house and really at home, where there were so many tokens to remind him of such select guests as Gerhart Hauptmann, Bernard Shaw, Bruno Walter and many others, he lived there like a startled hunted animal, and the man who had once had such a capacity for love became a hater and one who was hated. It was in these tragic circumstances that he died.

When I was still in Vienna I had not only repeatedly written for Swiss newspapers, but almost every year had given a talk or a reading in the Zurich studio for Radio Beromunster. Nevertheless it soon became clear to me that I was known in Switzerland more as Bernard Shaw's translator than as an independent writer. I had to reckon with this not very agreeable state of affairs, and I soon realised that although I was far from being at the age for it now, I must begin something like a new life from the intellectual point of view. I had certain literary goals in view, first of all (in order to bring the lesser part of my life's work to a conclusion) that of finally publishing a complete edition of the dramatic works of Bernard Shaw. Alongside this I wanted to publish a volume of poems that I had already planned in Vienna, and in general to be busy publishing feuilletons, articles and short stories. Yet if these plans were not to remain mere castles in the air, I had to succeed in finding a Swiss publisher for them. That was of course much more difficult than obtaining official permission to work.

At Pen Club Congresses I had already made the acquaintance of Dr. Eduard Korrodi, the respected literary historian and critic, who had published many a work of mine—above all, in the most prominent position in the *Neue Zürcher Zeitung*, the *Vermächtnis* (*A Legacy*), with which these chronicles end. Furthermore, I had also met Professor Robert Faesi, who was known to me from Vienna, as well as Dr. Bernhard Diebold, an acquaintance of the period of my youth that I had spent in Munich. In the house—much visited by artists and writers—of that highly cultured, sensitive and subtle woman, Frau Lili Reiff, I made the acquaintance of many eminent Swiss, among them Jakob Job and Ernst Zahn, with the latter of whom I have for years now had a warm friendship based on great mutual understanding.

I must make mention of a man who was the first to encourage me, with real sympathy, from the time when I sent in my first contribution. This is Dr. Otto Kleiber, the feuilleton editor of the *Basler National-Zeitung*. He published my poems, countless feuilletons, which I would perhaps never have written if he had not had the right way of stimulating me to do so, and a large number of short stories. Indeed, my novel, *Mord im Nebel* (*Murder in the Fog*), now, alas, out of print, also appeared in serial form in the *Basler National-Zeitung*. Since J. V. Widmann of Berne reviewed my early books as he did, showing so much affectionate interest in me, no Swiss helped me in my career as much as did Otto Kleiber.

About this time I happened to become acquainted with the neurologist and writer, Dr. Charlot Strasser. He, and likewise a short time later Bernhard Diebold, who, as a critic on *Die Tat*, had published some work of mine there, and with whom I had a number of meetings, gave me this advice, both of them in approximately the same terms: "I think the man who's the publisher for you is Dr. Friedrich Witz, who's in charge of the new Artemis Verlag."

So one day I set out on my way to the Rämistrasse and entered the building that I had known so long and so well, because it was also the Zurich Playhouse, where I had seen many a play of Shaw's produced by that careful director, Wälterlin, before him by Director Rieser, and before that again by Director Reuker, who had been well known to me. The head of the Artemis Verlag hailed my plan for a complete edition of Shaw's plays with enthusiasm, at the same time, however, drawing my attention to the fact that my proposal could only be carried out on the condition that the copyright situation was cleared up beyond any shadow of doubt.

I must now mention that Dr. Bermann had from the beginning of the war made it very plain indeed both to Bernard Shaw and to myself that we no longer interested him. He had not published another line by either of us, nor given any sign of life to either of us privately. He wrote to me, saying: 'I am entirely of your opinion, you ought to try to find Shaw a publisher in Switzerland.' Both Shaw and I therefore formally cancelled the contracts we had once made with this now silent publisher. The Artemis Verlag had, furthermore, got a university lecturer in international civil law to draw up a statement on the situation regarding the rights, on the basis of which they were able to decide to make a contract with me for a twelve-volume edition of Shaw's plays. The head of the firm that had now become my publishers reminded me, in a very confidence-inspiring way, of S. Fischer, and I soon began to feel thoroughly at home in the thought of working with him and for him, all the more since he had a young woman to do translations from the English for him who was an excellent English scholar, and whose young eyes were able to help my old ones, supplementing them in a really magnificent way.

To my delight Dr. Friedrich Witz had also begun to take a personal, human interest in our life in Zurich. He had in the meantime read poems of mine and had told me that he would gladly publish a volume of them in the event of there being such a thing. I could not but confess to him that there was indeed a volume, but in a drawer in a cupboard in Paris. We were, after all, burnt children who feared the fire and did not mean to experience a second time what we had been through in Vienna, where I had been robbed of so many precious manuscripts, letters, books, and documents of all kinds. I had to possess myself in patience until after the war, but then my first journey was to Paris and to the drawer in the cupboard containing my poems, which I was now at last able to take to a place of still greater safety. I had also been able to save Rodin's bust of Shaw and his many letters at that time, getting them to Paris under great difficulties.

At this period only strenuous work could rescue me from the horrors of war and from myself. I now dedicated many hours every day to the new edition of Shaw, for several years. It was only now that I set about translating a good many prefaces that had not previously existed in a German version, and I newly revised, checked, and corrected everything, wherever it seemed to me necessary, from the first to the last page. Since at the same time I did not stop writing and publishing things of my own, my days were now almost as full and busy as once upon a time in Austria.

But soon after I had embarked on this extensive activity, I suffered a very severe blow in the suicide of my friend Stefan Zweig, who had written to me as late as in July, 1941 :

'There is no longer any security anywhere, anywhere at all. Let us strike the word out of our vocabulary. Our world is past and gone, and with it our influence on things, and our happiness. Let us drag the tired carcase around just a little longer. In the end we shall, after all, be allowed to rest where no Hitler can disturb us any more. My dear fellow, you still hear our language spoken round about you, and that is a great deal. I feel myself boundlessly a stranger, an alien. Politics nauseate me and I avoid any form of sociability, living in a little place some way outside New York. . . . Our one piece of good fortune is that we have no children or grandchildren. We die on our own and in so doing, I am afraid, will cause few people much sorrow.'

Stefan Zweig, that clairvoyant man who had been spared even the slightest setback, the slightest diversion, on his course, which had led him straight on to considerable eminence, had now himself put an end to his life. From his youth he had snatched to his heart with rare *élan*, with positively tempestuous ardour, every mode of writing, every form of expression, that he felt he ought to make his own, and since he had from the very beginning been a darling of the gods, he had stormed the peaks that he had set himself the task of scaling, his fervent efforts crowned with the success that only heaven grants. He began, as almost every German poet does, with lyric poems; and people hearkened to him. He wrote a few stories of catastrophe, *Amok, Verwirrung der Gefühle (Conflicts), 24 Stunden im Leben einer Frau (Twenty-four Hours in a Woman's Life)*—to mention only outstanding examples of his manner—incomparable and unique writings that all connoisseurs found convincing, but also the great crowds, indeed throngs, of readers who flocked to him from the time of his first utterances.

It is well known that in his early years he drew Emil Verhaeren out of the mystic obscurity in which the great Belgian master lived, bringing him, by means of his accomplished adaptations, into the bright light of literary day; that he was one of the first to announce Romain Rolland's importance; and that he contributed to the select posthumous fame of that forgotten Frenchwoman, Marceline Desbordes Valmore.

One only needs to mention these few names—although it is impossible to pass over his *Balzac* in silence—which I pick at random out of the great wealth of his work, in order to recognise that in his endeavours, which were always the result of a profound insight and admiration, Stefan Zweig not only devoted himself to the study of the much-loved creative artists who belonged to his native Austria, but, gazing beyond all boundaries, recognised beauty and greatness wherever he met them. He only lauded his heroes and heroines all the more loudly when their figures were obscured in the shadows cast by ephemeral celebrities far below them in stature. It was his ambition to create reputations, not to win reputation for himself.

From these beginnings, these devoted endeavours, surely more was needed than to take only one great intellectual stride ahead, in order to bring Zweig to the works that were to make him world-famous: what was also needed was his tremendous capacity for hard work and his great and onward-urging gifts. Now followed the long and comprehensive essays on Balzac, Kleist, Nietzsche, Dostoevsky and others, which gradually took on the dimensions of a little encyclopædia, under the general title *Die Baumeister der Welt* (*Master Builders*). This important work was, however, only the first step towards the biographies that were the basis of his world fame. No living author was translated so often and into so many languages as this virtuoso translator and enthusiastic adapter of works in other languages. Meanwhile he wrote successful plays, essays, and in later years also a novel, *Ungeduld des Herzens* (*Beware of Pity*), returning ever and again to the great biographies, the last of which gave a portrait of that daring circumnavigator of the world, Magellan, while a large and comprehensive work on Balzac was to form the conclusion. "With this book I want to conclude my series of biographies," he said to me before we took leave of each other in London, "but I shall need a year only in order to get all the material collected."

I should however like to pass on from this all too fleeting enumeration of achievements that are, after all, world-famous and to be found in many books, and come to personal observations, to facts, and to the overwhelming events that had very nearly caused Stefan Zweig to lose his mental balance and composure even in the First World War.

Above all I should like to establish the truth on one point: like myself, Stefan Zweig was never a 'refugee' in the true, terrible sense of the word, not, however, on the grounds that he *could* never be that because he was more markedly a citizen of the world than anyone else I have ever known, but because his life and method of work protected him from that fate. I should therefore like at this point to refute the legend that he put an end to his life for some such reason as unendurable homesickness. His home was the great, wide, beautiful world and the freedom of being allowed to live anywhere in it and feel at home anywhere in it. That—in the technical sense

o

of the word—boundless world he was able to enter into through his work, which was at home in all the languages on earth. That world had opened its gates and its arms to him, everywhere welcoming him like a fellow-countryman, wherever he might go.

Stefan Zweig had only rarely been found at home in his native Vienna, however great his affectionate attachment was to its most prominent artists and the true character and temperament of the Viennese. Admittedly, he did spend happy years of his maturity in Austria, years that were rich in creative work; that was in his elective home, Salzburg, where once every year, at the time of the Festival, from all over the world there came the people whom Stefan Zweig called his friends, the people whose company he could never do without. In Salzburg he kept a hospitable house, and his days were passed in a wonderful rhythm of alternating hard work and intellectual recuperation, surrounded by his friends and his books, and with the delight of listening to music and the fascination of making plans.

When in the autumn of 1934 Stefan Zweig made the resolve—as, in keeping with his views, he had to—to leave Salzburg for ever, he did not do so by any means as a broken man, far less as an outcast; no, he went voluntarily, as a consequence of an anonymous insult which did, however, give him food for thought and—sensitive and easily hurt as he was—aroused his wonderful gift of foresight and vigilance, which afterwards never slackened.

After a somewhat lengthy stay in Paris, the new year found him in London, where his publisher had summoned him. Even at that time he came to the city on the Thames with the firm determination to become British, although his friends in Paris—among whom there were not only the most eminent contemporary writers, but also the most influential of France's intellectual spokesmen—positively vied with each other in their efforts to get him French citizenship. After all, a play of his had just had a long and successful run on the French stage. His drama *Volpone*, based on that of Ben Jonson, had been adapted by his friend—today his French biographer—Jules Romain, and in that adaptation had been an even greater box-office success than Zweig's own version had been some years earlier at the Burgtheater in Vienna. But Stefan Zweig did not want to have any advantage over others; he did not wish to owe any practical success to his fame; and it was for this reason that he always shrank from accepting the ribbon of the Legion of Honour. I have never known any creative artist who was less vain and less ambitious than he was. The intoxication of sheer ability, which was for him the profoundest of enchantments, bore him into loftier regions. He now made his way towards that harsher country, England; there it was that he wanted to fit himself in and fulfil the universal condition, which is: only after five years' domicile in England is one entitled to apply for British citizenship. Being still young enough to do this, Stefan Zweig meant to pass this test of patience that English law imposes on the foreigner.

The lot of the refugee, something that went to his heart so much and which he alleviated in a positively extravagant way wherever he could, was thus something that was spared Stefan Zweig in his own person. He was one who did good as quietly as he did it generously, as soon as he knew a friend or a man of talent—and for him the two expressions meant practically the same—to be in need. His ear and his generous hand were always open when it was a matter of giving help and making a hard road easier. The fate that so many others suffered as refugees he himself felt as though it were his own torment, which he soothed as well as he possibly could.

Stefan Zweig suffered indescribably from the collapse of our world and all the atrocities that it brought with it. When his time of waiting was at an end, he—the Austrian who was so extremely welcome even in England—received his British passport and could go out into the world as a British subject, or remain in his newly chosen country. He now took steps to settle down permanently and made a new home for himself in Bath, the well-known spa some two hours' journey from London. He lived there in completely happy partnership with his young wife, who was at the same time the guardian of his manuscripts and the great seal-bearer of his work finished and unfinished.

Although Stefan Zweig soon afterwards left England, this was not, of course, from any fear of the war. No, it was his popularity and his fame that once again pressed the wayfarer's staff into his hand and so brought about his doom. He could not bring himself to refuse the chance of a great lecture-tour through Northern America, and when at the end of it he arrived back, weary and rather exhausted, in New York, where he might have decided to make the return trip to England, he received an invitation, as tempting as it was pressing, to repeat the tour he had made through South America two years earlier, when it had reaped him high reputation and had been a thorough-going success. This time too he saw the job through, but he tried his strength too far. After returning from the long journey he suddenly found himself, tired, harassed by the terrible things happening in the world, infinitely far away from his dearest friends, in the foreign country on which he had just finished writing a book, which must be called a hymn to Brazil. He was undoubtedly one of the most fêted people in all that great continent of South America, and there was no wish of his that the governments there would not have granted him. Proof, if any is wanted, lies in the fact that only a very short time after his death there was a Stefan-Zweig Square in Rio de Janeiro.

If he sometimes suffered from homesickness under those tropical skies, it was homesickness for a few people and many books, manu-scripts and notes that had been left behind in Europe, in his quiet house in Bath. I am sure that this homesickness did not drive him to his death, although it may have done still more to depress the pessimistic melancholic that Stefan Zweig was all his life long. There is doubtless nothing that better expresses his mood at that time than his last letter to me, written to me a few weeks before his death, from Petropolis, where he was staying in Brazil.

DEAR FRIEND,

There is no better proof that I was sincere in advising you not to go to the United States than the fact that I did not stay there myself. Our kind of literature is something we shall never be able to adapt entirely to American needs. And then, too, as a foreigner in time of war one is subject to every imaginable sort of restriction and difficulty. So here I am now living in a sort of miniature Ischl. We have rented a bungalow with three tiny rooms, and I work as well as I can manage to. The life is pleasant, the scenery wonderful, and all that is missing is two of the most important things: first, books and, secondly, one's friends. The books one can in the last desperate resort, if necessary, try to write oneself, but it is difficult to make new friends at our time of life. One has to hold on to the old ones all the more. I have finished my auto-biography, which is to be out in a few months, and have been doing a bit of work at a little story about chess and also a larger thing. The real book, the Balzac, is something I can't get on with here, because I left all my notes at home and the books aren't to be had. This state of affairs, this living like a nomad, is a heavy burden to me. The others have established themselves in America and burnt their boats behind them, while I still have all my property, of which my books, my manuscripts, and notes are what is most important to me, over there, and so can't make any sort of home anywhere. In Switzerland anyway you still have two things that I miss here, friends and books, and also the chance to speak your own language. And as for insecurity—is there any place without insecurity? One ought to get used to living only for the next month or two. But I'm afraid we grew up with the idea of security and stability and feel the present state of things incomparably worse than those who have always swum with the tide. The main thing is to keep your health. "Survival is all," our friend Rilke said, who was not only a better poet than the rest but also one of the wise men who died in time to avoid this time. Till March my address continues to be: Rua Goncalves Dias, Petropolis, Brazil. And then? I can only answer with a question-mark. That is the cipher of our life.

And now it became the cipher also of his death. He kept the true reason for his violent voluntary departure a secret from us all, even if he knew it himself. Truly, he lacked any outward reason to abandon life. The large sales his books had all over the world meant that he was everywhere able to live in conditions of the utmost comfort; and there was no illness, no heart-ache, and no justified grief—except the mortally wearing grief about the collapse of our civilisation—to make him learn the meaning of despair. He remained a darling of the gods to his last hour. Who knows whether a rousing call from a friend would not have been enough to snatch him out of his death-sick mood or, say, from a melancholy mood brought on by the climate— a melancholy that transformed the instinct for self-preservation into an urge for self-destruction?

But the voice was not there that might have shaken him up and called him back into life in the crucial moment of his ill-fated death-sick mood, and so, in the grip of that mood, he plunged into the abyss. We shall, I suppose, never be able to fathom what it was that drove Stefan Zweig to that lamentable, grave last step which made inconsolable mourners of us all. That remains his secret; self-willed, he took it with him to the grave.

What else could I do, even though in the gloomiest frame of mind and rejecting the world in which I lived, but return to my work, which was once more, for the moment, for a friend's sake and not for my own? Apart from this, my lost friend scarcely imagined how right his intuition had been when he envied me for living in Switzerland, and not only exclusively because of the German language, which I was here able to write and speak. Naturally I can speak only of my own experiences and those of my wife, and here I must say that nowhere in the world were government departments and other official bodies more friendly and obliging than in Switzerland, the very country so feared by everyone because of its harshness and severity. There was another thing, which Stefan Zweig had not even mentioned, that I felt to be good fortune, and this was that during the whole of the war one could remain in contact with one's friends abroad. Without Shaw's agreement and co-operation I could never have taken on the great task that now associated me, in my work, with the Artemis Verlag; for I lacked many manuscripts, as well as any record of changes that he had in the meantime made for *his* complete edition, and also prefaces that he had only just finished. Furthermore, as a brand-new Frenchman I had of course to remain in touch with various official quarters in France.

The work went ahead faster than I had thought, because I kept to it as much as I could, only pausing to give form to the little ideas of my own that crowded upon me all too quickly.

In those very busy years I also became a contributor to *Die Tat*, and in this way had the pleasure of getting to know the great Swiss essayist and lyric poet, Max Rychner. In Berne my gravely ill friend Hans Müller-Einingen introduced me to Doctor Arnold Schwengeler, which resulted not only in my becoming a contributor to the *Berner Bund*, but also in a warm friendship, which has been a bond between myself and this highly-gifted dramatist (whose *Fälscher* (*Forger*) I regard as a little masterpiece) down to the present day, unmarred by any kind of discord.

What did a great deal to make the stay in Switzerland, and also the work, easier was the wonderful situation of the Hotel Dolder, where we lived. The forest in which the building stood produced a soothing and tranquillising atmosphere, and there was, of course, no lack of occasions when I went for meditative walks, on which I was able to come to some sort of terms with myself. The hotel was run on model lines, and, what was of more importance to me than anything else, my wife, too, was not left to her gloomy thoughts, for of course there were plenty of acquaintances from many countries passing that way, who stayed up there for longer or shorter periods and did something to provide the necessary distraction for this woman who was only gradually beginning to realise fully all that had in fact befallen her. I tried to capture this strangely composite atmosphere, which was also disagreeably marred by the many Nazis who stayed at the hotel, in a little book, which, however, for many reasons, but chiefly for the sake of personal peace and quiet, always so important, I hid away in the remotest depths of a drawer in my desk, without ever thinking of publishing it. What, after all, did it matter to me what other people thought? It was a heavy enough burden for me to have to bear my own thoughts.

During this time, in which I went to have a conference with Dr. Witz almost every week, chiefly because of the high speed at which my work was proceeding—it was now approaching completion after some three or four years—Bernard Shaw had not been idle either. He had written a long book called *Everybody's Political What's What*, which of course had to be published in a German version too, sooner or later. While I was still considering whether I could not shuffle off the good fortune of translating it on to someone else, I had a letter from the Swiss publishers Amstutz & Herdeg, informing me that they had bought the rights of this work in London, where they had, however, discovered from the Society of Authors that I was the sole authorised German translator of Shaw's work; and they asked me to come and have a talk with them.

I now set out to see Dr. Amstutz, whose wife was not only English but also a successful English author. It happened, however, precisely at that time that I became fairly seriously ill and on the advice of an eminent urologist was about to undergo an operation; and I also had to finish the complete edition for the Artemis Verlag somehow. I had at once realised, when Shaw sent me this fat book, that I should not be capable of undertaking that laborious work, for which I, as a person completely without knowledge of political affairs, was furthermore not in the least suitable. Hence Dr. Amstutz and I quickly reached the point of agreement that I would put my name to it as the editor, while the translation was to be undertaken by the Amstutz Verlag's house translator, Franz Fein, the brother of my friend the actress Maria Fein. I was very well content with this solution, and also with the proviso that I should collaborate in reading the proofs—which I faithfully did a year later, as a convalescent in the Hirslanden clinic, after the success of the operation I had undergone.

But this is somewhat to anticipate events. I should like to return to 1942, for I had not emptied the cup of that year's bitterness with Stefan Zweig's incomprehensible death. And with further reference to that I should like to add by way of explanation that there were in the main two forces that swept this excessively sensitive writer into the abyss. One was the quite unusually great fear he had of old age, of really growing old, something that he did not want to experience at any price. Ever and again I had to listen to him exclaiming in a trembling voice: "I don't want to be pushed round in a bath-chair like my father! I don't want to present people with the picture of an old man tottering to the grave!" And then, however much I appreciated his second wife, it must be said that she suffered from melancholia—though I am sure only as a consequence of her terrible experiences—and impatiently encouraged her husband in his desire for death. Young though she was, her weariness of life by far exceeded even his, and instead of distracting his thoughts—ah, and I imagine to myself that I might have been able to do it with a few games of chess!—she even encouraged him to dream of death and then, of course, in out-and-out loyalty, went with him on the last journey.

Scarcely had I, if not reconciled myself to, at least come to some sort of terms with, this sorrow when our old friend Felix Salten's wife died of the grave heart-disease from which she had been suffering.

Now I positively fled to the complete edition, burrowing into the work that afforded me distraction from myself, from the war news, which was, incidentally, anything but satisfactory, and from all the true stories of atrocities and despair that fluttered in the air around us. Now in another three years this work, which was close to my heart, but from which at the same time I wanted to free my heart, was really so far advanced that Dr. Witz could begin to have it set up in print.

But what was all that in comparison with the glorious spring of 1945, which brought mankind the liberation that we called 'the end of the war'? For at that time we all believed—and the fact that we

believed it did let something like joy enter into our shattered spirits—
that now peace would really settle upon the tormented world. We
did not yet dream that we were being granted a respite only in order
to be plunged into fresh uneasiness and alarm. Still, one thing had
happened: the world was open again. The barred gates of friendly
countries flew open, to let us hospitably in.

But two events now occurred that were as though designed to keep
my hopes well within bounds and to suppress my longing for travel.
One was my operation, which I survived thanks to the masterly skill
of Dr. Blangey, but which kept me tied up in the Hirslanden
Sanatorium for seven weeks. Scarcely had I left the sanatorium when
I suffered a new sorrow in the death of my friend Felix Salten, to
whom I had said good-bye before my operation, full of false
premonitions of death. At his grave-side here in Zurich I delivered
the second funeral address that I had held for a companion of
my youthful days in Vienna.

In those dismal hours it became fairly clear to me that we were
actually brothers-in-arms, and that if fate ordains that one shall
reach an advanced age, one sees one's comrades falling to right and
to left of one in the battle that life is. And if today I gaze back over
the figures I had known since my youth, all of whom are no longer
there, I really do feel as if we had gone into battle together shoulder
to shoulder, a battle from which, as though by some miracle, I have
always come out alive, even though covered with the wounds that
one calls 'sorrows'.

Now, with Felix Salten's death, the last friend whom I had had
since youth had been snatched away from me. Here I was now alone
upon this earth, except for the one man whom I still had: Bernard
Shaw. And it was to him that I set out on my first journey after the
war, even before I was quite recovered from my operation.

It was granted to us to see each other again after an interval of six
years and, as each of us said of the other, without there being any
particular change in two people who had experienced the collapse of
their world in such very different circumstances.

This reunion took place at a time when Shaw's ninetieth birthday
was approaching and a crisis had just compelled him to make a
complete change in his way of life. All those who have followed the
magnificent life of that man of great intellect know how entirely the
aged Shaw had over and over again done the right thing in questions

o*

of art, and also in matters of the conduct of life and the preservation of life. Hardness of hearing, failing sight, sleeplessness, heart attacks, and hardening of the arteries were all things he had graciously been spared. Nor had his capacity for work diminished, or his passion to master the growing problems of a new world still suffering its birth pangs.

I had to drop the ambitious hope of getting the greatest interview of his life, because there was scarcely any question left that this man, daily showered with questions, had not already answered. "I have written books and plays on the most important problems affecting humanity, and I really have nothing more to add," he remarked when I was about to produce my list of questions.

My visit was at the same time actually a kind of visit of condolence, too, for in 1943 Bernard Shaw had lost his lifelong helpmate, Charlotte, who had died after a long illness.

She was a great lady who was also a great woman. Herself an authoress and chairman of no mean quality, she condemned herself to profound silence from the moment when she recognised the genius of the man whose name she wanted to bear and in whose shadow she wanted to live and play her part. Anyone who had the privilege of experiencing what this noble-minded woman's favour and encouragement could mean, anyone who was distinguished by receiving occasional letters written in her hand, was enviable. She had a unique way of acknowledging one and showing the little throng of chosen friends her liking, a way that was a better proof of her attachment than words could have been, to say nothing of the usual social phrases.

In everything she did this woman, so eager for knowledge, showed an energy, an intensity, that swept one into her entirely independent sphere of thought. Her presence in itself was something convincing. How rarely did she practise criticism! But whenever she did begin to speak of a drama or a novel one was amazed at the sureness of her reasons for approving or disapproving. Totally unsentimental, she was kindly and helpful and in a very quiet way of her own dried many a tear. I once heard her exclaim about some false pity with which she had been pestered: "He's sentimental, and of course he doesn't realise how offensively unkind his interest is." She made the best use of her wealth; she levelled hard and steep paths, first and foremost her husband's, which at the beginning of his glorious career had indeed been a thorny one. Silently she managed her hospitable house, into which she permitted no one to enter to whom she was not in some way devoted. She immersed herself completely in her husband's work, and her advice was often decisive for his writing. It was, for instance, she who had once urged him to re-create the life of the Maid of Domrémy.

Charlotte Shaw loved sport and enjoyed riding and swimming. She was a brilliant cyclist and devoted to taking long walks. Her sister had in her youth been one of the best-known women riders to hounds in the British Isles.

There can, I think, have been few wives of great men who kept themselves so anxiously and eagerly in the background, in their husband's shadow, as Mrs. Shaw did. The more noise there was all round her husband, the more loudly his fame beat upon her ear, the quieter and stiller his helpmate became.

Her flight from publicity was sometimes intensified to the point of eccentricity. For instance, she would never let herself be photographed and ran away from troublesome amateurs; there is scarcely a picture of her in existence. Even the snapshots taken by her husband, who as a photographer was as good as he was enthusiastic, were something she took care to avoid. Pictures were to show him solitary in his greatness, a man alone; and it was for this reason that she would not grant Rodin's wish to immortalise her delicate features, cast in bronze, for posterity, after he had made his splendid bust of the writer. Modesty and pride were the yoke-fellows that drew her chariot up to life's heights.

She was present at first nights of Shaw's plays in the darkness of her box, and nothing in the course of the evening escaped her. Whatever went on upon the stage and in the audience, she noticed it and drew her conclusions as regards the work and its representation, recognising its high soarings as well as its weak aspects, and was never wrong. Her knowledge of human nature was amazing, her judgment a verdict that was a blend of wisdom, knowledge and kindness.

She understood German and had mastery of the French language. Her English translation of the three most important plays of Eugène Brieux, above all the drama *The Wrecked*, may stand as a model of the transmission of a work from language to language; on its appearance in London it aroused great interest and led to memorable performances at the Stage Society's theatre.

At the beginning of May 1940, when she was already ill, she was for the last time an eye-witness of the great success of a new comedy of her husband's. In Golder's Green there was a performance of *Good King Charles*, and sitting in Mrs. Shaw's box, together with her and her husband, I recalled those distant times when his old plays had been new and surrounded by the din of controversy, full of striving towards the future. She listened musingly, deep in thought, as though lost in dreams. . . .

Mrs. Shaw had an intense love of travel, an urge to get away into the far distance. She was well able to make it clear to her husband what advantages such tremendous new impressions must provide for him and for the welfare of them both. So the journey round the world was made three times, in very different directions, each time keeping them away from their native country for between six and seven months. The immediate fruits of these varied impressions were that delicious little comedy, written on board a gigantic ocean-going steamer, *A Village Wooing*, and the important drama *The Simpleton of the Unexpected Isles*.

The years following their last return home were dedicated to the unconscious preparation—overshadowed by the misery of war and by illness—for the most mysterious and greatest of all journeys, on which Charlotte Shaw started out at the age of almost eighty-seven, and yet, to our sorrow, all too early.

Bernard Shaw, who had now become a hermit in the truest sense of the word, listened to me with great interest when I told him about his books, some of which were on their way, that is to say, the first volumes of the German complete edition, and also that great book, *Everybody's Political What's What*, for which he himself had chosen the German title, on which he insisted with unusual obstinacy, *Politik für Jedermann*. He wanted to know more about the plans of the young Artemis Verlag and its chief, Dr. Witz, than I could tell him at that time. The thought of the twelve volumes of the German complete edition, with the twelve individual titles of the books, chosen by me on my own initiative, pleased him very much indeed, yet he was worried by the question whether it would be possible to distribute Swiss books without difficulty in Germany.

At this point I should like to record a statement of Shaw's that he made at the beginning of the ghastly period when the Nazis were in power. His reaction to my question, indeed my suggestion that performances of his works should be forbidden for the duration of the National-Socialist régime, was to oppose it violently, with the words:

"The performance of my works is something I don't want to have tied down to the condition that the governments concerned meet with my approval. It would interest me very much, for instance, to know what effect they have on cannibals. After all, the plays can only help to bring cannibals and dictators to their senses."

I naturally gave way before this attitude, but in the first years of the war almost all Shaw's plays were struck off the repertory of the German theatres and only replaced after 1945.

From England I then hurried to Paris in order to liberate my volume of poems (to which I had added about as much as half again during my years in Switzerland) from its captivity in the cupboard drawer. Admittedly, I needed all my documents and all my eloquence in order to attain this goal; but I did after all return happily to Zurich with these favourite children of my muse, and there instantly placed them at the disposal of the Artemis Verlag, which then published them, as fast as possible, under the title *Aus verschtüteten Tiefen* (*From Buried Depths*).

About a year later the young publisher Classen by chance came across my story, *Die Frau ohne Dienstag* (*The Woman who had no Tuesday*), and published it, without any change, in his series *Vom Bleibenden in der Zeit* (*Books that will Last*).

Meanwhile the complete edition of Shaw's plays was rapidly advancing towards its conclusion. Apart from this, the Artemis Verlag had published Shaw's profound and searching story, *The Little Black Girl in Search of God*, and I was busy translating the aged writer's last and in fact unexpected play, *Buoyant Billions*, into German, under the title *Zuviel Geld*, likewise chosen in dictatorial fashion by Shaw. A short time afterwards it was performed for the first time, at the Zürcher Schauspielhaus, and was a surprisingly great success, which was doubtless to be explained by the amazing topicality of the subject, for it was mainly concerned with the outrageous new English taxation laws, by which the highest income was precisely that which was transformed into the smallest. This play (fairly short by Shaw's standards) was also published by the Artemis Verlag, in a single small volume.

Now at last I could plunge into my own work again, which was so close to my heart and had for many years been luring me like forbidden fruit which I could now no longer resist plucking. On a journey to the South, which I took for my health, I wrote *Die Heimkehr des Diomedes* (*Diomedes' Return*) and had the good fortune to throw my publisher into raptures with it. He expressed his delight with this work by commissioning the famous Swiss illustrator, Hans Erni, to illustrate the book; unfortunately these drawings made it a somewhat too expensive thing of beauty. After Dr. Witz, however, there was another man whose approval I wanted to make sure of before the book went to press. This was Professor Emil Staiger, who instantly investigated the little work with microscopic exactitude and to my delight testified—in the most friendly terms—to its poetic validity and approved the liberties I had taken.

Now, however, it seemed to me the time had come to accept the many invitations I had received from my former country, and also to comply with a feeling of mingled curiosity and melancholy, and in spite of everything to visit Vienna, the city of my youth, once again. All my memories, all my sorrows and disappointments, all the terrible consequences of the political upheaval, were concentrated there, making my heart heavy, but so too were all my still surviving friends, and that made it light. It was Professor Schreyvogel, who once in the old days had organised an evening with the name 'The Discovery of the Poet Siegfried Trebitsch', who now went to more trouble even than anyone else to prevent my having any feeling of strangeness, far less of resentment. He had been accused of having collaborated with those in power at the beginning of those grim years; yet the fact was that this poet, who was physically excessively delicate, often ailing, had not put up a fight, but had only yielded to what was inevitably expected of him, in order to preserve himself and his family from the worst of fates. But no living person had suffered any injury through his doing; no one was robbed of his freedom or even his life in order to make his path easier; and that seemed to me to be all that mattered, mainly because none of us who were remote from it all know, after all, how *we* would have behaved if we had been forced to remain there and carry out our life's mission under a reign of terror.

In my native city I was hailed and welcomed in a quite unexpected way by all the newspapers and above all by my dear friends Franz Theodor Csokor, Oscar Maurus Fontana, Ernst Lothar, Erhard Buschbeck, and many others. The Pen Club and the Press Club held large receptions in my honour, with speeches of welcome, and most of the papers published very friendly articles. My friends all invited me to their houses and introduced me to the leading personalities present. Truly, I could not complain. But all this could not erase the terrible impressions that were made on me by the ravages I beheld, the changed appearance of the people, the unusual way of life, now too bustling, now too stealthy, and the awareness of being in an occupied city. Besides, it seemed to me there was a smell of blood wafted through the streets, and I still sensed a readiness to 'dance with the Devil', or imagined that I did.

In the summer that preceded this journey I had been in Gastein, accompanied by my wife, to a certain extent by way of preparation; but there, apart from the general public, almost nothing had changed, as little as in Salzburg, that best-loved city of my early years, which had intimidated me only by the noise and the overpowering crowds of tourists.

But now in my native city I was for the first time seized by an indescribable nostalgia for the Vienna I had left, which held the secrets of my youth and had also received the coffins of my parents into its earth. How neglected were the places that had once been most carefully tended, and how overwhelmingly distressing to set eyes again on the house in which I had lived, dreamed, and worked for thirty years of my life. Many a sight was more than I had the strength for, and among all the conflicting emotions a faint yearning began to glow within me, like a little flame pointing the way out of a labyrinth, a yearning for my new country, Switzerland.

Till then I had not known that the farewell to a city so dearly loved could be at once difficult and easy. Now I was to experience this, after it had become clear to me in an excessively painful way that, going on living there for the last years granted to me, any resumption of what was finally past and gone and utterly transformed was impossible.

When, then, in the company of Ernst Wiechert, who had given a reading to the Viennese Pen Club and shortly afterwards in the most touching way sent me copies of almost all his works, I had landed at the Zurich air-port once again, I felt a stronger sense of safety and of having returned home than I had felt in the old city of my birth. Here I had a modest, rather cosy little apartment, my wife's handiwork and one that did not give her over-much trouble, which was, after all, very important at this time; and now in this, the retirement of my old age, after the comparative bustle and stir of my life, I found perfect contentment. He who could manage to adjust himself to this life was spared the disappointments of which others, in a similar situation, so often complained to us.

In California we had, apart from Thomas Mann, many friends whom we believed to be particularly well and comfortable there. Alas, fate taught us that this was not so, for not only did Franz Werfel and Bruno Frank die in rapid succession, but Raoul Auernheimer from Vienna, the only one left of our Pen Club circle, who, already an ill man, had been a year in Dachau concentration camp, there closed his eyes for ever. In his seventieth year, in the most glorious of all parts of the world, he died of his old heart trouble, after having lived long enough to publish two eminently readable biographies of great Austrians. His heroes were Metternich and Grillparzer. It was not granted him to live long enough to see the effect these books had, which might perhaps have tided this tired and depressed man over his illness a little longer.

It was at Auernheimer's in Vienna that I often met that great savant, Rudolf Kassner, whose *Melancholeia* was at that time much talked of and who is today still alive and active, in the very best of health, in Southern Switzerland.

Returning from Vienna, where everything had reminded me of those distant days, I might perhaps have let myself brood a while longer on my mournful emotions, if it had not again been the last hero of my youth—Bernard Shaw—who snatched me back into the present with his virulent signs of life. Untiring as ever, he had written sixteen autobiographical sketches, which perhaps reveal more of himself and his life than his dramatic works do. He wanted to see them safely transferred into German as soon as possible, which meant that I at once returned to my accustomed work as a translator, and since the book, as I was glad to see, was not very long, I was in a short time able to place it at the disposal of the Artemis Verlag. Besides that, Shaw, who still had all his old delight in writing dialogue, an art of which he was such a master, was writing—as his last work—six *Far-Fetched Fables*, which, in spite of their wit and profundity, doubtless could not be performed because they would last no longer than three-quarters of an hour, a difficulty that could be solved only by performing some one-act plays together with them. But theatrical managements cannot make up their minds to do this, because they believe that only plays lasting the whole evening can lure a large audience into the theatre.

I myself visited Shaw at Ayot St. Lawrence on two more occasions and had long talks with him about these little works. But even at that time he turned out to be failing, in a strange way. He was impatient, was afraid of falling asleep when he leaned back in his chair, and at the same time, too, was afraid of showing this understandable weakness even in front of as familiar a visitor as I was. Intellectually he was as fresh as ever, and to my astonished delight his hearing had not suffered in any way at all. The difference in relation to the old days lay chiefly in the fact that he no longer walked so far beyond the house in order to accompany me to the taxi that had brought me, after a farewell that was kept light and airy, as he had always been so deft in doing.

But in these last years I was already feeling less attracted by London than by Paris, for one thing because Shaw was always emphasising the fact that he did not want to see anyone any more and, as I was often informed, remained invisible even to his oldest friends and acquaintances, but also for the reason that in Paris I knew there was a man who was full of friendly feelings for me, a man whom I had met for the very first time in Vienna, though only casually, some decades earlier, when he was still at the beginning of his career. He was at that time a very close friend of Hofmannsthal's. This was the Swiss Envoy, Minister Carl J. Burckhardt. This great historian, whose *Richelieu* in France ranked as the standard biography of that outstanding statesman, is undoubtedly among the most important Swiss writers of our day. In Switzerland I have not met any publicist with such a breadth of horizon, such comprehensive learning in all fields, such a knowledge of languages, and such inborn sureness of taste, as Professor Burckhardt, who was also President of the International Red Cross.

The visits I paid in Paris to this friend of Hofmannsthal, to whom he had once dedicated a work that was well worth reading, to this man who knew and understood the old Austria so well, were always uncommonly stimulating for me, and both of us only regretted that we had not more time for each other, for there was a superabundance of common interests and subjects on which we could gladly have had longer discussions.

When I had done my administrative errands in Paris, I never lost any time in returning to Zurich, where there was, of course, always a great deal of work waiting for me.

A man who gets on in years has, indeed, only the choice of either quitting the scene himself or bearing the sorrow caused him by the passing of dear friends. Again I was stricken by sorrowful news. After a painful illness, heroically borne, Hans Müller-Einigen had gone from among us. He died a few hours after a professional conference that had agitated him very much, though for no good reason. But his great excitability was a part of his disease, as it had once been part of his health and his over-brimming enthusiasm and energy.

For the sake of being able to work in tranquillity and in order to get away from all the things that he was too much inclined to let get the upper hand over him, Hans Müller emigrated to Switzerland in 1930, when there was as yet no sort of personal danger threatening him. He lived to be sixty-seven years of age, and for forty-seven of those years he was a poet, a creator, a writer who was in love with his mother-tongue, a man who served, with all the ardour of his fiery soul, the dreams that had marked him even in the nursery, as they do everyone of great gifts. His father was a prominent Viennese lawyer, and when Hans Müller had taken his degree in law, which he did with the greatest of ease, his father may well have hoped that he would see his son following his own profession and would be able some day to welcome the poet as his successor in the office. But, an impassioned theatre-goer and reader himself, the old gentleman was one of the first to recognise his son's great literary gifts and did all that was in his power to contribute to their development.

Like every real poet, Müller began with poems that were very original and convinced the connoisseur that here was a writer who was nobody's imitator. Then, when his first volume of stories, *Geheimnisland* (*Land of Secrets*), appeared, a larger circle of readers began to pay attention to him, and this still very young writer had 'arrived'. This volume contained a story that gave Oscar Straus' librettists the material for the text that was later to be known coupled with the well-known melodies of the 'Walzertraum'. But every fibre of Hans Müller's talent attracted him to the theatre. It was granted to him to have a work of his—a very audacious comedy, *Die Puppenschule* (*The School for Dolls*)—performed at the Burgtheater long before he had reached the end of his thirtieth year, and it was the superb acting of no less an actor than Adolf von Sonnenthal that helped this young poet to success. Perhaps it was a premature success, for now every critical gaze was turned on him—and what writer, and especially what dramatist, could claim to have risen ever higher, without a set-back, from his first to his last works? Hans Müller too was to discover the truth of this, above all when his plays very soon crossed the frontiers of his native land and earned great success for him in Germany. Hans Müller was born with a sense for great rôles and theatrical effects. He could not do otherwise than cause scenes to flicker with tension and burst into roaring flames at the right moment, even though, of course, the end of an act or some theatrical twist sometimes meant moving away from simple, natural human feeling.

The greatest German actresses, Ida Roland and Käthe Dorsch, owed their greatest successes to Hans Müller, both of them, above all, in that much-performed play, *Flamme* (*Flame*). Albert Bassermann counted Hans Müller's *Schöpfer* (*Creator*) among his favourite parts, and had great triumphs in this drama, both at home and abroad. It was not more than a year since Bassermann had said to me, speaking of the *Creator*: "*That* was a play! *That* was a part!"

The way to success has never been made easy for any Austrian writer. Hans Müller tried to avoid all public controversy, but it was his endeavour to convince his opponents ever again with a new work, and so to make them change their minds; and in this he sometimes succeeded, which heightened his vitality and self-confidence in the most wonderful way.

In Switzerland, which for him was a freely chosen sanctuary and not a place of refuge, he produced dramatic works that will live on in the memory of those who have seen them. The play about Dunant, *Der Helfer Gottes* (*God's Helper*), was perhaps the last success that he himself was able to enjoy here. The Stadttheater in Berne was putting *Der Liebling der Grazien* (*The Darling of the Graces*), his last work for the stage, into production at the time of his death.

But it was to Switzerland that Hans Müller owed the full development of his talent as a novelist, which only here came to its full, free realisation. His great work, *Jugend in Wien* (*Youth in Vienna*), is of course the story of his own youth, a story in which it becomes evident how modest this writer was, whom so many wrongly accused of being over-ambitious. This book, which was a declaration of gratitude and a confession of faith, was the swan-song of a brave pilgrim on this earth, one who, both in his virtues and in his errors, had fought the good fight to the last.

On my return from the deeply moving and distressing funeral in Einigen, at which Curt Götz spoke words that long afterwards continued to echo in my ears, as though to comfort me a very great joy came to me, something that I would never have dared to hope for. A long-lost, last manuscript of mine, a large volume of stories, which had been left behind in Vienna in a state in which it was quite ready to go to the printer, and which I counted among the most grievous of all the losses I had ever suffered, was found again as though by a miracle. This was thanks to my former, likewise long-lost secretary, who had received this work and, suddenly, after twelve years' silence gave a sign of life. Without explaining the mystery of why she had kept silence so long, she informed me that she was about to make a journey from where she lived in Salzburg to Vienna, in order to look for some of her lost possessions, among which she would probably find the volume of stories I had entrusted to her before my departure. And lo! she did indeed find the manuscript, squeezed in between two crates in the cellar of the house she had previously lived in—uninjured, undamaged, only a little yellowed with age. She at once sent me a telegram, which contained what was doubtless the happiest news I had hitherto received during my stay in Switzerland. I felt indeed as though God Himself had written a book for me: I had not to do anything with the half-forgotten text beyond reading it, approving it, and then setting about arranging for its publication.

At about the same time Bernard Shaw sent me a postcard saying he had just finished another little play of six scenes, which he referred to as a 'comediettina' and which bore the attractive title *Why She Would Not*. The little work was already in the press, he wrote, and would be sent to me from the printers'. But down to this day this has not happened, and the people who have had most to do with his affairs claim to know nothing of such a work's having been finished. I then received another card from him, with news of no importance, but instead of the creative sign of life that I have been waiting for in vain to this day there came the news of his fall and of its consequences, which today we all know, the last and gravest of them being his death on November 2nd, 1950.

Now the last, greatest and strangest hero of my life, whom I had always expected to outlive me, had gone the way of all flesh, and I do not feel justified in saying more about it here than I did elsewhere under the impact of the first grievous and upsetting news. But there is one thing that I believe I am entitled to confess in this melancholy hour: I am quite aware of what German literature owes to me. By this, however, I am far from asserting that the Irish master might not have succeeded in finding a better exponent of the art of translation if he had had the choice in time, instead of being dependent on a writer who was led to him only by his own enthusiasm and intense impatience to see an intellectual wrong righted, a writer to whom he then—perhaps to his disadvantage—who knows?—doggedly and with unswerving loyalty kept faith throughout a long life.

And if now I wish with wondering gaze to survey my own life, shadowy and lost in dreams, which I have tried to unfold in this book, and ask myself what this life was, I know no answer but the one:

Work, love, heart-ache, and—work!

These confessions really end my journey through life. But I feel it is my duty to offer just one more thing, a vision that came to me and in which I believe. It was my last. I call it

A LEGACY

Life's great verities cannot be proved—neither God nor love. They must be experienced, lived through and believed with the fervour of belief that is born in the heart and of the senses. They are perceived by visionaries, who even, indeed, see them with bodily eyes.

Perception is faith. But superstition can never arise out of a perception. What one who is elect recognises and experiences, what he believes he knows with emotion so profound that he does indeed know it, is always divine truth.

Despairing of there being any possibilities of offering others what he has uniquely experienced, or of communicating it to mankind, he often keeps it to himself, takes the encouraging, enriching, liberating revelation to the grave with him *unuttered*. Or once, perhaps, being overwhelmed by it, he shouts it forth upon the air where only Nature is, into the early morning freshness or into the mournfulness of evening, at the same time knowing that the birds, flowers, trees and leaves hear a voice blown on the wind and understand, because theirs is the kingdom of heaven that knows such understanding. But to the world of men he scarcely turns at all.

My solitary and hermit-like teacher was such a lonely walker on his own, one to whom grace had come, a man elect, to whom on his seventieth birthday something was revealed that he, the great physician, would have uttered only if there had been any possibility of proving it.

The sealed envelope containing the document that brings us nearer to the solution of the riddle of the universe bore, besides my name, only the instruction that it was not to be opened until I felt the limit of my own life approaching. My age, and many a sensation that concerns none but myself, today justify me—as it seems to me—in breaking the seal of the document entrusted to me. I read as follows:

'Do as you will with my discovery, this event in a man's progress to Knowledge. Keep it, re-experience it in the spirit, destroy it, or pass it on to the crowd, greedy for doubt as it is and nevertheless despairing—and under my name or yours or without a name at all. I wished to escape from having to make these petty, nagging decisions, and have escaped . . .'

A preference for remaining in obscurity, a love of achievement for its own sake, scorn of fame—this was the bond of our great friendship. In the spirit of that friendship let me be silent as to his name, which has long been known to the stars above us. This great man, now dead, left a legacy that is all that matters and which reads:

'There is nothing new in the statement that death and life are mysteriously related, like two buckets on the same rope, which descend into the same well, one of them rising into the light while the other is sinking into the darkness. But nobody before me has ever revealed the profound and great connection in all its truth. Hear then, my friend, and believe—believing what has not the slightest thing to do with the questionable dogmas of transmigration or reincarnation. A doctor swears to it.

'As truly as God has illuminated me and called me to proclaim it, every birth has its counterpart in a quite particular death, or, to formulate it better, every entering into life is the counterpart of a dying that it occasions, and every awakening of an extinction.

Invisible threads link the embryo with one who is enfeebled with age, link the infant with one who is in the throes of death. Anyone who, by his birth, has entered into the eternal cycle of evolving and passing away remains enclosed within it immutably. The new-born infant's first cry is coincidental to the very second with a death-rattle somewhere in the universe. It is not only the mother but some dying woman who helps a female being into the world, and not only the father but some man whose eyes are glazing in death who causes a new-born boy to utter his first cry. The well-known "peaceful smile" on the features of the dead is only the reflection of a rapturous vision conjured up by a new-born babe. Every death-agony is the reflex of a mother's travail; the pains experienced by a woman in labour are answered by the death struggle of someone who is dying, her counterpart somewhere in the world. In God's hand they lie close together, he who comes and he who goes. Only where these divine pendulum movements swing freely—not where they are violently disturbed and interrupted—is a human being's death peaceful and his birth a promise of happiness. Premature births, miscarriages, still-births— these are the counterpart of dying people who have had to take a violent leave of life, either by their own or by another's hand.

'Treble woe to those who give birth in times of war! Their catastrophic children lack the distant supporting and directing pole, they are and remain the most helpless of all who walk the earth, their first vibrations are not received, they enter into the void and gather into clouds of restless menace. From such as these, who are criminally withdrawn from the divine cycle of becoming and being extinguished, there come the sick, the heavy-burdened, the unstable, the criminals, the unbelievers, the lost, the reckless, the evil!

'When once this divine bond, and its eternal connection, now revealed, has been intuitively felt and has been recognised, the terror is taken from death. Death is at once the end and the beginning, the father's end and the son's beginning, the mother's end and the daughter's beginning, as it were—for in the highest sense we are, after all, ourselves the children whom our dying helps to bring into the world, we are the self-sacrificing allies of the mothers. We cease and begin, untrammelled by memories, our faculties heightened by intimations—if we have them—of higher things. The aimless and limitless yearning inborn in every human creature, the first emotion of each babbling infant, is a fading call to the strange, invisible kin that have helped to bring us into the light. No longer lament over growing old. Who knows? Already your new youth is being prepared for in some maternal womb.

'Every human creature whose development is not violently interrupted has two fathers, two mothers. The boy has his progenitor and his father-in-death, and the girl, besides her progenitor, her mother and her mother-in-death. United by the bond of universal love, they hold each other's invisible hands, made immortal by this immutable divine dance—and eternally. Such knowledge is prayer. Amen.'

I had been deeply shaken, filled with grace, and stirred by having received this revelation, and afterwards I was grateful for my own fate and the mission of that great man, my friend. Incapable of presuming to utter any view of my own, whether in agreement or, much less, in denial, when faced with such an illumination, I ask that I may be allowed to disappear among the whispering shadows that are slowly beginning to float down. . . .

January 10th, 1951.

INDEX

409